KU-182-468

WORKING MEN'S COLLEGE.

LIBRARY REGULATIONS.

The Library is open every week-day evening, from 6.30 to 10 o'clock, except on Saturdays, when it closes at 9.

This book may be kept for three weeks. If not returned within that period, the borrower will be liable to a fine of one penny per week.

If lost or damaged the borrower will be required to make good such loss or damage.

Only one book may be borrowed at a time

HIGHWAYS AND BYWAYS

IN

BERKSHIRE

WORKING MEN'S COLLEGE LIBRARY

MACMILLAN AND CO., Limited
LONDON . BOMBAY . CALCUTTA . MADRAS
MELBOURNE

THE MACMILLAN COMPANY
NEW YORK . BOSTON . CHICAGO
DALLAS . SAN FRANCISCO

THE MACMILLAN CO. OF CANADA, Ltd.
TORONTO

Abingdon Bridge.

WORKING MEN'S COLLEGE LIBRARY.

13573

Highways and Byways

IN

Berkshire

BY JAMES EDMUND VINCENT
WITH · ILLUSTRATIONS · BY
FREDERICK L. GRIGGS

MACMILLAN AND CO., LIMITED
ST. MARTIN'S STREET, LONDON
1919

PREFACE

A few words by way of preface are written, not because they are imperative, but because it is a pleasure to indite them. I cannot, like Mr. A. G. Bradley, in the preface to his admirable volume in this series, plead, if I have omitted matter of interest, the excuse of over-abundant material; yet my title, like his, involves no particular obligation to include everything, and the title is relied upon for what it is worth. The first object of this preface, however, is to offer a general apology, not for the existence of the book, although that conventional attitude ought possibly to be adopted, but to those who have given willing and abundant help concerning the history of localities of special interest to them. Many of them have provided ample materials for a monograph of respectable length, and it has been my aim to extract from those materials such gossip, ancient and modern, as might serve to fill part of a volume able to be read with pleasure, and perhaps not entirely without profit. Numerous men, no doubt, would have realised that aim more completely; no man could have enjoyed more thoroughly the occupation, not the task, of collecting the material; and, at the end of it all, I am astonished by the wealth of it existing in a county of no extraordinary repute, whose most promising records, those of the Mitred Abbey of Abingdon, and in a large measure of the

Corporation also, were in great part deliberately destroyed not many years ago. "I only know two neighbourhoods thoroughly, and in each, within a circle of five miles, there is enough of interest and beauty to last any reasonable man his life." I need not go quite so far, or confine myself quite so straitly, as our famous Berkshire hero, the author of *Tom Brown*; and it would delight me to see every part of the world that I have not visited yet; but the whole of a county, whereof a circle five miles in diameter (or radius) would have satisfied my old and honoured acquaintance, is surely enough by way of subject.

For the subject, then, I offer no apology; for shortcomings I crave indulgence; for omissions of facts imparted to me I excuse myself on the ground of my judgment of literary necessity. Finally, I acknowledge with warm gratitude the ready aid of many kind helpers, amongst whom I would mention particularly Lady Wantage, his Honour Judge Francis Bacon, Canon J. N. Dalton, Mr. John Eyston of East Hendred, Colonel Collins, the vicar of Denchworth, Mr. Paulin Martin, the late Mr. C. J. Cornish, and the Rev. James Cornish. The list might be extended indefinitely, but only one more name shall be added. It is that of Mr. Frederick L. Griggs, the artist, whose pictures adorn these pages, as amenable and suggestive a collaborator, well versed in the history of architecture too, as a humble painter of pictures and teller of stories in words could hope to meet. Perhaps, too, there should be an apology for occasional levity and lightness of heart. It is refused, for the deliberate purpose has been to eschew solemnity and to write in a joyful spirit.

J. E. V.

DRAYTON, BERKS, *October*, 1906.

CONTENTS

LIST OF ILLUSTRATIONS

MAPS

HIGHWAYS AND BYWAYS

IN

BERKSHIRE

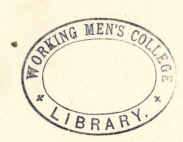

HIGHWAYS AND BYWAYS

IN

BERKSHIRE

CHAPTER I

OF THE FASCINATION OF BERKSHIRE

Armchair travel—The boundaries of Berks—Territory of the Atrebates—
The ancient Thames—Sinodun Hill—Associations of Berks—Saxon
kings — Battlefields — Amy Robsart — Abbeys — Kingsley—" Tom
Hughes "—Matthew Arnold—Hill-folk and Moormen—Topographical
divisions—Their faults—*The Scenery of England*—Its aids to appreciation.

> " *Ille terrarum mihi præter omnes*
> *Angulus ridet.*"

IT may seem strange that one to whom North Wales was
nursing mother, who has seen wonderful and beautiful sights in
every continent on the surface of the globe, should write with
so much of enthusiasm of the county of his adoption. Yet that
this is done deliberately, and not in cheap or unthought
rhapsody, is an indirect tribute to the wisdom underlying the
plan of the " Highways and Byways " series. I liked Berkshire greatly before the publishers were kind enough to entrust
to me this labour of love ; but I admire it tenfold more now

B

that the familiar spots have been revisited, and detours have
been made to others that were not familiar, to pick up stray
threads of history and legend, to study the people and their
ways, to drink in, as it were, the atmosphere that bathes the
Berkshire scenery. It is by this kind of process, and by it
only, that Englishmen (who are the most determined wanderers on the face of the earth, except American ladies) can
realise the complex interest of the country lying under their
eyes. The best thing they can do to this end is to study
this or that county, in leisurely fashion, for themselves, and
there is no district of England—or for that matter of Scotland
or Ireland or Wales either—in which they will not meet with
an ample reward. But there is also such a thing as travel, by
proxy, in an armchair. If it be not so healthy nor so enjoyable
as the genuine article, it is still not so irritating nor even so
mischievous as armchair criticism ; and it has its pleasures.
Amongst my acquaintance is a great editor, the greatest of
them all in my judgment, who, when he returns to his home
in the early hours of the morning, props up *Bradshaw* in
front of him as he breaks his fast and so, by indulgence
of innocent and waking dreams of tours to be accomplished,
drives from his mind those thoughts of political complications
at home and abroad which can murder sleep as effectually as
Macbeth himself. He is in truth a man of strong imagination,
for which there is no legitimate outlet in the columns under
his dominion. He can make the dry bones live in his
fancy, and my object in these pages is to do likewise in
relation to parts of Berkshire, to accompany the reader, in
the flesh or in the spirit as the case may be, to suggest, in
this place and in that, those memories and thoughts grave and
gay which are appropriate to the scene, and to direct his steps
into some of the many delightful corners wherein our Berkshire
abounds.

　　Numerous are the glories and the pleasures of Berkshire,
but chief of them all is its silent highway, the Thames, which,

for some 100 miles of its course, that is to say, from Lechlade to Old Windsor, forms the upper boundary of Berkshire in the maps. This, of course, is not to write with strict accuracy. It is not until the Thames joins the Isis hard by that splendid edifice at Dorchester, which all but tempts me to transgress the boundaries of my manor, that the combined streams become absolutely the Thames. But for all that it would be in harmony with general feeling, if a trifle Irish, to say that the Thames becomes the Thames below Dorchester, for the name Isis has fallen out of use save for poets and pedants, and the stream that passes Oxford, Nuneham, and Abingdon is incalculably the more noble of the two that join below Dorchester. In fact, for all practical purposes, it is the Thames, and Berkshire has a larger share in it than any other of the riparian counties. Moreover, Berkshire chose the Thames, so to speak, for its boundary. That is to say the Atrebates, who were the original Berkshire folk for our purposes, kept the line of the Thames against the Dobuni of a world more barbarian than their own. One cannot at first say the Dobuni of the North, save between Lechlade and Longworth, the home of roses; for from New Bridge, which is hard by unto Longworth, the river runs almost due north as far as Wytham Woods; then it takes a southerly direction with a shade of east in it to a point slightly beyond Radley, where it is pushed to the westward towards Abingdon of many streams, and of more than many memories. Soon it makes a meandering loop, intersected for purposes of navigation by the Culham Cut, to Sutton Courtney, and turns to the northward again, almost encircling those hills of Sinodun, better known as Wittenham Clumps, which perhaps the Atrebates held as fortresses against raiders from the outer world. To have traversed these reaches of the river very often, to have noted, wearily sometimes, with lingering pleasure at others, how they always dominate the scene, how one never can get rid of them, is to realise to the full how excellent a point of defence and observation they were. A few miles lower down the mighty stream turns southward again, past Wallingford and Streatley to Pangbourne, then eastward to Reading, northward again to Henley and Remenham, eastward to Bisham and Cookham, south and south-east past Maidenhead and Old Windsor; and so we have done for the moment with the upper boundary and the greatest highway of Berkshire.

It was, we need make no doubt, a magnificent and almost impregnable frontier to the territory of the Atrebates; so mighty indeed that imagination almost shrinks from the effort of reconstructing it. Father Thames has shown us some of his strength lately and the floods of 1903 will be remembered in the Thames Valley for many a long day, for their cost is to be reckoned in lives lost as well as in the devastation of smiling fields. But these were but the outbursts of a Thames cabined and confined, forbidden by multitudinous locks and weirs to make one wild rush for the sea. In these days, save in flood-time, there is no part of the river which a reasonably powerful swimmer may not cross with ease and without making leeway. But in the really old times, long before the locks came—they were introduced early in the fifteenth century in the interests of the mills and with little reference to navigation—the Thames in winter must have been almost impassable to skin-clad barbarians in coracle or corrach. The swollen stream was an ample protection and the watchers on Sinodun, if they kept their posts at all, were probably safe in little caves and hollows scooped out to shelter them from the driving winds and from the rain and snow which the storms carried before them. In summer it was another story. The stream must often have been sadly reduced; but on either side of it, where the ground lay flat and low, were vast marshes, not easy to traverse at all, and impossible to pass through without disturbing flocks of wild fowl which, to the ancient Briton on Sinodun, accustomed to watch every sign of natural life, would tell their own tale. It is pleasant even now to rest on Sinodun and to reconstruct the scene in imagination; to picture the group of bearded Britons, lightly smeared in woad—by the way, it is still grown commercially in Lincolnshire—straining their eyes over the flat country, where Dorchester and Clifton Hampden are now, noting the wild ducks circling higher and higher, and the bitterns and the herons flapping wearily away, and seeking to read the cause. Were barbarians, even ruder than themselves, drifting and paddling down either of the streams, now known as Isis and Thame? Or was the disturbance of the summer peace due only to the passing of some beast of prey? Time only could show, and what it might show does not matter in the least now; yet to think of it all now is at least innocent.

How the other boundaries of Berkshire came to be laid down is not clear, but there they are on the map, strangely and wonderfully irregular, marked sometimes by little rivers, but often by nothing in particular. They include, to be precise, a tract of land having an area of 573,689 acres, which can hardly be equalled even in England for variety of scenery or for wealth of historical and literary associations. Windsor, Cumner, Wantage, Reading, Newbury—a volume could be written about any one of them and, concerning Windsor, many volumes. Indeed many have been so written. The birthplace of the first real King of England at Wantage, the battle-grounds of Saxon and Dane, of Stephen's time, of the supporters of the Parliament and of Charles the First, the stateliest home of our Kings and Queens, of England first and of the United Kingdom later, the scene of the tragedy of Amy Robsart's death, should surely satisfy any writer, were he never so avaricious of facts. Of abbeys and monastic buildings too, as at Abingdon, Hurley, at Bisham, and Reading, Berkshire had some store, and of ancient manor-houses, beautiful, typical, and fragrant with memories of old time, she has still abundant wealth. Berkshire ground is hallowed in parts by Shakespeare and by

Sir Walter Scott, who by the way took many liberties with
Berkshire history. Charles Kingsley revelled in its southern
moorlands, and also, although not everybody knows this, in
its clear trout streams. Tom Hughes celebrated the fame of
the Vale of the White Horse in a book which bids fair to live
as long as the mysterious emblem itself, and to need no
"scouring" to keep it fresh in memory. Others there have
been, too, who have sung of our rivers and our downs, the
county's chiefest charm ; but our sweetest singer of all is
Matthew Arnold in "The Scholar-Gipsy." He realised more
fully than any other the joy it was to lie—

> " Moor'd to the cool bank in the summer-heats,
>   'Mid wide grass meadows which the sunshine fills,
>   And watch the warm, green-muffled Cumner Hills,
>   And wonder if thou haunt'st their shy retreats."

He loved "the stripling Thames at Bab-lock-hithe," and the

> " Maidens who from the distant hamlets come
>   To dance around the Fyfield elm in May."

He knew "the skirts of Bagley Wood," the lone homesteads
in the Cumner Hills," the ale-houses in "the Berkshire moors,"
the warm ingle-bench, and "the smock-frock'd boors."

Of these same rustic folk, whom Matthew Arnold called
"boors" *metri gratiâ*, that they might rhyme with "moors,"
there will be much to say. We divide them locally into
men "from the hills," and men "of the moors"—for the
great plain of Northern Berks, smiling cornland though it
be, is still called "the Moors"—and each class despises
the other with that complete mutuality which can only be
attained between near neighbours. They are, indeed, distinct ; but they are West Saxons all, denizens of Mr. Hardy's
Wessex. Saxon names linger among them, and sturdy lads
who tend the slow-moving farm-horses have been named
Cedric, Oliver, and Cuthbert, and so on, by parents who
never had time to dream of affectation in nomenclature.

They have their own traditions, their own dialect—and "precious" hard the stranger will find it to follow that dialect sometimes—and in large measure their own vocabulary. They are "just about pleased," when they are pleased at all, especially when "the feast," which is simply the annual village fair, comes round; they can dance at these feasts, round the Fyfield elm and elsewhere, as well as "arra one of 'em." Their phrases are of the old world. "Who bist thee o' 'thee and I'" was, for example, the rebuke addressed quite recently by a Berkshire parson's man to a presuming maid from the village; and "ee" will serve for any pronoun in every case save the possessive. As for the children's games, as usual the most conservative of survivals, they point back to immemorial antiquity. Thus, in one of them, seen and heard at Sutton Courtney, came the following dialogue:

> " *Shepherd:* Ship, ship, come 'oam!
> *Sheep:* Shaant.
> *Shepherd:* Ship, ship, come 'oam!
> The wolf has gone to Devonsheer,
> An' won't be back for seven year."

How many years have passed since the terror of the wolves was real and present in Berkshire? Perhaps four centuries; but the traditional rhymes and games of children are often the most unchangeable things on earth.[1]

Our people are easy of classification. In the north of the county they are the hill-folk and the people of the "moors"; these are ordinary agricultural population; the riparian inhabitants are in large measure hangers-on of those who take their pastime on the river; and there are the men and women of the towns, varying a little of course, but not very much. Thus Windsor, Reading, Abingdon, and Wantage, by virtue of their associations, their environments and their industries, where

---

[1] Since these words were written learned men have argued that many mysterious earthworks, including those at Dorchester, were constructed as a defence against the wolves.

they have any, influence the tone of those who dwell in them ; but your townsman does not possess so individual and characteristic a type as your countryman, and he is hardly the more interesting of the two. To divide the county under headings is a very difficult task, and perhaps there is no need to attempt it. Because Cæsar observed that Gaul was divided into three parts, his followers in writing of tracts of country have deemed it to be their duty to subdivide their subjects. Thus Mr. J. Meade Falkner, the really accomplished and learned writer of Murray's handbook, writes : " Nature has divided Berkshire into four parts : the Vale of the White Horse, on the North ; the Vale of Kennet, on the South ; the hill district of the Downs, between them ; and lastly all that part which lies East of the Loddon, and has been called the Forest District." But, having written thus much, Mr. Falkner appears to have seen that the divisions required some explanation, and this he gives in the form of a quotation, from some unnamed writer, in such a fashion as to lead to the hope that the division itself was not his own :

" Each of these four districts has its distinct characteristics and each has minor divisions of its own. Thus, the Vale of the White Horse comprises on its north side a low range of secondary hills, which run along the bank of the Thames from Faringdon to Radley, and include Cumner and Bagley Wood. These are sand-hills, whilst the soil of the Vale proper is for the most part a strong grey loam, mixed with large quantities of vegetable mould."

This, to start with, is a singularly inaccurate fashion of writing, least pardonable of all in the case of the Vale of the White Horse. The vale cannot " comprise a low range of hills," which make it, any more than it can include the White Horse itself, or than the wine can comprise the cup. Moreover, strangely enough, the *Century Dictionary* chooses the words of the late Judge Hughes about the Vale of the White Horse as the classic example of the meaning of the word. " I pity

people who weren't born in a vale. I don't mean a flat
country, but a vale; that is a flat country bounded by hills."
And that, more emphatically than in the vast majority of cases,
is precisely the right description of the Vale of the White
Horse, of which this secondary range of hills is the northern
boundary. This range is, by comparison with the Downs to
the southward, insignificant in point of size and in the matter
of association; but as a byway it is by no means to be despised.
Faringdon, Buckland, Hinton Waldrist, and Longworth are
well worth seeing, and the ridge which unites them is of surpassing beauty in its tranquil way. Cumner can by no means
be neglected. Inglesham Round House; Buscot, famous for
its Shire Horses and its Burne-Jones pictures, curious combination, is on the northern slope of the range beside "the
stripling Thames." So are Eaton Hastings, Tadpole, New
Bridge, and the woods of Wytham, famed in story. No, when
quiet byways are to the fore, we must away with these scientific
divisions, for they exclude not only many of these interesting
little places, but also the infant stream of Father Thames
himself, which is Berks *ad medium filum* at any rate.

So much for the first division. The second, the hill district,
includes "the high chalk range of which White Horse Hill
(893 feet) and Cuckamsley Hill (or Scutchamore Knob) are
the highest points. Towards the north the range is bold, and
the descent into the Vale steep, and the hills are indented with
a number of little 'cooms,' or meadows clothed with copse,
while towards the south it melts gradually away into the Vale
of the Kennet. . . . The outlier, Inkpen Beacon, in the south
of the county (959 feet), is the highest point reached by the
chalk in England."

Before offering a word of criticism, not in any carping spirit,
but simply for the sake of the honour of Berkshire, it may be
well to quote the description of the third division, since that
which must be said of the account of the second division
cannot well be understood without such quotation. "The

Vale of the Kennet comprises the low lands which lie along its
banks" (the word "vale" is used correctly enough this time)
"and includes clays, gravels, and a large and deep bed of peat ;
also the strip of wild and high sandy common land which runs
along the extreme south boundary of the county."

In what difficulties does not this infatuation for topographical
division involve him who feels compelled to classify? It
ignores that charming valley of the Lambourne ; it makes
inadequate individual account of the Enborne ; it gives no
indication of the mellowing influence of the Thames. Incidentally, too, it would be interesting to learn why, if Mr. Falkner's
authority prefers "coom" to "comb," "coomb," "combe," or
"cwm," he must needs define that which is essentially a hollow
in a hill, or a dingle, as a "meadow clothed with copse,"
which is simply a contradiction in terms. But that is matter of
detail, for a writer may classify the parts of a country under
headings without being guilty of misuse of language. That is
his own fault, not that of his method. The omissions, however, and the wrong inclusions, are the inevitable result of a
faulty and wholly unnecessary system.

Finally, we are told, "the Forest district comprises the small
outlying piece of the chalk which has strayed over the Thames
at Wargrave and leaves it at Maidenhead, and the Forest
proper, which, however, includes towns and flourishing hamlets,
and many hundred acres of good enclosed land, from Windsor
to the Loddon. Formerly the Forest stretched right away up
the Vale of Kennet to Hungerford, some 40 miles as the crow
flies." With this description, perhaps, it is not necessary to
quarrel much ; for it amounts to this, that, east of the Loddon,
there is a vast quantity of heath and pine land, altogether
delightful as a habitation, and capable of cultivation in many
parts, which is the survival from an ancient forest. But it is
really impossible not to protest against the expression "the
small outlying piece of the chalk range which has strayed back
over the Thames at Wargrave and leaves it at Maidenhead," as

needlessly, and even perversely, inaccurate and misleading.   It
was proper and poetical in the Psalmist to ask the mountains
why they skipped like rams, and the little hills like young
sheep ; but in later times Lord Avebury and others have told
us some wonderful things about the evolution of our scenery in
such language as to show that it is quite possible to be glowing
and truthful at once.

> " *Vidi ego, quod fuerat quondam solidissima tellus,*
> *Esse fretum : vidi factas ex æquore terras ;*
> *Et procul a pelago conchæ jacuere marinæ.*"

Thus wrote old Ovid, who saw the poetry of science and of
nature no less than of human passion, and his words have been
well translated by H. King :

> " Straits have I seen that cover now
> What erst was solid earth ; have trodden land
> Where once was sea ; and gathered inland far
> Dry ocean shells."

Ovid wrote, too :

> " *Quodque fuit campus, vallem decursus aquarum*
> *Fecit ; et eluvie mons est deductus in æquor.*"

This, since I have no metrical translation by me, I must
even versify for myself into—

> " Plain into vale was made by water's flow,
> Floods to the deeps have led the mountain low."

Thus Ovid has proved, if I have not, that there is poetry in
denudation, so that our authority cannot claim poetic licence
as " a way of necessity," to quote a lawyer's phrase ; and there
are romantic possibilities enough in all conscience supplied by
geology.   The course of the Thames from Wargrave to
Maidenhead may have been " planed out " by the sea, to use
Lord Avebury's phrase, or cut by fresh water after the
chalk was exposed to the air ; or Bear Hill and Ashley Hill

may have been upheaved by mysterious subterranean forces ; but the one thing which is absolutely certain is that they did not leap the river. It follows that this was the thing above all others which it was not so much wrong—that does not matter— but clumsy and unpoetical to write.

Let it be repeated again that these words have not been used in any spirit of carping criticism. Their purpose is, on the other hand, twofold. First to show that for the study of a county or a district, the habit of classification necessarily involves so much of omission or so much of wrong use of terms as to be in itself a vicious habit ; in fact that the desultory method, which does not contemn digressions but rather ensues them, is the better. After all the byways exist for the purpose of digression, and some of the best books that have been written, notably *A Sentimental Journey*, consist entirely of digressions. Secondly, it may be confessed, there is an underlying feeling that, where occasion rises, something ought to be said of the origins of scenery, that it becomes the more interesting from some slight knowledge of its history, and that Lord Avebury's *The Scenery of England* (Macmillan) is of no slight help to him or her who, loving the beautiful and romantic in Nature, would like to know how it came to its present shape.

Let an illustration be given in passing. Not long since I took an entirely delightful drive from Compton Beauchamp to Lambourne across the Downs, and back, passing Ashdown House and the Grey Wethers on the way back, and the next day I inspected Wayland Smith's Cave—the Blowing Stone and the White Horse were familiar friends already. Of all these, and particularly of the legend of Wayland Smith, common to many races, there will be something to be said later on, but for the moment the Grey Wethers serve best to illustrate my meaning. My companions were two very highly cultivated men and some ladies of more than ordinary intelligence. Not one of us had so much as an idea how the Grey Wethers happened to come flocking together at this point ; and some suggested glaciers—glacier is almost as blessed a word to him who has a smattering of geology as Mesopotamia is to the Divinity student. But the glacier theory was vague and unsatisfying. On the other hand, a feeling of contentment supervenes from reading, in Lord Avebury's book, that the Grey Wethers are Sarsen Stones, that the Sarsen Stones of Salisbury Plain (not to be confounded with the Altar Stone of Stonehenge, which is of grey micaceous sandstone) are probably indurated masses of sandstone from beds of Bagshot sand which have been washed away, and that you may find their like at Avebury, at Wayland Smith's Cave (where man has certainly handled them too), in Stonehenge, and near Maidstone in Kit's Coty House. You will find caps left by these same Bagshot sands on Highgate and Hampstead Hills, and they have been the making of the scenery of Eastern Berkshire. In like manner in traversing the Downs, of which more particular mention will be made very shortly, interest is added and enjoyment is heightened by knowing not only that this or that barrow marks the burial-place of a warrior, and that many a battle has been fought on their surface, but also that their lofty undulations were once submerged beneath the salt water and that their present form, changing surely if insensibly from day to day, is due partly to atmospheric changes and partly even to human agency. In fact a smattering of geological knowledge and scattered reading in history are the true conditions precedent to a real appreciation of the minor beauties of Nature. It is otherwise, perhaps, in the case of the stupendous in Nature. Niagara, for example, stuns the imagination of the visitor. He cannot analyse his impressions when he is on the spot or later. Then, and afterwards, the soft-toned but all-pervading boom of the waters, the sense of going on and of having gone on for ever which they convey, the paralysing feeling of human helplessness and of man's insignificance, are all that can be realised. But the ineffable sweetness of the Downs is one of the beauties that will bear analysis; and to know how the lynchets have assumed their shape, and

certainly "inferiour to none." He may indeed have had Windsor in his mind when he spoke of the air also, for Windsor naturally bulked large for him, and its similitude is printed at the head of his description, together with a list of the early Knights of the Garter. But this second sentence would certainly apply to the Downs, the prospect from which is certainly not inferior to that from Windsor, while the air is assuredly the sweetest and most delightful, if not always the most temperate, that is to be found in the length and breadth of England.

The fascination of Downs is a thing absolutely *sui generis*, more comparable, perhaps, to that of the Canadian prairie than to that of any other scenery in the world. But there is a wide difference between the two. Those who have lived long on the Canadian prairie, with its absolute freedom and boundless space and complete solitude, declare that it grows upon them, that in after life the desire to revisit it becomes almost irresistible. But this fascination is by no means felt at once by the new-comer, who is apt, at first sight, to be appalled by the savage solitude, to be wearied by gentle and monotonous undulations of poor grass which seem to go on for ever. On the prairie there is, so to speak, no view because there is nothing else but view, and nothing definite to look at in it. It is as changeless as a gently swelling sea, out of sight of land, and, on a brief acquaintance at any rate, not nearly so beautiful. The Berkshire Downs, on the other hand, attract the new-comer at once. They have space, sufficiently unlimited for all practical purposes, and, because they are an eminence, they have prospect in no common measure. Their deep and springy turf is a delight to the feet of those who tread them ; it is absolutely perfect for the purposes of the horseman ; and the fresh air that sweeps over it carries the faint fragrance of hundreds of tiny flowers, peculiar to the chalk downs, which repay minute investigation. Big treasures you shall find but few, here and there a gentian or an orchid, but every sod that, from a few yards distance, seems to consist of soft and elastic grass, contains many flowerets, each a joy to the eye, though it be no treasure to the collector.

Sweet thyme, potentilla, milkwort, harebells and the hum of bees, these are the characteristics of the Berkshire Downs, and Lord Avebury, who has lived all but in them and loved them, has a striking passage: " And if the Downs seem full of life and sunshine, their broad shoulders are types of kindly strength, so that they give an impression of power and antiquity ; while every now and then we come across a tumulus, or a group of great grey stones, the burial-place of some ancient hero, or a sacred temple of our pagan forefathers." Again, as Gilbert White wrote of the Sussex Downs in gentler mood : " I think there is something peculiarly sweet and amusing in the shapely figured aspect of chalk hills, in preference to those of stone, which are rugged, broken, abrupt and shapeless." One need not do more than pause to be amused at the last clause, reminding one of Dr. Johnson's hatred of mountains, in which, in his generation, he was not singular. It is enough that the prose-poet of Selborne, first of true Field Naturalists, felt the fascination of the open Downs, and felt it more and more year by year. " I think I see new beauties every time I traverse it," he says, after describing the Sussex Downs as a chain of majestic mountains ! Most paramount of all the superiorities of the Downs over the Prairie is that of association. The early history of the Prairie could be written in a few pages, and condensed into a few sentences. The real history is in the making now, and the Canadian Pacific Railway is making it fast, at the same time that it is changing the face of the prairie itself. The history of the Downs, and of the many great events of which they have been the scene, was made long ago, and it would fill many volumes : but their outward face remains substantially the same, save where they were cut up for corn early in the last century, as it was two thousand years ago. Even then, doubtless, they wore an air of antiquity similar to that which marks them now, and there were grass-grown tumuli and lynchets, marking ancient burial-places of heroes and primitive methods of cultivation. The Downs look the same now as they did when Briton fought Briton first (which was probably the first time he had the chance of doing so), when the Romans pushed their way along them from Streatley to the west, when Saxon and Dane marched and countermarched over them and fought that great battle of Ashdown—nobody knows exactly where—when Royalists and Parliament men met upon them again and again in deadly encounter. It is quite possible, in the light of recent theories, that the huge White Horse which puzzled the antiquaries of the Middle Ages may have been an enigma to Alfred of Wantage himself, as it really is to us all still. In fact an unchangeable antiquity and a spacious mystery belong to the Downs as to the mountains themselves, and in them alone can a scene of days gone by be reconstructed by the imagination with its identical surroundings. The cultivated country changes, woods vanish and fields come, marshes become the home of " waving furrowed corn "; cities are changed beyond recognition ; but the Downs and Mountains remain, for human purposes, the same ; although really they are changing all the time.

By no means the whole, perhaps not even the greater part of the Berkshire Downs is covered with the close and springy herbage which is their glory, although there is enough of that to satisfy any reasonable person. Cultivation has advanced and receded on them, and advanced again to recede again in these later days. The ancient cultivation has affected the outlines in such a way as to mislead competent geologists into entirely erroneous theories. ·Thus Lord Avebury, whose language certainly cannot be improved upon, says : " In chalk districts well marked terraces may often be seen running along the sides of the hills. These are locally (Wiltshire) known as ' Lynchets,' and have a certain geological interest, as they sometimes present a superficial resemblance to parallel terraces, and have indeed actually been described as raised beaches, as, for instance, by Mackintosh. Poulett Scrope has, however, clearly shown that they are really terraces of cultivation ; and, indeed, any one who lives in counties where they occur may see them actually in the process of formation. Wherever a chalk slope is under arable cultivation the ridge of soil raised by the mould-board of the plough has a tendency through the action of gravity to slip downhill, never upwards. This downward tendency is greatly assisted by the wash of rain on the sloping surface, and the consequence is that the soil travels slowly downwards.

"In early times much of this land was held in severalty by different owners or tenants—the same man often holding several detached strips. In such a case each upper cultivator would take care not to allow the soil of his strip to descend to his neighbour's below He would draw the lower limit of his strip by a reversed furrow, throwing the last ridge of soil up-hill. This process being repeated year after year would gradually give rise to a balk or lynchet, perhaps several feet in height, with a flattened slope above." Lord Avebury then quotes a case in which Scrope actually saw a lynchet from two to three feet high formed by the ordinary process of agriculture in about ten years.

This striking illustration of the manner in which civilisation, and a definite system of land tenure, may modify the face of a district, is particularly interesting in relation to the Berkshire Downs, where the lynchets are so numerous, and often, as behind Compton Beauchamp, on so vast a scale, that while their regularity suggests human agency, their size disposes the investigator to put them down to the credit of the unaided forces of Nature. It is true that in these times it is rare to see a lynchet in process of formation ; but the explanation is not far to seek. The coating of fairly fertile soil on the chalk slopes is very thin and peculiarly liable to be washed from the top to the bottom of the slope. Indeed, where a crop is grown on a slope it will be noticeably more abundant on the lower parts than on the upper. Chalk slopes, therefore, are by no means an ideal ground for the cultivator, though they will produce more than those who are not familiar with chalky soil might imagine. "Where there's stoans there's carn," said a Wiltshire labourer to me once when I questioned the quality of a ploughed field, recalling memories of schooldays and of Arabia Petræa. The stones do, as a matter of fact, act as a species of mulch, preventing the evaporation of moisture and shielding the roots from the scorching heat of the sun, while the foliage basks in the heat. That, incidentally, is why many a plant will languish in the border and thrive in the rock-garden, even if it be not by nature a rock-plant at all.

Still, for weight of yield, and even more for yield in proportion to cost of cultivation, the Down land is not to be compared for a moment with the rich and alluvial soil of the Vale. Why then was it cultivated in the days gone by, when the Vale was at hand? Why did generation after generation of peasants goad the slow oxen to and fro along the same strips of poor land on the hillsides, when the Vale with its vast and rich plain was under their eyes all the time? The answer is more or less historical. The Downs required no clearing, and they were at hand. The wide plain of the Vale, undrained and covered, no doubt, with all sorts of rank growth, probably not with timber, called for much labour before it would yield returns. Those plains of the Vale, which now show some of the very finest wheat and barley in England, were not only known as the Moors in days gone by, but are actually so described at this moment by the country folk.

Why then are lynchets rarely formed now, and why have those which were formed in days gone by been allowed to go out of cultivation? Partly because they would not pay; partly because Folkland (which led to cultivation in strips on the lowlands as well as on the Downs) is a thing of the past; and partly by reason of Enclosure Acts, of which, as

Lord Avebury points out, there have been as many as 4,000. But the traces of old tenures may be seen in thousands of districts by him who has eyes to see. The lynchets are perhaps the most conspicuous and permanent of these traces. The long and narrow "closes," each of an acre or there-abouts, fringing the ancient village of Drayton, in which these words are written, on the south side, beyond them being the wide and hedgeless expanse of Milton Field, are clearly silent witnesses of the date at which Folkland came under cultivation. Long Acre, itself in the very heart of London, is almost certainly the strip of Folkland which fell to the share of one individual of the community when it was first deemed worth while to persuade that tract of land to bear crops. Phœbus! how rich a man his heir in tail male would be now if he received the rent of the land which took its name when it first produced a few quarters of corn.

The lynchets, then, are "raised beaches" in one sense only. That is to say, they mark the levels of ancient tides of cultivation, not the action of the sea on land slowly raised above its surface, in spite of the fact that the chalk un-doubtedly was submerged once. Those ancient tides of cultivation receded, in obedience to purely economic forces, and never rose again in the same form. But another, and a far more considerable tide of cultivation, a tidal wave in fact, submerged a great part of the Downs centuries after the little strips of plough land had gone so long out of use that their very origin was forgotten. At the end of the eighteenth century, and during rather more than the first half of the nineteenth century, huge fortunes were made by growing wheat. This was especially the case during the early years of the last century and "at the time of the Russian War," to which aged farmers of the present day refer still as a period of inconceivable prosperity. So it was for them, if not for the labourers who served them, nor

for the country at large. While wheat, falling a little now
and again, and then rising, maintained an average of price
which sounds fabulous in these days, the temptation to bring
every available tract of land under the plough was irresistible.
Large areas of Down land suffered under the ploughshares
of those who yielded to this temptation, and there need be
little doubt that, from a purely commercial point of view,
the act of ploughing was profitable in the extreme. True it
is that arable Down is worth very little now and that there
are wide extents of such land which let at sixpence by the acre.
Equally true is it that the skin of thick and close herbage
formed on the Downs when they are left alone is the growth
of man knows not how many years, insomuch that it is to
be doubted whether Down that has been once broken will
ever, under any treatment, recover that skin. But, if it comes
to a pure question of economy, the breaking up of the Down
pastures probably paid well enough. That is to say, it most
likely produced their freehold value in the course of a couple
of years, in which case the act of ploughing was certainly
defensible on economic grounds, for the pasturage of the
Downs, to judge by the uses made of it, is worth very little
indeed. Still, economy apart, the breaking of the Down
pastures was and is matter for abiding regret ; and the only
consolation is that a vast area never was broken at all.

For hundreds of years, however, there have been considerable farms in the recesses of the Downs. I have two such
farms particularly in mind now. One, a large house and
steading, with adequate buildings, and surrounded by a wide
zone of cultivation, lies in a hollow but in full view of him
who rides or drives, as drive he can even in a heavy carriage if
he pleases, over the green turf track from Compton Beauchamp
to Lambourn. Another comes into view of him who goes
over the Downs from Aldworth to Blewbury, of neither of which
this is the place to speak. Both houses are of standing, both
present an appearance of appalling loneliness and solitude, both

are possibly relics of a system of agriculture subsequent to the division of Folkland, but long prior to the existing system. The great farmers of old times, it appears, had often two holdings ; the one, mainly for summer use and of wide extent, up in the hills ; the other, where crops were sown and reaped and garnered, and flocks and herds were safely sheltered in the winter. For, it must be noted, the Downs are peaceable and beautiful exceedingly in the summer, but in the winter, and when snow is falling, the angel of death hovers over the lonely wayfarer. In fact it is no uncommon, at any rate no unheard of thing, for even grown men to lose their sense of direction on the Downs in snow, and to lose their lives also.

There is, indeed, a pathetic little story of a tragedy of this kind told in connection with the first of the lonely Down farms which have been mentioned. Not many years ago, on a deceitfully smiling day in winter, the solitary household was in need of coal ; and waggon and team were assigned to the task of fetching it from the more inhabited world, most likely from the ancient community of Shrivenham, which stands on the main line of the Great Western Railway, not far short of Swindon. At the farm was a little boy, perhaps a son of the house, perhaps a guest, who begged to be allowed to accompany the carters for a treat ; and obtained leave. Whether the coal was ever loaded or not my story does not tell, and it is obviously, as the sequel will show, one too full of painful memories to justify inquiry on points of mere detail from those who would feel the pain most deeply. While the expedition was on its outward or its homeward journey—it matters nothing which— the clouds gathered and the silent snow began to fall. On and on it went, obscuring all prospect, muffling the familiar outlines in a mantle of monotonous and deadly whiteness. Very soon bearings were lost and the little party was as hopelessly ignorant of its whereabouts as if the waggon had been a ship in a fog at sea and without a compass. The very excellence of the Down turf added to the misfortunes of the travellers. Even in summer it is not too easy to discern the track, for the grass springs up over the wheelmarks as soon as a heavy vehicle has passed. In the snow it was hopeless to attempt to find the way, and the only course open was to wait until the snow had ceased. The short winter's day crept away quickly; the pitiless snow continued to fall. The carter and his mate did all that was possible. They unharnessed the horses and huddled themselves and the boy among them for warmth; they covered the boy up as best they might; they themselves suffered untold misery; but in the morning, the sullen and grey morning, the boy was dead, and the strong men with him were in parlous state. That is a typical tragedy of the Downs, and, moreover, it is one which may happen, probably will happen, again.

This brings me to a curious little point, almost to be digni-fied by so grandiloquent a word as philological. It has been written that

> " 'Tis a very sad thing to be caught in the rain,
>   When night's coming on upon Salisbury Plain,"

and, years ago, I remember at the Academy a clever picture illustrating this distich, which represented the figure of a man and a woman cowering behind the shelter of one of the great stones of Stonehenge in the dusk amidst a storm of wind-driven rain. But it is very much worse to be caught on the Downs in snow, which turns them into one lonely and track-less desert. That view of the Downs seems to have impressed itself upon the Berkshire folk of old times. It was, indeed, in all probability, a lesson emphasised by Nature in her usually calm and relentless way, by lives exacted as a penalty of carelessness. So, being wise and prudent men, they eschewed the Downs in winter, but used them, and lived among them, and kept their flocks and herds among them, in the summer. But for winter there was another and a safer homestead, at the foot of the Downs or in the Vale. Sub-

East Hendred.

stantially, in fact, the practice was analogous to that of the
Swiss peasants, only the thing was done on a larger scale and
the homestead on the Downs was a considerable affair. Where,
then, is the philology ? Possibly it may be in the words that
follow. Between Steventon, which is quite at the foot of the
Downs, on the east, and Lockinge House, on the west, are two
villages named East and West Hendred. They are, as is
shown elsewhere, interesting in various quaint ways and of
immemorial antiquity. Thus in East Hendred a certain plot
of land was called Paternoster Bank, says Lysons, in 1805—it
is still so called—and it had taken its title from the fact that
one John Paternoster – who doubtless took his name from the
nature of his tenure—held it in petty serjeanty, the service
being that he should say a paternoster every day for the soul
of the king ; and the king who took this step towards his own
salvation was Edward I. Now, having been born in Wales,
and being well aware that the Britons were before Roman
and Saxon, I have a tendency to suspect a British origin for
old place-names when the derivation is not obvious ; and that
is the case of the Hendreds ; and in Welsh, which, apart from
Saxon and Latin corruption, is British, the word Hêndre or
Hêndref, meaning "old town" or "old house," is in quite
common use, in connections which show it to be ancient.
Thus, at Caernarvon, formerly Segontium, the vicarage stands
on a hill and on the site of the house of the Roman Governor
of years gone by, and on the slope of the hill to the south is
another house entitled Cefn Hêndre, or back of the old town.
Bron Hêndre, again, is another house on the " breast," or the
little hill over, the old town. So, at first, it occurred to me as
quite possible that the two Hendreds were old towns or
hamlets which had kept their British names through all the
ages. Then it seemed prudent to refer to my only Welsh
Dictionary, compiled by the worthy Thomas Richards, curate
of Coychurch, wheresoever that may be, in 1753, and printed
in Bristol, and there, first, came what seemed a disappoint-

ment. Richards does not mention "Hêndre" in the sense which I know it; still, for all that it is as certain that "Hêndre" means "old town" as that "Newgate" means "new gate." But his book contains the following passage: "Hendref. K. H. *the same as* Gauafdy, *a winter house in which the husbandmen house their herds and flocks*"; and K. H., on investigation, is found to be a reference to the laws of Howell the Good, otherwise Cyfraith Hywell Dda. When I read this the practice of winter and summer farms held by the same tenant was unknown to me, and it seemed that the modern Welsh derivation suggested by my own bias towards Ancient British explanations was every whit as suitable as that towards which the worthy Mr. Richards seemed to point. But when the practice became known to me, it appeared that the key had been supplied by Mr. Richards. Here were two hamlets, separated, it is true, from the Vale by a fold in the Downs, but still in fertile ground and remarkably well sheltered, bearing a name of which nobody seemed to know the meaning. Here, on the other hand, was a Welsh word, of the date of Howell the Good, substantially identical with them (for the final f, which would be pronounced v, is of no importance), carrying a meaning which will fit the position and characteristics of the Hendreds like a glove.

It is only fair to say that one English antiquary of repute, to whom this idea was broached, flouted it; but merely on the ground that in the heart of Wessex British words and place-names could not possibly have survived. The answer is that they have enured, as a matter of fact, all over the most English parts of England, as all the "Avons" show, for "Afon," in which the f is pronounced as if it were v, is simply the Welsh for "river." After all a place-name is precisely what one would naturally expect to live through changes of occupation; nay, more, it is, as we find in Canada and in the United States, of great vitality and permanence. Waves of qualified barbarism, such as that of the Ancient Britons – who were in some respects certainly more advanced than the Roman chronicler was able to perceive—of formal civilisation, such as that of Rome, of heathenism, like to that of the Saxon and Danes, to say nothing of the Norman wave, have flooded the land and receded again. They have left their marks on the face of the country in barrows, tumuli, roads and camps. Of the last-named many have doubtless served several races in their time. They have left their seal upon our language with its many traces of Latin and Celtic, as well as of Anglo-Saxon ; and the place-names in particular are of polyglot and often hybrid origin. All the -chesters and Chester are as Latin as they can be ; Avonmouth is hybrid—in British it would be Aber-afon ; and Latin, Danish, and Saxon endings to names of places occur at every turn. Surely it is well that this should be as it is, since it turns our minds to the variety of races which have gone to make the English stock. Surely, too, the antiquary who is not suffering from Saxon bias will forgive one who has some Welsh blood for maintaining that this suggestion about the origin of the two Hendreds is certainly a pretty conceit and by no means over-strained.

Since writing the foregoing words I have found, through the courtesy of the learned Mr. Henry Bradley, that in old charters Hendred appears as *Henna rid*, which would mean the " Hen's brook " ; and it is true that there is a brook running through both the Hendreds, which may or may not have been famous for its water-hens. But, being master of my own pages, I flatly decline to expunge a passage embodying a pretty fancy merely because philologists do not care to go back beyond the Anglo-Saxon for derivations. " Hen's brook " is not particularly taking as a derivation at the best ; for domestic hens are not fond of any brooks, and water-hens like all brooks indifferently. For the life of me I cannot see why the explanation should not be that the Saxons found these two places called Hendre, and spelled Hendre in their own way. Their descendants have acted in like fashion in India until quite recently, and it is only now that we are beginning to humour the orthographic caprices of the mild Hindoo.

Let me go one step further, this time without any help from derivations, probable or certain. It is my honest belief that there is still a great deal of ancient British blood running in the veins of the Berkshire peasantry, and that the type of some of them is neither Saxon nor Danish. Blue eyes and fair hair and ruddy complexions are by no means usual in the villages that I know best ; indeed, when they occur, they are the more striking because they are unusual. Straight-cut or even aquiline noses, dark eyes, dark hair, and lean faces are, on the other hand, very prevalent ; and it may well be that they point back to absolutely British ancestry. After all the old theory that successive hosts of invaders exterminated the aborigines here, as we have all but exterminated those of Australia and North America, is no longer held. To Roman civilisation it is, indeed, matter of history that the Britons adapted themselves very largely, and, although the Saxon ideal of colonisation was lower than the Roman, and far more ruthless, nobody now believes that the Saxons succeeded either in driving away all the British to the fastnesses of the mountainous West, or in killing them all off. Their system of law, their constitution, their land tenure, they imposed universally in Wessex ; but the probabilities are that among the lowest, or at any rate the most down-trodden, of the people of Berks there remained a considerable number of Atrebates. Even if the Saxons succeeded in killing or driving into exile the able-bodied men, they confessedly kept the women and children as slaves, and the blood of these captured women probably runs in Berkshire veins to-day. There is therefore nothing fanciful or strained in the view that the Berkshire type of face is, in part at any rate, British ; and the theory is strengthened by the historical facts that the Saxon invasion was littoral, that the Isle of Wight and Winchester, wrested from the Jutes, were the strongholds

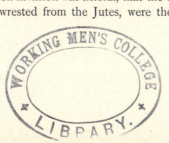
WORKING MEN'S COLLEGE LIBRARY

of the Saxons, that Berkshire was on the northern fringe of Wessex, and that the Saxon sway over Berkshire was not for very long after all. A tough race of natives, who had shown under the Romans their faculty for adapting themselves to imperious circumstances, are not likely to have been extirpated altogether ; and, if they were not destroyed, we may be sure that their blood told. Certain it is that you might take many a Berkshire labourer or shepherd of to-day, and put him down among the country folk at a Cardiganshire fair, and he would pass muster easily as a true "Cardi" until he opened his mouth. Then his drawling Berkshire tongue would be a puzzle even to the most English-speaking Welshman, for the Berkshire language, which is strange and peculiar, and the Berkshire cadence and accent, are by no means to be picked up in a day. More than once, indeed, my guests from other counties, after visits more or less prolonged, have confessed that the Berkshire dialect has baffled them altogether.

We have wandered, it must be confessed, some distance from the Downs. But away with that word "confessed" ; is it not of the essence of a volume of this kind to encourage the mind to wander and the imagination to roam ? Still, let us return to the Downs. It has been observed already that their spacious solitude is not the least of their charms. It is a solitude which, away from cultivation, is as nearly absolute as may be, for even the domestic animals are rarely seen. To a Berkshire farmer or shepherd, indeed, the song about lying on "a sheep-trimmed Down" would seem a wild flight of poetic fancy, and he would probably describe it in uncomplimentary terms. Substantially speaking, the Berkshire Downs are not grazed at all, although it may be conjectured that, if they were, the mutton would be passing excellent. Our Berkshire sheep are not of the hill-climbing type ; and they are hardly ever allowed to graze at large. Except along the roads, which they spoil abominably with their cloven hoofs when they are driven from place to place, they take practically no exercise. The system is to pack them on good feed, grass, clover, turnips or what you will, practically as close as possible, until they have eaten it bare, and manured it well, and then to pass them on to the next plot. Some years ago, for example, I had a rank aftermath of about an acre and a half, which, as a favour to me, a farmer neighbour permitted his sheep to eat. He hurdled the little area off into two equal plots, put 300 sheep into one of them for one day and night, and into the next for the same time, and, behold, every vestige of the grass had vanished. Had they all lain down simultaneously, no ground to speak of would have been visible. That is the way we feed sheep hereabouts, and one rarely sees the Downs dotted with sheep singly or in groups. The Berkshire sheep lives between hurdles, and seldom knows freedom from the day when he, or she, is born in the sheltered lambing yard, to that on which the Saxon sheep is converted into the French mutton. Hence comes it that the coat of the Downs is never, or very rarely, that hard, close, and velvet-like turf which one finds where sheep have grazed at their will.

The only animals one sees are horses and hares; but the latter only are at large. Of horses we have no ancient breed like the ponies of the New Forest, of Exmoor, or of the Welsh mountains; for that matter the county is one in which it is passing hard to obtain a sound pony for love or money. There is, perhaps, no particular reason for the non-existence of such a breed, for it would probably thrive very well on the Downs, except that it has never existed and that, as the fences, of Northern Berkshire at any rate, are few and far between, it could not very well be started now. But ever since the days when " William Duke of Cumberland " built large stables at Kate's Gore in the parish of East Ilsley " for his running horses," the value of the Downs as a training and exercise ground for thoroughbreds has been recognised to the full. Their popularity, indeed, is second only, and perhaps not reasonably second, to that of Newmarket for the purpose;

and certainly better galloping ground and purer air cannot be
desired by any trainer. Newbury, Lambourn, and East
Ilsley are all of them headquarters of trainers, and the strings
of horses going out to exercise are a pleasant sight. To see
them at full gallop over the springing turf, to hear the thud of
their hoofs, is one of the glorious sights and sounds of our
county. *Evehit ad deos.* Moreover, even in the driest
summers, the going is never hard on the Berkshire Downs ; and
that cannot be said of Newmarket. Since these words were
penned Newbury has become the site of a race-course that
may easily rival Newmarket.

Ground game Acts and poachers may have been the de-
stroyers of the hare elsewhere. On the Downs he is in an
ancient haunt which is, by reason of its abundant space, a
genuine fortress. Traces are abundant in history, and,
curiously enough, in ecclesiastical architecture, of the esteem
in which the hares of the Berkshire Downs were held by hunting men in the days when the fox was regarded as a mere
beast of vermin and not worthy to be hunted. Thus the
manor of Bockhampton, in the Lambourn parish, was held in
grand serjeanty by the De Bathe family, the service being that
they should maintain a pack of hariers—to spell the word in
the old-fashioned way—for the king's use when he came that
way, at the king's charges. Nor was Bockhampton the only
manor in the Down land held on these easy terms. Moreover, in the days of the Saxon monarchs, who were sportsmen
when they had leisure from fighting, Berkshire was even more
of a Royal County than it is now, for they had royal palaces
at Abingdon, Faringdon, and Wantage, as well as at Old
Windsor and one or two other places. Coursing also, a pretty
form of sport when it is pursued privately, although there is
little to be said for public coursing, has been a pastime of the
Downs from time immemorial. Of it, or of hunting—it would
be rash to pronounce upon the breed of a hound represented
in a bas-relief some hundreds of years old—there are traces in

the churches. All round the arches of Lambourn Church, for example, are unmistakable hares in stone, fleeing before the jaws of straining dogs, which might be either greyhounds or hariers, but are certainly dogs. This coursing has fallen into disrepute in these later days, mainly, perhaps, because it has come to be practised by persons of low repute. The reference here is not to farmers, to whom no man could grudge any enjoyment that is open to them in these hard times, but to publicans and the like, and to the betting men who tend to deprive of healthy charm any and every sport which involves competition. For the sport itself, privately pursued by small parties of gentlemen, with two or three couples of greyhounds for separate use, I know nothing prettier, especially in Down country, where the hares are strong and able to use the upward slopes of the hills to their advantage. The greyhound, fully extended until he seems a mere line of black, grey, or fawn colour that flies over the grass, is the very embodiment of the idea of pace ; the quick double of the hare, while her pursuers shoot onwards for twenty yards or more with a momentum which they cannot resist ; the skill with which a clever greyhound will turn the quarry from her upward course ; finally, the welcome fact that the hare, in country of this sort, has a chance of escaping with her life—all these things are, to one not superior to the weaknesses of humanity, a sheer delight. It was Aristotle who wrote that man was by nature a political animal, meaning, of course, not that he was a creature given to talking politics, though there be men who do that in mixed company and live, but that he was inclined to assemble in communities. It is by no means certain that Aristotle was right, and that the gregarious aptitude does not come later, when the savage has learned that his fellow-man may be trusted occasionally. But if he had written that man is by nature a hunting animal, he would unquestionably have been accurate, for the hunting instinct, implanted in the savage by nature, and cultivated by him for the sake of his own existence, sur-

for taking hard exercise, however, walking up Down partridges can be recommended without reserve.

Perhaps this chapter, dealing with the charm of the Downs in general, without detailed references to this or that place in or on them, may close with an impression of hunting on them, gained, oddly enough, with gun in hand. The scene was a modest shooting manor near Catmore, in the Down country, but not in the unenclosed part of it. It is an ancient seat of the Eystons, the Roman Catholic squires of East Hendred, to which they used to retire when persecution grew severe. We had enjoyed a fair day among the pheasants, which gave some sporting shots ; we had organised an impromptu partridge drive with the usual result ; that is to say, the majority of the birds had disappointed all calculations and had gone the wrong way. Then, suddenly, while we were shooting a covert on the side of a hill, the sound of a horn was heard, and on the other side of the little valley the hounds streamed past in full cry, and the scarlet coats, the black coats, and the ladies in their habits in close pursuit. The coincidence was one which I had never before seen in any county of England, and the moving scene, as it unfolded itself quickly before our eyes, and, as rapidly, vanished again, was like an old sporting picture suddenly endowed with miraculous life. It was the kind of picture that lives in the memory, and it was certainly a characteristic impression of the Downs.

CHAPTER III

THE STRIPLING THAMES

WHILE there are parts of Berkshire which may best be studied with the help of horse or bicycle—a motor moves too fast for intelligent travel—and other parts in which, after travelling by train to the spot to be investigated, days may be spent with profit in some number, there is one part of the county which can be studied in one fashion only. That part is the Berkshire margin of the Upper Thames, from Inglesham, which as a matter of fact is just outside Berkshire, to Oxford, a distance of forty-five miles or thereabouts ; and the only way to travel over it, in worthy and satisfactory fashion, is by boat. Roads following the course of the Thames there are none, for the good reason that no man save the lover of natural beauty wishes to go that way, and for him the river serves better than any road. Villages, even hamlets, are few and far between on the banks themselves, and the course of the stream, running for the most part under the steep shelf of hills that makes the northern boundary of the Vale of the White Horse, is tortuous as that of classic Meander itself. Cross-roads there are, from Buscot, which really is on the river, to Lechlade and onwards; from Faringdon to Bampton and the Cotswolds, two of them following different lines; from Kingston Bagpuze to Witney; and from Oxford, behind Wytham Woods, to Eynsham. Also there is a splendid high-road, worthy of the palmy days of coaching, which runs fairly straight, albeit by two lines, from Abingdon to Kingston Bagpuze, and thence to Faringdon; but that is far out of sight of the river, and, even when detours are made from it to Hinton Waldrist and to Longworth, the stream is still invisible. Nor, in fact, is either one or the other easily accessible from the river. So, for the present, let us be navigators of the Thames.

And first, to open in Baconian style, we must be leisurely navigators, pausing from time to time to note that which is of interest, so long as it be not too far from the boat, and not given to hurry. In truth it is impossible to hurry on the Upper Thames, for the navigation, although it is safe enough to satisfy the most cautious, since shallows are the only obstacle to it except weeds, is far from easy. Often, when the water is low and the boat grounds, and the banks are marshy so that man cannot tow from them, the only way to make any progress is to wade and drag. Moreover, when it comes to a matter of shooting weirs, as it does at Hart's Weir for example, and the voyager has to work the weir for himself, expedition is out of the question. The way to accomplish the little voyage with any approach to comfort is to send a boat—clearly it must not be too large a one—by train to Lechlade, which is in Gloucestershire, and to row down stream, spending at least one night on the way, at Tadpole or at New Bridge. The accommodation is not luxurious, but, if notice be given providently, it is adequate to human needs and clean ; and the scenery is simply unrivalled of its kind. Never, while memory remains, shall I forget one afternoon and evening in 1884, and in the month of August, spent between Tadpole and New Bridge. The river was low, the sun was so scorchingly hot that when it sunk in the West one hardly knew whether to rejoice most in the departure of the heat, or in the unspeakable beauty of the long reaches of water between the reeds and the flags as they blushed under the last kisses of the sun. Nay, they did much more than blush. No opal, not even the "noble opal" which "exhibits brilliant and changeable reflections of green, blue, yellow, and red," ever shone with such varied and evasive glow. It was lovely beyond comparison. All too quickly, while progress grew more slow, and we had to pole the boat along, or sometimes wade and drag her, the light faded. Then soon, from the marshland on either side, rose herons complaining hoarsely that their sanctuary was invaded in the night season, and wild ducks innumerable started from the reeds with clanging wings and circled round about us high in the air. The quacking, the whistling of countless wings in the half-darkness, the minor difficulties of the voyage, and its final accomplishment with success, are among golden memories.

Then the reception at New Bridge, which, by the way, is one of the oldest bridges over the Thames and of well over 600 years' standing, was quaint. On the Berkshire side, in the little "May Bush" Inn, the goodman and his wife were gone to bed ; but they took us in kindly, vacating their own bed and remaking it for the purpose, and gave us what they had to eat, which in truth was not much. From the "Old Rose," on the

Oxfordshire side, came sounds of revelry, which were explained
to be due to "them there Conservatives," who in their

New Bridge.

turn were found to be simply the workmen of the Thames
Conservancy.   They were relaxing themselves after their

labours in the bed of the stream ; labours sadly needed, but, it is to be feared, not so effectual as they might be.

Being comparatively young at the time, having indeed not long left the bosom of Alma Mater of the Isis at Oxford hard by, I was more interested in the mallards and the ducks, in the chance of bringing some of them to bag in days to come, and in the ways of the inn folk, than in the bridge itself or in the history of the place. Yet the bridge, with its six narrow and pointed arches, its niches for foot-passengers to take refuge in, its buttressed ribs to meet and divide the floods of water, is one of the best remaining bridges of the Thames. It was there when Leland wrote in Tudor days, exactly as it is now, " lying in low meadows, often overflowed with rage of rain " ; and the " May Bush," nestling under it on the right bank of the river, is old and picturesque and clean, although it must be admitted that a matutinal request for soap elicited, as it might in France, the saying, " They mostly brings their own soap." New Bridge has its little corner in history too, although nowadays, in spite of standing on the main road from Abingdon to Witney, it is not on a living artery of communication. Before railways were in the land this was an important road, the best perhaps between Oxfordshire and the country south of the Berkshire Downs—for south of Abingdon, at the foot of Steventon Hill, it begins to climb the Downs, and passes through East Ilsley to the valley of the Kennet. Also from the bridge leads a road to Wantage and so across the Downs. Hence came it, no doubt, that the Royalists made a successful stand here in May of 1644 against the Parliament men, who retired to Abingdon and consoled themselves for their defeat by iconoclasm, as was their wont. That is to say, they broke up the Market Cross, and the lost beauty of that cross was as much greater than that of those which were left as the weights of the trout that have broken away were greater than those of the fish that have found their way to the landing net and the creel.

The Royalists, however, seem to have made no provision for holding New Bridge, for, in spite of their victory in May—the day was the 27th—Sir William Waller marched over the bridge unopposed on the 2nd of June. That mattered, as it happened, but little, for Waller was badly defeated far away at Cropredy Bridge before the month ended. Now, perhaps, even that is a matter of small moment; but it is more than commonly interesting now, in these essentially and, one might almost imagine, eternally peaceful parts of the country, to think what it was like in 1644, when harassed Charles held his Court and semblance of a Parliament at Oxford, and Berkshire was as much harried by troops as she is every autumn now. New Bridge was then in the centre of the active world; it is now as far from it as it conveniently can be, except of course when it happens to be useful in the course of military manœuvres. In passing there is a temptation to pause and consider what those dashing Cavaliers and those stern Roundheads would think of the soldiers who are their successors to-day, if they could but revisit us. On the whole, perhaps, the machine guns and motor-cars dashing to and fro, with umpires or generals for passengers, would astonish them less than the system for compensating farmers for damage done to crops by the military. That would indeed seem to them marvellous, and by it they might account for the fact that the British army of to-day is a thousandfold more welcome on a country-side than either party of them ever was.

By no means least of the fascinations of the Upper Thames is its solitude. Should fortune be favourable a little party of voyagers may move slowly downwards all the long day without encountering any others of their kind, hearing no noise, vexed by no voices of men. It is the very place for those who, like the Scholar-Gipsy, "love retired ground." It is shunned by the tripper, the desecrator of the sacred calm of the river, partly, no doubt, because it is lonely, partly because the navigation is really troublesome. For the first reason, doubtless, Kelmscott was chosen by William Morris as a peaceful resting-place. Of Kelmscott, since it lies a little inland on the left bank of the Thames, it is not mine to speak. But Buscot, with its church standing modestly at the waterside, with its ancient rectory embowered in noble trees, is safely inside Berkshire : and surely it is one of the most restful and soul-satisfying haunts of ancient peace in this England of ours.

The little church, a mixture of many styles, Early English, Transitional, and Perpendicular, is interesting from the architectural point of view, and it would be easy to speak too harshly of the work of restoration that has been effected. In many cases, indeed, this kind of criticism is futile as well as unkind ; and it would be no bad thing sometimes if the critic would try to put himself into the places of those whom he censures for "restoring" (the inverted commas are of course bitterly sarcastic) an ancient edifice. He might remember that it could not be permitted to fall into decay ; that funds are not always available locally ; that the ill-paid incumbent is often personally liable for repairs ; and that those who are most eager to raise an outcry against Vandalism or lack of taste are not always the first to find the money which is necessary for harmonious restoration. At any rate Buscot Church will remain notable for many a long year as one of the few which show glass windows designed, in admirable and characteristic taste, by Sir E. Burne-Jones : and its situation among the trees and amid

> "Those wide fields of breezy grass
> Where black-winged swallows haunt the glittering Thames"

is, in a single word which this time is not misused, perfect.

Hard by, on an eminence in a fine deer park, stands Buscot House, built in the closing years of the eighteenth century, more substantial and imposing than it is beautiful. But those who have the opportunity will do well to cultivate the acquaintance of the owner, Sir Alexander Henderson, for the sake of the acquaintance, of course, in the first place. Then shall they see the wonderful series of Burne-Jones pictures. They are the famous Briar Rose series illustrating the story of the Sleeping Beauty, shown in a room designed especially for them, though it must be admitted that the light is poor. Between the pictures, which of course were once exhibited, are panels expressly painted by the artist, and almost as beautiful as the pictures themselves, less known since they have not been exhibited.

Is it wrong to add that Sir Alexander Henderson is one of those numerous and valuable persons who, having amassed riches in commercial or industrial life, have done yeoman's service to the country by taking up farming in a serious and scientific spirit? The Buscot shire horses stand at the very top of the tree, and "Buscot Harold," who won the first prize and the championship at the London Shire Horse Shows of 1898, 1899, 1900, and was bred at Buscot, was (perhaps is) probably the finest specimen of that noble breed, descended from the "Great Horse" of days gone by, that ever was foaled. Agriculturally, in fact, the farming and the farm buildings at Buscot are in all respects model, and that means not a toy but a thing to be copied and studied. Buscot, too, is a place at which, under cherishing influence it may be, some of the old sports flourish. So late as September of 1903, in connection with a local flower-show held in the park, there were all kinds of old village sports and pastimes. The best of them was the pursuit of a pig, with his tail greased, by maids and matrons in a spacious paddock, the condition being that the animal should become the property of her who should grasp the tail and capture its owner. It was, as Mr. Pepys would have said, mighty diverting to the spectators, and, apparently, not distressing to the pig, who was in fine running condition and led the panting women a merry dance. It was satisfactory, too, that the porker, a genuine Berkshire gem, black, and with snout " tiptilted like the petal of a flower," remained at last in the hand of a woman possessed of many children. The knowledge provoked visions of children feasting on various delicacies at killing time, of hams and flitches dependent from the rafters of a rose-clad cottage. For our Berkshire cottages are really rose-clad, and the vicinity of Longworth, from which a fine collection of roses was exhibited at this very show, is in evidence on many a cottage wall. Not Gloire de Dijon only —that is omnipresent and always welcome—but Rêve d'Or and Longworth Rambler, and a score of more rare and precious roses, clothe the cottage walls, and there is hardly a cottage garden but boasts its little collection of capital standard roses. Almost every labourer, too, can practise the occult art of budding with fair success; and that adds much to the charm of the country dwellings. In Buscot they are quite at their best, and " jasmine-muffled lattices " are frequent as flowers in May.

From Buscot, passing down stream, through flat land first and then under the sharp brow by Eaton Hastings, one soon reaches another Early English church, and a village, now in the midst of fine trees, which for one reason or another has changed its site. The " old town," still marked by a humble habitation or two, is pointed out by tradition ; but who Teucer was, and why Salamis stands not where it used to stand, the inhabitants have clean forgotten. Radcot Bridge, with pointed arches on either side, and a blunter arch for the main stream, is a beautiful stone structure now, and was more striking once when it carried a stone cross. Good Mr. Henry Taunt, of Oxford, to whom all those who use the Thames owe much gratitude for careful charts and amiable riverside gossip past and present, notes a battle of Radcot which has escaped the observation of most historians. In it the barons under Henry of Derby, afterwards Henry IV., had the better of Robert de Vere, the favourite of Richard II., Earl of Oxford and Duke of Ireland. Radcot Bridge, too, an important thoroughfare in those days, had its

Radcot Bridge.

share in the excitement of the Great Rebellion, for it was held by the Royalists as an outpost of Faringdon House, and it was marked by a minor victory of the Parliamentary troops some time before Sir Robert Pye, one of the few persons in history to whom it has fallen to lay siege to his own home, received the surrender of Faringdon House from the King to the Commons in June of 1646. But of the story of Faringdon, and of the Pyes, the stout soldier Robert, and Henry, the worst of the Laureates, but, be it hoped, not an inefficient police magistrate, this is hardly the place in which to write. They belong to the Vale.

Buckland too, lying a mile or more inland from Tadpole, where the fishing is good, has too long and too interesting a story to come into a river expedition; and Hinton Waldrist, the beautiful, with Longworth of the roses, belong rather to the road than to the river, since both are on the crown of the hill which has pushed the infant Thames into its course. But Duxford is a pleasant little resting-place, and Harrowdown Hill, reaching the commanding height of 325 feet, over the remains of an ancient weir, quite dominates the landscape. Does anybody whisper that 325 feet is no great eminence? Truth to tell it is not, in a mountainous country or in a land of hills. But all depends on environment, and, as a plain matter of fact, this mere hillock, crowned with trees, looks grand as it rises a sheer hundred feet and more above the slow-moving stream. Also from almost any point along the ridge which, more or less, borders the river Harrowdown is distinctly commanding.

Of New Bridge mention has been made already, out of its place perhaps, but designedly so, since it gave the opportunity of describing a typical episode in such a river tour as is here suggested. Appleton and Besselsleigh, some little way from the river, are reserved for a road pilgrimage, partly because they are not conveniently accessible from the river, more because there is so much to say about both. But Bablock

Buckland Church.

Hithe is still absolutely charming, and it has changed very
little since Matthew Arnold wrote that stanza of which a line
has been quoted already :

> " For most, I know, thou lov'st retired ground !
>   Thee at the ferry Oxford riders blithe,
>   Returning home on summer nights, have met
>   Crossing the stripling Thames at Bab-lock-hithe
>   Trailing in the cool stream thy fingers wet,
>   As the punt's rope chops round ;
>   And leaning backward in a pensive dream,
>   And fostering in thy lap a heap of flowers
>   Pluck'd in shy fields and distant wychwood bowers,
>   And thine eyes resting on the moonlit stream."

Change there has been some, and for the better. That is to say, the inn on the Oxfordshire side is better than it was in the 'seventies, when this deponent knew it first, and yet it is no palace of luxury. For the great punt, substantial enough to carry a waggon and horses, worked in primitive fashion by a man hauling at a cable, it may easily, by its looks, be the same vessel that Arnold knew. Seated on the bank it is easy to reconstruct the scene, and sometimes one may see the "riders blithe," more often on bicycles than on horses, crossing from Oxfordshire into Berkshire, in order to reach Oxford, distant only five miles, in time for Hall. They will have come, most likely, from Stanton Harcourt, the stately but deserted manor-house of the Harcourt family, beloved of Alexander Pope too, but, sadly be it written, outside my limits ; and they will go by Cumner to the city of dreaming spires. Otherwise they would have to go a long way round, for nothing is more striking than the manner in which Berkshire and Oxfordshire have been content to let the river be as absolute a bar to communication between them in these parts as it was in the old days of the Dobuni and the Atrebates. Until quite recent times the rustic ferry was the only means of crossing the river between New Bridge and Eynsham, a distance of fully eight miles, save by scrambling across a weir. Now Skinner's Weir has vanished, to the sorrow of all who remember its quaint beauty, and a "gallows" bridge stands in its place, and Ridge's Bridge, a commonplace

Eynsham Bridge.

E

structure enough, has come into existence a mile below New Bridge.

So on the boat and its passengers go, the bow pointing almost due north, until at Eynsham Bridge the course becomes north-easterly, and Wytham Woods, fringing their 478 feet of hill, dominate the scene. Here one may pause to think of many things, but most of all, in the season of the year, of strawberries ; on which, indeed, it is not necessary to meditate only. Nowhere, unless it be in Kent, where the flavours of various kinds of strawberries are discussed with as much nicety of knowledge as our fathers showed concerning vintages of port and claret, does the strawberry flourish more abundantly, nowhere is it eaten with so much of abandon, as at Wytham. For the growth, it is probably due to the deep alluvial soil ; the zest is that of youth, for those who feast are undergraduates who, a year or two ago, were boys at school, not ashamed to debauch themselves on ices and sweet things of all sorts. And now they have but changed their *status* ; their nature and their years are much the same ; and at Wytham boyhood's healthy appetite for fruit may be indulged in without compromise of dignity. It is curious, when one comes to think of it, how rapid is the change of habits in the boy who, going to Oxford, becomes a man. In June and July, he could eat "sock" at Eton, or "suction" at Winchester, or frequent the "tuck shop," perhaps under some other name, at Harrow or Rugby. In October he is supposed to put away childish things. But if the summer be not too long delayed, and he has the luck to hear of Wytham, he may renew his lost youth next year. The distance is but short for a summer walk, or, if it seem more pleasant, a boat will carry him from "the primitive abodes of the Bossoms and the Beesleys"—a beautiful phrase of the sporting papers in the 'seventies—to Godstow, and thence he may walk, leaving his boat at the inn. Then the strawberries are a sheer delight, because there is no nonsense about manly dignity, or refinement, or delicacy of appetite. Crushed in a wide bowl with the base of a wine-glass, they emit a delicious fragrance, not dissimilar to that breathed out from bracken trodden in the hot sunshine, and, with sugar and rich cream to taste, they are a meal meet for gods, but enjoyed no less by young men and maidens, the latter from that Northern Oxford which has recently been condemned by the Union as detrimental.

Strawberries take first place in the thoughts of the traveller in their season. After all, why should they not do so? Does not every wanderer over the globe's surface admit and protest that no fruit grown in the open air, neither mango nor mango-stine, neither persimmon nor custard apple, neither guava nor banana, possesses a taste so clean and unquestionably delicious as that of the strawberry of England at its best? But, when the strawberries are eaten, if they are to be had, or at once, if they be not available, there are some other points to think of. Here is a manor of Wytham, once the property of the Wight-hams. Did they take their name from it, or did it take its name from them? That is a question which raises itself over and over again in Berkshire, where place-names and those of families long passed away are very often identical, except in point of spelling—a detail which never worried our ancestors. The last of those Wighthams vanished, the antiquarians know not how; and in 1480 one Alice Denton—she may have been born a Wightham—died, having been seised of the manor. To her succeeded her kinsman Sir Richard Harcourt, and here we are on firm ground. Old Fuller tells us that "the lands of Berkshire are very skittish and apt to cast their owners"; in other words, that there were few landed estates in the county in his time which had been in the same families for many generations. The Lysons, taking up the tale in 1805 (the copy of their work which I have used is dated 1868), tell the same story, noting that the Cravens date back two centuries, the Reades, Heads, and Southbys longer, the Englefields, Eystons, and Clarks longer still. But they do not mention the

Wytham Abbey.

Harcourts or the Lenthalls, perhaps because both were always and principally Oxfordshire folk. Still the Harcourts are, in respect of Wytham, a Berkshire family; they are still in the land; and their handiwork remains in Wytham Abbey, although it is now the property of the Earl of Abingdon. That is to say, their arms are on a ceiling there, and one of them, tradition has forgotten which, was the first builder of it. It is to the Bertie family, however, that Berkshire owes a debt of gratitude, and Oxfordshire very much the reverse, for some of the grandeur of Wytham Abbey. It was an Earl of Abingdon who pulled down the palatial house at Rycote, hard by Thame, built by Lord Keeper Williams, which had housed Elizabeth, James I., Charles I., and his son Charles also, and the gentle Anna. He had some excuse, perhaps, in the fact that the house was enormous and that a whole wing was burnt down in 1750. At any rate, somewhere about 1800, Wytham was, to use Mr. Meade Falkner's words, "enriched with much of the spoil of Rycote," and Oxfordshire's loss is Berkshire's gain. Wytham Church, too, is enriched with transported materials, but here the lover of Berkshire gains nothing, and loses much. Cumner Hall ought to be one of the most interesting places in Berkshire, but as a matter of fact Lady Warwick is overstating the case when, in her handsome book on Warwick Castle, she describes Cumner as a ruin. It is not even that, for the best of the stones were taken away in 1814, and Wytham Church was rebuilt with them and the rest are gone. But the inscription on the churchyard gate, "*Janua vitæ verbum Domini*," is as appropriate at Wytham Church as at Cumner Hall; perhaps more appropriate.

Between Wytham Wood and Wytham Village, if one follows the exact course of the river, comes Hagley Pool, and with it the beginning of a reticulation of streams which is somewhat intricate. The main stream proceeds due east to King's Weir, formerly a ford (where a bridge was built about 100 years ago by the then Earl of Abingdon), and is then turned sharply to the right or

south-east. From that point it proceeds, meandering, and
with various bifurcations, natural and artificial, to Godstow
Lock, where the forked streams re-unite and continue as one to
Medley Lock, about two miles above Folly Bridge, Oxford.

Wytham

After Medley there is fresh ramification caused by junctions
with the canal and the necessities of navigation, but the main
stream is that which passes a quarter of a mile, or less, to the
west of the Great Western station from Tumbling Bay and
through Osney (the bells of whose abbey are now at Christ
Church), and then curls round to be united with other streams
as the main river above Folly Bridge. But from Hagley Pool,
past Wytham proper and west of Medley, is yet another and

perhaps the most ancient channel, which appears to become
the main stream at Tumbling Bay.   All this is mentioned, not
with a view to a historical dissertation on the alterations which
the ages have seen in the course of the Thames, but because
here there comes in a question of county boundaries.   Thus
the river is the boundary of Berks and Oxon to King's Weir
and for half a mile below.   Then the dividing line leaves the
river, goes inland from the right bank, almost if not quite cuts
through the ruins of Godstow nunnery, passes due south to the
west of Binsey Church, and, a furlong or so further south,
impinges on the branch of water between Hagley Pool and
Tumbling Bay, of which mention has been made.   This it
follows, and we have once more a boundary, clearly defined
by running water.   If the original course of the river, or the
eldest known course—for there is no such thing in geology or
geography as an original course of a river—was the branch
from Hagley Pool, then Berkshire has poached some of Oxfordshire in the past.   If the elder stream be that from King's
Weir, which is the more ample of the two, Berkshire has been
the sufferer, and that, having regard to the greatness of
mediæval Oxford, is the more likely explanation.   Thus much,
at least, is certain, that man has done so much to guide and
hamper the course of the Thames immediately above and
through Oxford that it would be difficult, if not impossible, to
produce a map of Oxford and its environs showing the various
watercourses of the tenth century, which was the period in which
most counties took their present shape.   Perhaps it might not
be particularly interesting either ; but the fact that, for this
little space, the Thames ceases to be a boundary is worthy of
notice.

Still, Oxfordshire cannot be allowed to exclude me from the
Benedictine nunnery of Godstow, the ruins of which still
remain, although the building was used as barracks during the
civil war, and afterwards burnt.   It is, of course, in accordance
with the perversity of human nature that nobody cares in these

days about Editha, who founded the nunnery in 1138, whereas most people are interested in Rosamond Clifford, otherwise known as " Fair Rosamond," with the name and fate of whom

Godstow Bridge.

the memory of Godstow is indissolubly connected.   'Tis true, 'tis pity, that wicked women are, as a rule, far more interesting than those who lead saintly lives; and it is quite sure that Rosamond Clifford was not quite good.

How much of her romantic story, as told by Higden the monk, is myth, is more than will ever be known ; but opinion is agreed that the episode of the poisoned cup is false, which is fortunate for the reputation of Queen Eleanor. Mr. Falkner, in his *History of Oxfordshire*, says : " It would be perhaps as injudicious to deny it (the story) *in toto*, as to believe all the romantic additions which have gradually clustered round it." It would, indeed, for Rosamond's tombstone and its inscription are undoubtedly historic ; and the advancement of her sons, William Longsword, who married the daughter of the Earl of Salisbury, and Geoffrey, who became Archbishop of York, would be proof enough that Henry II. regarded them as his sons also, apart from the close association in which Geoffrey was seen with him at his death. In fact there is no doubt that Rosamond Clifford, daughter of Walter, Lord Clifford, of Hertfordshire, was Henry II.'s mistress, and that she bore him children. She may, also, have been educated at Godstow Convent, in which case, seeing that it had been but nineteen years in existence when she entered it to end her days in 1157, after some years of association with Henry, she must have been one of its earliest pupils. Mr. Falkner suggests, very reasonably, that Henry did not, as some have it, make a clean breast to Queen Eleanor when he married her, and that Rosamond Clifford accompanied the Court from place to place, but was discovered by the jealous Queen at Woodstock, more or less by chance.

That may be the reason why legend points to so many bowers connected with this lady's name. Legend indeed has been almost as busy with her as fiction itself, and Sir Walter Scott, in *The Talisman* and in *Woodstock*, has used her as freely as that other lady, Amy Robsart, in whom Berkshire is interested. Dryden, too, wrote, one knows not on what ground :

> " Jane Clifford was her name, as books aver,
> Fair Rosamond was but her *nom de guerre*."

At any rate Rosamond was the name under which she was buried

in the conventual church, after she had remained an inmate of
the convent for twenty years; and all that one has read of conventual life in those ages tends to the belief that, if her sins
were capable of being atoned for, she is likely to have ex-
piated them to the full.   Her epitaph, too, is historical.

> " *Hic jacet in tumulo Rosa Mundi non Rosa Munda,*
> *Non redolet sed olet quæ redolere solet.*"

Mr. Falkner thinks there is reason to believe that this
epitaph, which seems so distinctly and personally appropriate,
was not composed expressly to meet the case of Rosamond
Clifford, but was the stock couplet used by monumental masons
of the Middle Ages for the tombs of all Rosamonds, and that
the allusion, in the first line, as well as the second, was to the
natural state of the body after death.   But is it necessary to be
quite so matter of fact as all that?   The couplet is very neat
and apposite as it stands ; there have been hundreds of other
Rosamonds, mediæval Rosamonds too, to whom it was not
applied, and surely, in ages when Latin was generally understood, and men were rough, so flagrant a departure from the
salutary maxim *de mortuis* would have been likely to invite the
chastisement of the tomb-maker.   The probability is that
Rosamond Clifford was so cruelly and epigrammatically
insulted on her tomb because, like most of her sisters who
have erred in like fashion, she had no friends, especially
amongst her own sex.   True, the excellent and imaginative
monk Higden says that Henry decorated her tomb lavishly ; but
Henry was a busy king ; and it was a hard age.   How hard it
was, Hugh, Bishop of Lincoln, proved in 1191, for he caused
the remains to be removed to the outside of the church.   They
were taken back again, however, and there they lay in peace
until the dissolution.   Leland, who was very much alive at the
time of the dissolution of the monasteries, informs us : " Rosa-
munde's tumbe at Godestow Nunnery was taken up a late : it is
a stone with the inscription *tumba Rosamundæ*.   Her bones were

closid in lede, and within that closid in lether; when it was openid there was a very swete smell came owt of it."

Here Mr. Taunt, of Oxford, who has been quoted already, is of assistance, but it is a pity that one who has clearly spent much pains in research does not quote his authorities. After describing the action of Hugh of Lincoln, he adds: "But after a while the sisterhood collected the desecrated bones and laid them, enclosed in a perfumed leather bag, in the abbey church again, where they were found so preserved after the dissolution of the monastery." So Leland's words are amplified and made intelligible, and the rather singular story of an exhumed corpse which breathed forth sweet savours is not dissipated by the light of research, but confirmed and, at the same time, improved in poetic quality. That, in an age which would have William of Wykeham no architect, and revels in describing Edward VI. as a spoiler of schools, is distinctly refreshing.

And now we are very near the end of the little voyage. From Wytham to Oxford, being tied to navigable water more or less, it is best to go by way of King's Weir, halting, perhaps, for tea at the "Trout" inn at Godstow. This stands on an island, and a little detour must be made to reach it. But *Consule Planco*, which being loosely interpreted in this case is, "When Dean Liddell ruled in august fashion at Christ Church," the digression was worth making for tea, or for spiced beer, cunningly made in vessels of tin, funnel-shaped for thrusting between the glowing coals, and for the really fine old English game of skittles. Other memories, indeed, than those of Rosamond Clifford are associated with Godstow in the minds of many of those who were once irresponsible undergraduates. They are memories of days of fresh air in the rain and the sun, when the pleasant perils of the voyage from over against Binsey to the "Trout" up-stream, or across the flooded surface of Port Meadow (which the citizens of Oxford have enjoyed since the time of the Confessor, at least), had been encountered triumphantly in a cranky centreboard sailing boat. Winter was the best season, for then there was the better chance of wind and water, and shipwrecks were many in number. It was real joy, then, to be skipper of one out of perhaps thirty boats which pushed up river gaily after luncheon, and to be one of two or three which won to the haven where they would be under the willows of Godstow. Then, indeed, spiced beer—appalling thought now !—was thrice welcome, and *sequelæ* there were none, since *dura messorum ilia* were not a circumstance to the digestion of a nineteenth century undergraduate. They are more fragile and indulge in hearts and things now. Nor was the homeward course, plain sailing as it was by reason of the aiding stream, whatsoever might be the airt of the wind, rendered any the less enjoyable by the sight of the half-inverted hulls of less fortunate craft that had capsized by the way and of the other wrecks stranded on many a lee-shore. No harm had been done to men, save what could be cured by a change of clothes, and none to boats that "Jupiter"—for so the attendant on sailing boats had been named by others than his sponsors—could not repair before the morrow. A genuine "character" was "Jupiter," full of strange sayings and laconic sailing directions, and even able to prescribe for the wounded. Once a sudden gibe—inevitable but none the less stupidly unforeseen—caused the boom of the good ship *Romeo* to break my head rather severely, and "Jupiter's" prescription was immense. "When you gets yer dinner fill a spoon with butter, an' melt it in the candle, and pour it on the wownd." It is, perhaps, almost a pity that the advice was not followed. The dent in a battered skull would probably not be less deep than it is to-day, for the knock was a shrewd one, but the scene in Hall, if a Junior Student had suddenly anointed himself with butter *coram populo*, would certainly have been merry in retrospect.

These things are changed now. Sailing on the lowest reaches of the Upper River has become systematic. There are clubs and regattas and the like. In fact the sailing of the 'seventies was to that of what, some day perhaps, we shall call

the 'noughts, as the croquet of the 'sixties and—a closer
analogy really—the cricket of the 'twenties were to those of
to-day. But it was the best of fun and a good school of petty
seamanship. To have learned to mark the influence of shelter-
ing objects, a hedge, a pollard, or a haystack, in stealing the
wind, to have realised how much can be done in the way of
coaxing a boat round an awkward corner up-stream and up-
wind, was to have acquired knowledge of value in a wider
sphere. The experience was worth acquiring, apart from the
enjoyment, and, if the yachts were not exactly *Valkyries* or
Shamrocks, they were at least as good as the seamanship of
their crews deserved.

Surgit amari aliquid. I cannot part from the Upper River,
particularly in a volume of the "Highways and Byways"
Library, without remembering that it was the favourite haunt
and the familiar topic of the bright and sympathetic author
of the London volume, the late Mrs. E. T. Cook, whose un-
expected death in the spring of 1903 was widely mourned. It
is a topic upon which, for personal reasons, I cannot dwell.
But, just because of that, it is possible to say that an
unsigned article of singular grace on "A New River,"
which appeared in *The Cornhill Magazine* of September,
1893, was her work ; and, just because it and others were not
signed, it was not until some years afterwards that my friend
and connection won the reputation to which her rare beauty
of mind and her flashing intelligence entitled her. (It is a
curious but almost universal experience, by the way, that the
literary weaklings are always anxious for their names to appear,
whereas the men and women who have genius, as the "names"
Henry Seton Merriman, Anthony Hope, George Eliot, and
John Oliver Hobbes demonstrate sufficiently, are content to
hide their personality under anonymity or a pseudonym for
their early ventures. They are, as Mr. Henry James might
say, "of a modesty," which in time causes their real names to be
forgotten in connection with their fame.)

For the article, written in 1893, be it remembered, is as good as that kind of production can be ; it is the cheerful and natural talk of a clever and highly cultivated woman. Exaggeration there may be in it, but it is the happy exaggeration which fits the theme. The Upper River is not really "as silent, as secluded, to all intents and purposes, as a South American forest stream, or a Californian creek"; but what does that matter? The true spirit of the river-lover, the seeing eye, is there ; and it contains some of Mrs. Cook's most essentially characteristic passages :

" After Eynsham Bridge—a solid, not a beautiful structure—the real charm begins. It is curious to notice in this connection how the only signs of life, the only human beings you come across in your wanderings, are invariably to be found looking over a bridge. It reminds one of the child's early drawings. Tell him to draw a bridge, it is never a bridge to him until he has placed a man on it—ergo to the rustic a bridge is not so much a bridge as a place for a man to stand on and from which to survey the world at large. The average rustic seems to spend all his holiday-time in this enthralling occupation. To him a bridge seems to be a scene of wild dissipation. Bridges, however, are comparatively scarce on the Upper Thames, which may perhaps account for their popularity."

She goes on to tell a delicious anecdote of the ruminating apathy of an Oxfordshire rustic, and I only hope he was not one of our Berkshire folk.

" On one occasion, above Eynsham, one of these rustics was, as usual, on the bridge, when an upset occurred in a boat passing underneath it. . . . The stream happened to be deep at this particular place, and enclosed between high mud banks, sparsely covered by dry reeds. These reeds snapped when grasped, like tinder, and it accordingly took the submerged ones some time to extricate themselves from their difficulties. But the man on the bridge did not budge an inch. When at last one of the sufferers, impelled thereto by an imperative desire for dry clothes, went up to him and accosted him, he slowly removed his pipe : ' There wus a young man,' he said, ' drowned in this very place six weeks ago to-day, and they ain't found his body yet.' "

That is Oxfordshire all over, and, it is to be feared, Berkshire also ; and the deft touch, introducing a piece of human interest,

so lightly and so easily, was Mrs. Cook's very self. She
always saw the pathos and the oddity of things at the same
time ; but she saw the poetry in them too. Indeed the

Eynsham Bridge.

concluding passage is so beautiful that it must be quoted at
length. In truth it is all too short.

    "But alas ! our holiday is ending, and we must, however reluctantly,
turn our faces homewards. Again we must see the stream widen and

> ' Flow, softly flow, by lawn and lea,
>   A rivulet, then a river,'

as our boat slips quickly down towards Oxford. But not too quickly ; we
must not unduly hurry, for here, no less than on the Lower River,

> ' Where'er you tread is haunted, holy ground.'

The ruined walls of Godstow Nunnery, within which Fair Rosamond once
dreamed away long enchanted days, the manor-house of Stanton Harcourt,

where Pope wrote and suffered and writhed under cruel criticism, *mens curva in corpore curvo* ; what tales they could tell you out of the far distant past ! Here, in the fragrant meadows of Kelmscott, Rossetti made himself sweet imageries through the livelong day ; here William Morris thought out *The Earthly Paradise*, and here he clothed his idea of a social Utopia in beautiful description. You drift down towards Oxford thoughtfully, and almost sadly ; the heat of the day is past, the sun sinks in bands of orange and purple behind the Cumnor Hills, and the mysterious twilight comes on. But you are no longer alone. The ' shades of poets dead and gone '—all the dim memories and associations of the past—draw from out the vast solitude and accompany you on your way. Here, in the gloaming, you see no shepherd boy, but a rural Pan, dipping his lazy feet among the water-reeds ; and there, waiting listlessly by an osier-clump, his drooping figure melting into the evening mists, can you not see the Scholar-Gipsy himself,

> ' Trailing in his hand a withered spray,
> And waiting for the spark from heaven to fall ' ? "

Of a truth, with her help, for she had such a gift of easy and apt quotation as is seldom given to man or woman, I can see them all, and I can see also the shade of her who has helped to open my eyes more widely to the inner meaning of the Upper Thames.

So, with a note of sadness, we have done with this expedition on the boyish breast of Father Thames, for to the oarsman the passage from Godstow to Medley Weir is easy and dull, and here, if he is wise, he will entrust his craft to a hireling if, as the chances are, he has taken it from below Folly Bridge ; for the navigation through Oxford is intricate, noisome, and not in the least picturesque. There have been those who have spoken of this aspect of Oxford as Venetian ; but that was an example of mechanical hyperbole. In plain truth this part of Oxford has nothing in common with Venice except water and dirt, and that is not enough to justify a simile.

Below Oxford the river of course continues to be a highway of Berkshire, to be indeed its most noble highway, the use of which is the purest of pleasures. But in this our cruise upon paper it shall not be used as a highway,

for the present.   For a while at least, let us be content to keep
our feet on the firm earth of Berkshire, pausing only to
note that, strangulation of canals by railway companies
notwithstanding, the Thames is still used not a little for
purposes of commercial navigation.   Many a heavy-laden
barge comes into Oxford from the North.   Although the old
Berks and Wilts Canal is a waterless ditch, of some three years'
standing as such, the farmers at the mouth of the Vale of the
White Horse still send their corn to Reading by barge from
Sutton Courtney and elsewhere, and commercial Reading makes
intelligent use of the river.   But here I must needs draw rein,
since I have mounted a favourite hobby, and there is no intention
of being unduly serious.   Only, if men would reflect that
haulage by rail costs roughly fifty times as much as carriage by
canal, which is every whit as effectual in the case of heavy
articles, and that the interest of the railway companies is
bound up in the effacement of canals, they would realise how
irretrievable a blunder has been committed by the body public,
which needs cheap transport, in permitting the railway companies to annex a large proportion of the canal mileage of the
country and that in central districts.   It is that which makes a
deserted waterway, like the Berks and Wilts Canal, which
used to enter the Thames at Abingdon, after running through
the heart of the Vale, one of the saddest of sights.   It is worse
than the talent buried in a napkin, which may be dug up
again, for it is good money absolutely thrown away.

CHAPTER IV

THE NORTH SIDE OF THE VALE—ABINGDON

FATE and the infatuated perversity of some Berkshire folks
in the early part of the last century have contrived that two of
the principal towns of Berkshire, Abingdon and Wallingford,
should be served sadly ill in the matter of railway communication. The original scheme of the Great Western Railway was, to put the matter shortly, that Steventon should be
what Didcot is, that is to say, the point of bifurcation for the
lines of rail destined to serve respectively the purely western and
the midland and western parts of England and that Abingdon

South and West. In fact Didcot is now a convenient starting point for almost any part of England. But, in spite of that, Didcot is not likely to become a popular resort, mainly because it is so ugly. Once, I remember, it was in my mind to take a house in Essex, since good houses were cheap there; but a house-agent dissuaded me, saying, "You can't live in Essex; it is not a residential neighbourhood." For quite different reasons Didcot is not a residential neighbourhood, and you cannot live in it; although it must be confessed that there are villages in the vicinity in which you can. We shall reach them too; but not *viâ* Didcot; that would be too depressing.

It would not have been reasonable to expect the railway company to make New Didcot beautiful, or to place it where it might have been made beautiful, because they did not desire to create it at all. As has been said, they wished to make their line bifurcate at Steventon, one of the quaintest and most picturesque villages in all Berkshire, to proceed across the tableland, known in various parts as Steventon, Milton, and Drayton Fields, to Abingdon, and so to Oxford. But the worthy folks of Abingdon did not desire communication with Oxford in those days, since they thought that the Oxford shops, being better than theirs, would take away their trade, and the University authorities at Oxford did not desire the railway at all, lest youth might be corrupted by ease of access to places beyond the range of the Proctor and his "bulldogs." Perhaps, indeed, they were shy of Abingdon itself, which, in the days of the *Shotover Papers*, was not without reproach of gaiety. So two petitions, the first as frankly selfish as it was wanting in provident insight, the second well meaning, but foolish, were presented with success. The result was curious, annoying to the Great Western Railway authorities at the time, and inconvenient to the greater number of the inhabitants of Abingdon even to this day. In order to reach Warwick, Birmingham and its surrounding industries, Shrewsbury and Chester, the line had to be diverted at right angles at

Steventon.

WORKING MEN'S COLLEGE

Didcot instead of Steventon, to cross the Thames twice, by
bridges of more than common hideousness, whereas it need
not have crossed it at all by the projected scheme except
to reach Oxford. By the planned course it would have
tapped at first hand the considerable community of Abingdon.
Through the perversity of those who were permitted to speak
for Abingdon it was driven through a long stretch of purely
agricultural and pastoral country, and the bridge below Nuneham Woods, at any rate, did all that was possible to deface a
beautiful stretch of river. The line had to pass near Oxford,
but it was long before Oxford possessed the convenience, or
suffered the indignity, of a railway station, and Abingdon was
in the like case. A station, situate close to Nuneham Bridge
and known as Oxford Road, served both Oxford and Abingdon,
with mighty inconvenience to both. Late in time Oxford
secured its station, since the line ran near it : but three miles
separated Abingdon from the Great Western. Hence came
the construction, by enterprising men of Abingdon for the
most part, of a ridiculous little line from Abingdon to the
main line to Radley, where there is a junction at which the
traveller to and from Abingdon must always wait a good many
minutes in circumstances of indifferent comfort. Rarely, as
he waits, does he omit to reflect that the isolation of Abingdon
from the Great Western system is a piece of fatuity hardly to
be matched even in the annals of railway companies, and to
say that is to say much. Nor has he the consolation of hoping
for any great improvement in the future, for the Great Western
is never likely to be diverted from the existing and inconvenient line into its natural and reasonable course ; Radley
will always be a junction ; and the Great Western directors
may be pardoned if, as some folks allege, they bear a hereditary
grudge against Abingdon. Meanwhile, since the line was,
until January, 1904, owned in Abingdon, but the traffic was
run by the Great Western on terms very advantageous to the
shareholders, who held the Great Western in the hollow of

their hands, the shareholders were very well satisfied. For
delay in their own movements they had the consolation of a
ten per cent. dividend, which is not easily to be obtained in
these hard times, and this solid comfort enabled them to bear
with even more than common fortitude the misfortunes of
others. And now, late in time, they are remarkably well
pleased with themselves in that they have forced the hand of
the Great Western, compelling it to pay through the nose for
the freehold of their trumpery little railway, every shareholder
in which has received something like thrice the par value of
his shares. So there are visions of decent accommodation at
Abingdon Station and of a better service of trains. But the
inconvenience of a line laid down in a direction not suited to
the distribution of population will always remain.

To Abingdon, none the less, would I conduct the visitor
by rail, having duly explained to him why he is entitled to
say as much as he likes concerning the petty discomfort of the
journey; and at Abingdon, for other reasons than that it is
as tiresome to leave it as to reach it, I would detain him some
time. Just because it is inaccessible it is a place of which
the world at large knows little. More often than not, on
requesting that sundry goods and chattels should be forwarded
to an address of which Abingdon forms a part, have I found
the apparently cultivated assistants of great shops in London
ignorant how to spell the word at all, innocent, apparently,
of the very existence of the town which has stood at the
junction of Ock and Thames (or Isis) since the seventh century
at any rate. If the railway had been allowed to go straight
through it, it would, by virtue of the splendid stretch of river
between it and Sutton Courtney, one of the best sailing
reaches of the river, and the vicinity of Nuneham Woods,
have been " a popular boating resort." That it is not so may not
be altogether matter of regret, except perhaps to its keepers of
hotels and to its tradesmen. Of the former it has a fair supply,
and there seems to be no reason why the faithful guide should

not speak frankly in the matter. The "Queen's," in the central square of the town, looks the most imposing of them, and it is certainly the most modern. But, in the matter of hotels, the personal equation counts for not a little, and the "Queen's" has changed hands, or at any rate management, so often of late, that it would not be prudent to speak confidently of its merits. Murray, usually to be trusted, recommends the "Crown and Thistle"; I cannot speak from experience in this case, but Mr. Ruskin lodged there habitually when he was Slade professor. On the other hand, the "Lion," which is the kind of hotel that changes ownership through death only, is a thoroughly comfortable hostelry of the old-fashioned type, and it is absolutely in keeping with the old-world atmosphere of Abingdon. Others there be, but they cannot be spoken of on the ground of experience, and some of them have strange names. There is the "Nag's Head," a common enough name; but the "Old Bell," the "Happy Dick," and the "Old Air Balloon" are distinctly peculiar titles.

At any rate the visitor can stay in Abingdon quite comfortably, although none of the hotels or inns is a Hotel Ritz or Carlton; and he will find it worth his while to do so. It is a place, surprisingly little familiar to Englishmen, or even to Americans, of extraordinary interest in itself, and of remarkable beauty also; and it is within easy access by good road—the roads of Northern Berkshire have fallen off sadly in the last lustre, but are still among the best known to me—of a large number of attractive and historic places and hamlets. So let it be head-quarters for the time being.

The best way to make Abingdon strike the imagination of the visitor would be to take him captive at the railway station, blindfold him, and lead him say half a mile through the town and to the Oxfordshire side of the ancient bridge. From that point of view the sight, in summer or winter, is an exceptionally fine one. The bridge alone, credited to Henry V., but really built early in the fifteenth century by worthy Geoffrey Barbour

and others, or at their expense, from stone furnished by Sir
Peter Besils, of Besselsleigh, one of a race of much importance
in the history of Berkshire, is a thing of beauty. Concerning
it Colonel Cooper King, in his *History of Berkshire*, makes
two blunders. He describes it as a "bridge of six pointed
arches," whereas the principal arch, through which the navigation
passes, is not pointed at all; and, after telling us of Sir Peter
Besils and Geoffrey Barbour, of John Huchyns and of William
and Maud Hales, who were also benefactors, he goes on to say,
"They built another (bridge) at Burford too, and so there arose
a stream of trade by the Cirencester route." It is amusing to
note the difficulties into which an initial misconception will lead
an ingenious man. Colonel Cooper King had heard of the
two hexameters, atrocious even for the Middle Ages, which
once adorned one of the windows in St. Helen's Church.
They were:

> " *Henricus Quartus quarto fundaverat anno*
> *Rex pontem Burford super undas atque Culham-ford.*"

Now Burford, that little treasure-house of ancient buildings,
worthily celebrated in Mr. W. H. Hutton's *By Thames and
Cotswold*, a town which cannot be matched in consistent
antiquity for its size in England, let alone elsewhere, is miles
away to the north-west in Oxfordshire, and the only bridge it
ever needed was one across the Windrush; and Burford is no
more on the way between Abingdon and Cirencester than
Croydon is on that between Greenwich and Windsor; nor was
there any reason why the Squire of Besselsleigh, which is so
close to Abingdon that we shall visit it soon, should be at
pains to benefit the inhabitants of a far-away place in the
Cotswolds. In fact, neither he nor Geoffrey Barbour departed
nearly so far from the principle that charity begins at home.
The simple truth is that the bridge at Abingdon is Burford, or
Borough-ford Bridge, and Culham-ford is another across the
old river a mile below; so the whole ingenious edifice of

explanation tumbles to the ground. The case is one in which, on the whole, sympathy must be denied to the gallant writer, since, as anybody may see by comparing the positions on the map of Abingdon, Burford, and Cirencester, the explanation is so far-fetched and ludicrous that the mere exercise of examining it might easily have turned the historian into the right track.

Burford Bridge at Abingdon and the bridge over Culham-ford were, then, all that Besils and Barbour built; and Burford

Abingdon, from the river.

Bridge alone was quite enough, for it extends for some hundreds of yards, across the branching river and over the often-flooded meadows, and it is an extremely graceful if not a commanding structure, as well as an excellent example of the skill and care with which our ancestors built. How great a benefaction the bridge was, in the days when locks as yet were not—the first was built in 1723 for mill purposes and without reference to the navigation—when floods were even worse than they are now, and when ferries and fords were the only means of crossing the Thames between Wallingford and Oxford, might be imagined if the effort of imagination were necessary. But it is not, for in very early times a ready rhymester commemorated the benefaction in verse which is full of gratitude, if it be given to a king to whom no credit was justly due :

> " King Herry the fyft, in his fourthe yere,
> He hath i-founde for his folke a brige in Berkshire,
> For cartis with cariage may goo and come clere,
> That many wynters afore were marred in the myre.

> " Now is Culham hithe i-come to an ende
> And al the contre the better and no man the worse.
> Few folke there were coude that way mende,
> But they waged a cold or payed of her purse ;
> An if it were a beggar had breed in his bagge,
> He schulde be ryght soone i-bid to goo aboute ;
> An if the pore penyless the hireward wold have,
> A hood or a girdle and let him goo withoute.

> " Culham hithe hath caused many a curse,
> I-blyssed be our helpers we have a better waye,
> Withoute any peny for cart and horse.

> " Another blyssed besines is brigges to make
> That there the pepul may not passe after greet schowres,
> Dole it is to draw a deed body out of a lake
> That was fulled in a fount stoon and felow of owres."

It is to be noted that the hexameters attribute the bridge to Henry IV., while the jingle assigns it to Henry V. ; and it is curious that both Colonel King and the author of Murray's Guide, knowing both verses and hexameters, omit to notice the discrepancy. No doubt the hexameters are wrong, and Harry of Monmouth—1416 was his fourth year of reign—was the bridge-builder by proxy, for what that may be worth to the memory of a monarch of good repute. Of that there can be no doubt from the history of the bridge as recorded otherwise. For the verse, there is little in it needing explanation, save that " hithe " means a " ferry," and that " fulled in a fount stoon " means " washed in font," otherwise " baptised." But there is just one other little point to be noted. Besils and Barbour, if there is anything of trust to be placed in the verse, showed the almost unprecedented generosity of founding a free bridge. *O si sic omnes!* Even now, in the opening years of the twentieth century, there are other bridges leading from Berks into Oxon which are not free; of some of these mention is made in their proper places.

Of the bridge we shall hear and see more when we reach Christ's Hospital, nestling under St. Helen's Church, of which

Christ's Hospital, Abingdon.

the airy, flying-buttressed spire is already in full view, present-ing a graceful vision. So is the old gaol, of which the latter observation cannot be made. Indeed, it is a positive eyesore, since it hides all but the crowning cupola of the beautiful Town Hall, perhaps designed by Inigo Jones. Of that which remains of the abbey much is visible from this standpoint, and some of the riverside houses, washed, frequently more thoroughly than the inmates relish, by the passing Thames, are old and of noble proportions. Also the vista of Bridge Street is more than pleasing. It is narrow and many-gabled, with here and there a timbered house—there are many such in Abingdon—and the lines of its roofs and gables are many. But they have one characteristic in common, and it is negative. Hardly any one of them is either horizontal or perpendicular, and this peculiarity makes for beauty if not for stability.

The end of the bridge furthest from Abingdon, and all that part of it destined to permit the passage of flood-water beneath, and of men and women above, rests on Andersey Island. This is formed by the channel of the old river, which diverges from the present and navigable stream a mile or so above Abingdon or Burford Bridge, at a point where there are the remains of an old lock, and re-enters the navigable stream about a mile below the bridge. Both streams, it is probable, follow natural courses, and the island is a natural island. At any rate, it has been an island for more than 1,100 years. Why it should be assigned to Oxfordshire on the map and at law, it is not easy to see, for its whole history is closely connected with that of a Berkshire institution which was the making of Abingdon, and a glance at that history is of distinct assistance to him who would realise the atmosphere of Abingdon. Andersey probably means somebody's Island, Andrew's perhaps. Originally, it is to be presumed, it was no man's land, but in the days of Offa it was the property of the Abbey of Abingdon. Every school-boy knows that Offa, King of Mercia, succeeded to the throne of Ethelbald, who was the first sovereign to style himself King of Britain, not long after that redoubted warrior slept with his fathers, having been killed in battle with the men of Wessex, in 755; but those who are not schoolboys will not, perhaps, object to a reminder. One may well imagine that Offa was very glad to secure the islet from the abbey, for it lay on the fringe of the country of the West Saxons, with whom, as with most of his neighbours, he was at loggerheads when the wild Britons of the West gave him any leisure time. Indeed, he had made some of their country his own. It was, therefore,

LIBRARY

just the place for a fortress, and it is not surprising to find Leland noting that there was one there "in olde time." Also Egfrid, Offa's son, built a palace on Andersey. But Andersey soon intrudes itself in amusing fashion into the abbey's story. The abbey doubtless thought it had been wise as the serpent in exchanging the frequently flooded plot for the fat manor of Goosey, also in Berks. The exchange turned out to be a sad error of judgment. Offa's successors in Mercia were not great as kings, but they were eager sportsmen; and the hounds, being kept on Andersey, as were the king's hawks also, marred the cloistered peace in a manner readily to be understood by those who have lived anywhere near a kennel of foxhounds. Of course they were not foxhounds, for that noble breed had not then been developed, and the fox was vermin, not a beast of the chase. But, whether they were southern hounds, as they may have been, or wolf-hounds, or whatever they were, they became an unbearable nuisance to the abbey; and in the time of Kœnwulf, Egfrid's successor, the Abbot Bethunus was glad to buy back Andersey, and peace, for the Manor of Sutton, now Sutton Courtney, and 120 lbs. weight of silver, or £120 in silver—opinions differ. Sutton was adjacent, so that a sporting monk, prototype of the sporting parson (if such a thing there was), might yet join in the chase, but the kennels were at least out of earshot of the abbey.

Abingdon's early story, as may be imagined, is that of the abbey, founded in the seventh century, from which it took its name. By this is meant Abingdon's early story so far as it is known, for legend alone tells us of Seovechesham, "a wealthy city, a royal residence, and a religious centre" in British times. Generally, indeed, there is enough of vagueness about the records of Abingdon to give colour to an otherwise incredible story that, not so long ago, the good folks of Abingdon, finding that their muniment rooms were over-full of ancient documents which seemed to them of no value, caused the greater part of the accumulation to be destroyed after some had been selected by a committee for preservation. (Subsequent inquiry has shown this story to be absolutely accurate.) Thus the experience of those who wish to dig into antiquities at Abingdon is a degree worse than that of antiquarians who have rescued precious parchments, in fragments, from the tops of the parson's wife's jam-pots, or have found them used as leaves in his reverence's fly-book. But there is no good in crying over burned documents; they are gone, and there's an end of it; and so much is known about the abbey still that, from a literary point of view, the act of Vandalism may have been a blessing in disguise; for a congeries of facts clogs the flow of ink. It is enough to know from the *Abingdon Chronicle* (which, being in the custody of the Master of the Rolls, is safe from wanton destruction) that the original site was close to Sunning-well, near Abingdon, upon a little hill, called, according to the Chronicle, after one Aben, a holy man, who escaped from the massacre of Stonehenge; and there is little difficulty in accepting Mr. Falkner's suggestion that Aben is probably mythical, and that the hill was called after the Benedictine abbey which had its first home upon it. The site was changed and Abingdon assumed the name which, spelled in many ways, it has borne ever since, in the reign of Edred, who brought St. Ethelwold from Glastonbury to be abbot of the transported abbey. From that time until the dissolution the establishment, much favoured of successive kings, throve amazingly. It was a mitred abbey; it owned thirty manors in Berks and lands in other counties also at the date of Domesday; it was visited by the Conqueror; it was the school of his son Henry Beauclerc; its abbots sat in Parliament as of right. In short, it was an abbey of almost unexampled magnificence, and, as was natural, it excited enmity as well as admiration. The author of *Piers Plowman* gave expression to this feeling of revolt against the greatness of the abbey and the pretences of its abbots :

> " Ac ther shal come a kyng
>   And confesse yow religiouses,
>   And bete you as the Bible telleth
>   For brekynge of your rule.
>
> " And thanne shall the Abbot of Abyngdone,
>   And al his issue for evere,
>   Have a knok of a kynge,
>   And incurable the wounde."

A remarkably accurate prophecy was this, considering that it was made in the fourteenth century and not fulfilled until the middle of the sixteenth. The king came in the shape of Henry VIII., of course, to find the abbey possessed of the princely revenue of £1,876 10s. 9d., which, as some say, was about £30,000 a year of our money ; but from the moment one begins to enter into detail, it is plain that to attempt to state an income of the past in terms of the present is very delusive. For example, the Abingdonians of the fifteenth century—for which statistics are handier than for the sixteenth —could buy lambs at 1s., geese at 2½d. each, and eggs at 5d. a hundred ; but other things which are cheap to us were dear to them, or perhaps not to be obtained at all, so that comparison of significance and exactitude is impossible. And surely, from a general point of view, one might say that thirty manors in Berks, manorial privileges, and lands in other counties, must have been the sources of an income more considerable in those days than £30,000 a year is now.

In one amusing particular the prophecy in *Piers Plowman* was qualified, if not falsified. The last abbot " had a knok of a kynge," it is true, but, like his fellow Berkshireman of slightly later times, the Vicar of Bray, famed in song, he was wise in his generation. He saw the " knok " coming, and took all measures to mitigate its severity by ready acceptance of the Royal Supremacy in 1534. His was certainly not the temper and the spirit of Bishop Fisher or of Sir Thomas More, whom the Eystons of East Hendred proudly claim for ancestor, who paid for their faith with their lives, and acquired imperishable fame. The abbot could not know of the glory to come in this world from a display of steadfastness; perhaps, indeed, he would have cared little for it, seeing that he could not live to enjoy it, if he could earn it by death only. At any rate he took a more tangible payment for his easy complaisance, in the shape of a life interest in Cumner Place, Amy Robsart's Cumner to be, until that time the summer-house and the sanatorium of the brotherhood whom he had been wont to rule. Besides that Henry, always generous to those who bowed to his will, rewarded the time-serving abbot with a handsome pension. So Abbot Rowland or Pentecost—there seems to be some uncertainty as to his exact name—suffered a "wounde" indeed, but hardly one that was incurable, and became the first individual owner of a house which was to bulk large, perhaps somewhat too large, in history and in romance.

That Seovechesham, the community planted at the junction of the Thames and the Ock, at the mouth of a rich valley and by the side of the waterway, had an individual history and character may be presumed. But it is certain that, when the abbey migrated from the hill at Sunningwell to the flat land by the river's edge, the lay community by the abbey's side lost its individuality as well as its name. We have seen from *Piers Plowman*, of which the author was certainly not a Berkshireman, though he may have been reared in Oxfordshire, what one who was in advance of his age thought of the splendour of the abbots. The lists of the property of the abbey, the buildings which remain, all that we know of the position and the influence of the abbeys of old time combine to make it certain that Abingdon, the town, was nothing more than a dependency of the abbey, and that its people were hangers-on of the abbey. Trouble there was from time to time between the abbey and the town, the occasions being the privileges of markets and of fairs granted to the abbey, privileges which could hardly fail to press hard on a community

G

the authority of the boy king his successor, wielded by Isabella and Mortimer. In any case too much blood was being shed recklessly elsewhere for the hanging of a few rioters at Abingdon to be a matter of public interest. Yet again in 1431, when public attention was concentrated on France (for it was the year of the capture and cruel execution of Joan of Ark), the Abingdonians, headed by their bailiff, William Masdeville, rose against the abbey, and swore that they "would make the heads of the clergy as cheap as sheeps' heads, 3 or 4 a penny." But these were passing storms, and the abbey continued to prosper, to hold the fairs and markets, and to exact its dues until the dissolution.

The markets, on Mondays, so that they do not interfere with the more important markets of Oxford, still remain, but they are free. The fairs also endure, taking the form of mild Saturnalia, partly for the purpose of hiring, for two autumn days, with a supplemental day, entitled the "runaway fair," a week later. Other fairs there are, too, but the first-named is the real institution. Your Berkshire labourer takes little notice of Bank-holidays and like festivities, but his village "feast" and "Abendon Fair" are to him as sacred institutions, and on the days allotted to them he will by no means work. Cost what it may, he will walk into Abingdon, or jog thither in the carrier's cart, in his Sunday suit, accompanied by his whole family, and "just about" enjoy himself in the market square by the abbey gates. His spirit is probably much the same as that which animated his forefathers, and some of the amusements are substantially the same. Roundabouts and biographs are modern of course, but harmless. But fortunes are told, and boxing is exhibited in a booth to patrons of the "noble art" at threepence a head, and beer is drunk as freely as in the days of yore. The effects, also, are the same, as they will continue to be to the end of time ; and it cannot be denied that, of those who wend their way homewards from the fair, more than a few find Ock Street (which is nearly as wide as Whitehall in these days) inconveniently narrow. It is a pity, no doubt; and the custom is not defended for a moment; but if monotony of daily life and miserable inadequacy of wage are an excuse for occasional indulgence in beery hilarity, the Berkshire labourer of the Abingdon district may claim it to the full. Hard by Abingdon wages are 11s. a week on an average, with a little extra in harvest time—not much, for machines are everywhere—and the rent of a cottage has to be paid in addition. It should be added that "Abendon Fair" is still a genuine hiring fair, and that, in October of 1904 and 1905, young men with whipcord in their caps were to be seen in front of the Lion Hotel with farmers, some of them actually in top-boots of the John Bull type, scanning them with a view to employment. So the fair has its uses no less than pleasures.

The fairs have taken us thus far, from the abbey to the labourers; let us follow that train of thought one step further before returning to the abbey and the town, and let me justify the digression on the ground that *Homo sum, nihil humani a me alienum puto*. Leland wrote of Abingdon, "the town stondeth by clothing." Colonel Cooper King writes: "The clothing trade and manufacture that flourished in Berkshire at Newbury, Hendred, Reading, Abingdon and elsewhere, fell off and decayed with the disappearance of the monastic edifices of the country." Mr. Falkner says: "This industry has long ago forsaken it, and it is now mainly an agricultural centre." Happily this is not strictly accurate. Hard as the Berkshire peasant lives, compelled, as he often is, to include the field-service of his wife and children at harvest time in his meagre wage, he simply could not support existence on that wage alone, and, although it may not be true any longer that Abingdon "stondeth by clothing," the Abingdon district does stand by clothing to a large extent. In Abingdon is a clothing factory, in itself of no imposing appearance, but representing a large industry. It has, indeed, no call to be imposing, since most of those who sew do their work at home. But the carriers, those old-world gossips of the country-side, who are a great institution in Berkshire, carry out to the outlying villages every week vast store of pieces of cut cloth, to be brought back again in due course as finished garments; many women too fetch their allotted tasks in perambulators; and the sums which the women earn in this way, small and hardly won as they are, become items of real importance in a weekly budget which is itself almost microscopical. A reduction of the rate of pay (there was one not long since) spreads consternation through a dozen villages or more, amongst scattered workers whose circumstances are such that they could not possibly resist, even if they were organised. Also, since we are on the subject of manufactures, let it be mentioned that Abingdon produces malt, carpets and reed matting, not wanting in artistic merit, and, like most country towns, a sufficient quantity of sound and wholesome ale.

Strangely enough, this topic of ale has brought us back to the abbey. The monks left it perforce, and betrayed by their abbot, in the sixteenth century; at the end of the seventeenth century King Beer entered to reign in their stead, and remained in possession almost until the end of the nineteenth century. Incredible as it may seem, most of the abbey buildings which remain were actually used as malt-houses and the like from 1690 until after 1890. After all, perhaps, that was no great misfortune, for malting is a clean business, and, if the buildings had not been in use, they might have disappeared altogether. That has been the fate of the magnificent abbey church, 434 feet long, which has vanished so as to leave no trace. It has not been the fate of the thirteenth-century house called, rightly or wrongly, the Prior's House, nor of the Guest House, probably fourteenth or early fifteenth century, nor of the Abbey Gateway. The last-named was convenient and therefore it survived; the two first were used, as stated, for trade purposes, and so preserved, although in some measure defaced.

How the Abingdonians were wont to use the fragments of portions of the abbey which were not converted to base uses, the visitor may see in many an adjacent wall: but in the "Prior's House" he may still notice the buttresses, the vaulting to a central pillar of the ground floor, some fine stone-carving, and the striking chimney; and in the "Guest House" he may trace the marks of the partitions for the dormitories. The "Guest House," then, is probably rightly named; not so the "Prior's House," which is both insufficiently considerable and too near the "Guest House" to have been the dwelling of the prior. It is far more likely to have been the habitation of the steward. Curiously enough, the very ground once occupied by the abbots is now the house of a twentieth-century ecclesiastical personage, the Bishop of Reading.

Let us enter Abingdon, pausing to inspect the Police Court, which, like many another building in venerable Abingdon, has a history. In these days minor malefactors are tried in it, the magistrates hold their meetings, and the remarkably handsome Corporation plate is stored in the building, which, according to tradition, was once the chapel of the Guild of St. John the Baptist. A year after the foregoing words were written came an opportunity, easily to have been made before, of inspecting the Corporation plate of Abingdon under the guidance of the Mayor for the time being, Alderman Shepherd. It is certainly worthy of something more than passing notice, of more space than can be afforded here, of greater store of special knowledge than is available in this instance. It would make a collector's mouth water. Fascinating little silver maces of Edward VI., James I., and Charles I.; salt-cellars of 1600; goblets, obviously chalices and probably from the abbey, but "*Ex dono Lionel Bostock*"; a seal of 1609; a bowl presented by John Lenthall in 1659; a "dog" tankard, having a hole in the base of the handle, so that it could be used as a whistle when duly emptied of some two quarts of liquor, and the Corporation mace are among the gems. The mace, a colossal affair, was

The Town Hall, Abingdon.

presented by a keen Royalist " in the twelfth year" of Charles II. ; for the Commonwealth is completely ignored in the legend. A remarkable feature in other pieces of plate, of interest in themselves, is the fact that they were presented by Berkshire magnates not closely connected with the Corporation, so that they are an indication of the respect in which it was held. Martha and John Stonhouse, of Radley, gave a bowl; and Admiral Sir George Bowyer, also of Radley, presented the huge vase given to him by "Lloyd's Coffee House" in celebration of his part in Howe's victory. Sir George Bowyer and the Stonhouses we shall meet at Radley. A large bowl of Benares silver, presented in modern times by the Earl of Abingdon, is a testimony that county respect for the ancient Corporation has not entirely perished.

Somewhere hereabouts, too, was the Hospital of St. John, but it has been established for the last century and more in that northern part of Abingdon, near the singularly insignificant railway station, which is known as the Vineyard. In the County Hall above the Police Court are preserved a number of royal portraits, Charles II. and James II., George III. and Queen Charlotte, the last-named a true Gainsborough, the standard measures of Elizabeth's date, and a print, dated 1727, of that noble building the Town Hall. This last-named edifice is one of the most striking pieces of architecture in all Abingdon, and, although its date (1677) was more than a quarter of a century later than that of the death of Inigo Jones, its form and proportions speak eloquently either of an original design by or of the abiding influence of that renowned exponent of Palladian principles. The Town Hall was restored, but not spoiled, in 1857. It is, however, reputed not to be over-sound now ; still it is a rare pleasure to the eye, which sees in it a building of fine proportions, with no side walls at all to the ground floor, but with the chamber, as often occurs in work by Inigo Jones, and by Christopher Wren also, supported by a colonnade of pillars. The effect is distinctly airy and attractive, and the shelter to be obtained under the chamber is much appreciated both in the rain and when the sun is fierce. In 1903, during a fair, this space was being used, profanely perhaps, for the purposes of a miniature " roundabout," where children of tender years could ride revolving cock-horses at a dizzy pace for the sum of one farthing sterling. Here, too, the men who have no work, or the men who do not want work, as the case may be, are wont to stand " in the market-place."

The Town Hall, then, was built in 1677 ; and it filled a gap which must have been a source of bitter memories to the Abingdonians of the day, if they possessed any of that feeling towards memorials of antiquity which ought to be, but seldom is, natural to those who have been nurtured amongst old and lovely buildings. Perhaps, having regard to the cheerful fashion in which they used fragments of the abbey and its church for buildings of all kinds, they may be inferred to have been a people without a nice and sensitive taste in these matters. Still, surely they must have had a regard for their Market Cross, erected, so to speak, as a memorial of the incorporation of the town in the reign of Queen Mary, the place of proclamations, and the scene of an extraordinary escapade on the part of a Dean of Christ Church. Aubrey is responsible for the remarkable story that Richard Corbet, then " *Reverendus admodum doctissimusque vir* "—that is how an epistle craving leave to depart for the vacation had to be addressed, in accordance with immemorial tradition, to Dean Liddell and to the present Bishop of Oxford when he succeeded him— broke out in most undecanal and even unclerical fashion. Dean Corbet—he was afterwards Bishop of Norwich, if you please—" being one market-day with some of his companions at the taverne by the Crosse, a ballad-singer complayned that he had no custom and could not put off his ballads ; whereupon the jolly Doctor puts off his gowne, and puts on the ballad-singer's leathern jacket, and being a handsome man, and having a rare full voice, he presently vended a great many and had a great audience." Well, for that matter, Liddell was a handsome man, and he possessed a fine voice, and doubtless, if he had ever dreamed of a like performance, he would have collected as great an audience. To those who knew him, or the stately Gaisford, it will seem almost strange that one of them did not contrive to be born before his time in order to rebuke his ribald predecessor.

A more delicious picture, or one which emphasises more acutely the change for the better, if the more dull, that has come over England, it is impossible to conceive. When did it happen? Without digging into the records of Christ Church to find when Corbet desecrated Tom Quad, one can tell within a hundred years or so; for the Cross, which was put up in Mary's reign, was razed to the ground in the days of the Great Rebellion. Waller was the Vandal in this particular case, and, without sympathising with him in the slightest degree, one may realise that everything connected with it was calculated to raise his Puritan and democratic gorge within him. It had been erected in the days of a Papist queen. It boasted no less than three rows of what he doubtless called graven images. These represented six grave kings, past wielders of the monarchy against which he was arrayed; the Virgin, four female saints, and a mitred prelate, all of course rather more odious to him than the monarchy; and a number of apostles and prophets, who had to go with the rest, and would have been hammered to bits in any case, since they were "graven images." Still, one is tempted to think that the prophets, in their denunciatory moods, were more to Waller's mind than the apostles. Clearly with its carved work, its octagonal form, and its coats of arms, the Cross must have been a thing of beauty which should have been a joy for ever, and one can well credit the story that it served as a model for the Cross of Coventry. A rude picture of it is still preserved on the river side of Christ's Hospital. Its destruction was one of those futile and exasperating outrages which have an almost irresistible tendency to make our judgment of those who were, after all, the founders of our liberties, more harsh and less grateful than it ought to be. One who thinks that, if he had been alive in the 'forties of the seventeenth century, he would have fought for Charles, can yet understand the execution of the king who betrayed Strafford, but for the life of him he cannot forgive the brutal and senseless destruction in which the Puritans revelled. This particular example of it occurred in May, 1644. The gap which it left remained an eyesore for precisely thirty-three years ; and then in its place the stately fabric of the Town Hall—it is really all that—sprang "like some tall palm." It is admirable still, albeit not too sound internally ; but the loss of the Cross is none the less grievous.

Passing the ancient house of the grammar school founded by John Roysse in 1563 (or, as Colonel Cooper King says, in 1571) and leaving St. Helen's Church unvisited for a while, we go, by a quiet path through the churchyard, to the curious and ancient structure in one story known as Christ's Hospital. It is a long range of chambers, built of mellow brick and immemorial oak, having in their centre a small hall, darkly wainscoted, the very table in which makes a collector sinfully covetous. In front of the modest doors of the chambers, inhabited by almsmen and almswomen, runs a tiny cloister with oak pillars, so that the inmates may visit one another dryshod in any weather. Each door, too, bears a text from the Old or New Testament. A more typical relic of the old world, a more sequestered haven of rest, than this row of lowly buildings, looking up to the great church in front, and with its windows opening on to green turf bordered with flowers in the rear, it could not enter into the heart of man to imagine. Ancient as it looks and is, it is honourably and indissolubly connected with all that is best and most energetically useful in the history of Abingdon, and that perhaps is why the *genius loci* is more inspiring to those who visit that miniature hall than it is to those who linger among the scanty if interesting relics of the vast abbey.

Towards the end of the fourteenth century, it would appear, the best men in Abingdon, that is to say, those laymen who had the temporal and spiritual welfare of the community at heart, formed themselves into a gild, entitled "The Fraternity of the Holy Cross." Amongst the earliest members was Geoffrey Barbour, of whom mention has been made in connection with Burford Bridge. A great man of business was this, for he was Mayor of Bristol once, as well as Abingdon's best friend. Associated with him in the gild were the other bridge-makers. So, although the gild did maintain from the beginning a priest and two proctors, and although they decorated St. Helen's with a handsome cross at an early period, its members were clearly men who had an eye for the temporal well-being of the community. In 1442 the good work of founding the bridge being already to the credit of the gild or of its founders, came incorporation and endowment, the trustees being Sir John Golafre and Thomas Chaucer. It has been the pleasant fashion to assume that this Thomas was the son of Geoffrey; but the better opinion is that this theory, based upon purely heraldic premises, is quite inconclusive. The matter is one of those, in fact, on which we must be content to have no certainty. The incorporated gild was, indeed, a typical mediæval institution of the best kind. It built, or took in charge, the bridge that was the making of the town commercially; it kept the road, which the bridge rendered highly useful and important, from Abingdon to the ancient Cathedral of Dorchester; and in 1446, four years after incorporation, it built the hospital as a quiet resting-place for thirteen poor men and thirteen poor women: and there the hospital stands, fulfilling now the beneficent purpose of its founders more than 450 years ago, for thirty-eight inmates. The gild also maintained, from 1457 onwards, two separate chaplains, the Rood Priest and the Bridge Priest, to pray for the souls of the two sets of benefactors indicated, and these priests received the annual stipend of £6 13s. 4d., and probably had lodging found

for them into the bargain. If we compare this with the income
set aside by the reigning king for the Provost and the Head
Master of Eton, we shall find that these priests had a remarkably good position.

The gild feasted, too, in the month of May of each year,
and we know they ate well and cheaply. Here is part of the
raw material of their menu with the cost computed :

	£	s.	d.
6 Calves at 2s. 2d.	0	13	0
16 Lambs at 1s.	0	16	0
80 Capons at 3d.	1	0	0
80 Geese at 2½d.	0	16	8
800 Eggs at 5d. per 100	0	3	4
	3	9	0

No mention is made of beverages, but we need not doubt
but that they were consumed in abundance, nor, probably, but
that the poor men and women had their share in this
Gargantuan feast, which was eaten not at the hospital but at
Banbury Court, afterwards the judge's lodgings, when Abingdon
had assizes, in East St. Helen's Street hard by. It may be
worth while to note that West St. Helen's Street and East St.
Helen's Street, picturesque and quiet thoroughfares both, keep
their titles to this day. In 1539 too, to judge by the date
on the corbels, the gild built the aisle of Holy Cross in St.
Helen's Church.

Naturally a gild so rich as this, and semi-ecclesiastical to
boot, did not escape the attentions of Henry VIII. ; and it
was dissolved in 1547, the year of Henry's death. But early in
1553, Edward VI., being then in the sixteenth year of his
age and near to his early death, granted a new charter,
whereby the gild and some others were appointed Governors
of Christ's Hospital, and Colonel Cooper King records the
interesting fact that Laud, not yet a bishop, preached a sermon
in commemoration of the benefactors. This charter was

granted on the entreaty of Sir John Mason, whose portrait, as well as that of Edward VI., is preserved in the ancient hall. John Mason, son of a cowherd and a sister of a monk of Abingdon, graduate of Oxford, favourite of Henry VIII., Privy Councillor, Ambassador to France, and Chancellor of Oxford, never forgot the place in which he had his humble origin. In the hall, too, one may see the portraits of good Sir Peter Besils, John Huchyns, also of bridge fame, Geoffrey Barbour, Tesdale, of Roysse's School, who founded Pembroke College in Oxford where the school still has scholarships, and others. There are also coats of arms in the windows, the picture of the building of the bridge, and the table already referred to, which is as sound now as it was in Elizabeth's day, when it was made, and probably a good deal harder. Also, on a panel let into the wall to the visitor's right as he enters, is the vellum scroll containing the verses that have been quoted concerning the bridge, and an obliging attendant is glad to show a quaint silver badge which the almsmen wore when they possessed a uniform dress. The dress, more's the pity from the picturesque point of view, was relinquished some time ago, probably because the almsmen objected to it. The badges were given up because, to put it gently, it was found difficult to persuade the kinsfolk of dead almsmen to yield possession of them. Still, the effect of this tranquil backwater on the mind is very deep and stimulating. It enshrines much of what has been most noble in Abingdon's story. Long may it continue to do so in unchanged form. Nor, perhaps, is it in much peril, for the land on which it stands has no special value for commercial purposes, and, further than that, the Charity Commissioners, the supreme authority, whom it is often the fashion to disparage, are really a very worthy if somewhat dilatory body, and by no means wanting in regard for the ancient and the picturesque. It is perhaps worth mentioning that this Gild of the Holy Cross, this association of good Englishmen to do work that was useful in this world, as well as

F L GRIGGS - 1906

St. Helen's Church, Abingdon.

to prepare themselves for the next, was not a peculiarly Abingdonian growth. There was one of similar character at Stratford-on-Avon ; and, when one comes to think of it, there is no reason in life why, with or without the religious side of the system, similar gilds should not exist locally in these days, as well as on a national basis. They would serve to stimulate that local patriotism which has a value of its kind and is not less useful in its small way than the national patriotism having far wider aims.

It is in the churches of Abingdon, particularly in St. Helen's, that one sees the kind of good effected by the spirit of local patriotism that the gilds fostered. The whole of the very peculiar inside shape of St. Helen's is the result of the work of the gilds, which must needs build whole aisles to the glory of God, so that here we have a church nearly as broad as it is long (105 feet by $86\frac{1}{2}$ feet), and boasting no less than five aisles. Even those who complain that it has been " restored," with an infinity of bitter emphasis on the inverted commas, are fain to confess that the effect is remarkably good, that the people of Abingdon have loosened their purse-strings generously for the adornment of their historic place of worship. Writing as one who "in another place " is asked to sanction the restoration of sacred buildings, and as one who knows both the liabilities and the difficulties of clergymen in this matter of buildings, I have not much patience with these commas sarcastically inverted, even where a church has been, from the artistic point of view, spoiled. The lovers of the picturesque are usually wanderers who ignore the value of a sound roof to those who possess the right of worshipping in a church, who have little sympathy for a rector saddled with a liability to repair the chancel of his church, a liability of which his parishioners are nearly always willing to relieve him when occasion arises, but still legally subject to the liability. Repairs must be done, as a matter of imperative law, when they become necessary ; and repairs frequently and perforce involve alteration and recon-

struction. The most that he who cherishes the antique has the
right to demand is that, where the indispensable funds are
available, that which is beautiful in form and detail should be
preserved as carefully as may be. That this has been done
wonderfully well in St. Helen's is plain to the eye. The
tower supporting the graceful spire is Early English ; nearly
every porch and arch and doorway is full of good old work ;
the Perpendicular pillars of the five aisles, standing at some
distance from one another, are of remarkable elegance, so that
the whole building has an appearance of airiness and lightness
rarely to be found in a church. A church ought to be—
unfortunately it often is not—a good auditorium, and St.
Helen's is precisely that.

Thus it was that it impressed itself on the parishioners when
Mr. Powell, now long dead, occupied the Jacobean pulpit,
insomuch that his somewhat grandiose epitaph begins :

> " Within these sacred walls where thousands hung,
> In awful silence, on thy hallowed tongue,
> Powell ! repose."

It also impressed itself on the Abingdonian mind as a church
to be honoured and extended as their local Valhalla. So grew
the five aisles, the northern, or Jesus aisle, with the Jacobean
font at its eastern end, and, in order from the north, Our
Lady's aisle, St. Helen's aisle, St. Catharine's aisle, and the
aisle of Holy Cross, of which Our Lady's and St. Catharine's
are remarkable for their excellent oak roofs. Our Lady's,
moreover, boasts a picture of the Nativity, and the east end of
St. Catharine's, behind the carved organ—on the side of
which a wooden saint, David probably, carries a brightly
gilded harp—conceals quite a little treasure-house. For here
is another picture of Christ bearing the Cross ; and "a sort of
picture," as Lord Halsbury might say, representing, in the form
of a family tree, the issue of stout William Lee, of the seventeenth
century, and their issue, and so on. On November 5th, 1657,

William Lee, who had married three successive wives and was, by his portrait, still a hale old man, had begotten seventeen children, all of them the issue of the first or the second wife. He had seen no less than seventy-eight grandchildren and 102 great-grandchildren born into this world; and his family tree, looking somewhat like one of the old Jesse windows, but more refined in conception, names them all. It is adorned also with those numerous texts from the Old Testament which are, perhaps, better appreciated in a thinly populated country than in one like ours of to-day. For one man to be the direct progenitor of no less than 197 persons during his life time is surely remarkable; and it is fortunate—*pace* the Bishop of London—that not all men are now so prolific. But those were troublous times, when population was sparse, bloodshed was frequent, and life was held cheap; and it is more than likely that some of stout William Lee's progeny met face to face, as soldiers in different armies, at Newbury, at Marston Moor, at Edgehill or at Naseby.

Elsewhere one may see a memorial of Geoffrey Barbour the bridge-builder, and the tomb and arms of John Roysse, the founder of the useful grammar school in 1563, and of a dole of bread, which used to be distributed at the tomb itself: and it is pleasant to note that his generosity is still held in grateful memory, and that his good work endures to this day. The school has, wisely no doubt, been removed from the vicinity of the abbey to a spacious building on the outskirts of the town, where there is room for a playing field, and it flourishes; but the tomb was restored so recently as 1873 by old boys of the school who had been beneficiaries of a trust created more than 300 years before. As one who was educated for six years, free of cost, through the liberality of William of Wykeham, I may be permitted to say that all such honour paid to the founders of education seems to me absolutely right and touching. Away at the north-west corner is the square tomb of Richard Curtaine, another local benefactor, who died in 1643, a year before Sir William Waller saw fit to break Abingdon Cross into small pieces. What Curtaine's good works were I know not, but the front slab of the tomb records them thus punningly :

> " Our Curtaine in this lower press
> Rests folded up in Nature's dress :
> His dust perfumes this urne, and he
> This towne with liberalitie."

So solid is the tomb that a wanderer of A.D. 2005 may very likely find it as fresh and quaint as it is now. Should such a one come he will see also the brasses of Abingdon heroes of yesterday, brave young fellows who volunteered for South Africa and fell there for their country ; and no doubt, those of Abingdon heroes as yet unborn who will fight for their country in her time of need. Our Berkshire lads may not be quick-witted, but they are hard and steady fighters, who have given a good account of themselves in many a great battle since Copenhagen and Talavera ; and this is not one of the counties in which the lad who takes the recruiting sergeant's shilling is held to have disgraced his family.

Many other parts of Abingdon are interesting in themselves, or simply by virtue of their names. St. Nicholas's Church (how many persons forget that St. Nicholas and Santa Klaus are one and the same) is well worth a visit, and the Vineyard, albeit desecrated by the town gas works, reminds us that time was when the monks cultivated their own vines, and, probably, made their own wine. After all, why not ? Fair wine of the champagne type is made from Lord Bute's vineyards in Glamorganshire in most years, and, though this last fact is little known, from grapes ripened in the open air, hard by the old Physick Garden at Chelsea. But the real charm of Abingdon is in its all-pervading atmosphere of the old world and in its way of revealing unknown treasures at odd times. You may dig in the gravel near Abingdon, and you will not need great luck to find a mammoth's tooth ; a local friend once had fifty such in his possession ; and in like manner, if an Abingdon house of moderate age is pulled or falls to pieces, it often happens that highly interesting pieces of old stonework are discovered. Sometimes they are fragments of the despoiled abbey, which, as already stated, occur in all sorts of un-expected places ; sometimes they are entire portions of ancient buildings which have been overlaid with rubbish, modern by comparison to them, but less enduring than them all the same.

It is a curious little fact also, and one well worthy to be known, that, by reason perhaps of the age of many of the buildings about Abingdon, and of the constantly recurring necessity for repairing them, the craftsmen of the Abingdon district are really artists in preserving that which is old by sheer patching. They are, in fact, the best men I know at restoration without any inverted commas at all, and at trans-ferring buildings from place to place. This, it is to be feared, is the result of practice, not of taste ; of a laudable desire to humour the fancies of "the quality" rather than of veneration for the antique. When, for example, I wanted old tiles and not new to replace some which had vanished from my house, my worthy craftsman took them off his own house, replacing these with new ones at my expense, and the transaction was eminently satisfactory to both of us. When a new-comer to Abingdon, a year or two ago, caused a really hideous modern house, battlemented and otherwise odious, to be demolished, it reappeared, battlements and all, in another part of Abingdon, having, no doubt, been sold as builder's rubbish and then taken to pieces and put together again like a Chinese puzzle. Under wise direction, however, this power of patching what nine builders out of ten would pronounce to be beyond repair is invaluable.

As the town is so are the people, old-fashioned, slow-moving, and comfortable. Save in the way of fighting—and in that way there has been nothing very sublime—Abingdon has no astonishing record of great work done for the country. It has

bred no statesmen, no generals, no admirals, no poets, no
novelists, and, so far as I know, no artists of commanding
fame.   I used to think that George Morland was an Abingdon
man, for the Morlands are a great Abingdon family, and many
of his pictures savour of Berkshire.   But alas ! though he may
have been of the same stock, he was born in London, and
certainly lived there much of his not altogether creditable life.
He would assuredly not have been appreciated in Abingdon,
if the Abingdonians of his day were at all like those of ours ;
and the chances are that they were, for the Abingdonian
manner gives one the impression of having descended from
father to son for generations.   There are families of lawyers,
doctors, brewers, estate agents and auctioneers, butchers,
grocers and the like, which go on for ever, overlapping sometimes, but not very often ; and between them they rule the
little town kindly enough.   There is a Corporation of course—
there has been one since the days of Queen Mary—and the
Council meets regularly ; but it is a very peaceable Council and
by no means given to startling movements.   Improvements are,
indeed, discountenanced in Abingdon, for the simple and
sufficient reason that most of the inhabitants have an interest
in the old enterprises which the improvements, if made, would
displace.   It is unreasonable to expect the shareholders in gas
works to foster a scheme for electric lighting.   After all life
would not be any happier, and no more money would be made
in Abingdon, if the streets were lighted by electricity instead
of gas, and the paperhangers and painters would lose much of
their work.   Abingdon is probably better off and more
comfortable under the rule of an unprogressive Corporation
than many another place in which a corporation of tradesmen
and hotel-keepers show "enterprise."   This usually consists in
"developing" the town, by laying out recreation grounds or
constructing winter gardens or piers, as the supposed need
may be, and in advertising the town, at the expense of all the
ratepayers, as a health resort or a golf centre, for the sole

benefit of the tradesmen and the lodging-house keepers. In fact I could name many an English or Welsh town where the ratepayers, especially those possessed of fixed incomes independently of trade, would hail the slow-moving councillors of Abingdon as saviours.

Abingdon, in a word, does well to be provincial, steady-going, and contented. Isolated, through its own irretrievable folly, in the matter of railway connections, it can hardly aspire to popularity for a few months in a fine summer as a boating resort. Far removed from coal—although one Lord of the Manor of Radley was ruined by looking for coal three miles away—it cannot, in the present state of scientific knowledge, become a vast centre of industrial enterprise. It is, in fact, essentially a county town and rural centre, although it is not the capital of Berkshire; and it fulfils its functions as such to the satisfaction of the district which it serves. That is to say, it is a busy place on market-days, and it keeps a half-holiday religiously on Thursdays. But it is really only kindness which induces the tradesmen not to keep a half-holiday for at least four days of the week, since always, on any other days than Saturdays and Mondays, the shopkeepers inform the chance customer with an air of gentle surprise that "the town is very quiet to-day." That is its charm, or one of its charms. But, unless I am very much mistaken, these good, easy tradesmen, of whom most, except the butchers, charge more than London prices, do uncommonly well for themselves, and it is reasonably clear that new-comers into the ranks of Abingdon tradesmen must fight an uphill battle for many a long day. No doubt the story would be the same in the professional life of the little town if any "foreigner" should venture into competition with the established practitioners. Indeed, it has even been whispered, and something more, that the recent advent of a medical man who strove to establish himself in Abingdon was resented bitterly by his brethren of the order of the leech, inasmuch as he had received no formal invitation from them. The story may not be true; but it is quite true to the character of a community, which behaves as if it had a freehold of comfortable prosperity without undue effort. Another story, equally characteristic and credibly reported, is that a lady who tried to make some local board or other do its obvious duty was informed that, if she did not like the place, she would be well advised to return to London. That is Abingdon all over; but for all that it is no bad place to stay in for a while, and quite tolerable as a residence when, as they say in Berkshire, you have learned " to put up with " its little ways; and this you may as well learn soon as late, for Berkshire changes little and slowly.

Near Bablockhithe.

CHAPTER V

THE NORTHERN SIDE OF THE VALE—AN EXPEDITION.

It has been explained that the intelligent traveller in his or
her own country, or for that matter the intelligent foreigner,
can stay in Abingdon for a while in mighty ease and comfort.
Amusement is to be found there too, antiquities apart, on as
fine a stretch of the river as is to be found for sailing or rowing
boats. Only, if the former be needed on hire, it will be necessary to make arrangements beforehand with some of the
amphibious folk over against Binsey, which is above Oxford.
In this chapter, however, there is no boating expedition.
Suffice it that the distinctive features of the Abingdon reach

are that it is not one much affected by fashion, so that ladies may wear sensible clothes on it without fear of being out of the mode, and that it is to be avoided on Thursday afternoons. They are holidays, and in summer the shop-attendants of both sexes are apt to throng the river. They do no harm ; no humane person would grudge them their innocent pleasure ; but, for the time being, they do not make for restfulness.

As has been suggested at an earlier point, Abingdon is an admirable starting-point for expeditions by road, which may be taken afoot, or on bicycles, or in carriages, or even in motors, according to taste ; and the excellence of the roads in Berkshire makes any of these methods pleasant. And first, to begin in Bacon's convenient style, we will take quite a modest expedition, leaving Abingdon by way of the Vineyard, and keeping to the right hand at the point where the Oxford roads bifurcate. A couple of miles or a little more bring us to Radley. The road, which passes through rich corn-lands, is somewhat annoyingly circuitous, in which respect it resembles many another road in Berkshire ; the surface is usually good, and the gradients, which are of the switchback type, are not severe enough to try even a weak or an indolent cyclist. It is worth while, however, if the weather has been at all wet, for the cyclist to make a detour in the direction indicated by a signpost in the words "to Radley Station." That is not advised because the station is an object of beauty, but because, by so proceeding, one obtains a glance at Radley village, which is pretty and old-fashioned, and the going is better than by the other route, which is shaded. Also it is well to cross the railway to the old village, for it is picturesque. The church, too, is worth some careful study for its wealth of fine oak-carving, for its pillars of dark and solid oak, and for the fine altar tomb of William Stonehouse, who flourished in the seventeenth century. This is one of the cases, indeed, in which a manorial story is interesting.

Originally, that is to say, originally for our purposes, the manor of Radley naturally belonged to the great Abbey of Abingdon. At this point I was near to being led astray by the statement "after the dissolution it was purchased by George Stonehouse, one of the clerks of the Board of Green Cloth *temp.* Elizabeth"; for of course it is conceivable that a rich young man, who bought at the dissolution, might have lived to be a Court official under Elizabeth. But a reference to *Fifty Years of S. Peter's College, Radley*, by the Rev. T. D. Raikes, undertaken originally simply for the purpose of making sure of this interval, showed that "after" meant "long after," and that the interregnum between the abbey and the Stonehouses was interesting. The hunting lodge of the monks—grand hunting it must have been with Bagley Wood close at hand—was granted first to Lord Seymour of Sudeley, Admiral of England, and brother of the Duke of Somerset, Lord High Protector of Edward VI. So, oddly enough, the first lay Lord of the Manor of Radley was a sailor. He was also a good many other things. He had the courage to marry "Katrin the Queen," as Catherine (*née* Parr) used to sign herself when she lived at Chelsea; and she hated the Lord High Protector, whose face she wished to "scratt" (the cause of quarrel being the Crown jewels), as much as her ambitious husband hated him. The Admiral too, when "Katrin" died in childbirth, had the audacity to court the Princess Elizabeth before she was sixteen; and he came to his end, like many a better man, on Tower Hill in 1548. Radley, we may take it, had seen little of the ambitious and plotting sailor. But it saw something of the next owner of the manor, Princess Mary, afterwards the Queen who, let historians strive as they may to show the good points in her character as well as the bad, will be "Bloody Mary" so long as England remains England. It was not, in fact, until 1575 that George Stonehouse, "Clerk of Green Cloth," obtained the property, and in truth no man can tell whether he received it as a free grant or bought it. Possibly, Mary's residence at Radley may account for the fact that Abingdon was incorporated by charter in her blood-stained reign.

The Stonehouses, who lasted as Lords of the Manor almost into the nineteenth century, did well by Radley. They rebuilt the chancel of the church at any rate, in 1635 or thereabouts, and they beautified the edifice with a stately altar tomb. Moreover if the original George was but a commoner without a title, his son was created a baronet. In 1792 his descendant, Sir James Stonehouse, left the property to Captain George Bowyer, R.N., his nephew (the second and best sailor who held the manor), and two years later, as a reward for gallant services under Lord Howe against the French, Captain Bowyer also received a baronetcy. Let us hope that while London was illuminated, and George III. with his family visited the fleet at Spithead, and Howe was receiving a diamond-hilted sword at the hands of the King, there was rejoicing also in the retired Berkshire village whose chief, so to speak, had been honoured by the sovereign. Nor is Radley likely to have been forgotten, for the Bowyers, Bucks family although they were, clearly had a strong affection for the great house at Radley, and the carving in the church comes of their generosity. In no church have I encountered so many massive beams and pillars of black oak within a narrow space.

Interest in Radley, however, concentrates itself upon the Hall, now St. Peter's College, and its history. George Stonehouse built him a house there, of which traces are visible in the gateway and in the walled garden. Sir John Stonehouse, Comptroller of the Household to Queen Anne—the Stonehouses were Court officials still—built him a new house in 1726. Good Thomas Hearne, disliking the Queen Anne style perhaps, wrote, "'tis nothing near so pleasant nor snug as the old house"; and before the century was ended the Bowyers were installed   But the Bowyers fell on evil times.   "Sir George

Radley.

WORKING MEN'S COLLEGE LIBRARY.

Bowyer being persuaded by fraudulent methods that there was coal on the estate, and induced to begin extensive works, including a canal to carry the coal from the pits to the river, soon got into difficulties. The estate was heavily encumbered, and the mansion was let for a middle-class Nonconformist School." That school appears to have been a failure, and the house was without a tenant when that wayward but wonderfully good man, Dr. Sewell, was looking for a home for a school which might be partly middle-class, but certainly would not be Nonconformist.

This was in 1847, and the whole scheme of the foundation, in its earnestness and its eccentricity, is one of the most striking examples of the habits of thought prevailing in the middle of the last century. Dr. Sewell had already helped to found St. Columba, in Ireland, "to secure in the College a full exhibition of the principle of the English Church," and he was in the thick of the Oxford Movement. He, and Singleton, the first Warden of St. Columba, had severed their connection with that institution mainly because a secular spirit was being introduced, and so it came that Sewell, Singleton, and others, "drinking tea together in the Turle at Oxford" on March 5th, 1847, determined to found a new Salamis. The time came, not once but often, when they had need to take all the courage they could from reflection on Teucer's motto of "Nil Desperandum." Their ideal was difficult of attainment by reason of its complications. Churchmanship was to come before all things; that might have been pursued *ab initio* without commercial obstacle; for there were plenty of parents holding Dr. Sewell's somewhat extreme views, and to observe the fasts of the Church is, after all, cheaper than to disregard them. Closer association between boys and masters than at other schools was to be a part of the system; and the present flourishing state of Radley, in which this principle is still followed, as are Church principles also, shows that from a business point of view there was nothing amiss with this principle. The old manor-house of the Stonehouses was, and is to this day, a magnificent centre for the school-buildings. But Sewell, never the man to count the cost, began the life of Radley College on August 17th, 1847, with three pupils and, including Singleton, whom he made Warden, three masters, and immense ideas. He had good support, it is true. Singleton advanced £4,000 and offered to devote his private income of £500 or £600 a year to the scheme; Mr. Sharpe, of the old-world firm of Goslings and Sharpe (formerly trading under the sign of the Three Squirrels, now amalgamated with Barclay's,), Mrs. Sheppard, sister of the famed Dr. Routh of Magdalen, and others, were ready with ample contributions.

But Singleton was a fanatic and Dr. Sewell was a refined and extravagant collector of things beautiful and rare because he believed in the value of artistic association for boys. Doubtless he was right; but he had to build a chapel, dormitories, a school-room, and the innumerable appurtenances of a great school. Moreover, both Sewell and Singleton were convinced of the essential necessity of music as part of education, and of the paramount need of a fine organ. They ordered one, at the modest price of £1,000, within a week of obtaining the lease of the Hall. They bought "seven magnificent old chairs," twelve selected pictures for £110, great stores of Turkey carpets, "a magnificent walnut wardrobe," "four chairs which had formerly been in Carlton Palace," "a fine carving, in solid walnut and of large size, of the four symbols of the Evangelists, and *Salvator Mundi* in the centre," "sixteen old panels exquisitely carved with Scripture subjects," "a wrought-iron chest with an elaborate lock," portraits galore, curtains "from the Queen of Portugal's private chapel at Belem," "a Thibet carpet made of the material of which Cashmere shawls are composed," wonderful stained glass, and the priceless reredos, which was rejected at first because its gold and colour gave it "a Popish air" and then scraped and cherished. Some of these treasures are gone now, for reasons which shall be explained, although in truth they are fairly obvious ; but others remain, and amongst them is the Thibet carpet, highly prized, and used as a "Pede-cloth" in chapel on high festivals : at other times it is hung on the chapel walls. Mr. Raikes, by the way, uses the word "pede-cloth," which is quite new to me, as if it were the most familiar in the world ; but it may be worthy of observation that it has escaped the notice of the usually accurate and exhaustive *Century Dictionary*, and I can only guess that it must mean a cloth or carpet on which somebody's foot, probably that of the officiating priest, is placed on special occasions. Once it was put to humbler uses, being, in fact, used as a bath mat. Then it occurred to somebody that it might make a tolerable rug if it were cleaned, and it was sent up to London for the purpose. Its arrival in London was followed by a letter asking at what value the Radley authorities desired that it should be insured during the process of cleaning ; and so its value of £700 or thereabouts was rediscovered.

Radley, then, began as a school which was a treasure-house of art, under a Warden who was a fanatic, with its buildings in a very incomplete state, and with a mere handful of boys ; not enough, in fact, to play any of the principal games of boyhood. Of the treasures of art some, a large number indeed, still remain, and, looking back upon a long and wide experience of public-school boys, I venture to say that Sewell's theory of the value of artistic association to boyhood has been in large measure justified. That is to say, Radley boys, or men who have been at Radley, have, either for the better or for the worse, rather more of refinement as a body than the men who have been educated at other schools, even at schools which can boast the associations of many centuries. But the cost of this result may possibly be considered to have been excessive. Dr. Sewell was unfortunate in his first Warden, as single-hearted a man as ever lived, but a fanatic and a crank ; and his own views were too high for this world. His administration, too, was faulty in the extreme, and the natural, indeed the inevitable, result was that, by the year 1860–1, the debts of the college, for all of which Dr. Sewell was personally liable, were more than £40,000. Fortunately that sound man of business, Mr. J. G. Hubbard, M.P. (afterwards Lord Addington), was not only the largest creditor, but also a friend of the school. Its indebtedness was a shock to him, but he took the whole of it on his shoulders, extricated the college from debt to others, sold a good many of the treasures, and put the whole affair on a business footing, so that now Radley is a prosperous institution standing on its own freehold ground. It owes its remarkable interest, as it now stands, to the idealist William Sewell; it owes the fact that it exists at all to the practical mind and the firm will of Lord Addington. It may here be noted as a curious coincidence that another of Berkshire's three public schools, Bradfield, also the foundation of an idealist, was once within a hair's breadth of bankruptcy. Finally, from Radley have come a fair number of brilliant men, the best of them, perhaps, being the late Rev. S. H. Reynolds, one of the original three boys. He took two " Firsts," won the Newdegate and the English Essay prize at Oxford, was a Fellow of Brasenose, editor of Bacon's *Essays* and Selden's *Table Talk* for the Clarendon Press, a student of Dante, a writer of leading articles for *The Times*, and an earnest clergyman in the East End. Radley has produced also Mr. W. B. Woodgate, *rude donatus* as an oarsman, and a notable critic of oarsmen. Radley, indeed, may share with Eton the glory of turning out " wet-bobs " who are better watermen than any other school in England can produce. She turns out also her annual contribution of exceptionally pure-minded English gentlemen, and that is best of all. In fact the Radley tone, the artistic associations, the beautiful environment of trees and the adjoining River Thames, make Radley eminently desirable as the nursing mother of boys.

Quite recently, too, the Warden of Radley pointed out that the three senior Admirals on the Navy List were not only all of

them old Radleians, but also contemporaries at St. Peter's
College in Sewell's first year of Wardenship. They were Lord
Charles Scott, Lord Walter Kerr, and Sir Edward Seymour.
It is a curious coincidence in itself, and still more interesting
when it is remembered that the first Lord of the Manor of
Radley, and probably the worst, was Admiral of England, and

Bishop Jewell's Porch, Sunningwell.

that the first of the Bowyers, for Radley's purposes, was a post-
captain in the Royal Navy.

From Radley we go to Sunningwell, making a slight detour,
in order to glance at Bagley Wood, from the high-road to
Oxford from Abingdon, and perhaps going on to the end of
the wood, and to the top of the hill above Hinksey, to look
down on Oxford. That is all that can be done now, without

I

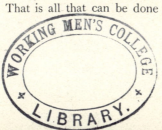
WORKING MEN'S COLLEGE LIBRARY

special leave from St. John's College, the owners, and probably from the shooting tenant also, for the wood, haunted by highwaymen in bygone days—they caught St. Edward of Abingdon there once—and later by the great Dr. Arnold, who was better than many a saint, is now sacred to St. Pheasant. Nor is it a very hopeful enterprise to attempt to trespass in disregard of notice-boards, for the fossa and vallum, a combination of hedge, stakes, wire-netting, barbed wire and ditch, are thoroughly businesslike. Long after Arnold's time, as late as 1879 in fact, to my knowledge, the glades of Bagley Wood were a favourite place for picnics during Commemoration : but now one must gaze from the high-road, and a very beautiful and tempting sight it is, especially when the " blue bells " (which are really squills and not, as some have it, wild hyacinths) are in full bloom. Owing, perhaps, to recent clearings of underwood, and to thinning of trees also, and consequent open spaces, they present a glorious sea of colour in the season of the year. It is not, perhaps, more particularly a characteristic of Berkshire woods than of those of any other southern county, that raw surfaces left by periodical clearings of underwood are, in the course of a few weeks of late spring and early summer, carpeted with flowers innumerable so suddenly that, as in the case of the Arctic springs of which we read in travellers' tales, a miracle seems to have been worked. But it is a most precious trait of all English woodlands none the less.

This first day's ride, if ride it be, need not be a very long one ; for 'tis prudent to get into condition gradually. There has been lingering at Radley, because it was worth while ; and perhaps it would have been well, before glancing at Bagley Wood, to make first the very slight detour needed to reach Bayworth and Sunningwell, both of them sweetly pretty places which enjoyed greater fame in days gone by than now belongs to them. Hereabouts, as already noted, was the first home of the mitred Abbey of Abingdon. To Bayworth, in

1659, walked Anthony Wood, the antiquary, to visit the house inhabited by " the Lord of Sunningwell called Hannibal Baskervyle, Esquire," father of Thomas, the traveller. The said Hannibal was one of those dispensers of charity who are a nuisance to their neighbours. " A melancholy and retired man," he built a barn for the accommodation of tramps and devoted a third or fourth part of his income to the sustenance of the poor. And the people of " Abendon "—we spell it differently nowadays, but the country folk stick to the old pronunciation—found the aggregation of beggars so troublesome that they indicted Hannibal at the sessions for harbouring beggars. Thus early were the evils of indiscriminate almsgiving recognised. Sunningwell Manor, like that of Radley, passed into the hands of the Stonehouses and the Bowyers, and the church, which has an octagonal porch well worth looking at, is celebrated as the burial-place of Samuel Fell, D.D., Dean of Christ Church, and a native of Longworth in Berks. Fell will be remembered for all time as a disagreeable man by virtue of the familiar jingle of the nursery, which one need not quote. Very likely it represents nothing more than the spleen of some undergraduate of Christ Church whose high spirits were not appreciated by the choleric dean ; but tens of thousands of folks know the rhyme for one who has read that the dean, who may have been a worthy and good-natured don, is reported to have died in a passion of grief on hearing of the execution of Charles I.

Hence let us go back to the high-road to Oxford, and on to the top of the hill of Bagley Wood, whence may be obtained an unrivalled view of a scene not to be surpassed in England. It looks best, perhaps, in time of flood, as in June and October of 1903, when the trees, the spires, and the cupolas seemed to rise out of a gleaming lagoon. But the sight is fine, too, when the whole picture is bathed in sunlight, and the sinuous river gleams like a ribbon of silver twined among the green of the meadows and the willows. In fact Oxford is always a sight glorious and provocative of a thousand memories.

Here there is no real need to leave the county, but the chances are that a run downhill, which is too good to miss, takes the traveller, but must not take me, down into Oxfordshire, into Oxford itself *viâ* Folly Bridge, where he is asked to proceed straight up St. Aldate's to Carfax, turn to the left there, and go on until he meets me again on the Berkshire border at Botley. The chances are that he will seize the opportunity of lunching at Oxford, but no matter. Cumner Hurst is always worth looking at, with its clump of trees rising more than 500 feet high, and the climb to Cumner itself, with a bicycle for companion, is the kind of enterprise one does not mind postponing for an hour or two. At Botley you are 187 feet above the sea, at Cumner 415, and the distance is roughly two miles. But it must be climbed for the sake of romantic (and romancer's) association. The church, which has pieces of almost every style of architecture in its composition, a chained Bible, a Jacobean pulpit, and wonderful carved work, not to mention a figure of Queen Elizabeth and relics of Amy Robsart, is of remarkable interest. Of Cumner Place hardly a vestige remains ; and the exact truth of the story of the tragedy enacted there in 1560, shortly after the last and the most complaisant of the Abbots of Abingdon came to the end of this life's comforts, will never be known. However, it is certainly an occasion for a brief digression, and it is the more imperious on our attention in that Lady Warwick, in her beautifully equipped volumes on *Warwick Castle and its Earls*, has entered into the controversy with an ardent desire to make as good a case as possible for a Dudley.

The facts, up to a point, are common ground. Robert Dudley married Amy Robsart in 1550 ; and on September 28th, 1560, Amy was an inmate of Cumner Place, under the care of its owner, Anthony Forster, who was Robert Dudley's steward. On that day Amy met her death at the hands of men under Dudley's orders, according to Ashmole, whose opinion is but the reflection of the popular talk of the time. Motley, who

Cumner Church.

was a careful historian, as well as a picturesque, notes that the
coroner's jury, at an inquest demanded by Dudley, a jury composed of Dudley's enemies and of strangers to him, found
Amy's death to be due to accident ; but he opines that the
calumny, having endured for three centuries, is likely to survive
for as many more. Moreover, shocking, from the historical
point of view, as is the disregard for history shown by Sir
Walter Scott in *Kenilworth* generally, the mere fact that, perhaps for the sake of romance only, he adopted the theory of
murder, is enough to make that theory generally accepted for
ever ; and the picture by Mr. W. F. Yeames, R.A., which is
full of power, appeals yet more strongly to the popular
imagination.

"Was it accident ? Was it suicide ? Was it murder ?"
asks Lady Warwick. We may eliminate suicide surely. If
there is any truth in any part of anybody's story, Amy was
found dead at the foot of the staircase in the hall by the
servants when they came back from Abingdon Fair ; and to
throw herself downstairs would have been too stupid and too
uncertain a method in which to court death, though she may
have had reason enough to wish for it, poor soul. Besides, it
would be an unfeminine action. Students of suicide have
observed that women rarely choose a disfiguring fashion of
self-sought death. Accident it might easily have been ; and it
were a piece of poor historical judgment to pay much attention
to the popular rumours of the time or to the pamphlet known
as *Leicester's Commonwealth*, although from its sensational
character it served the purposes of Sir Walter Scott very well.
But Lady Warwick marshals the other known facts so well
that she upsets her own conclusion. Dudley heard the news
at Windsor, in the same county as Cumner, though at the
farthest point of it. He did not hurry to the spot, as any
husband of decent feeling would have done, but he sent his
cousin Blount who, after tarrying for a night at Abingdon,
wrote a letter which, judging by Dudley's answer, clearly

showed some apprehensions as to the possible finding of the
jury. The letter itself contains no direct evidence save that it
makes one reflect " he doth protest too much " ; but Lady
Warwick adds extracts from the correspondence, quite clearly
proving that both Dudley and Blount were in close communication with the jury. " There is plenty in it to suggest, and very
little to contradict, the idea that Blount and Dudley bribed the
jury " (they might have intimidated without bribery for that
matter) " to defeat the ends of justice—or at least that Dudley,
only giving Blount half his confidence, bribed the foreman behind his back, while hypocritically parading a desire to get at
the truth, the whole truth, and nothing but the truth. A
modern judge, discovering such a correspondence in the course
of a case, would hardly fail to suspect something of the sort.
But there is only a presumption, and it is quite impossible for
us to pass the boundary that separates presumption from proof.
Dudley's equivocal behaviour may have been—and probably
was—due to fear that his enemies, who were numerous and
powerful, would twist facts against him. This would have been
moral cowardice ; but nothing that we know of Robert Dudley
warrants us in crediting him with moral cowardice."

Why " moral cowardice " ? If Dudley, being innocent of
his unfortunate wife's death, trafficked with the jury—as he
undoubtedly did—for fear his enemies should twist facts
against him, or for any other reason, that was not moral but
physical cowardice of quite an ordinary type. The plain fact
is that such trafficking affords a presumption of guilt so strong
that, unless rebutted, it is absolute. It is impossible, having
regard to the scanty array of facts that could be twisted against
Dudley, who had been away at Windsor all the time, to regard
it as the act of an innocent man ; and it is difficult to agree
with Lady Warwick's charitable conclusion, or to avoid a
word of comment. She says : " On the whole, therefore, the
fact that Dudley's enemies could not convict him, and did
not even try to convict him, is the historian's best reason for

acquitting him." His enemies did not know of this correspondence; if they had known it, conviction would have been certain; and Lady Dudley omits to remember that Anthony Forster was Dudley's steward, a fact which might have been used against Dudley legitimately, without any twisting at all. Nor is it fair to make quite nothing of the accusation made in 1567 by John Appleyard, Amy's half-brother, and withdrawn with apologies when he was examined by the Privy Council. "Possibly," says Lady Warwick, "the retractation was made under pressure." That, indeed is more than possible, even probable. Moreover, part of the accusation, which was that Dudley had bribed the jury, was at any rate very near to the truth. In fact, while absolute certainty can never be reached on the evidence known to exist, Lady Warwick's verdict, "there is no good reason for believing that he murdered her, and there is fairly good reason for believing that he did not," cannot be accepted. It is distinctly more likely than not that Dudley caused his wife to be murdered, and his conduct after her death goes to support the theory. If so, the unhappy lady's crime was simply that she stood in the path of a magnificently ambitious and unscrupulous man who, but for her, might perhaps have been the King Consort of Queen Elizabeth. So, in this respect, Sir Walter Scott may have been historically correct when, in writing *Kenilworth*, he exercised his right of selecting the most picturesque and romantic theory of Amy Robsart's, or rather Amy Dudley's, death. The rest of *Kenilworth*, of course, is full of mistakes, or of legitimate liberties taken with accurate history.

In these days, as has been stated, hardly so much as one stone is left on another of "the haunted towers of Cumner Hall," towers which never had any real existence save in verse and in *Kenilworth*; but there is a tale of recent times worthy to be told again for its humour. It is to the effect that a gentleman with a fancy for ghosts bought a house at Cumner, called Cumner Place, in the faith that it was the house in which Amy Robsart died, and in the hope that it was haunted. The faith was based on definite representations, and that was a little unfortunate, since Anthony Forster built a new house in the place of the one which was fatal to Amy, and of that new house there is not enough left to satisfy any self-respecting apparition ; and the credulous gentleman won his action for rescission of contract. He was doubly fortunate, for, associations apart, there are few places in Berkshire more dispiriting and woe-begone than Cumner. Emphatically it is not " residential." Almost, indeed, does it seem like a hamlet on which a curse has rested, and our little tour to it has been undertaken simply because it was unavoidable. The wise man will not really go there at all ; he will read, and believe. The sceptic will go, as I did, and depart believing, and " sick and sorry he came," as the Psalmist has it.

So good-bye to Cumner and its memories, and down the hill to Besselsleigh and Appleton. Both these places are fragrant of Berkshire history as the homes of the Besils (they are spelled in many ways) and of the Fettiplaces. Besselsleigh is of note, too, as one of the houses of the Lenthalls. Appleton, originally granted to Giles de la Motte, Groom of the King's Chamber in 1308—but Lysons notes that the house of his day was much older —was one of the many homes of the Fettiplace family, whose argent chevronels are to be traced in half-a-dozen Berkshire churches or more. These same heraldic emblems may be seen also in many another county.

> " The Tracys, the Lacys and the Fettiplaces
>   Own all the manors, the parks, and the chases "

says the old rhyme : and as to the Fettiplaces, who alone concern us, it is not far from right. The first of them known to fame was, curiously enough, Adam, Mayor of Oxford in 1240, and they passed out of existence as a family in 1805, when Charles Fettiplace died of apoplexy in room 11 of the Bull Inn

at Burford, having been a victim to a seizure on his way back
from Burford races. In the interval, at one time or another,
they seemed to have acquired, sometimes by marriage, land in
no less than fifteen counties ; but Childrey and Little Shefford in
Berks, and Swinbrook in Oxfordshire, were their principal
seats. " Though the family was of vast local importance,"
says the historian of Oxfordshire, " its members seem to have
taken comparatively little part in national affairs." That this
may have conduced to the obscure prosperity of the family is
pointed out in connection with Childrey, long their principal
seat. For the present let it suffice to make the attempt, not
really difficult, to conjure up the picture of their lives. *Mutatis
mutandis* it was on the same lines as that of many of the
nobility of our day. I open the Peerage at a venture, and the
name of Lord Penrhyn discloses itself. At the end of genea-
logical and heraldic matter appears a list of his residences,
between the lines of which it is easy to read. Penrhyn Castle
serves for principal residence ; it is near the huge slate quarries
which have attracted no little attention of late. Glan Conway,
hard by, and Banchory, far away in Scotland, serve for shooting and fishing ; Wicken, Stony Stratford, suggests hunting ;
Mortimer House is for the London season and Parliament.
Similar is the case of other peers and persons of position ; only
my Peerage has been kind in opening where I could read
between the lines with ease. For the Fettiplaces there was
no London season ; Oxford or Burford, or perhaps even
Abingdon, sufficed. But, when they were weary of the glories
of Swinbrook, which was of extraordinary splendour, they
could and did proceed, by infamous roads, to one of their
other manors, moving their whole households with them, and
the change was every whit as complete, and at least as troublesome to the family, as are now the migration of the households
of, shall we say, the Duke of Devonshire and Lord London-
derry to Lismore and to Seaham.

Appleton was one of the manors which the Fettiplaces

Wootton.

acquired by marriage, from the neighbouring Besils, in this case, and the remains of Appleton Manor, formerly theirs, are of remarkable interest, especially the doorway of the hall. Besselsleigh is the ancestral home of the Besils, of whom good Sir Peter, the bridge-builder, has already come under notice. Leland knew the Besils well by repute, as men of "activitye in feates of armes," who came "out of Provence in France." Here again, not by marriage apparently this time, the manor passed from the Besils to the Fettiplaces, and from them Besselsleigh passed in 1634 to Speaker Lenthall, of the Long Parliament, whose descendants still survive.

Now, returning to the high road from Appleton, let us go straight to Fyfield, Fyfield of the famous Manor House, built by John Golafre in the fourteenth century, modernised, so to speak, in Elizabeth's time ; Fyfield whose modest house of public entertainment shelters the wayfarer within walls that served for nobler and holier purposes in the fourteenth century. This same John Golafre was a great man of his time, being chosen with Thomas Chaucer as one of the trustees of the Gild of Holy Cross at Abingdon. His arms, too, were on the cross which Waller's soldiers wrecked at Abingdon. A charming little place is Fyfield, but here the curious persistence of inexplicable error compels a personal digression. Murray's Guide states that inscriptions in the church show it to have been repaired in 1632 by William Lenthall, the Speaker ; in 1788 by William J. Lenthall ; and in 1888 by Mr. E. K. Lenthall, "who died at Besselsleigh in 1892, and was said to be the last person (1821) born in Burford Priory." Again, Mr. W. H. Hutton, in *By Thames and Cotswold* observes that Burford Priory was sold in 1828 by " the last of the Lenthalls." As a matter of fact, Mr. Edmund K. Lenthall was very much alive at Besselsleigh Manor on the third Sunday in 1905, and, if he had been dead, he would not have been the last of the Lenthalls, for, at Boar's Hill, hard by, lives another descendant of the Speaker in the direct line, possessed of a son, a young

Besselsleigh.

man in the prime of life, to say nothing of daughters, so that to
speak of the last of the Lenthalls is at least premature.   Now
the Lenthalls are a remarkable family.   Concerning the quality
of the Speaker's character opinions may vary.   Some hold that,
in signing the warrant for the execution of Charles, which he
clearly did against conscience, he was acting ministerially and,
therefore, blameless ; others think that, having so behaved, he
did but sum up his own character justly when he directed that
his tomb should be marked by the humble legend *Vermis Sum*.
But concerning the quality of the stout old Lenthall of
Agincourt fame there can be no question.   The five fusils in
the Lenthall arms are the record of five knights of various
degrees whom he took prisoner by the strength of his good
right arm at Agincourt ; and with their ransoms he built to himself a noble house in Herefordshire.   In this connection
I doubt not that Mr. Lenthall, of Boar's Hill, will forgive the
repetition of an anecdote.   Early in the nineteenth century the
Lenthalls, or some of them, fell upon evil days through
extravagance, and Mr. Lenthall's father emigrated to Australia ;
and there Mr. Lenthall himself rose to high office in the New
South Wales Police Force.   To him once a shrewd Australian
put a question concerning the deeds of his Agincourt ancestor,
and on learning of the five prisoners observed, "I don't see
why you should think much of your ancestor.   You have most
likely taken up five hundred prisoners, let alone five."   There
is all the difference in the world between taking prisoners and
taking them up.   It is, however, consoling to find that Mr. Lenthall has been able to retire in his old age in comfort, to a fine
house from which he can look down on the Vale wherein his
forefathers were great men and reflect "*et nos aliquid,
nomenque, decusque, gessimus.*"

Of Besselsleigh Manor House all has perished save the
pillars of the gateway, standing near the church, and the
chapel, which is the church ; and the present manor-house is
modern.   The old house and chapel were, in all probability,

designed by Inigo Jones, and portions of the old house were transferred to the Home Farm. But the surviving Lenthalls still believe that they can point out the site of the "listes" where, according to Leland, the head of the Blessels (or Besils) family *tempore* Edward I. "faught in listes with a strange knyghte that challengyd hym, at the whiche deade the kynge and quene at that tyme of England were present."

For the Fyfield Elm, Matthew Arnold's elm, we must go to Tubney, half a mile off and on our direct route to Abingdon. The elm is the ruin of a magnificent tree. It is a pity, really, that legends should be allowed to cluster round elms, short-lived trees, and treacherous while they live. As a nucleus for legend there is nothing like an oak, a yew, or perhaps a white-thorn growing in an exposed position. From Tubney, then, let us hie back to Abingdon easily, for there is some fifty feet of fall in some four miles of excellent road, and let good eating and good sleeping crown a well-spent day.

Churchyard Cross, Cumner.

WORKING MEN'S COLLEGE LIBRARY.

Faringdon. Part of Church Street, now demolished.

CHAPTER VI

THE NORTH OF THE VALE—SECOND EXPEDITION

Abingdon to Marcham—"Ware glass"—Interest of Marcham—The
Priory—Grateful gluttony—Longworth and its roses—Sir Henry
Marten—His "ungodly son Harry"—Hinton Waldrist—Elizabethan
manor—Buckland—Its antiquity—Thomas Chaucer—The Throckmorton coat—Pusey—Tenure by cornage—Traditions of Canute—The
Pusey horn—Description—Paternoster land — Puseys extinct—Dr.
Pusey on Bouverie—Cherbury—More Canute traditions—Stanford-in
the-Vale and its glass—Faringdon "Folly"—Pye the Laureate—
Faringdon a centre of roads—Its place in history—Home of Wessex
kings—Siege during Rebellion—Sir Henry Unton—Great Coxwell—
Little Coxwell—Lyford—Goosey—Denchworth—An admirable clergyman—The *Denchworth Annual*—The vicar's library — The Hyde
family—A wonderful brass—Providential vandalism—Rare books in
library—A Caxton lost and found—A "chipping" cross—The clergyman as social adviser—Struggles for water—The hard case of the Vale
—A punning epitaph—West Hanney—Quaint brasses—"Files" of
children kept in stock—Sir Christopher Lytcott—Steventon—Curious
buildings—Causeway—The Black Monks—A view of Abingdon.

THE next expedition to be taken from Abingdon may not
occupy many pages here, but it will be found fairly satisfying

in the flesh, by reason of the amount of road it will involve. In fact to do things in comfort—and that is the only way in which it is worth while to do things for pleasure at all—it will be prudent to send on a supply of clothes and necessaries for the night to Faringdon, where reasonable entertaiment for man and beast is to be found at either of the inns, the "Crown" or the "Bell." But it must not be taken that, because these pages are going to travel lightly over the chosen route, it is therefore wanting in interest from any standpoint. In truth there are few prettier rides than this which lies before us, few in which the country traversed is more characteristically English, few in which the hamlets by the wayside have more stories, in stone and of other kinds, to tell to the wayfarer. But it is necessary to push forward, for Berkshire is an extensive county, and if, as one of old time wrote, it resembles "a sandall for a man's foot" in form, the man must have been a giant indeed.

So this fine morning, we will start betimes from Abingdon, setting our faces to the West and keeping straight on, turning neither to right nor left, when the end of Ock Street is reached. Here a small piece of practical advice may be offered to the cyclist. In Ock Street "Ware glass." The ingenuous children of Abingdon have a playful habit of breaking mineral water bottles of a familiar type on the road for the sake of the marble which serves as a stopper. The fragments, though they flash like a weak emerald in the sun, are a frequent cause of puncture, but they are easily avoided by those who know what to expect, and they are usually nearer to the sides of the wide road than to the centre. It is well, too, to keep in mind the fact that the Berkshire rustic, although obliging in giving way, usually makes a point of driving on the wrong or off side of the road, especially in turning corners. Gratitude for these hints is neither asked nor expected ; but unless they are remembered annoying accidents are probable.

For a matter of two miles the level road is quite

uninteresting. Then we reach Marcham, whereof, and of Garford, Mr. Falkner writes : "The churches are rebuilt and the villages are without interest." That is a little hard on Marcham, though it is true enough of Garford, which is a mile or so off, along a branch road, and across the River Ock, to the left. But Marcham, with Sheepstead House and Park in rear, and the remains of a grand refectory at the house known as the Priory, is a passable village with a good deal of old domestic architecture about it, and Marcham Mill, lying down in the water-meadows, is not entirely wanting in association. Like most things in these parts, it once belonged to the abbey, but, unlike them, it was given away by the Abbey ; for once on a time there was an abbot who loved good fare daintily prepared, and the said abbot actually granted Marcham Mill in fee-simple to a cook of the abbey who had pleased him mightily. When it is remembered that the tenants of the manor were bound to use the mill, and to pay the miller accordingly in kind, it is plain that the guerdon was great. One small part of the mill looks as if it had been built in the days before the dissolution. Also, from the churchyard of Marcham for half a mile or so, there is one of the most charming little walks along a tree-lined path that the county can show. After this, save for a glance at Kingston Bagpuze in passing, it will be as well to push on, turning to the right soon, and then to the left, for Longworth.

Longworth, indeed, is to me an oasis in the fields. It has a pretty church ; it was the birthplace of Dr. Fell, of Christ Church and of the nursery rhyme, and of Sir Henry Marten, Dean of Arches, whose "ungodly son Harry" was one of the regicides and came to a bad end. The ungodly Harry, as portrayed in Lysons—that is to say, in Lady Wantage's magnificent and Grangerised copy—had rather a pleasant face. But at Longworth, if so be it is near the season of "the roses and the longest day," or indeed at any time before the frosts have been severe, one may lay aside the past in the joy of the present. "*Laudabunt alii claram Rhodon aut Mitylenen.*"

Others will praise Hitchin, Cheshunt, Newtownards, or Colchester; but for roses give me Longworth.   You see them in their beauty in many a cottage garden, perhaps because the brothers Prince preach the gospel of the rose among the poor, perhaps because everybody at Longworth can bud roses and make them grow. Standards in the plots by the houses, climbing roses against the walls, show blossoms fit for exhibition, " an' good zarts too," as they say at Longworth.   Inside the domain of Messrs. Prince they are to be seen by the acre, and always of every variety, new and old.   Of course it is not the best way of seeing roses for artistic effect, for these are the gardens of a grower.   But the true rosarian will find abundance of perfect blossoms, and the gardener who is not of the strictest order of rosarians, the man or woman who will not sacrifice a rampant bush of roses for a few fine blooms, will hardly fail to conjure up scenes to be created elsewhere out of this raw material, as he wanders among the flowers.   A Bardou Job, with its wondrous petals of dark red velvet, will suggest itself as a robe for the old apple-tree ; a Rêve d'Or, cunningly grown against a wall, staked, not nailed, will bring to mind that naked wall at home that needs a covering so sadly ; and the tea-roses, the strongest feature of the garden to my mind, will be full of temptations.   But, if you have a garden, by no means enter unless you mean to buy, for buy you surely will, although nobody will pester you so to do. You will be welcomed as a visitor in any case ; and you will depart with a gladly given bunch of roses at your handlebars if you so desire.

On we go, along the crest of the hill, amongst stately trees too, to Hinton Waldrist, hardly suspecting that the infant Thames is within a mile, and at a level about a hundred feet lower, on the right.   For sylvan beauty, restfulness, and commanding views, the ancient seat of the St. Walerys is not to be surpassed ; and if their manor-house is gone, the Elizabethan structure which one may see from the road, without invading any man's privacy, is still satisfying.   So is the mound on

which the keep of the castle stood, for hence the eye ranges
over the whole breadth of the Vale. It is a sea of corn and
grass land, in which, as one looks southward, clumps of green

Stanford-in-the-Vale Church.

trees, and occasional towers of churches, mark the sites of
Charney Basset, Lyford, Goosey, the two Hanneys, Stanford-in-
the-Vale, and Denchworth.   Beyond them, distant perhaps ten
miles, is the undulating rampart of the Berkshire Downs,

looking blue and mountain-like in the distance, historic every
acre of them, though it be not easy to locate all the history with
precision.   At their feet nestle, mostly in a veil of trees, half a
score of places to be visited another day.   For the moment,
nay, for the hour, if inclination calls, that grand stretch of rich
plain absorbs the whole attention and delights the mind.
Verily, if one desired to live forgotten, by the world forgot, in a
lovely environment, and in fresh upland air, Hinton Waldrist
would be a place more than suitable, for it is nearly six miles
from the nearest railway station at Faringdon, and that is but
the terminus of a branch line.

The very name of the next village, Buckland, is a guarantee
of antiquity.   The manor was granted to Hugo de Bocland,
says Lysons, in 1227.   It is more likely that it was granted to
one Hugo, to hold as *boc-land* (that is to say, land held by an
individual), as distinguished from Folkland.   A later, and perhaps a more interesting holder of this *boc-land*, was Thomas
Chaucer, but whether Geoffrey Chaucer was the father of
Thomas, as well as of English poetry, is, as has been seen, by
no means certain.   A fine house there is here, too, in which are
curious relics of the Throckmortons, a chemise once worn by
Mary Queen of Scots, a gold medal of Charles I., and the
famous Throckmorton coat which has been celebrated in many
an agricultural journal.   It was made, from the shearing of the
sheep to the putting on of the coat for dinner, at Newbury, in
precisely thirteen hours and twenty minutes, in the year 1811.
Similar stories, of rapid conversion of standing corn into bread,
for example, are not uncommon ; but here is the original coat,
serving to remind us that Newbury, like Abingdon, once
" stood by clothing."   The church, too, is full of quaint things,
including the dried heart of William Holcot, some time Lord
of the Manor of Burcote in Buckland, a reformer in religion,
who combined prudence with zeal, in the days of Edward VI.,
Mary, and Elizabeth.   Moreover, the church, though it was
reduced in height during the eighteenth century, is a stately

piece of Early English work, and the whole village is embowered
in trees. Buckland should certainly not be passed on one side.

Still less should Pusey; Pusey, the classical example of
tenure by cornage, which in its turn is one of the very oldest
forms of tenure by knight service. Perhaps one ought to
adopt the sceptical attitude concerning the silver-mounted horn,
still in existence and bearing, according to Mr. Falkner, the
inscription ".I King Knowde geve Wyllyam Pecote this horn
to hold by thy lond," or, according to Colonel Cooper King,
"Kynge Knoud geve Wyllyam Pewse hys horne to hold by thy

Buckland House.

Londe." (The vast difference between these two authorities
upon a matter of fact illustrates the difficulties which have to
be encountered by one who uses them for reference, and I
regret that I have had no opportunity of seeing the horn.) That
is to say, Canute the Dane may not have been the giver of the
manor to the original Pusey; but at least one need not reject
it for Colonel Cooper King's reason, "that the custom of holding manors by such curious tenures is rather Norman than
Saxon [*sic*]." To start with, Canute was a Dane, as Colonel
Cooper King no doubt knew, if he had but thought. To go
on with, "the elements of feudalism so far existed in England
under the Anglo-Saxon and Danish Kings as to make it easy to
introduce in full at the Norman Conquest." So writes " J. W."

in the ninth edition of the *Encyclopædia Britannica* (I had hoped that "J. W." would conceal the identity of Joshua Williams, *par excellence* the authority on the history of the law of real property; but it appears to represent James Williams, who may have known quite as much). Moreover, Mr. Falkner has unearthed, and by the look of the English has modernised, a passage from one Dr. Hickes, who, writing in 1681, alleged that horn and manor were owned by Charles Pusey, who actually produced the horn in the Court of Chancery before Jeffreys.

"The horn itself was produced in Court, and with universal admiration received, admitted, and proved to be the identical horn by which, as by a charter, Canute had conveyed the Manor of Pusey 700 years before" (665 really at the most—but 35 years are a trifle). "The horn is that of an ox of middling size, mounted in silver gilt, in workmanship of the latter part of the fifteenth century. The colour of the horn is dark brown, which proves it to be a real ox horn, and not, as was sometimes the case, made of ivory. It is 2 ft. 6 in. long, and 9½ in. from its feet; the circumference at the largest end is 1 ft., in the middle 9¼ in., and at the small end 2½ in. The dog's head at the orifice was formerly moveable, turning upon a joint, so as to make it either a hunting or a drinking horn."

The "feet" referred to are fixed to the central ring, which bears the inscription. It is clear, then, that men accepted the horn, apart from the mountings, as genuine in Jeffreys' time, and that was more than two hundred years nearer to Canute's epoch than ours. But the interval has added to, rather than taken from, the knowledge of the learned concerning early history. Still, it is a very attractive story, and, in the absence of any cogent argument against it, there seems to be no adequate reason for denying ourselves the pleasure of accepting it. In any case, it is not a little curious that while Buckland retains in its name the traces of one of the most ancient forms, if not the most ancient form, of individual ownership of land, Pusey, within a mile or so, should have this venerable relic (for it would be venerable even as a forgery) of early tenure, and that, as there will soon be occasion to note, Canute tradition is very prevalent in this district of Berks. Moreover, in Pusey, as in other Berkshire parishes, there is evidence of what, for lack of a better title (unless, indeed, that title has been given to it already), may be called Paternoster Land. Alice Paternoster held lands in Pusey on the terms of saying a Paternoster five times a day for the souls of the ancestors of the King (Edward I.); and Mr. Falkner speaks of a Richard Paternoster, and John his brother, who said the Lord's Prayer (Pater Noster, of course) three times before the Barons of the Exchequer instead of paying a relief. A similar case is noted in relation to certain land at East Hendred. But it is puzzling to notice that the Lysons, with plenty of space at their disposal, and the later commentator, treat "Paternoster" gravely as a surname throughout. Nothing could be more plain than that it was originally a *sobriquet*, or than that it was bestowed, probably in envious derision, on all those who held land on these easy terms. That, be it said in passing, is one of the many points concerning that extraordinary place, East Hendred, on the far side of the Vale, comfortably treated; and this, having regard to the fertility of East Hendred as a topic, is a great relief in advance.

The original Puseys, naturally mentioned in Ashmole, are quoted by Colonel Cooper King as being among the few old Berkshire families who survive; but Mr. Falkner, who is much the more trustworthy, points out that the present Puseys of Pusey are, in the male line, Bouveries, of French Protestant origin, who changed their name to Pusey on obtaining the property through a marriage. Still, Pusey House is a fine example of eighteenth-century architecture, and the Park is none the less enjoyable for change of owners; and to have been the birthplace of Edward Bouverie Pusey in 1800 is to have produced an English divine whose influence on his generation during a life of eighty-two years was equal to that of any Pusey from the days of Canute until now.

Cherbury Camp, close by on the east, has also a legendary

connection with Canute, and is perhaps correctly diagnosed by
Colonel Cooper King as having been an earthwork to defend
an ancient road from Oxford, *viâ* Cumner, Besselsleigh, Kingston Bagpuze, and Buckland to Faringdon. But against this
theory must be set the fact that the original routes of traffic, on
the south side of the Vale at any rate, were on the highest land,
probably because the Vale in old times was marshy and liable
to floods. It was, as has been stated, known as "the
Moors," and, except in the case of Pusey, the villages ending in "ey" (Goosey and the Hanneys, for example) were
certainly islands from time to time. Again, Colonel Cooper
King writes of the tradition that Cherbury was a palace of
Canute, "but this is improbable," and no more. That is a
somewhat curt way of disposing of a legend, for it must
have its origin in something. After all, why should not
Canute have had a palace there? Mainly, it seems to me,
because military roads are a ruling passion with Colonel
Cooper King, and he could not think of two things at one
time. It is a hobby amiable and natural in one of his profession; but that is all.

Is the day so far advanced that time cannot be spared for a
detour to Stanford-in-the-Vale, with its interesting church
and relics, and its fragments of ancient glass in the windows?
If not, it is quite worth while to ride to its somewhat lower level
from Pusey, and then to take the Wantage road to Faringdon.
Otherwise, it will be best to return to the Abingdon road and
turn to the left for Faringdon on reaching it. Whichever
way be chosen there is a stiff climb to be faced; for, although
the town itself lies in a cup, it boasts a hill, known as
Faringdon Folly, rising sheer and high from the Vale, and to
be seen from a vast distance from the south side. From
White Horse Hill, for example, it and its clump of trees
look distinctly imposing. That is the effect of its position,
for, supposing it to be 500 feet high (the nearest point marked
on the Ordnance Map is 443 feet), that is not exactly a

mountain. But, both to the north and to the south, the drop
to the two hundred and fifties or thereabouts is rapid, and
that, of course, makes for prominence. The trees on the
hill, which were the real "Folly" in the view of those of
old time, were, oddly enough, planted by the Laureate Pye,

Faringdon Folly.

and they have lived longer than his verse has endured, save as
an object of derision; but the Pyes were great folk at
Faringdon in their day, as we shall see in due course.

If Abingdon be isolated through its own fault, Faringdon
has been left out in the cold by fate and the railway system
only. It is connected with the main line of the Great Western
by a miserable little branch; but a glance at the map shows

that it is to the road system of Berks and the adjoining counties as the centre of a spider's web is to the radiating filaments. From Buscot and Lechlade, from Highworth, Shrivenham, Wantage, Abingdon, and Radcot come good high-roads, all of which are concentrated on Faringdon; but the railway has left it on one side, being doubtless well advised from a commercial standpoint in so doing. It has left Wantage on one side also, but not quite so far. The consequence is that Faringdon, being a thriving town and a great meeting-place for the farmers of the Vale, retains none the less an air of the old world which is hard to match: and to this the domestic architecture generally, and the old Town Hall in particular, contribute not a little. It has been written by somebody that the history of Faringdon is unimportant; but that is a matter of opinion. The Wessex Kings had a palace there; that was some-thing. Robert Earl of Gloucester built a castle there, but Stephen captured it after four days' siege; there was enough history in that to be inconvenient to the inhabitants. It was held for the King in the Great Rebellion by stout Sir Marmaduke Rawdon, and during the siege the church lost a transept and a spire; Faringdon House, too, was actually held for the King against its tenant in fee, Sir Robert Pye, Hampden's brother-in-law, and the Laureate's ancestor, and was only surrendered finally, by the King's orders, when the Royal cause was irre-trievably lost. Surely therefore it is hardly fair to Faringdon, having regard to the sufferings of Faringdonians of the past, to attribute to it the ignoble happiness that belongs to places as well as to people having no history. In the Unton Chapel of Faringdon Church also is buried the body of Philip Sidney's friend, Sir Henry Unton, the challenger of Henri de Guise, the defender of Queen Elizabeth's honour, and a hero of the Battle of Zutphen. So the associations of Faringdon are amply sufficient to satisfy, and it is no mean delight to take ease at the inns, which are old, or to wander reverently in the church, which is older, and to think over the scenes that

Church Street, Faringdon.

have been enacted in and round a town now the very embodiment of the idea of peace. Nor is it reasonable to say that
its history in the days of the Rebellion was unimportant. Its
command of five great roads, in the heart of a district where
there was much fighting, was no trifling matter to the Parliamentary generals.

At Faringdon we stay a night, or perhaps two, making it a
centre for expeditions to a number of little places in the Vale,
all of them worth seeing, but not so conveniently to be
invaded when, some time later, headquarters are moved to
Wantage. They are Great Coxwell, where the stately barn
of the Cistercians, and the adjoining farmhouse of the
sixteenth century, are hardly less attractive than the church or
than the ancient camp of Badbury Hill, which very likely
served in turn all the races that overran Berkshire; Little
Coxwell, with its clipped yews; Charney, nestling on the bank
of the Ock, with its village cross, its curious little church, and
its monastic remains; Shellingford, with its remains of the
once gorgeous mansion of the Packers, who disappeared in
the eighteenth century; Lyford, where again is an ancient
farmhouse, and the traces of the manor-house of the Yates
family wherein Campion, the Jesuit, was taken; Goosey,
which the monks of Abingdon got in exchange for Andersey
Island, only to repent them of their bargain later; Denchworth
and the Hanneys, East and West. They are all well worth
some expenditure of time, except East Hanney; but of places
that must by no means be missed Denchworth and West
Hanney come distinctly first.

Denchworth, a tiny hamlet having a population of 232
persons in 1871, is lucky in that it has not lacked its *vates sacer*,
although he sang but to a thin audience. To Denchworth,
too late to avert a great deal of mischief, came in the
'seventies of the last century the Rev. C. H. Tomlinson, of
Worcester College in Oxford, to which the living has belonged
since 1758. Mr. Tomlinson appears to have occupied himself

Faringdon Church.

in his seclusion not only by looking to the spiritual and temporal interests of the rural parishioners, but also in studying the antiquities of the parish, embodying these in a publication entitled *The Denchworth Annual*, continued for several years. These are now very rare; indeed, the only copy

Faringdon Church, South Door.

of them known to exist is in the "Vicar's Library" at Denchworth; but they are of such fascinating quality that no apology is needed for lingering over them, though it should be to the exclusion of some other topics. Note first that Denchworth is invariably referred to in the Saxon charters as "the place which the country people call by the ridi-

culous name of Denceswurthe," and that "Denceswurthe" is
neither more nor less than Duncetown. It had originally
three manors, of which one only belonged to the great family
of the Hydes, who were reputed to hold it by a grant of King
Canute. Whether the tradition was true or not, it is certainly
impossible not to be impressed by the number and the
persistence of Canute traditions in the Vale. Then, gradually,
the Hydes added field to field until by 1383 they held all the
manors, and they continued to hold them for two centuries
and more before retiring to their great seat at Kingston Lisle.
To them succeeded by purchase the Geerings, who had
actually been their tenants, and the Geerings lasted from 1617
or a little later till 1758; and after the Geerings came
Worcester College.

Now the Hydes, no doubt, did many noteworthy things in
their generations. For example, they built a great manor-
house with fish-ponds—the Hydes built often, but never without creating fish-ponds—and they had the same arms as the
Fettiplaces, which, seeing that the two families flourished
simultaneously, is as confusing as it is odd. But far the most
interesting thing about the Hydes at this time of day is the
brass of William Hyde, who died in 1557; and he and his
brass are of the first order of importance simply by reason of
an almost providential chapter of accidents. It fell out that
in the year 1852, in the time of Mr. Tomlinson's predecessor,
Denchworth Church stood in need of restoration. That the
case was a pressing one may readily be imagined from the
present aspect of the restored edifice. Either it has sunk, or
the ground has been raised by burials (of which more than
3,000 can be counted) inside and out, until the bases of the
pillars have disappeared from view altogether, and many of the
arches, but especially the chancel arch, are all askew and
wonderfully out of plumb. For the like reason, from the
outside, the whole structure looks strangely low as well as old.
So in 1852, funds being in all probability scanty, the late

The Market Hall, Faringdon.

L

Mr. Street, then a local architect of Wantage, was called in. Now occasion has been taken before to urge, by way of gentle protest, a few arguments worthy to be considered by those to whom "restoration" means ruthless destruction; and it has been suggested that it is hard to condemn unheard the parson and architect who were pressed at the same time by the absolute duty of repairing and, in most cases, by the cursed need of pence. But when it is clear beyond doubt that restoration has been "restoration"—that is to say, senseless destruction without saving in expense—then not even regard for the memory of a dead man who attained some fame will permit criticism to be silent.

Let us see what Mr. Street found, and what he left. Properly embedded in stone in the floor of the church he found first the Hyde brasses; and one of them, that of "Wyllm Hyde Esquyer," who died in 1557, and Margery his wife, who died in 1562, bore the inscription also:

> "Quisquis transieris pro nostris ora animabus
> et junctas tumulo tu prece junge Deo."

The "animabus" alone, being none too frequent, should have warned an architect of taste that this was a brass worthy of some special care. But it was not proposed to replace the stone in the floor, it is now covered with encaustic tiles of no merit, and metalling was wanted for a field path close by. So the brass was torn from its resting-place in the stone—really it sounds almost like an interposition of Providence—and on the back was a found an inscription far more important than any words commemorating the death of a Hyde. It ran thus, and it constitutes, says Mr. Tomlinson, the oldest dated brass in England. Mr. Tomlinson may have been right according to the state of knowledge in his day. Older brasses are known now, but none more interesting than:

> "Edward Roy danglete qe fist le siege deuant la cite de Berewyk et
> coqjst la bataile illeoqs et le dite cite la veille seinte Margarete lan de gae

F.L. GRIGGS – 1906

The Abbey Dormitory, Abingdon.

L 2

WORKING MEN'S COLLEGE LIBRARY.

MCCCXXXIII mist cest pere a la requeste Sire William de Mountague foundour de ceste mesoun."

" Ceste mesoun " was the Priory of Augustine Canons at Bisham, founded by William, Earl of Salisbury, on the site of the preceptory of the suppressed Templars, refounded in 1537 as a Benedictine abbey and finally surrendered in 1539. One can imagine shrewd William Hyde, picking up the brass cheaply, and laying it aside until such time as it might come in useful for him and his wife. Such conduct was not unusual in those times ; that is to say, men often had memorials of themselves in readiness. But it is really extraordinary to think of the strange way in which this priceless historical document was brought to light. At present it can be read by the eye of faith only, for the side of the brass, now fixed to the chancel wall, which is visible is, perhaps properly, that bearing the Hyde inscription. It would not be over-safe from collectors, who have no consciences, but for the fact that the present vicar, at the request of the Berkshire police, keeps the church locked save on those rare occasions when an intelligent visitor penetrates to the lonely hamlet.

Mr. Street, however, found more in another part of the church, and left even less. Above the porch was a chamber, a parvise, built in 1693, during the vicarage of Ralph Kedden and the church-wardenship of one of the Geerings, in which was housed the library, " to be held in trust by the vicar for his successors for ever," collected by the above-named persons and " E. Brewster, stationer of London." It was a library of 100 volumes, all chained, including Cranmer's Bible (the fourth edition, with Cromwell's arms omitted and the fly-leaves of the Old and New Testament designed by Holbein) and *The Golden Legend*, a genuine Caxton of 1483. Here, it might surely have been thought, was a rare example of a wise usage of old time, to preserve which every care should have been taken. But what happened ? Porch and chamber were destroyed. The books, chains and all, were taken to the vicar's study, where those of them which remained have been preserved with scrupulous care by Mr. Tomlinson and by his successor. Amongst them is the Cranmer's Bible, but the Caxton, alas for Denchworth, disappeared before Mr. Street destroyed its home. Fortunately, however, it has gone to a worthy resting-place, for, having been sold to an Oxford bookseller, it was eventually bought by the Bodleian. A rib of a "mermaid," really a manatee, is still preserved.

The church, with its traces of Early Norman architecture, as well as of Early English, and of a rood loft and stair-case, and good gurgoyles, is still interesting in spite of restoration. So is the "preaching cross" in the churchyard; and in the village is the bottom of another cross, at the junction of four ancient roads, supposed to be a "chipping" or "cheapening" cross, at the base of which the chapmen offered their wares. It is pleasant, too, to note the other activities of Mr. Tomlinson as illustrated in the Annuals, his prudent advice to labourers whom Trade Union agitators were trying to seduce, his incessant efforts to secure a water-supply. Here indeed he was upon the most dire want and the greatest grievance of the Vale, although it is gradually disappearing. At the foot of the chalk there is no trouble, but successive issues of the Annual deplore the insuperable difficulty presented by Kimmeridge clay, two, three, and even five hundred feet deep, and the perversity of the inhabitants in polluting and then drinking from a shallow brook. Their case was, and to some extent is—thanks to Mr. Tomlinson a hydraulic ram makes the water of the Hyde Moat available, and they are to that extent provided for—that of many a village in the Vale. That is to say, there is no reasonable chance of obtaining pure water *in situ*, and no organisation for obtaining it from a distance. Indeed, I do not hesitate to say that there are villages in the Vale where the water-supply is so bad that, if they were in India or South Africa, instead of being within fifty or sixty miles of

London, Parliament and the newspapers would ring with their grievances.

One more epitaph of the Hydes, the same lady and gentleman apparently, may be quoted for its quaintness first, and next to bring brasses back to mind, for at West Hanney, our next point, brasses are to the fore.

" Here lye we two now in erth not far a parte
Husbande and wyfe whiles we had lyfe who only death could pte
My name Willm her's Margery by surname called Hyde
Which name accorde to us lyve and deade who now ye erth doth hyde
While we did lyve God gave us grace to harbour cloth and hyde
The naked poor folkes injuryes we did defend and hyde
Now beyng deade we crave mercy of God that he wyll hyde
His face fro owre synnes and wyth his arme he fro ye diuyll us hyde
And that wyth saynts and happy sowles our sely sowles may hyde
In heven wyth God, good folkes we pray to pray to God for Hyde."

Hydes there are to this day, albeit not in Denchworth, and one of their number has given to the little church a remarkably good window by Messrs. Morris, of Merton Abbey.

Close to Denchworth are West and East Hanney, of which the nearer, and the former, is the more worth visiting. It has some interesting and sufficiently ancient examples of domestic architecture, and the church is remarkable. The cursed need of pence probably accounts for a wooden screen that blocks away a whole transept ; and, from workmen who were there when it was last visited, it was gathered that invasions of surface water were a constantly recurring trouble. The West Hanney brasses are numerous and remarkable on the face of them. They will be found within the rails of the altar, covered with loose mats, and they relate for the most part to the Ayshcombes and the Wellesbornes, who flourished in the sixteenth and seventeenth centuries, and intermarried not a little, amply fulfilling the scriptural injunction to increase and multiply. For example, John Ayshcombe married Mary Wellesborne and begat ten sons and four daughters, all of whom are shown on the brass in tidy rows. Also it is a curious little fact that behind the fourth daughter is to be seen the front part of the skirt of a possible fifth. Clearly this case and the similar one at Shottesbrooke prove that rows of sons and daughters were kept in stock by the tomb-makers and cut off as required. Another very taking brass is that of Sir Christopher Lytcott, "husband of two wives," between whom he stands. They were Jane

Buttress Window, East Hanney.

Essex, of Beckett, widow, and Catherine Grey, widow. He was a man, clearly, of some courage in domestic life, for he faced two successive widows, and a notable warrior in public life, for he was "knighted in the camp before Roane by Henry of Navarre," in 1591. After serving with distinction under Essex, one may take it, Sir Christopher found West Hanney distinctly restful. He certainly so found it if, in his time, it was at all like it is now; for, as it stands, it is exactly the

kind of place in which a tablet recording the fact that one
Elizabeth Bowles saw the light of three centuries causes no
surprise.   She died in 1718, aged 124.

And now, having penetrated so far south as almost to render
the title of the chapter misleading, let us return to Abingdon,
leaving the rest of the southern side untouched for the moment.
The route will be along a level road through East Hanney,
which need not detain us, to Steventon; and there a halt must be
called, for, *experto credite*, the gems of beauty in Steventon are
very easy to miss, from whatsoever direction it be approached.
Resist, therefore, the temptation to turn "stunt" to the left
on reaching the main road between Abingdon and East Ilsley,
and do not be at the pains to study the road to the right,
which leads towards the station, as well as to Ilsley, but halt at
the corner.   From it, to the church on the east and to Milton
on the west, meeting the high-road at right angles, leads what
is called in these parts a "causey."   It is a cobbled path (a
"pitched" path locally), raised several feet above the level of
the surrounding ground, quite narrow, and having fine elms
set close on either side; and a tablet in the church records
that it is maintained out of moneys left "by two sisters, by
ancient report."   Originally, no doubt, it was built by the
Black Monks, who had a priory at Steventon attached to the
Abbey of Bec, but were suppressed by Edward III.   The
elms at one point are poor by reason of a lawsuit of bygone
years, for payment of the costs of which some fine trees were
felled and sold.   Time was when, knowing Berkshire in
dry seasons only, I was amused at these elaborate precau-
tions against flood, but glad that they had been taken,
since the vista of the "causey," flanked for the most part by
the tall elms on either side, dappled by the sunlight penetrating
their dense shade in patches, is, especially on the way to
Milton, unspeakably beautiful in a quiet way.   But 1903
proved that the monks had made and the two sisters had
maintained the "causey" for real and sufficient reason.   Then

F L GRIGGS · 1906

At Steventon.

one learned that the little River Ock with its tributaries, and
the other brook, called at various parts of its course the Gynge,
Steventon, Milton, and (again) Gynge brook, entering the
Thames at Sutton Courtney, were quite inadequate to carry
away the water that came coursing from the slopes of the
Downs on the south of the Vale, and down the northern ridge
from Faringdon to Cumner. Then it was that the high-road
from Steventon to Abingdon was, until it reached Drayton, a
tawny flood, three feet deep in parts, although the road is full
twenty feet above the level of the Thames, a mile or so away.
Then it was, finally, that the "causeys" were an unmixed
blessing, as practical as they were picturesque.

But the "causey" is a footpath only. Parallel to it, at a
level six or eight feet lower, runs the road to the church, and
it passes a series of old timbered houses, one of them once the
vicarage, of the sixteenth and seventeenth centuries, with gay
gardens in front of them. These houses would certainly be
hard to find fellows for in any county of England in point of
quaint beauty, antique timbering and pargetting, and for the
memories of the old world which they suggest. It used to be a
delight—here is a confession of ignorance—to assign this or
that one among them to Jane Austen; and it was almost
annoying to discover later, what everybody else knew before,
that Jane Austen's Steventon was in Hampshire. But the
houses are none the less entrancing, and, well as I know
Steventon now, I usually find, if there is half an hour to spare
there, that an entirely purposeless detour reveals some pretty
corner that has been missed on previous occasions. That is all
that needs to be said of Steventon, save that its copse is
haunted by nightingales in the season of the year and that the
church is worth a visit by reason of its noble roof.

So, with an easy gradient to help us from time to time, and
only one natural hill to climb, let us ride on to Abingdon, passing the hedgeless corn-land of Milton Field on the right, and that
of Drayton Field on the left; enjoying, too, such width of view

The Priory, Steventon.

as is rarely to be seen in England.   Let us remember, in riding, that, but for the perversity of Abingdon, sleepy Steventon would have been, from a railway point of view, Didcot ; and the wide view would have been spoiled to a certainty by com- monplace houses all the way.   As it is, after leaving Steventon Green—an exceptionally fine one in a part of the county by no means well provided in that respect—we pass no houses until Drayton is reached (but we will not visit Drayton to-day) ; and after passing Drayton there are again no houses until Abingdon. But before that there has been time to enjoy a new view of the spires of Abingdon, rising, as it seems, out of a sea of red roofs and green foliage, against a background of wooded hills, and from a foreground of rich corn-land, green, golden, or chocolate in hue according to the season of the year.   It is a glorious sight ; but why, now that the Berks and Wilts Canal has gone definitely out of use, horse and man should have to ascend and descend the very steep pitch of the bridge which left room for the navigation is, as Lord Dundreary used to say, " one of those things no fellow ever could understand."

are felt. Else will the former surely be missed ; and some of them deserve a far better fate.

Westward along Ock Street is the first marching order, and at the bridge over the Ock turn to the left, and ride two miles or thereabouts to a point where a modern stone cross under a group of ancient elms marks the head of the long street—they call it a street—of Drayton, Berks, not to be confounded with Drayton in Oxfordshire, only a few miles off, or with any of the other Draytons in Middlesex or elsewhere of which no man seems to know the derivation.

There will have been three turnings by the way, after the irritating little ascent of the disused canal bridge, not one of them worth taking. The first leads to a farm ; the second to the hamlet of Sutton Wick, remarkable principally for its walnut trees—we are here in a country prolific of walnuts—and for the large number of farmhouses and cottages, falling or fallen into melancholy ruin, within its limits ; the next leads past a few cottages and houses, of which one only is curious, and then past the church into the main street of the village. The church, if desired, can be reached later from the main street, and it is better so reached, since Church Lane, which is the road (so-called) under consideration, is not usually good for travelling. Nor is its one curious house, within which, as it happens, these words are written, at all a show place. It is, indeed, peculiar only by reason of the fact that, viewed from the back, it is seen to be built round three sides of a little square, that it has mighty beams of elm, and that some of its sixteenth-century casements are strangely beautiful. Its walls could probably tell strange tales, but no man can say with truth even why a certain attic in it is called Dr. Johnson's room. It is about as unlikely a place for the great lexicographer to have visited as can be conceived. The ceilings in some places are as low and inconvenient as those in Shakespeare's house or Ann Hathaway's cottage at Stratford-on-Avon. Still, it is clearly a pity that the walls cannot talk to fill in the spaces between the lines of the scanty records preserved by lawyers, which simply show that, on the dissolution, the manor (including this close) was granted to Sir Anthony St. Leger, K.G. ; that it was sold in 1561 to John Southcote, Esquire, Serjeant-at-Law; that the Southcotes were succeeded in 1758 by the Jerninghams, from whom this close was bought in 1808 by my predecessors in title. But the chances are that none of these interesting folk actually lived here. Nor are they likely to have lived in the fine old manor house lying off the main street, for that, now the property of Lady Wantage, formerly belonged to that interesting family the Eystons, of East Hendred.

Entering Drayton, then, not by Church Lane, but at the head of the main street, the traveller sees only a long, straight, and wide road flanked by scattered houses, some of them timbered, of no very striking character. If, instead of going down that street, he proceeds a couple of hundred yards or more in the direction of Steventon, and then takes the path to the left as soon as hedges cease and the open corn-land shows, he will be at the back of a series of "closes," long and narrow fields (mostly planted as orchards now), but all clearly relics of ancient village tenure, and a striking example of the revolution in village life. Time was when the holders of these closes in severalty ploughed them—they are of about the traditional acre—and turned their beasts on to the rough moor as common pasture. Now that which was common pasture is the plough-land of one farmer, and the closes, though some of them are still held in severalty, have an almost immemorial "skin" of grass upon them.

There are still left, too, a few men, labourers mostly, and bearing really old Berkshire names, who retain the freeholds of the cottages at the street end of the closes, and there may be some who hold the closes themselves ; but all, or nearly all, speak longingly of the days when their fathers, or their grand-fathers, had their little stake in the country in the shape of the closes, which were first mortgaged and then lost. I do not know that any of the great writers on village life in days gone by have ever noticed these particular closes; but, then, Drayton, Berks, is as near to being *terra incognita* as any place I know. Its very existence was once denied in my hearing by a superintendent of Berkshire police, although the then Chief Constable lived within four miles of it. What more shall we say of it? Well, its Manor House looks well from without, with its fine gateway; but it looked better, no doubt, in the days of the Eystons; distribution of the trees in the neighbourhood clearly points to the existence of a park, or at the least a pleasaunce, in days gone by. The Manor House had, as that at East Hendred still has, a private chapel; but the chapel, as such, has perished. The church has interesting points, a Jacobean pulpit and an alabaster reredos disinterred in 1814, for example; but somehow or other it fails to arouse interest.

Also Drayton possesses an undoubtedly loud peal of eight bells, on which, according to records preserved under the tower, "astonishing campanological exploits" have been achieved. But, if the truth may be told, active campanology is not always an unmixed delight to its passive audience. There was a certain farmer in Wales who, interrogated on the subject of an absentee landlord, observed that he had no objection to absenteeism in moderation. "I would rather see him in his riding-boots than in his slippers," was the homely way of putting it. In like manner a peal of bells, capable of "astonishing campanological exploits," which are not suffered to lie idle, are better five miles than five hundred yards off. They charm the occasional visitor, but to the constant resident fours hours of them at a stretch, on a summer's evening that might have been quiet, are a weariness of the flesh. The "sweet church bell" is in its right place when it "sounds over hill and dell," but clanging and crashing at short range for hours together, it distinctly palls even on the ear

F.L.GRIGGS .1906.

Lime Close, Drayton.

M

of the robust, while to those who have headaches it appears to cause unmitigated agony. Moreover, lest I be accused of airing an individual fad, be it added that when the campano-logical professors go on tour to neighbouring villages, as happily they do on occasion, similar opinions are expressed there. In fact bell-ringing seems really to appeal, like many other noises, principally to those who cause the din.

In the matter of water-supply Drayton is as badly off as Denchworth, and possibly worse ; that is all that can be said. An irregular substratum of Kimmeridge clay, a small rateable value—no railroad runs through the parish to help the resid-ents—and lack of enterprise parochially, are the explanation ; and they are likely to continue to be the only explanation of a grievance likely to last until the time comes for the rule of the heaven-born Minister of the Interior for whom rural England waits. Drayton, indeed, is one of those typical com-munities on a small scale in which it is hopeless to expect any practical results to follow from the pressure of public opinion upon or through local and nominally representative institutions. Possessed of a church, it necessarily boasts a clergyman ; having schools, it also maintains schoolmaster and mistress ; it has two general shops, two public-houses, a brickmaker, a blacksmith, a jobbing builder, a wheelwright, and a very small percentage of middle-class residents. But the over-whelming majority of the inhabitants are entirely dependent upon two farmers, inhabiting respectively the Manor House and the Grange, and the will of these farmers is law. It is, indeed, or perhaps, more emphatically law than they wish it to be, for no man accuses them of tyranny. Still, the villager is always face to face with the fact that his scanty wage depends on the goodwill of one of the two largest ratepayers in the parish, who is also, more often than not, the owner of the cottage which the villager inhabits. To displease his employer might not, almost certainly would not, involve loss of shelter and employment ; but the labourer as a rule prefers to keep on the safe side of the hedge, and he is timidly reluctant to take any step which might offend. Besides, he cares little, if anything, about sanitation or about pure water, regarding those who cry for either as faddists and a nuisance, and looking upon visitations of typhoid or diphtheria, which are by no means uncommon in the district, as the act of God: and so, no doubt, they are, if the laws of nature be of divine-origin, for they are the inevitable penalties exacted for gross neglect. It would be a great thing if some of our rural clergy, instead of preaching on the " Higher Criticism," as one preached recently here, would instil into our villagers the sanitary teachings of Leviticus, for they are sound and sadly needed.

Normally the life of the village is dull in the extreme, and, as one generally finds, when one knows a rustic community well in any part of England or Wales, by no means moral. That is an ugly truth which cannot be ignored ; but it is not necessary to enlarge upon it save by way of suggestion that immorality may be the result of dulness. The young men do not drink much, partly because they have next to no money ; very few of them smoke, probably for the same reason : but illegitimate births are startlingly numerous ; and the case is the same in many adjacent villages. Sheer lack of occupation out of working hours is not and cannot be conducive to good habits ; and a village without a village green, big enough to play cricket or football on, and possessed only of a lodge, or species of parish room, not run on democratic lines, for winter evenings, has every excuse for being in a bad way. But it has, it is true, its merry seasons also. There is the annual Feast and Guy Fawkes is never forgotten. On Mayday the children make a house-to-house visitation with their garlands ; at Christmastide the mummers are to the fore ; and, although Mayday, mummers, and mendicants have something more than an initial letter in common, the mummers at any rate are a highly interesting survival in most parts of Wessex.

It happens that only a week or so before the moment of

M 2

writing I was engaged on an earlier page when interruption
came in the shape of a question whether I would like to see
and hear the mummers. Of course the answer was "Yes," and
proceedings began at once. Into the hall walked a plough-
man's boy, white-bearded, in a tall hat and an overcoat of
immemorial age, who reeled off a long speech in broad and
rapid Berkshire, of which the intelligible part was a fervent
hope that "Father Christmas won't never be forgot." Next
entered "King George," and after him a "knight from furring
parts," both gaudily attired, partly in portions of cast-off
uniforms of the British army (for Berkshire, you shall note, is
military—perhaps because Berkshire wages are poor). Followed
a terrific combat with wooden swords, after the first bout of
which King George fell, "wownded in the knee" and grinning.
But a doctor, summoned from without, after a recital of the
merits of his medicines, some of them "strong enough to kill
any tu," cured King George and bade him "rise and foight thy
foe agin." So King George rose and laid about him with a
will, until the foreign knight fell. Him a stranger, fantastically
attired, tended, and the combat ceased. Next came "Merrian,"
a carter's boy with a shirt over his muddy corduroys, and bright
blue eyes brimming over with fun, who recited at breakneck
pace a number of lines consisting, so far as they could be
followed, of wild paradoxes. "I zaw a cow black as snow"
was one of the few phrases that could be distinguished, and
then, upon modest largesse, followed singing. But the taint
of the Music Hall is over the country, and the "Honeysuckle
and the Bee" failed to please, even in the broadest Berks.
What it all meant was a puzzle. The verses and the play are,
it is said, traditional, handed down from father to son as those
of Homer were from bard to bard. St. George had
probably become King George, in the time of the gracious
monarchs of that name, and the dragon had been developed into
the foreign knight, by process of evolution. "Merrian" was
probably a survival of Maid Marian; on a principle that she

ought to appear in a rustic piece whether she has any real connection with the action or not. The rest of the business may have been founded on the yarns of some forgotten Draytonian who had crossed the line with full honours. The only objection to this theory is that, to the mind of the peasantry of these parts, who have never seen the sea, the idea of the ocean is apparently quite inconceivable and absolutely terrible. My daughter went to Italy for a short time last summer. "Will young miss have to go athurt (athwart) the sea?" and, on hearing that she would, "Ah! I shouldn't like that; I'd liefer bide at home." So universal is this shrinking from the unknown sea that it is almost impossible to think of a North Berkshire peasant lad as a bluejacket. However, I have seen bluejackets, apparently very much at home, in Abingdon.

Down the village street we will go, after this digression, past the walnut-tree-shaded wheelwright's house, and other houses of old time, glancing through the gates and over the lawn at the broad front of the Manor House, and on till we reach a little brook in a hollow, once no doubt utilised for stewponds. Then, to the left, is a pretty green lane, shaded by tall trees, as English as anything can be; and to the right runs the road to Milton, which we will take. But first note some gravel-pits on the right and left of the road; in them, some years ago, were found not only human bones but gold ornaments also; and the latter, I am informed, went to the late Lord Wantage, the then Lord of the Manor. (This part of the rumour turns out to be inaccurate.) Human bones are no rarity in that gravel, and I myself possess a skull recently disinterred there, without having the knowledge of the peculiarities of skulls necessary to determine the approximate date at which it held the brain of a more or less thinking being. One to whom the occurrence of skulls in his gravel-pit is no novelty, the digger of the gravel in fact, says that on occasion his pick-axe has disturbed whole skeletons, usually lying in a crouched attitude, which have fallen to pieces at once. That, of course, is no evidence against sepulture, for that interesting personage, the Neolithic Man in the British Museum, is seen crouching ; and the Britons buried corpses in this sort of shape. But an expert pronounces my skull, the one I bought for half-a-crown, not the one I have always had free, to be a very fine one and of Saxon type at the earliest.

As for the beds, no doubt they are post-tertiary, and that is "recent" in a geological sense; but the recent times of geology are apt to be, humanly speaking, prehistoric. Local tradition, the tradition, that is to say, of the peasant, not of the antiquary, attributes all human remains in stray places to "the Wars," and by "the Wars" it always means those of the Great Rebellion. But, if many things are uncertain about these remains, it is at least certain that neither Royalists nor Parliamentarians buried in this fashion, when they were at the pains to bury at all. Possibly some of these burials, however, may be referred to the period of the Black Death.

Milton is the most tranquil of villages, an oasis of elm-trees at the edge of the plain of the Vale, with the Downs rising behind it, and from it to Steventon, whither we have fared before, runs an avenue of elms, shading the "causey" of which mention has been made, and following the course of the brook of many names, the only natural channel for the escape of surplus water from this southern district of the Vale. The approach to that "causey," along the garden wall and the magnificently wooded grounds of Milton House, has a peculiarly quiet if sombre fascination of its own. Milton House, too, which the wayfarer may see from the public road, is an Inigo Jones house, a noble structure, possessed of a private chapel ; and the village inn will serve for purposes of wayside refreshment, welcome as the glorious trees of Milton, if the time of year be summer, and if summer be worthy of its name.

On the way to Sutton Courtney, indeed, a bare road across a hedgeless plain, bearing such crops of wheat as would make a prairie farmer stare, the wayfarer is tempted to long for clouds ; and then comes a long stretch, surely almost a mile, of Sutton

The Thames at Sutton Courtney.

Courtney. It is by no means, however, "a mile of human pig-stye," as the poet once said unkindly of Combe Martin in Devonshire; for many of the cottages are old and pleasing to the eye. As we near the river, the road is shaded—and of course spoiled, but that cannot be helped—by splendid trees, and the houses grow bigger. Evidence there is, too, in a certain spick-and-span air of renovation and trimness about some of the larger houses, and in the appearance of the passers-by at times, that the world, which is not of Berkshire, has invaded Sutton Courtney: and well it may, for on all the banks of Thames there are few villages more charming, none more sequestered, none more fragrant of quiet history. After all, perhaps, it is the fascination of the scenery and its absolute tranquillity which is of principal importance to the traveller; and this tranquillity is assured to Sutton Courtney for many years to come at any rate. Those who look at any reasonably large map of the country through which the Thames runs will perceive that a "cut," starting from the left bank of the river, some two miles below Abingdon, carries the navigation across country, so to speak, directly to Culham, while the old river meanders for a mile or two round all sides but one of an irregular polyhedron. The boating man goes always by way of the "cut"; indeed, he must so do if he is proceeding down river, for there comes a point, a short mile below the upstream entrance of the "cut," where not even portage will serve him. A huge paper mill, long disused, spans the whole of the stream, except so much of it as pours into a spacious and remarkably beautiful lasher; and there is literally no access to the stream below from the upper reaches. But those upper reaches are of extraordinary beauty. On the right bank is the little isle of Otteney, created by the bifurcation of the Gynge brook before it reaches the Thames, and Otteney, one knows not why, is Oxfordshire, not Berks. Still its lush pastures, its grey and green pollard willows, and its waving bull-rushes are none the less delicious; and in the deep waters under the banks lie many great fishes.

especially chubs, from which sport of an easy-going kind may be obtained. So, according to our master, Walton, may good eating be obtained; but that is matter of taste, or of cooking. But of the chavender or chub, and how to catch and cook him, fuller mention is made in another chapter.

Yet another reason there is for confident hope that the tranquillity of Sutton Courtney may be assured for years to come. Practically all the land not occupied by houses and gardens already is necessary to the amenities of the Manor, and the owner of the Manor, who resides in it and appreciates its rare beauty to the full, is the last man in the world willingly to permit those quiet amenities to be destroyed.

The Manor, indeed, is the glory of Sutton Courtney, but, as Mr. Murray's Guide observes, "it is not shown." Substantially it could not be shown, consistently with the comfort of the occupants. To have been an inmate of a great house, even of the most noble proportions, on the day when certain rooms are open to the inspection of the curious, is enough to make the considerate man resolve that never again will he take advantage of the kindness of an owner by looking over an occupied house in any other capacity than that of a welcome guest. On such occasions the scene within the house, and out of sight of the invaders, is much what, one may guess from subterranean rumblings faintly heard, is enacted when a ferret is at work in a big "bury." The family scuttle from room to room, never knowing when they are safe from intrusion. One would not willingly introduce such discomfort into the house of a perfect stranger, and it is perhaps worth mentioning, since many persons are apt to forget the fact, that the owners of beautiful houses are, after all, our fellow-creatures. Also Captain Lindsay's Manor House at Sutton, beautiful as it is, and filled with the spoils of a cosmopolitan collector, who has also been a great shikari, is not spacious enough to render any intrusions of the kind conceivable. And after all the wayfarer can see a vast amount that is charming from the road. If he cannot see

The Abbey, Sutton Courtney.

the exquisite entrance hall, or the banqueting hall with its
oaken wainscoting and its minstrels' gallery, he can feast his
eyes on the stately front, which looks passing well, framed as it
is by the two successive gateways, and he can see enough of
rampant roses, and hear enough of the peacock's cry, if there
be a threat of moisture in the air, to realise that within those
walls is an old-world paradise.   We have met this manor before.
It is the same manor that the monks of Abingdon were fain
to give to a Saxon king in exchange for Andersey Island, which,
in its turn, they had bartered for the Manor of Goosey, and
this makes it somewhat difficult to follow Mr. Falkner when he
says that as the abbey, a neighbouring edifice in private occupation, was once·a hospital to Abingdon Abbey, so the Manor
House was once a country seat of the abbots.   Certainly, in
my judgment, no part of the existing Manor House, old as it is,
can possibly date back earlier than the Conquest, and there are
enough records of the history of the Manor House to show that
the Crown and not the abbey dealt with it long prior to the
dissolution.   Henry II. granted the manor to Reginald
Courteney, ancestor of the Earls of Devon, whence its name ;
and, though the Courteneys lost it once or twice by attainder,
it came back to them more than once also.   Then it was leased
to Sir Richard Hyde by Elizabeth for sixty years ; and Lysons
has it that "the see [*sic*] was granted by Charles I. to some
citizens of London who sold it to the first Lord Craven "—of
whom more later.   Of its intervening history, except that it
came into the possession of the late Lord Wantage, V.C., and
that it now belongs to his kinsman, Captain Harry Edith
Lindsay, I have no knowledge.   But it is none the less one of
the most choiceworthy houses of its size in England, both for
appearance and situation.

   Inside the grounds is an ancient edifice, with a fine Norman
door, formerly known as the Manor Farm, and actually
occupied a few years ago by two farmers, rude partitions
having been erected in the interior.   These have now been

removed, and the inside has been cleared of modern rubbish, with the result that the noble proportions of that which was once, most likely, the Hall of Justice of the great Manor of the Courteneys, stand revealed. It has now, by process of building in the rear, become the hall of a riverside country house. Lately, during the restoration of the church, it was used for divine service; but in relation to the restoration of

Norman Hall Doorway, Sutton Courtney.

the church no inverted commas are required, which is good news, for it is of remarkable interest. Reverence for antiquity has been the paramount feeling of those whom necessity compelled to set their hands to this ancient building, with the result that it has been improved, not spoiled. Removal of plaster from the roof has exposed some fine oak timber, and it has been supplemented; under the whitewash on the walls have been found something more than traces of ancient frescoes, some of them apparently representing George and the dragon, which, since oil is not the medium that was employed, can never have been really suitable to our climate. Still, with its mixture of styles, its fine altar tombs, its parvise over the south porch with its store of books, calling Denchworth to memory, the Early English font and the beautiful oaken pulpit, an ancient one presented by Captain Lindsay, Sutton Courtney Church is by no means the least interesting in the diocese.

The extinct paper-mill at Sutton Courtney is a sad spectacle; and it cannot even be called picturesque. Why it is suffered to remain, or why so much water-power is allowed to run to waste, is not quite clear. The only thing to be said is that it probably would not pay anybody to pull the mill down, even if he had the right, and so it continues to stand.

From Sutton, for so it is called locally, we proceed a couple of miles to Appleford, and here the vagaries of Berkshire roads become really distressing. In this case we desire to reach Long Wittenham (was there ever a place with name more Saxon in sound?), but it naturally often happens that folks wish to pass through Appleford to Didcot. At any rate, the Applefordians, though to be sure there are but few of them, must often have cause to go to the one or the other. But to reach Didcot by road one must go round three sides of a parallelogram, which seems needless, and to arrive at Long Wittenham by road is nearly as tedious and circuitous. However, to Long Wittenham on foot, or with a cycle that can be lifted over stiles, one may proceed by a pleasant path across the fields, saving at least seventy-five per cent. of the distance by comparison with the road, and gaining a glimpse of Long Wittenham's backwater of the Thames, which, for idleness and fishing, is by no means to be despised. But that we shall reach by boat on another day, as is proper in the case of a backwater.

Of Long Wittenham the main features are its length, which is colossal, its church, its backwater, and its village cross, probably, like that of Denchworth, a "chipping" or

" cheapening cross." Many years ago considerable excavations were made at Long Wittenham, with the result that several
hundreds of Saxon graves, or, at any rate, of graves containing
human remains and Saxon weapons, were disinterred. Were
they warriors who fell in stark battle on the slopes of the hills
dominating the landscape, known in old times as Sinodun, a
style which has been revived for a time, at any rate, in the
Ordnance Map, and by a famous picture in the Academy, and
locally by the name of Wittenham Clumps or by a more homely

Sinodun.

title still? That, it seems to me, is the probable explanation;
for, first, the interments were of some hundreds of bodies, and
Long Wittenham is hardly likely ever to have been a place of
sufficiently populous character to need a cemetery on such a
scale in Saxon times; and next, the interments were
undoubtedly Saxon, since, by the kindness of Dr. Martin, of
Abingdon, I have been in possession of several relics of
arms and ornaments, found with the bones, which are
undoubtedly Saxon and, some of them, military. There
might be some doubt as to rusted fragments of iron knives,
as to some peculiar and interesting shears; and that which

WORKING MEN'S COLLEGE LIBRARY

has passed for an Anglo-Saxon forceps or pair of tweezers is too like the lynch-pin of a modern cart to support any weight of argument. But the fine circular boss of a shield, showing the rivets at its outside edge, and a beautiful bronze fibula, of a familar and elegant Saxon shape, leave no room for hesitation. These were the graves of Saxon men, warriors most probably, and they are more than likely to have fallen in some great battle, hidden in the depths of history, around the great camp of Sinodun. Who built that great earthwork? Was it, with the almost obviously connected work on the Oxfordshire side of the river near Dorchester, constructed by the Atrebates as a fortified post to be used in keeping watch and ward against the Dobuni on their frontier? Or did they find it ready to their hands? That is one of the secrets hidden in the obscure recesses of time, and no man may answer it with accuracy, although some may do so with assurance. The one thing as sure as death itself is that the original purpose of these works was military, and that successive generations of warriors, aye, and of distinct races of fighting men, used them as a fortress. With their absolute command of a sea of plain, entirely devoid of cover save where the one hundred acres of Wittenham Wood invade their lower slopes, Sinodun hills would be an ideal stronghold even now.

It would be no great stretch of imagination to fancy that some such thoughts as these had passed through our minds as we sallied forth, guns in hands, from Long Wittenham over the flat lands towards Little Wittenham on a fine morning in golden September. It is an ideal country for the partridges, whose name is legion, and, barring one or two drawbacks, a paradise to the partridge-shooter. The drawbacks are the scantiness of covert, for the clover is fed off early as a rule, and, in normal years, the turnips, which are rarely ridged, remind one of the pawky Scots laird's saying that he had never been asked to shoot in fields of radishes before. Further

disadvantages are the almost complete absence of hedges and the difficulty of learning the boundaries. The absence of hedges and of covert tends to make the birds become wild and fly far very early in the season, and to render scientific driving very difficult. As to the boundaries, I have found it impossible to induce my friends to believe, but it is the fact, that in what appears to be one vast and unbroken stubble there may be a boundary between two owners; in fact, there was one in the late 'nineties, indicated by nothing at all except a change in the direction of the curtailed stalks representing the original courses of the drills of two separate tenants holding under distinct landlords. Many a time have I walked over this boundary unwillingly, to be recalled with the warning that I had trespassed on the ground of some Oxford College, St. John's, if memory serves correctly. To a West-countryman or to a Northerner this will seem incredible; and I have no hope of being believed; but it is a familiar experience that true stories, worth telling for their strangeness, are seldom believed, while others, improved from truth in order to be worth telling, are accepted readily. It is the old fate of the midshipman whose aunt believed in the wheel of Pharaoh's chariot picked up on the shores of the Red Sea because it was in harmony with scriptural record, but considered the mention of flying-fish to be an insult to her intelligence.

On the flats, and in Wittenham Wood, which would give grand shooting if it were nursed for a few years, and if the foxes were not present in such vast numbers, we are, in a literary sense, poaching upon the manor of my lost friend, the late Mr. C. J. Cornish, whose *Naturalist on the Thames* is devoted largely, and in a singularly attractive fashion, to this tract of land. I owed to him my introduction to its shooting amenities, the one chance I have ever had of bagging a woodcock and a cock-pheasant right and left, and the sight of four red robbers, and never the sign of a bird, issuing from the last square of covert, which had been expected to be

Abbot's Wittenham.

the best. His book may be commended, heartily and without hesitation, for he had eyes to see, and a pen to describe the things seen. Equally to be commended, if in another way, is an organised drive of hares and partridges round and from the great hill of Sinodun to guns cunningly posted at the upper edge of the wood; for hares are numerous, and the partridge of those parts is quite a woodland bird, especially where the underwood, which is felled systematically, is in its first or second year of growth. The only drawback is that the drive is often spoiled at the critical moment by the advent down the hillside of a party consisting, according to the shooters, of "trippers," according to its constituent members, of ladies and gentlemen in the exercise of their just right to inspect one of the most interesting examples of early earthworks, undoubtedly military, to be found in the kingdom. Mount it yourself, study the colossal scale of the threefold circumvallation, and scan the wide view on all sides, and the "tripper" will be forgiven; but the student will be no wiser than he was, and he never will be wiser.

As for Little Wittenham, it is a pretty little village, once the site of a manor-house belonging to the family of Dunch, who bulked large in their time. Edmund Dunch supported Cromwell, whose first cousin he was, to say nothing of being connected with Hampden; but he also aided in the restoration of, says the really wonderful Colonel Cooper King, Charles I. (*sic*). He was created Baron Burnell by Cromwell, holding, said the Royalists, "a patent to be lord of the Lord knows what and how little he deserves it." In 1688 the Dunch of the day helped in promoting the Revolution, and so won his way to Court office under a new *régime*; in fact, the Dunches, trimming not a little, did well for themselves all round; but their habitation is now desolate and has been so this many a long day. In truth it has practically disappeared. But there could be few more choiceworthy sites for a country gentleman's house than Little Wittenham, with its wide prospect, its background of gently rising hills, and its almost private reach of the

Thames at the foot of them. Some day, perhaps, a family will establish itself there, and the memorials of other notable folk will be added to those of the Dunches in the pretty little church on which, as on St. Mary's at Oxford, creepers are permitted to grow. Little Wittenham (need it be added?) was once Abbot's Wittenham, and the manor was owned by the Abbey of Abingdon; but there are no legends attached to the church save one, held locally by the ignorant, and wrongly, of course, but in such manner as to amuse. Somewhere in the tower is a small opening of a form familiar in architecture, but

Sinodun from Abbot's Wittenham.

also identical with that of the ace of clubs; and the story told to me, in a rambling sequence and in broad Berks, is to the effect that one of old time, having amassed great moneys through the ace of clubs—fairly, let us hope—built the tower with the proceeds and caused this little window to be left as evidence of his liberality and of his repentance. An inscription shows that the living was in the gift of Exeter College from 1322 onwards, and it remained with the college, and was invariably held by a Fellow of it, until 1885. An uncommonly nice and quiet college living it must have been, in which a clergyman might do his duty to the full without undue exertion;

from which he might easily make many a visit to the comfortable Common Room of his graduate days.

Abingdon is still our headquarters, so we return thither by way of Long Wittenham, Clifton Hampden Bridge, and Oxfordshire as far as Burford Bridge, which is at Abingdon, a total distance of seven or eight miles at the most, and very easy going. True it is that the next group of towns and villages to be examined is much nearer to Didcot than to Abingdon, and it might have been well to lie for the night at Didcot. But, although the hotel at Didcot is clean and sufficiently comfortable, to lie at Didcot is not necessarily to sleep there ; for the hotel is within a poor stone's throw of the station, and, *experto crede*, trains seem to run all night, there is much shunting of goods waggons, and so long as trains stop at Didcot there is stentorian shouting of their destinations, to say nothing of shrill and desperate efforts to part with a local dainty. After a night spent at Didcot the brain rings with " Change for Oxford " and " Banbury Cakes " ; and at Abingdon the night is always peaceful. So to Abingdon let us return for the last time, for tomorrow it will be well to lie at Wallingford.

CHAPTER VIII

Up then betimes, or according to taste and inclination pre-
ferably, for an easy morning's ride upon a perfect road to
Wallingford. The baggage may go by train, changing at
Radley and also at Cholsey, but that is not the way for white
men to travel. The route, once Burford Bridge is crossed, lies
almost entirely through Oxfordshire, and it passes through Clifton
Hampden, Burcot, where Jabez Balfour built to himself a great
house (but the resources of civilisation found for him another and
stronger one), and Dorchester—Dorchester boasting the great
cathedral of days gone by from which the pen can hardly be

restrained, so attractive is the subject. From Dorchester we
go through Benson or Bensington to Shillingford, and there,
crossing the river by a beautiful bridge, we re-enter Berkshire
past the Swan Inn, but it belongs more justly to the chapter on
the river. Leaving the "Swan" and climbing a somewhat tiresome hill, we are soon at Wallingford, "an historical town with
many comfortable burgher-like houses."

Near Burcot.

At Wallingford the "Lamb" is a distinctly good inn of the
old-fashioned type, and in Wallingford the Oxfordshire and Berkshire farmers meet. Emphatically it is a great agricultural
centre, if agricultural centres can be great in these days, and it
has every appearance of flourishing life. If the "Lamb" may
suffice for the needs of the traveller, the ancient earthworks of
Wallingford have more than sufficed to puzzle the antiquaries.
That there was a ford there, from the earliest times—of course

VIII DUBIOUS DERIVATIONS

no impression about ancient fords can be gathered from the modern river—is certain ; and there is some evidence in masonry of a Roman occupation ; but, eager as I am to find traces of the Britons in English place-names, it is difficult quite to follow the writer who says, of the date of the Norman conquest : " Like all great military nations, the Normans had a keen eye for ground. The possible Celtic or British *Gualhen-ford*, or old fort by the ford, had become Romanised, had changed to Saxon *Wallinga's-ford* and so to *Wallingford.*" *Gwâl*, it is true, is Welsh for " wall," but similar words occur in old Frisian and old Saxon, and the Welsh probably made their word from *vallum* as they made *ffenestr*, " a window," from *fenestra*, and *maneg*, " a glove," from *manica*. *Hên*, it is true, means " old," but the part of Carnarvon named after the ancient walls of Segontium is called *Hênwalia*, not *Gwaliahên* ; and *fforda* means a " way," not a " ford," which is *rhŷd*, a possible derivation of Reading. So let us be content to be uncertain as to this point, and to deal with a part only of the things which are certain, since they are not all of thrilling interest, or would not be if they were told at length.

Wallingford enters into Alfred's story, and it was destroyed by the Danes, in 1006, when Alfred was dead and gone. Exactly sixty years later, when Norman William was making good his hold of England, Wallingford was an important post held by one Wigod, who was wise, if not heroic, in his generation, for it seems to be reasonably clear that Wigod had trafficked with William beforehand. Certain it is that he invited the Conqueror to the stronghold, where the submission of Archbishop Stigand and the Barons was received, and that he bestowed his daughter upon Robert D'Oyley, one of William's generals. This same D'Oyley is an important personage in the history of Oxfordshire, also ; but at Wallingford, by William's command, he built a strong castle, which, besides being used as a State prison, played a part in practically all the wars. Here the Empress Maud was besieged by Stephen ;

here was struck the treaty which secured the succession of
Henry II. ; here died the widow of the Black Prince ; here
Queen Isabel lived during the absence of Richard II. in
Ireland ; and here dwelled Catherine, the widow of Henry V.
Twice only was Wallingford Castle besieged and taken, once by
the Barons when John had seized it in his brother's absence,
and once by Fairfax, in 1646, after stout Governor Blagge had
stood a siege of sixty-five days. Of a truth, then, Wallingford
has its historic and military memories, for all that it looks so
restful and isolated a town.

It has its peaceful memories also; for the Black Prince
attached to the Castle the collegiate Chapel of St. Nicholas,
afterwards known as the King's Chapel at Wallingford, some
small parts of which still stand ; and this, according to the
Lysons, who are usually trustworthy, was bought by the Dean
and Canons of Christ Church in 1548 to be a place of retire-
ment and rest.

Mention, too, must be made of a curious privilege once
possessed by the natives of the borough, long before it was
incorporated in the time of James I. It was that a native
of the borough might compound for a first offence by electing
to have his eyes put out and to be mutilated. Of a truth this
very local First Offenders Act compares quaintly with that of
the present day, and one is inclined to wonder whether any
man was ever disposed to avail himself of it even in days
when hanging was the punishment for larceny, and the idea of
mutilation was not so horrible as it is in our softer times.

Why Wallingford has been passed on one side by the
stream of riverside fashion is not easy to see, unless the whole
explanation is to be found in indifferent railway accommodation, for the bridge is a beautiful old-world structure, and the
river above-bridge is quite pretty enough for the enjoyment of
man or woman. Still, just because Wallingford stands on a
railway backwater, it is a restful place for a few nights, when it
has once been reached, and, while one stays, the narrow and

Wallingford Town Hall.

tortuous streets impress one almost with the idea of a foreign city. The people, however, especially the farmers who come into market, are English of the English, and their talk is of sheep, which they call "ship," always, save when it is of the roots and other foods of the said "ship." It was Solomon (was it not?) who asked scornfully, "How can he be wise whose talk is of oxen?" But I have never noticed yet a tendency on the part of cattle-breeders to grow like to their charges in physiognomy. That may be my fault, and John Bull may sometimes look bovine. Even if this be so, it is surely better to look bovine than to look ovine, for your ox has character in his features; there is a refinement of the Jersey, a plain nobility of the shorthorn, a devil-may-care expression of the Highland or Welsh bull, a cut-and-come-again look about the Hereford. Sheep, on the other hand, look monotonously simple and foolish; their standing epithet is "silly," and a glance at the features of any lowland breed of sheep, at the fatuous curve of their noses and lips especially, justifies the epithet, superficially at any rate. Mountain sheep may be, indeed they are, capable of developing a measure of intelligence; for example, they know their own runs and will drive trespassing sheep away. (It may be worth while to observe in passing that this peculiarity of mountain sheep has been proved by expert evidence and has won judicial recognition at Dolgelly Assizes.) Mountain sheep, however, living almost a wild life, have opportunities of developing their natural intelligence; lowland sheep have no such chances. The consequence is that they look as silly as they are; and that they are as silly as they look, as they prove when they are encountered on the road.

Now it is not my own idea only, but also that of many " foreigners " who have made their homes in Berkshire, that the Berkshire sheep-farmers distinctly resemble their sheep in feature. In the course of the afternoon preceding the evening on which these words are written, I observed casually to a

friend that a certain farmer had precisely the expression of one
of his own wethers, and the answer was, " Yes, of course he
has ; but did you ever meet —— the great sheep-farmer of —— ?
He is the image of a sheep." Nor are these instances
exceptional, so that there need be fear of giving offence to any
particular producer of wool, fleeces, and mutton ; for the phenomenon, if not universal, is certainly very generally noticeable.
Its existence is beyond question, even though its explanation
be somewhat hard to discover.   Is it that constant association
with sheep causes the sheep-farmer's mouth to be drawn down
as that of the sheep is ?   That is just conceivable.   There are
those who maintain that husband and wife, after long association, grow more similar than they were at marriage, and most of
us can call to mind many a married pair of standing who are
absurdly alike.   Or is there, science notwithstanding, good
natural history in the story of Jacob and the flocks of his
father-in-law ?   It will be remembered that Jacob, having been
promised as his portion all the ring-straked and spotted lambs
(which, by the way, would be by no means so exceptional in the
East as in our uniform and carefully bred flocks), set up peeled
and striped wands before the ewes when they were heavy with
young, and that the results exceeded all anticipation.   Jacob,
in fact, invented and illustrated the theory of suggestion, in
which country folk continue to believe as implicitly as in
telegony, calling the latter " throwing back."   Science says
this is all nonsense ; and it may be all that, and a pretty
idea notwithstanding.   The fact remains that the wives of
Berkshire farmers have the sheep always before them, and that
they produce sons, ay, and often daughters also, who develop
a distinctly ovine cast of features.

Here the resemblance ends ; for in wits the Berkshire farmer
is at least equal to his contemporaries in the like calling,
having the same virtues of patience, and, strange as it may
seem to the urban critic, some readiness to adopt new methods
of agriculture, and the same faults, of which absolute neglect of

the minor sources of possible income is perhaps the worst. In many districts of agricultural Berkshire, for example, fresh milk is simply unpurchasable, and nobody who knows anything of farming will deny that, where there is a ready sale for milk at threepence a quart, it is a very profitable business. "But," say the farmers, "it is not worth while to make these small profits"; and the result is that our rural population of the present generation is growing up, far more frequently than the townsman is likely to believe, absolutely without the nourishment which is, above all others, essential to the health of children.

These are the topics, the one half-playful, the other most sadly earnest, into which the mention of the farmers who meet, and chaffer, and talk of "ship" and of "feed" at Wallingford have led me. Let us now to the open country for a while, making our first expedition to Streatley, and thence climbing the hill of the Downs to Aldworth. After that, be it understood, the expeditions may be many or few, according to taste, provided always that it be remembered that none of the places mentioned can be missed without loss. To Streatley is an easy ride by a good road and at Streatley the traveller finds himself at one of the most fascinating of the many riverside villages that are the pride of the Thames. There is no place more ideal at which to eat the lotus than this spot, sheltered by the swiftly rising brow of the Berkshire Downs from the west and south-west winds, where the Thames grows wide and embraces an island, where the weir and lasher are ever vigorous, where every English flower flourishes amazingly. Streatley, however, again belongs most properly to the river chapter; and it must suffice to mention it at this point and no more.

Somewhere here it was, most likely, or possibly a little higher up the stream, that the famous Icknield or Ickleton Way, the *Via Iceniana*, crossed the Thames from the Chilterns to the Downs. It is spelled in many ways, it has been attributed to

many makers, but it can be traced with reasonable certainty
from Icklingham in Suffolk, the ancient capital of the Iceni, to
Bath and, perhaps, to Exeter ; although there are points, such
as this at Streatley, where the precise track of the ancient road
cannot be laid down within a mile or two. In climbing
Streatley Hill we may be treading where Britons, Romans,
Saxons, and Danes trod before or we may not, but once we
are fairly on the top, the track becomes clear and we are on
classic ground. Having looked more than once at the
unrivalled panorama of plain and hill and river, and having
looked long also, since Streatley Hill would tend to appreciation
of a poorer view, let us for the moment leave Aldworth on the
left unvisited, and, standing on the summit of the green hill
half a mile to the north of it, survey the grand sea of the all
but desolate Downs. Immediately below runs the Icknield
Way, a defined road at first, then possessed of a green surface ;
and some will tell you that here it forks and pursues two routes
westward, the one, on the top of the crest of the Downs,
being called the Ridgeway, the other, to the north and at a
lower level, being called the Port Way, and that the two unite
again in Wilts, after crossing the width of Berks. Where no
two authorities, literary or local, and very few independent
maps, agree, it is clearly not worth while to quarrel about
names ; the simple course is to say there is one wide track
along the top of the Downs, locally called the Ridgeway in
parts, which we shall call the Ridgeway throughout, and that
the Port Way, according to a map of Mr. Stanford's, is the
excellent road running more or less at the foot of the Downs
through East and West Hendred, or rather slightly to the
north of them, and then, under the name of the Roman Way,
through Wantage past Childrey, the Blowing Stone, the foot of
White Horse Hill, Compton Beauchamp, and Ashbury, and so
into Wiltshire. From the Blowing Stone to Ashbury it is
within a mile of the upper track, described in Stanford's map
as the Icknield Way, but to which the title Ridgeway seems

Compton Beauchamp.

more apposite, and the Ridgeway is about 300 feet higher up on the average.

From our green hill we see the beginnings of both ways, and the first of many ancient fortifications marking the upper route; but of these the more important occur further to the westward, and the very real difficulty of dealing with them satisfactorily from a historical point of view may be postponed. Raised high in this sweet and vigorous air, with the wondrously elastic turf under foot, and very likely a " string " of thoroughbreds in sight at exercise to inspire the thought, man is apt to cry " My kingdom for a horse." It may be true that, as a satirical electrical engineer of poetic name (Mr. James Swinburne, M.I.C.E.) has written : " The chief drawback to street locomotion is the horse. He is nearly as foolish as the hen, and he is dirty and insanitary on a larger scale. He has been with us over five thousand years, and has not learned even manners or decency." But the Downs are not the street; they are indeed its absolute antithesis in every conceivable respect, and until somebody invents a trustworthy flying machine, cantering across the springy surface of the Downs will continue to be the absolute poetry of motion. They can be traversed, *experto crede*, on and off a bicycle; but only at the cost of much pushing of the bicycle by hand and of much bumping, and general uncertainty what is going to happen next, when it is mounted.

The air is full of history of an elusive kind. Somewhere on the Downs was fought Alfred's great battle of Ashdown, but nobody knows exactly where. Time was when I might have written with authority that it was fought beyond the " Roman Camp " lying close to our green hill to the north-west; but that time is past, and the authority has lost its weight. Here and there a barrow speaks of ancient British deaths and burials; a Grimm's ditch to the north-west may mark an ancient tribal boundary—again, nobody knows exactly what story the Grimm's ditches, occurring in many counties, ought to tell. Let it suffice then, for the time at any rate, to enjoy the free

air, the sense of space, and the unsurpassable turf, to think of
the Ridgeway in general terms, as the great track between east
and west, for military and peaceful purposes. Of this Ridgeway,

Compton Beauchamp Manor.

indeed, it may be said without much fear of contradiction that,
saving only the rivers, and other ways passing over Downs, it is
and must be incomparably the oldest highway in the kingdom.
It has been there always, from a human point of view. It

needed no making and it has never been made by man. It was never masked with trees nor clogged by marshes. It offered itself as the obvious path from east to west and from west to east from the very beginning of human time. It is, if the phrase may be permitted, God's own road that needs no mending, that cannot be improved; and if it has rung with the clash of weapons and with the shouts of warriors from the days of the Atrebates even until those of the Stuarts, it has also accomplished its purpose as a road of peace. For it will hardly be credited, but it is true, that there are men living in the Vale of the White Horse now who remember the days when coal came from South Wales along the Ridgeway by waggon, and the residents in the Vale sent their teams up to the Ridgeway to fetch it.

Now let us turn to some of the villages. Aldworth must by no means be neglected. The name looks as Saxon as Saxon could be, and probably it is *Ealdwurth*, although Domesday makes it Elleorde—which goes to prove how little one can rely on the etymological derivations that seem, once again, to be in fashion. It is emphatically a picturesque place, famous for its gigantic yew, 27 feet in girth and festooned with chains whereon lamps are hung to guide those who may attend evensong in winter; for its well, going down 372 feet into the chalk; and for the monuments, mostly of the De la Beche family, in its church; and the church is otherwise interesting. They were great people in their day, these De la Beches, and they met with the ups and downs of life that seem to have been taken as a matter of course in the Middle Ages. Sir Nicholas, for example, was Lieutenant of the Tower and Guardian of the Black Prince. In 1340 the erstwhile Lieutenant was a prisoner in the Tower, instead of Lieutenant, because he had either been remiss in collecting, or in sending in to the Treasury when collected, the moneys of which the ambitious King Edward III. was in grievous need. But the King needed men, too, for the wars, and in the seven years of life that remained

O

to Sir Nicholas, for he died in 1347, he fought under his royal master's banner in France, and became a Member of Parliament, as well as Seneschal of Gascony.

Aldworth has received once at least the honour of a royal visitation. There is a firm tradition, which there is no particular reason for disbelieving, that Elizabeth, being then the guest of the owner of Ewelme Palace, in Oxfordshire, and distant about ten miles *viâ* Wallingford Bridge, rode to Aldworth on a pillion behind Leicester to see the to bs. Doubtless then she was entertained royally in the castellated house of the De la Beches, now perished as completely as the Palace and moat of Ewelme, and doubtless she saw the yew, a a reputable tree even then, and the finest collection of recumbent figures ever collected in a small church. There lay in stone Robert, knighted in 1278 ; John, his son ; Philip, the son of the John and builder of the south aisle and the chancel; John, the son of Philip, who was captured with his defeated leader, Lancaster, at Boroughbridge in 1321, but was not deemed sufficiently important to be beheaded ; Isabella, the wife of the last-named John ; Nicholas, whose career has been touched upon briefly ; John, the son of John and Isabella, and Joan, his wife ; and Philip, the brother of Nicholas, and also of John, the husband of Isabella.

At the head of one of the female figures, believed to be that of Joan, are two angels, emblematic, according to tradition, of the fact that she died in giving birth to twins. But here comes a difficulty, never to be solved, which cannot be explained better than in the words of Captain Symonds, the Royalist and diarist of 1644, who, indeed, tells us something more concerning Aldworth Church, in the following entry : " May ᵉ, 1644, Aldworth vulgo Alder. In yᵉ E. ende of yᵉ S. yle did hang a table fairly written in parchment of all yᵉ names of yᵉ Family of de la Beche, but yᵉ Earle of Leicester coming with yᵉ Queen Elizabeth in progresse tooke it down to show it her, and it was never broughte againe. Yᵉ common People call

Wallingford Bridge.

WORKING MEN'S COLLEGE LIBRARY.

y^e statue under y^e outside of y^e Churche John Everafraid and say further that he gave his soule to y^e Divil if ever he was buried either in Churche or Churchyard, so he was buried under the Church Wall under an Arche "—which arch may still be traced. So to the carelessness of Leicester for others, while he was in attendance on the Virgin Queen, we owe it that the stone figures, although still remaining, cannot be identified with any certainty ; but there are distinctly compensations in things, for the careful note of the Royalist Captain, made at a time of the most severe storm and stress, is really more interesting as a human document than it would be to know precisely how the figures are to be distributed among the De la Beches. Need it be added that sceptics—there is no romance in the soul of your true antiquary—have attacked the Aldworth figures, pointing to so-called unconvincing details of dress, and to clumsiness of general treatment. They may be right, but at worst it seems unlikely that, since the time of Elizabeth, anybody would have been at the pains to supply spurious statues on so large a scale, and that they were *in situ* in Elizabeth's time is quite reasonably clear.

Three miles to the west of Aldworth, and down a cruel hill, the modest village of Compton lies in a dimple of the Downs ; and here the ghost of Alfred's crucial battle of Æscesdun, or Ashdown, begins to flit and hover about our path. Topographically it is a most elusive ghost, a tricksy sprite indeed, but it has risen in our way, and so it must needs be laid sufficiently for our purposes or at least discussed. Asser is the authority for the details of the battle, and Asser was the preceptor and companion of Alfred, who rewarded him by making him an abbot many times over and Bishop of Sherborne into the bargain— the see of Sherborne was afterwards transferred to Salisbury, the minster remains as a vision in stone. But Asser was a Pembrokeshire man, and the chances are that, although he had the evidence of eye-witnesses to help him, he did not hesitate to allow his imagination to help him when a tale seemed wanting

whole army of the Pagans was put to flight till the night, and even to the following day, until those who escaped arrived at the citadel, for the Christians pursued them until night, and overthrew them everywhere."

Leaving the question of the single thorn-tree on one side for the moment, the topographical guidance to be extracted from this account of a battle grim and stark is that the Danes held a high position, and that it was a long way from their citadel. " The Pagans were put to flight till the night, and even to the following day, until those who escaped arrived at the citadel " —those are words to which the sceptics who pour contempt on the ancient theory that the battle of Ashdown was fought near Ashdown, on the place now known by that name, at the western end of the Berkshire Downs, seem to have paid inadequate attention. Very likely, almost certainly indeed, the White Horse had been carved on the hillside long before Alfred's victory was gained, in which case the old theory that it commemorated the victory must be wrong ; but that is no sort of argument for or against the view of the ancients that the battle was fought thereabouts. Let me illustrate bluntly. If in the year 3000 A.D. some antiquarian asserts that London Bridge was built to commemorate King Edward's triumphant progress over the Thames in the autumn of the Coronation year, the antiquary will be wrong, that is all ; but the progress will none the less have been made. Of this particular kind of fallacy in argument I was once compelled to realise the danger by a shrewd observation of the late Lord Esher, who, when he was Master of the Rolls, said, at the hearing of an appeal, " You must not be too sure that, although every ground on which the learned judge based his judgment was wrong, his conclusion may not have been right." In like manner here, if I am able to dispose of every ground upon which it has been decided by some that the Ashdown we know was not the scene of the battle, it must not be supposed, therefore, that Ashdown really was the scene or that we shall ever know exactly where it was fought. But let there be no false profession of indifference on

the point. I have no predilection for Ashdown or for any
other place, but, when I roam over the Downs trying to set the
battle in array in imagination, it would be a great comfort to
have some definite tract as a scene to animate.

Perhaps the *Saxon Chronicle* helps us a little. In connection with the battle it informs us that the Danes " turned along
Æsced unto Cwichelmslaw and there awaited better cheer ";
and in connection with the later invasion of 1006, " when the
Danes had ravaged and destroyed Wallingford, they spent the
following night at Cholsey, and from Cholsey they went along
Ashdown to Cwichelm's Hill." Now two of these places are
still easily located. Cholsey, not particularly interesting, though
it dates back to the Heptarchy, is the big village we passed
by rail in going to Abingdon from the South, near Moulsford
Asylum. Cwichelmslaw is a commanding eminence of the
Downs, boasting the remains of the very fine barrow of the
West Saxon King Cwichelm, lying about four miles south of
Lockinge House and a little further, south-east by south, from
Wantage. The distance between the two points is, roughly,
ten or twelve miles along the Downs, and that from the
present Ashdown to Cwichelmslaw, or Skutchamore Knob, is
about the same. The legitimate inference from this, it seems
to me, is that, as many hold, the term " Æscesdun " refers to
the whole ridge rather than to any part of it ; in fact, that
Æscesdun and the Berkshire Downs are more or less
synonymous terms.

But Colonel Cooper King goes too far. Taking for text the
sentence, " When the Danes had ravaged and destroyed Wallingford, they spent the following night at Cholsey, and from
Cholsey they went along Ashdown to Cwichelm's Hill," he
says, " As there is no doubt about the position of the latter
point and of Wallingford "—for that matter there is none about
Cholsey either—" the field for conjecture is at once narrowed."
But is it ? If I ride from Streatley to Wantage on the high
road it does not quite follow that places beyond Wantage on

that road are not on it. If Æscesdun means the ridge, it means the whole ridge. Nor will the rest of the argument bear examination. "Most of the writers of old time have placed the site of the battle near Ashbury, at the western extremity of the ridge, both because of its name, and of the false local tradition of the origin of the 'White Horse,' and also because there was a fortified position in front of it. But it seems somewhat hazardous to assume that these rude clans, in such rapid and partial operations as these, necessarily made earthworks. To cover their point of embarkation was natural ; but to assume that so many cubic feet of earth and chalk could be thrown up by inferior tools in the brief time at the disposal of either party seems an error "—and so on, upon the same lines. Possibly such an assumption might be an error ; but how stands the matter if the earthworks were there already ? They certainly were, if the Danes did not erect them, for they assuredly have not been constructed since 971 A.D. Probably, indeed, they had been there since early British times as a part of the chain of hill-forts, perhaps, of the Atrebates. If they were in existence, and, as the Irish would say, "convenient" to the place of battle, we may be very sure that the Danes, who were much addicted to earthworks, would make use of them ; also, if there were earthworks ready to hand, as there surely were, the Danes could go lightly equipped and might very well have covered a great deal of ground "in these partial and rapid operations."

Colonel Cooper King goes on to argue that the Western Ashdown was too far, and that to reach it they would have had to pass by Wantage, "where presumably Alfred would be collecting his forces." On the point of distance, perhaps, there is something to be said; but the other point does not go for much. Nothing would be easier, nothing is easier, than for troops to pass unseen in the folds of the rolling Downs ; and after all, on the question of distance, it has to be remembered that the Downs offer at all times of year a perfect

surface for marching, and, as we have seen, that it took the
Pagans a long time to reach their citadel when they were fairly
put to flight.

Colonel Cooper King has two other points, one of which
may possibly indicate a battle-field opposed to his beliefs. In a
note, of which the authority is not given, he prints the words :
" Eadred is also said to have given eight hides of land at
' Cumtune ' (Compton) near the hill called Æscesdune."
Again let a favourite question of the late Lord Esher be quoted :
" Well, and what then ? " This present Compton, between
East Ilsley and Aldworth, is but Compton Parva, of which
the true history, if it ever had one, is forgotten, while the oldest
brass in its church is of but 1500. At Compton Beauchamp,
which positively nestles under the shadow of the White Horse,
the church is mainly Early English, and there is glass as well
as architecture of the fourteenth century. So, if the hides of
land which Eadred gave at " Cumtune " are to help to locate
Æscesdune, it may as well have been near to Compton
Beauchamp, as Ashdown and Ashbury are, as to Compton
Parva. So also the sword, believed to be Saxon, and the two
skeletons found in Hagley Wood (which appears to be near
the modern Ashdown) may, after all, corroborate the view that
there may not be much difference between the positions of the
ancient and the modern Ashdown.

Precisely the same observation applies to Colonel Cooper
King's last point. He writes : " There is one clue to the
mystery. Asser, in his account already quoted, refers to the
single thorn-tree (*unica spinosa arbor*, *brevis admodum*) that
stood on the hard-fought field. And curiously enough
Compton, one of the ancient hundreds of Berkshire, is
named in Domesday as that of Nachededorne—that is, the
Hundred of the Naked Thorn. Unless this tree were well
known, it is scarcely likely that it would have been selected
as a title ; and seeing that it "—the hundred presumably, not
the thorn—" was afterwards divided between Faircross and

Compton, and that in the survey the manors of Contone and
Assendone are mentioned as part of the now extinct hundred,
there seems at least sufficient evidence to connect this district
and modern Compton with the above places." So be it ; but,
although Colonel Cooper King's index contains no mention of
Compton Beauchamp, it exists, and, if Colonel Cooper King
had ever taken the delightful drive or ride across the Downs
from it to Lambourne, he would have passed close to White
Horse Hill, Uffington Castle, Ashdown Park with "Alfred's
Castle" and a camp in rear, Wayland Smith's "Cave" and
Letcombe Basset ; and midway he would have seen a number
of gnarled and stunted thorns, some standing singly, some in
groups, which would fit in with the story admirably. Also, at
Compton Beauchamp, mark you, is a charter of 955 A.D. which
settles argument on this point. "This sind thæs landes
gemære æt Cumtune."

The result, then, is that argument has not disposed of the
western site favoured by the ancients, although it has weakened
some of their grounds for believing in it, and that the argument
is, indeed, sometimes favourable to the western site when it is
intended to be unfavourale ; but that positive certainty is not
attainable. The balance, to my mind, is if anything in favour
of some place near the modern Ashdown, but not sufficiently
so to enable us to go forth, as the Trojans did during their
short-lived period of hope that the Greeks had gone away,
saying—

"*Hic Dolopum manus, hic sævus tendebat Achilles*," or, "Here fell King
Bægsæg, and Sidroc, the ancient of evil days."

Returning to Compton Parva, from which we have not
really moved, we are in the midst of the Downs at their very
best, not far from Churn Hill, haunted by military in the
summer months, military to whom it is a matter of small
interest that one Birinus, a saint, once preached to Cynegil
and the West Saxons from this very "green hill without a city

wall." Military camps of old time are abundant and no man knows their history. There are no enclosures worthy of mention, the turf is perfection, and race horses out at exercise often add just the necessary touch of life to the scene.

Amongst places which should by no means be missed are Catmore and East Ilsley, both places of note and charm. The former is situate on the Downs; that is to say amidst an ocean of gently undulating hills; but the abundance of woodland, and of cultivated land in between the woods, renders the environment less Downlike and characteristic than in parts where the scenery is open. Here are an ancient church and a house, belonging to the Eystons of East Hendred, of whom there will be more, and much that is interesting, to say presently. Both were of supreme value to the Eystons, who have always been staunch adherents to the Roman Catholic faith (as might be expected of lineal descendants of Sir Thomas More), in days which may now be described as those of Protestant persecution. "Catmore lies in a very remote position." It does indeed, and that is why it served the needs of the Eystons when it was not safe for them to remain at their great house at East Hendred. It is a curious state of affairs that their interesting old house brings to mind. It recalls an age in which men who believed themselves to be conscientious hunted others from place to place simply because they held other views than theirs; and it is difficult to realise it in an era of tolerance. The bitter memory of those Protestant persecutions still rankles at East Hendred. Whether it is quite logical that it should so remain is another matter. After all, Protestantism did not inaugurate persecution, but found a very complete Roman Catholic model ready to its hand; nor was the persecution concerned fundamentally with differences of doctrine and religion, for the temporal pretensions of Rome were the real provocation to the mass of the English people rather than divergences of creed.

East Ilsley, given over entirely to sheep-sales and to

racing stables, is a place of extraordinary quaintness. It has been mentioned before that "at Kate's Gore in this parish were large stables built by William, Duke of Cumberland, for his running horses," but this is the point at which to note that Ilsley is to the racing world as Stratford-on-Avon is to men of letters. Ilsley was the birthplace of "Eclipse," that racehorse honoured as the best, so far as it is possible to compare animals of different epochs, that ever came of the blood of the Darley Arabian. And here kind chance has led me to a happier phrase than was planned. That Ilsley was to racehorses as Stratford-on-Avon is to literary men had been written when I knew no more than that "Eclipse"[1] was born on the 1st of April, 1764, the day of a great eclipse of the sun, that he did not race until he was a five-year-old, that he never was beaten, and that he was the ancestor of a noble strain, of which Blair Athol was probably the brightest example. But in choosing my chance trope I little hoped that research would prove it to be far removed from the commonplace; and it was joy to find a suspicion among the genealogists of the turf that "Eclipse's" sire may have been Shakespeare (by Aleppo ex Hobgoblin—not William) rather than Marske, to whom the studbook gives the credit. "Eclipse" was bred by the Duke of Cumberland. Naturally the birthplace of "Eclipse," and the neighbouring villages of the matchless Downs, are favourite places for training stables, and there are those who regret this fact on the ground that association with racehorses inevitably tends to encourage the pernicious practice of backing horses. It may be so, but to the unprejudiced observer, who knows not only the rest of Berkshire but also the manufacturing towns of England, two points are plain. First, in the training villages of Berkshire, so to speak, there are no outward signs of that grinding poverty which is the curse of the agricultural

[1] Since these words were written it has been suggested, on the basis of a tablet at Windsor, that "Eclipse" was born there. But the tablet may have been moved when the Ilsley stables were given up.

hamlets of the county; on the contrary, they look comfortable and well cared for; and so do their inhabitants. Next, the habit of betting, for which there may be some excuse in persons who are constantly associated with racehorses, is not a tenth part so prevalent as it is among the artisans of the North of England, who hardly ever see a racehorse.

Of about equal importance with the horses, from Ilsley's point of view, are the sheep, and it is the volume of the sheep-markets and fairs which causes Ilsley to present its unique appearance. Situated in a dimple of the Downs, as Compton is, but on a larger scale, it has its fine church and its ancient houses, and probably a larger supply of old-fashioned inns than any other place of its normal population in inland England. That, however, does not make Ilsley look strange: its peculiarity consists in the fact that the main street, running up and down the face of a fairly steep hill, is lined with row upon row of permanent sheep-pens, in the midst of many of which grow shade-giving trees. These, and the multitudinous angles of the ancient houses, make Ilsley decidedly picturesque and singular in appearance even when the sheep-pens are empty, and the streets and inns are deserted. Very different is the aspect on a fair day, when as many as 80,000 sheep are driven into Ilsley and out again, and the farmers do a roaring trade. But let him who would see this unique and diverting sight take heed lest he go to Ilsley by bicycle or even by motor. The roads into Ilsley, from Steventon to the north or from Compton to the east, are not bad in the ordinary way; but they are made of chalk and of flints; and there is nothing equal to the passage of flocks of sheep on such roads for destroying the surface, or for churning up the little flints into the position of the sword of Ajax when he was going to fall on it, "that in which they are most cutting." No one will willingly repeat such an experience. But let us be just even to roads. To approach East Ilsley from the north when the sheep have not destroyed the surface of the road, and there are no "strings" of horses to impede the cyclist's swift course, is to attain something near akin to the poetry of motion on wheels; for there is a downward slope of a mile or more, not over-steep but yet sufficiently so for exhilarating speed without effort, and a clear prospect obviates the danger of running into any thing or body unexpectedly. Such was the last experience of approaching Ilsley, and at Ilsley itself, in an inn roomy and ancient, with a trophy of Boer Mauser's hanging in the hall, was a luncheon—they called it dinner—and a welcome helping the luncheon to make man bid defiance to fate for that day at the least

West Ilsley, some two or three miles to the west—the distance depends upon the point selected to represent each village—has none of East Ilsley's peculiarity, though it is not wanting in peaceful charm. Chilton, to the north, is a training or racing village, possessing a nice little church of many periods and a quaint epitaph which seems to have escaped the notice of the hunters after such curiosities. Indeed, until a rosarian's budding knife had played the part of Old Mortality's chisel, by removing moss and lichen, the piteous brief story of W. Goddard, who died in 1794, aged eighteen, was not in such case that he who ran might read. It runs thus:

> " In health I went away from home,
>   But did with life no more return.
>   My horse he stumbled and fell down,
>   And threw me lifeless to the ground.
>   Short was my life, my pain the less,
>   God took me home as He thought best."

Simple resignation could hardly be expressed in more homely words; but one cannot help doubting whether poor young W. Goddard, if time had been given to him to consider his fate, would have been quite so resigned as his friends made him out to be. Indeed, there is unconscious humour about these epitaphs placed by relations and friends in the mouths of those who have died unexpectedly. Here, since we are on the subject, is another such—and a very funny one—from Lam-bourn :

> " In the morning I went forth well,
> Brought back my death, took by a smell.
> Therefore in health always prepare
> To meet your Lord and Saviour dear."

Perhaps it was a recognition of the general existence and of the unsatisfactory quality of this kind of vicarious resignation which induced many of those of old time to compose their own epitaphs and to construct their own tombs during life-time. In these two cases at least the buried men could not have composed their own epitaphs.

Some little way back we discarded for the time the idea of a definite itinerary, but, having found ourselves at Chilton, we must of a surety make the easy run to Harwell, and then visit the Hagbournes, East and West, before returning to Walling-ford *viâ* Blewbury, Aston Tirrold, and North Moreton. Four or five years ago the quiet waters of Berkshire society were stirred by a peculiarly brutal murder at Harwell. That is to say, a crowd looked on with callous apathy while a policeman, who had attempted to stop a fight, was overmastered by one or both of the combatants and beaten to death. The unpleasant episode is only mentioned because on that occasion the local paper produced an epithet worthy of old Homer himself. " Fruitbearing Harwell " was designated as the scene of the tragedy ; and " fruitbearing " is absolutely appropriate to the whole of this upland district. To parody Leland's words of Abingdon, " Harwell stondeth by cherries," and the same words are true in large measure of the other hamlets named. Now this sounds ideal. It conjures up visions of cherry blossom in the spring ; and he who visits Harwell and the Hagbournes at that jocund season of the year may feast his eyes on them with impunity. It conjures up also dreams of lips, as well as eyes, feasting on black hearts, white hearts, and bullocks' hearts (they are really heart-shaped, with a pointed end of juicy

cherry-meat), which are the best of all. But those feasts are
not to be enjoyed quite with impunity, for, when the fruit is
ripening, a walk in this district is comparable, in point of
danger, to participation, in the company of many careless guns,
in the sport of shooting rabbits in covert. The reports of the
ancient weapons of the bird-scarers are heard on every side, nor
are they content with *bruta fulmina*, which is surely the
classical equivalent of blank charges. It has been found that
they must use shot. If they do not, then the thrushes, the
blackbirds, and the starlings, to say nothing of the smaller
birds, will barely take the trouble to fly from one loaded tree
to another. About cherries there is, for birds, an irresistible
fascination, which there is no great difficulty in understanding.
The starlings are the worst offenders, for they travel in flocks and
will strip a tree in a very short time ; but the thrushes and
blackbirds as individual robbers are not to be lightly regarded.
In 1903 all stone fruit perished and the district suffered
from frost, but it could be studied more safely than usual ; but
in 1904 the crop was abundant, and so was the sparrow hail.

Harwell Church is fine, too, full of those quaint things such
as squints and double piscinæ, a delight to the architectural
enthusiast ; but that which takes the untrained eye captive is
the splendidly timbered roof, of the kind known as king-post,
that is to say, possessed of a single vertical post to each truss.
Candour suggests the admission that, having seen the roof and
admired it, and having read a description of it, I was
compelled to look out this expression "king-post." It would
have been easy to affect knowledge ; but it is kinder and more
honest, even at the risk of telling to the learned that which
they know already, to confess and explain. Leaving the
church we go along the wide but not particularly interesting
street of the village, and, not being desirous of traversing West
Hagbourne twice, go by Didcot to East Hagbourne, by far
the more interesting of the two Hagbournes.

East Hagbourne has a future. It has been described by an

East Hagbourne Cross.

P

author not given to rhapsody as "one of the most picturesque
villages in the country, and almost theatrically old English."
I confess that I do not quite understand the word "theatrically," unless, indeed, some scene-painters have actually
sketched corners of East Hagbourne and reproduced them for
stage purposes, for there is nothing more noteworthy about
Hagbourne than the substantial impression given by its
architecture, and "theatrical" carries a notion of flimsiness.
There are many things here which are noteworthy : the curious
outline of the Grange, and one or two other houses of considerable size and even more considerable antiquity in the village ;
the crosses (most likely chipping or "cheapening" crosses
all) ; and, above all, the church, with its beacon-turret and
sanctus bell-cot, and its significant carvings within. To judge
from the view over the country to be obtained from the tower,
that beacon must indeed have been seen afar in the days when
it blazed, if it ever did so, and, although nothing could be
further from the purpose than to make this a handbook to
churches, one cannot miss anything so characteristic of the
district as the greyhound chasing a hare and the deerhound
pulling down a stag, which are to be seen carved within.
Before parting with East Hagbourne let me justify the opening
observation that it has a future. It is within easy reach of
Didcot, which is now an extremely good starting-point for
almost any part of England ; there is land between it and
Didcot, land capable of infinite possibilities in the way of
horticulture, yet now quite plain and ugly, which could be built
over without being spoiled, and even to advantage. Also
East Hagbourne has been discovered by artists of real merit,
who may be relied upon to "boom" a district effectually, in
inverse ratio to their desire to do anything of the kind, and
with the minimum of result in the way of substantial compensation to themselves.

To reach the main road from East Hagbourne we pass through
a tortuous maze of miry lanes, for the improvement of which local

reformers have striven in vain. "There have always been floods in Hagbourne" was the stolid answer of a local representative to a suggestion that something might be done, made in council during the autumn of 1903. As for West Hagbourne itself, without being in any sense remarkable, it is just one of those tranquil villages making the true country of England the home of placid pleasure. Blewbury, which we reach next, for it is hardly worth while to turn aside from the high-road to reach Upton, will repay the loiterer abundantly. The first impression its long and wind-swept street, with the bald down rising 200 feet behind it, gives to the traveller is one of bleak exposure, and one is not surprised to learn that when John Wesley rode to Blewbury in the first month of 1750, and in the teeth of a north wind, he could "scarce feel" whether he had any hands or feet. What is surprising is that he preached to a large congregation, for, in these days, if every man, woman, and child in the parish of Blewbury were gathered together, they would hardly make a large congregation. But, it must be remembered, Blewbury was then situate on an important artery of inland communication ; and it is now left out of the world. Also it was in a district where Nonconformity had taken root early. Even then, in the adjoining parish of Aston Tirrold, an Independent chapel had been standing for nearly a hundred years, so that there would be attendants from other places than Blewbury in all probability ; and Blewbury has fallen in population so steadily since the introduction of the railway system that, a century and a half ago, it may have been quite an important place. It was officially described as "venerable" so early as the tenth century ; and it may be that it has a future before it, for imagination faints before the attempt to realise definitely what motor traffic and touring may do for the decaying villages of England, and the high-road is, as high-roads go in these days, a markedly good one. Off that road, and to the left, if West Hagbourne be in rear, one finds, as a few wise and country-

need not boast to excess its superiority to the seventeenth. Play is less savage than it used to be when the "lusty plough-boys" would "salute so rudely, breast to breast, That their encounter seemed too rough for jest," but spectators are as fierce as ever, and "Ould Gunter" has his successors in the crowds which, in many parts of modern England, have mobbed referees in cowardly spite. After all "Ould Gunter" fought single-handed for his own offspring; and it is quite possible that he retired to Wallingford for the night, as we do in the spirit, with a comfortable consciousness of honest work done. He had disposed of his son's enemies; we have disposed of a very substantial and sweet-savoured slice of the county of Berks.

CHAPTER IX

KING ALFRED'S COUNTRY

KING ALFRED of blessed memory was born in the palace of the Kings of Wessex at Wantage, as his statue in the market-place testifies every day and all day. The statue, like the excellent one representing the late Emperor Frederick in St. George's Chapel at Windsor, is the work of that capital sculptor the late Count Gleichen, and it was presented by the late Colonel Sir Robert Loyd-Lindsay, V.C., afterwards Lord Wantage, in 1877. Of the palace of the West Saxon Kings not one stone is left lying upon another, and even the manor-house of the Fitzwarrens, which succeeded it, has vanished completely. Again, although Alfred was beyond question born at Wantage, and perhaps did some of his fighting from it, it was with Winchester, and not with Wantage, as a centre, that his life's work was connected. For Wantage itself, it thrives in a modest way, and is not unpleasing to the eye ; but it has not the old-world atmosphere that lends an undying charm to Abingdon, and there is not much in its records to appeal in stirring tones to the imagination. Among little items of quaint interest two may be mentioned. The old Market Cross bore the inscription :

> " Praie for the good Earle of Bathe
> And for good Master Willm Barnabe
> The Beldar hereof, Ano. D. 1580
> And for William, Lord Fitzwarin."

But *The Gentleman's Magazine* in 1796 avowed that the cross had certainly not remained standing for more than a century, and, as it was adorned with sculpture, or, in Puritan language, with graven images, it probably perished during the rebellion. The chances are that, as at Abingdon, Waller was the vandal, for he was not the man to miss a chance of destroying things beautiful for conscience' sake. Another pleasing little item is a passage extracted by the Lysons from the parish register, which shows that it is not necessary to travel to the Far East for a kind of marvel usually associated with Siam :

"Septem. 1598. A strange miracle ! The 19th day were buried 2 male children growing together from the breast to the navells, having all their right members each of them, being the

F. L. GRIGGS. 1906.

Wantage Church.

was starved by James I., who desired to encourage Ilsley; would do justice to the Benedictines as the agricultural missionaries of England; and, finally, would occupy scores, perhaps even hundreds, of pages fragrant of the old world.

For us, since space is limited, some salient facts stand out. The occupant and the owner of Hendred House in 1904 is John J. Eyston, Esquire: the occupant and the owner of Hendred House in 1450 or thereabouts, as it then stood, was William Eyston, Esquire; and the property was an old one then, for the fifteenth-century squire—we still talk of squires without affectation in these parts—obtained the property with his wife Isabel from the Stowes, and the private chapel, which is the glory of the house, had stood there then since the thirteenth century at least. There it stands still, having an entrance for the congregation from the grounds and a private entrance from the squire's library, with the sacred lamp burning in front of the altar, as it has continued to burn for more than six hundred years. There, every day, is held such office of prayer and praise as the Roman Catholic Church prescribes, and there the considerable Roman Catholic population of East Hendred attends on weekdays with a regularity that might put professing Protestants to shame. A very plain building is this, with walls of enormous thickness, a gallery for the Eyston family, and a few fragments of ancient glass carefully preserved, besides some stone figures in the vestry. Still, on him who shall enjoy the rare privilege of entering it, even though he should be of another form of faith, the simple dignity of the edifice must needs impress a feeling of reverence deeper than comes from presence within many a more majestic church. Six hundred years at the least—that is a long time; for six hundred years and more, through good report and evil report, in the days when Rome was all-powerful and persecuting, in the time of her humiliation and of her persecution; when the Squire of Hendred was the unquestioned head, so far as layman might be, of a Roman Catholic community; when the Squire of

Hendred must needs flee to remote Catmore for safety and the consolations of his religion; and now in happier times of toleration, this little chapel has stood, inviolate, to be the centre for a religious life of varying intensity and volume. It has never, say the Eystons, I am told, been "desecrated"; that is to say, no Protestant service has ever been held in it; and there are those who resent the word; but surely to know all is to pardon all, and Eystons who have grown to manhood in the atmosphere of this chapel, who have heard how their forefathers suffered for their faith, may well be pardoned for using such a word in such a connection, because it is so very easy to understand their attitude. The great house of the Stonors in Oxfordshire has a chapel of which the same boast may be made, and there is one of like character at Hazelwood in Yorkshire; but the history of the Eystons' chapel is at least one century longer than that of the Stonors' chapel.

Such were the feelings inspired by a visit to the private chapel, not open to visitors in the ordinary course, and to the public chapel, for which a resident parish priest, a canon in his own church, is maintained. But they were strengthened ten-fold by seeing the interior of the house and by remembering that, if the chapel was spared by Cromwell's Puritans—perhaps it escaped their notice—it was profaned, if not "desecrated," by Orange soldiery at the time of the Revolution. Even now it makes the gorge of a member of the Church of England rise to read how these rude barbarians "supped out of the chalice and, taking some of the church stuffe to Oxford with them, dressed up a mawkin in it, and set it up on the top of a bonfire."

It seems inconceivable, childish, vulgar, and contemptible. What then are likely to be the sentiments of the Eystons touching this senseless profanation of their holy of holies? They are, beyond doubt, descendants of Sir Thomas More. They have many relics of him, including a portrait, a Holbein which there seems to be no reason to doubt; a family group, like to the

Champ's Chapel, East Hendred.

famous one at Basle, only the picture of Lady More has been cut out; and more than one rare print of the one Roman Catholic martyr to conscience who has an unquestioned place in the heart of every Englishman.   Very curiously interesting it is to note in these portraits the difference between the expression of More's face in youth, and that of the same features in his sorely tried middle age.   More's drinking cup is there too, and a portrait of Cardinal Pole, and the stick on which Fisher, the Cardinal Bishop of Rochester, leaned as he walked to the scaffold at the Tower, exactly a fortnight before More met his fate at the hands of Henry VIII.'s headsman.   So long as human nature remains human, until it becomes entirely divine, it will be idle to expect men bred and nurtured in such an atmosphere as this not to bear a grudge.   Shall it be said that the majority of us, who are Protestants, do not feel particularly bitter, save when we reflect expressly upon the matter, concerning the doings of Bonner and of Mary Tudor ? Let it be remembered that we have the upper hand, which makes a vast difference ; that our immediate forbears have not suffered from disabilities ; that the Catholic Emancipation Act was assented to by George IV. only as one of his last public duties; that it is not a century old by a long way ; and that the features of Ridley, Latimer, and Cranmer have not been before all our eyes incessantly since we were in the nursery.   Surely, then, it must be a small mind—for that matter there is no lack of such — that fails to perceive something of dignity and of pathos in this survival of a Roman Catholic family and of no inconsiderable Roman Catholic community of good citizens, in the very heart of rural England ; and there will be many to whom it will be joy to learn that the little and ruined chapel in the middle of the village has been acquired by Mr. Eyston and will be treated with due reverence.

The English church is of considerable proportions, and noteworthy chiefly for its internal evidence, in the form of brasses, showing that East Hendred was really a commercial centre, wool being the staple of commerce, in the fifteenth century. Not everybody may enjoy the chance of entering the rectory garden; but all may see from outside that it has great store of the yews for which, as for box-trees and hollies, Berkshire has always been celebrated.

West Hendred has a pretty little church, in good repair, although most fortunately it has not been restored, with some fine and ancient oak in it; and it may now fairly be said that West Hendred possesses literary associations. It is best reached from East Hendred by a path across the fields which, according to some, is not open to cyclists. Be that as it may, a cycle will travel on it not amiss. The village is ordinary, but the church and vicarage, lying together, are the very embodiments of ancient calm. On the slope of the Downs, but sheltered by a belt of trees, some of them beeches, which thrive in the chalk, lies the parsonage; at the bottom of the slope, by a little brook, and with abundant trees near, is the church. Here, as at East Hendred, were several manors—one is apt to forget that a manor was often little more in extent than a large farm, and less than some modern farms—and one of these manors was acquired in exchange by Corpus Christi College in Oxford from Henry VIII. in 1536. The college holds the living to this day; and so it fell out that, many years ago, the Reverend Frederick Hayden was presented to it. He died at an advanced age in November 1905, having begotten many sons and daughters, of whom one, Miss Eleanor Hayden, has achieved a measure of quiet but decidedly well-earned fame within the last few years. Her books, *Travels Round Our Village, From a Thatched Cottage, Turnpike Travellers,* and *Rose of Lone Farm,* show not only that she has the literary gift, but also that, by close and sympathetic study, she has attained to such faithful and complete knowledge of the tongue and of the thoughts of the peasant folk as few have been able to acquire. The books have humour too, although their world is necessarily narrow, and they are perforce somewhat overweighted by dialect. Above all, they are true. But let me not make the mistake of rating Miss Hayden's work too high. She has not the relentless strength of Mr. Thomas Hardy, which makes for grandeur ; perhaps it would be a pity if any woman had quite that ; but, if the generation to come has any leisure, there is no reason why it should not value Miss Hayden in much the same way as we value Miss Mitford, if not quite so highly. Certainly those who desire to know the ways of the Berkshire peasantry, their old-world customs, their hard life, their matter-of-fact attitude towards marriage and death, cannot do better than face the struggle against their dialect in Miss Hayden's books, and win (for it is not really very difficult) and be entertained. On occasion, too, they will be even touched.

Away behind that reposeful parsonage the road goes slanting up the side of the hill to one of the fascinating manor-houses, a little one this time and of Elizabethan date, in which this country abounds. It is called Gynge Manor, probably after the brook, unless, indeed, the brook be named after it, and is occupied ; with its powder-closet, and its priest's chamber, and its small size, it may be fairly described as an exquisite pocket edition of a sixteenth-century manor-house. Curiously enough, after some recent excavations, the uncovered ground brought forth Columbines from long dormant seed of a type so old as to be quite novel.

Now we are within sight of a big subject which is personal, but not therefore by any means a cause for apology. High above a wooded eminence in the centre of Lockinge Park, if Lady Wantage be in residence, flies the flag of the Lindsays, and it is my purpose to mention a few interesting facts not generally known concerning the late Lord Wantage, V.C., as a Berkshire man. All the world knows that he won the Victoria Cross by personal gallantry at Alma and at Inkerman ; that he was specially selected by the Prince Consort, by reason of his strong and pure character, as an associate for King Edward when he was a young man and Prince of Wales ; that he

WORKING MEN'S COLLEGE LIBRARY

performed all sorts of meritorious public service as a Member of Parliament, in connection with military affairs, as chairman of the National Rifle Association, and in founding the English Red Cross Society. A smaller circle of the world knows how hard he worked, how good was his influence, and how large and discriminating was his generosity in relation to local and county affairs. He and Lady Wantage—there is no need to distinguish between them, for in mind they were one—were associated with every local movement of value in Wantage, to which they gave the site of its Town Hall, to say nothing of bearing a large part of the building expenses, and the Victoria Cross Gallery, containing an interesting series of portraits. But perhaps the most princely and thoughtful benefaction of all was the purchase and extension of the Wantage Iron Works at a time when they were in danger of passing out of existence. By this the local calamity of sudden cessation of work for a large number of men, in a district which is not industrial, was converted at one stroke into the local blessing of more work for more men in a neighbourhood where, apart from agriculture, employment by no means goes begging.

These are matters of more or less public notoriety, which, if there had not been much more to be said, would perhaps not all have been worth saying. When Robert Lindsay, V.C., a most worthy scion of the fighting stock of the Lindsays of Balcarres, married the only daughter and heiress of the first Baron Overstone and became Loyd-Lindsay, he was a comparatively poor man, and, to quote the old song, "she had gold, and she had land," almost beyond the dreams of avarice, according to Cis-Atlantic standards ; and she received in return the lifelong affection and devotion of a man whose soul was as pure as his features were handsome, whose intellect was as keen and clear as his blue eyes. Of their financial arrangements I prefer to know nothing that is not public property ; perhaps, indeed, it is not necessary to know even the whole of that. Suffice it that at Lockinge, with its surrounding estate of many thousands of acres, Lord Wantage (he was raised to the Peerage in 1885) was always supreme. From the earliest moment he set himself to work to do his duty as a landowner to the full; and there is no duty which is better worth doing. Whole villages were practically rebuilt—Ardington is, perhaps, the best of them—co-operative stores were established, so that the country folk might obtain provisions at fair rates and of fair quality, and all went merry as the marriage bells that had but lately rung. The hero of the Crimea, the chosen associate of the Prince of Wales, the accomplished connoisseur, as we shall see later, in matters of art, the busy statesman and the still busier Englishman, set himself vigorously to work to learn all that there was to be learned of agriculture in England and of its potentialities. In him there was but one more example of the truth that he who is most occupied can find most time for useful work.

Those were piping times for farmers; but, as we all know, they ended; and the next part of the story was imparted to me long years ago by the late Mr. John Walter, of Bear Wood and of *The Times*, and for many years the colleague in the House of Commons, as a Berkshire Member, of him who afterwards became Lord Wantage. In passing it may be added that Lord Wantage was wont to say of Mr. Walter that he was the most absolutely honest man he had ever met. Well, the piping times ended, and the lean years came to Lockinge farmers in the late 'seventies, as they did elsewhere. The tenants on the Lockinge estate, or the mass of them, protested with one voice that they could not live on their farms and pay their rents. Whether Lord Wantage had recourse at first to the mere palliative of temporary abatements of rent, or whether he granted permanent reductions, I cannot say, since I do not know. It would be easy to find out; but it is not worth while, because it does not matter, for a cause which can best be made clear by a personal reminiscence, quoted to that end only. When I had the honour of representing Welsh landowners before Lord Carrington's Welsh Land Commission, it became plain to me that many estates, the representatives of which claimed credit on the ground of large abatements and reductions during the period of acute distress, were really more highly rented, and harder to live on, from a farmer's point of view, than others on which the abatements and reductions were small, or even non-existent. On estate A, which had not been revalued for purposes of rental for a century, tenants had enjoyed virtually hereditary succession in occupation, and had secured the full benefit of good times on low rents ; it was fair that they should share the burden of bad times. On estate B there had been many revaluations with consequent increases of rental ; and abatements or reductions were imperatively necessary. Of each class of estate there were numerous examples, and every particle of evidence of abatements and reductions in class B was forced on the Commission. This was, perhaps, a trifle unjust to class A ; but class B were my clients also ; and, in dealing with a Commission, four-ninths of the members of which did not know the first thing about agriculture, while two-thirds were believed to be hostile to land-lords, it was desirable to provide the kind of material for reasoning which they would believe themselves to be capable of digesting. It is really only by experiment that it is possible to discover whether a given rent of a given holding is fair, in the sense of leaving a livelihood to the farmer, or not.

On the Lockinge estate we have one of those very rare cases in which the experiment was made on a large scale, and with intelligence, and with triumphant success. Lord Wantage found himself with some 6,000 or 7,000 acres of land, of which by far the larger part was arable, and believed to be only fit for wheat, thrown on to his hands by tenants who vowed they could not farm at a profit. Did they imagine that they could force his hand? Too many years have passed for an answer to be possible ; but if they did so imagine they were sadly out of their reckoning, since those thousands of acres became, and they still are — for Lady Wantage keeps up everything as in her lost husband's time—the most colossal home farm on record, and probably the best. Lord Wantage had capital at his disposal, it is true ; there is no sort of good in trying to farm in the Vale or on its fringes, or, for that matter anywhere, without capital ; but he had intelligence and an open mind also, and he was the last man in the world to sit down under depression. Much of the land that would not grow wheat to a profit was found to produce first-rate barley of a good malting sample ; the best agricultural machinery was introduced ; high cultivation (and basic slag) extirpated the thistles that had been rampant ; a classic race of shire-horses was established ; great herds of white-faced Herefords grew fat on the broad pastures near the Great Western line ; and above all, far above all, the new and vast home farm paid and continued to pay right down well, after all proper deductions had been made. Incidentally, of course, Lord Wantage had also provided for the county and for the country an object lesson showing what still may be done in English agriculture by the application of energy, intelligence, business methods, and the employment of capital.

Socially the result has been somewhat curious. Here is a large tract of country, well farmed, employing at least as many labourers as it can carry, having regard to modern conditions, producing more than it would be likely to produce under separate tenants ; but it is a tract of country from which one class, that of the tenant-farmer, has practically vanished by its own will, if not by its own fault. It would be idle to say that such a state of things is universally popular in the county. Farmers and minor corn-dealers, and men of that stratum in society, complain of it a good deal, and it is fruitless to remind them of its history and explanation. In like manner it is useless to argue with a village tradesman who holds that the Ardington Stores established by Lord Wantage are "unconstitutional"—a lovely word this, and faithfully quoted. But the sum of the whole evidence is that Lord Wantage did excellent work locally and did it on a grand scale. Another definite piece of work which he effected was the provision of a great reservoir in the Downs above Lockinge, fed by a wind-mill pump from the boundless moisture of the chalk below, for a supply to neighbouring villages of that pure water which is all too rare in Berkshire's rural parts.

Take him for all in all, Lord Wantage lived a noble life and a useful one, and the cross erected by Lady Wantage on the highest point of the Downs within Lockinge Parish is indeed a "landmark to be seen from afar," and will be "a memorial in years to come of one who served his country faithfully in the Army and in the State, and whose influence for good was felt not only in his own home but throughout the county of Berks." This, it may be mentioned, is thirty-three feet high, and an exact copy of the ancient fifteenth-century cross of San Zenobio at Florence.

Lockinge House is the country home of Lady Wantage, and was that of Lord Wantage in life. The manor of Lockinge is ancient, but the laborious search of the author of a monograph has failed to discover in the history either of its occupants or of the parish anything of romance, or anything that is fantastic, save a playful habit of a parishioner of past days who frequently turned a mean, hardly honest, but legitimate penny by informing upon those who failed to bury their relatives' bodies in woollen according to law. In 1853 the manor, and much surrounding property, was bought by Lord Overstone, and from 1858, as soon as the necessary enlargement had been effected, it became the home, since enlarged, of Colonel and the Hon. Mrs. Loyd-Lindsay, afterwards Lord and Lady Wantage. It occupies a peculiar and remarkably attractive position. The peculiarity of its situation is the close juxta-position, to be found in but few cases, of the house and the church, the latter going back in parts to the thirteenth century and dedicated to All Souls—until recently the living belonged to the college of that name at Oxford. From house to church

Lockinge House.

WORKING MEN'S COLLEGE LIBRARY.

is but a few steps through a conservatory and across a lawn. The attractive character of the situation impresses itself forcibly on one who approaches house and church in the ordinary way from Ardington, or from West Lockinge, the rectory of which is a perfect haven of rest at the edge of the park. Formerly the rectory was situated within the grounds.

On the left of him who approaches is a swelling knoll, crowned and fringed with beeches and other trees; and below it the greensward of the park, on which Herefords or Jerseys are mostly to be seen grazing, comes quite up to the little enclosure of shrubs and gardenage in the immediate vicinity of the house. On the right the turf continues, broken by here and there a stately tree, to the verge of an irregular lakelet of fair size, and on the far side of that is a sheer cliff of rugged rock, or rockwork, one cannot say which. Herein are the remains of a grotto, excavated and fitted with shells and rockspar now vanished by them of old time, in deference to fashion; and scattered about the gardens formerly were not a few leaden figures of which one, a copy of the Vatican "Ariadne," still remains. Modern fashion in garden adornment has not come back to grottos yet, but it has returned towards a fancy for honouring these figures of lead, and some may regret that the rest have gone. Others, perhaps, will agree that if, like many others, they were sown far and wide in the form of bullets during the Napoleonic wars, they were put to good use. Few, if any, will dispute that the rock, or rockwork, much of it muffled in ferns, with here and there a splash of colour, the grey church, the reflections in the still water, the green lawns, the waterplants at the edge of the pool, and the fine, if unpretentious, house, combine to make a strangely pleasing scene.

And what shall be said of the inside of Lockinge House? It is not a Chatsworth, or a Badminton: it was never intended to be one of "the stately homes of England," most of them really not homes at all; but it has a distinct character of its own, in which that of its makers, who were its occupants for many happy years, is clearly reflected. It has its entrance hall, its tapestry hall, panelled and galleried from the spoils of one of the City halls, and with carved Italian work in walnut, both good and ancient. Let into this is the famous Murillo, " La Vierge Coupée," the Virgin and Child in which were cut out from their place at Seville during the Peninsular War, and acquired later by Lord Overstone, while the rest of the picture, which was taken to Paris by Soult, was secured by Lord Overstone in 1862. The top of the hall is glorious with sixteenth-century tapestry, and the great drawing-room, and the garden room, with its corridor leading to the conservatory, are among the best lighted rooms, and also among the rooms which are, by virtue of their contents, best worth lighting, to be found in all the length and breadth of England. In fact Lockinge House is the ideal combination of a home and a picture gallery, which latter, as the late Mr. Strong, the accomplished Librarian of the House of Lords, has written, has all the merits of its recent origin, merits which made its pictures " the objects of constant companionship, and the unfailing delight of the latter years " of Mr. A. G. Temple, now the Director of the Guildhall Art Gallery. These are the words used by Lady Wantage, of Mr. Temple, in her preface to the catalogue of the collections at Lockinge and in Carlton Gardens. To improve upon the language would be difficult ; to say that the pictures were to the late Lord Wantage, and are to her, " the objects of constant companionship, and the unfailing delight of their latter years," is to speak simple truth. To write that they lived for their pictures would be foolish injustice ; they lived to do their duty, and they achieved the purpose of their lives ; but they lived up to their pictures, and Lady Wantage continues to live up to them, in the fullest sense of the words. Lord Overstone was a discriminating collector and a highly trained connoisseur. Those who came after him possessed discrimination and trained taste in equal measure. They were picture-loving, picture-acquiring folk ; and the growth of their house was probably due to, as it was certainly planned with definite purpose of suiting, their increasing collection.

But the catalogue, a superb work of art, and a joy for ever to those who possess it, occupies a hundred and eighty folio pages irrespective of plates, and its language is never diffuse. True it is that many of the pictures named in it are at Carlton Gardens, but the number at Lockinge is so considerable that any detailed description of them is out of the question. Also, although some of the best of them have been lent for exhibition from time to time with that free generosity which would be noteworthy in one owner of noble pictures, if it were not characteristic of many, the pictures are not, in a public sense, on view. So, perhaps, a detailed account of them would be out of place ; but some striking treasures may be mentioned. The Murillo, already alluded to, is surely the picture of pictures in which the prince of Spanish painters best obeyed the instruction, " Our Lady is to be painted in the flower of her age, with sweet, grave eyes, a nose and mouth of the most perfect form ; in a word, with all the beauty that a human pencil can express." Posterity may be thankful indeed that Lord Overstone's pertinacity had the effect of reuniting, after the lapse of half a century, the two parts of this glorious picture. It is not the only Murillo at Lockinge, still less the only one in either collection, but, with its romantic history and its perfect execution, it is perhaps the most treasured picture possessed by its owner. To my mind, one aiming to be guided by Mr. Ruskin in matters of art, but often falling sadly short of its ambition, "The Enchanted Castle" of Claude, the inspiration of some melodious verse of Keats, appeals with irresistible force. " A perfectly genuine and untouched sky of Claude is indeed most perfect, and beyond praise, in all qualities of air . . . such skies as those of ' The Enchanted Castle.' " That, surely, leaves nothing more for man of common prudence to add. Next, to follow inclination merely, may oe placed the Van Dyck, that unsurpassable "Henrietta Maria," wherein the lustre of the dark-brown eyes is hardly more admirable than the sheen of the pearly satin and the elaboration of the lace collar.

Tintoretto, Canaletto, Hobbema, Perugino, Bassano, Teniers, Lancret, Romney, Burne-Jones, and even Turner must be passed by. We can but glance, in print, at portraits by Shannon, Watts, Richmond, and Ouless, the last a joyful reminder of Lord Wantage in 1877 ; for it is necessary to push on to the rare Pesellino panels and the four characteristic Corot landscapes. To the former, to these "panels painted in *tempera* on a partially gilded ground," for wedding chests, "with the delicate jewelled gold-work on the dresses, trappings, &c., done by a process of working over with tooling the gold ornamentation laid on a preparation of 'Gesso,'" the late Mr. Strong gives the first place in point of antiquity and merit. And certainly there is in them a "combination of simplicity and alertness" quite Chaucerian, to borrow Mr. Strong's apt analogy, giving to them a rare attraction. They live in the memory, with all their richness of quaint incident, as an illustration of the career and exploits of David the son of Jesse that is full of old-world merit and curious particularity. Jean Baptiste Corot never painted better pictures, and he certainly painted many worse, than these "Les Quatres Heures du Jour," painted for his friend Decamps, which were acquired by Lord Leighton first, and then, on the sale of Lord Leighton's pictures, after his death, by Lord Wantage ; and of Corot, at his best, one need not hesitate to accept the authoritative pronouncement that "he ranks with Titian, Rembrandt, Claude, and Turner among the great interpreters of landscape."

Amidst such treasures as these, and many more of almost equal worth from the artistic point of view, Lord Wantage lived with Lady Wantage, and Lady Wantage lives now, continuing to collect with discernment when the opportunity offers. The collection is, of course, an exceptionally grand one, made by persons of far more judgment than is usual even among collectors. But it is similar in point of character to collections to be found in many other great houses, and these may serve to explain a little feature in our upper classes or aristocracy —call them what you will—which is not without interest. It is that many of the " Barbarians," as Matthew Arnold used to call them, men and women of capacity by no means above the average, who have studied little of anything, and least of all of the principles of art, have in fact a far nicer judgment in art than the average men or women in other classes of society who have read more, and possessed better brains to read withal. The phenomenon is, on reflection, too generally prevalent to need demonstration. The explanation is to be found, not in instinct or in heredity, but in the value of association, on which, it will be remembered, the strange founder of Radley College insisted in season and out of season. These persons spend their lives, when they are indoors, in the companionship of the kind of pictures which the middle classes as a rule can see only at exhibitions. They naturally, and without thinking, learn to distinguish a good picture from a bad, just as a shepherd learns to know the individuals in a flock appearing to us to consist of many sheep of identical form and appearance. And one is tempted to carry this a little further. Among the members of this upper class are a number of men who in the ordinary way are not above the average of intelligence, men who could no more be Senior Wranglers, or First Class men, or successful in a competitive examination, than they could fly : yet of them a considerable proportion show more than common aptitude for the art or science of politics. May not that also be due to environment? Would not a commonplace youth nurtured at Hatfield or at Hawarden, living always in a political atmosphere, be compelled to take in political ideas, or ideas about politics, through the pores, so to speak, and so start in political life with an advantage over men of far greater capacity who had not enjoyed his opportunities. The train of thought, it may be asserted confidently, is worth following. *Non sequitur*, however, that this is the place in which to do more than suggest it.

"Immediately to the east of Lockinge House, a grove of venerable elms, bordered by a clear chalk stream, leads to the Manor House of Betterton. Environed by ancient fish ponds, and magnificently timbered glades, this house, originally quadrangular, but now decreased by the removal of a wing, is an interesting and picturesque specimen of Tudor domestic architecture. A huge tithe barn close by is probably co-ëval. A lease of Betterton was granted by the Prior of Poughley to John Collins in July 1521, but there are evidences of the family possessing property in the place at a much earlier date.

Successive generations rest in the chancel of Lockinge church. Their monuments are clustered on its walls, and from the latest, in memory of John Ferdinando Collins, we read, 'at his death—1889—the estate of Betterton, held by the Collins family, from father to son, for upwards of four centuries passed from their possession.' It passed into the possession of their life-long friend and neighbour Lord Wantage."

For the preceding words I am indebted to Colonel Collins, a representative of the ancient family, nor can his simple statement be improved upon. With it he sends a document, so full of the spirit of the old world that it must be given in full, a document too, calling attention to the fact that Abingdon, peaceful to a fault as it is now, had something approaching to a fast reputation in the seventeenth century as well as in the days of the *Shotover Papers*. The curious orthography and punctuation are retained.

Letter from Jo: Collins to his son Charles Collins 1682.

CHARLES,

I am sorry to hear that you should have soe little discretion to run yourself into such danger, as to goe to Abingdon and especially at such a time, I shall say nothing of y^r behaviour there, but advise you to leave off such frolicks, you wrote to me, that it would be unhandsom for one of your quality not to have money in y^r pockett, I should account myself indiscreet to enter you a gentleman, and not to maintain you there accordingly, but let me advise you in this according to the proverb, to cut your coat according to y^r cloth, t'is true you are placed in the same rank with Gents: but you must know y^t there is a great difference in the estate of Gents: there be som t'is probable y^t you may bee in company with, y^t have ten times more estate than I have, or ever you will have, and therefore must not thinck to spend with them, and truly I must stretch

Arthurus Collins de Betterton
in Com Berceriæ.

hard to maintaine you in this quality, & therefore pray be frugall and discreet as you can, and to come as seldome amongst them as you can possibly come off with creditt, and by God's blessing you shall not want to maintain you in y^t equipage, with good husbandry, and following your study will prevent the spending of mony, besides the advantage y^t will accrue to you during your life. I received a letter from a Gent: this last week, wch was of y^r quality and newly come from Oxon, in wch was scarse a word of Ortography, but I hope better things of you. I have here enclosed, sent you my coat of arms, wch you may place up in y^r study, & because you may be able to blazon it, for there be many y^t cannott, wch seems rediculous, & because I suppose you have but little scill in it, I will do it for y^r knowledge, wch is, Vert, a Gryphon passant, or, a cheif ermin, the crest is a Gryphon's head, erased, vert, crowned or, & because to many arms there is a mysticall meaning, I will likewise declare it to you, once for all, and I desire you not to forgett it ; The field vert, signifys husbandry, the Gryphon, in authors, is an emblem of watchfullness, his being passant signifys diligence & industry, his colour, or, denotes riches, the cheif, ermin, signifys honour in cheif, wch put together resolves into this, y^t, by diligence & industry in our calling, we attain to riches, the foundation and way to honour, where the Gryphon is not rampant, as whereby a man should attain to riches and honour by rapacity and ambition, but by honesty and humility, all wch is aptly enpressed in this Mottoe ; per Callem, Collem, such Motto's belonging to arms not only enpressing the mystery of them, but alluding to the name of the person y^t beard them, soe one D^r. Collins, a famous Cambridge man, took for his Motto, Colens Deum et Regem, now look into your Roman history and there you shall find a great and noble family of the Collini, wch took theyr name a porta Collina, & the gate soe called, because it led in Collem, soe y^t, as I s^d before, their Motto, per Callem, Collem, takes in the mystery of the Coat, as much as to say, per Virtutis callem, honoris collem ascendimus, wch y^t you may attain to, to live vertuously att the beginning, y^t you may gain reputation hereafter, or rather, y^t you may pray to God to give you sanctified vertue here, wch is Grace, y^t you may attain everlasting glory, is not only the advice, but the prayer of,

y^r loving father,
Jo: Collins

Imprimis venerare Deum.

May 5th, 1682

So the expedition is ended, none too soon, perhaps, so far as mere print goes, although those who are able to make it in the flesh will not be in a hurry to return from it ; and we are back again at Wantage. Whither shall we fare next ? Surely, since we are under the shadow of White Horse Hill, and hard by the Blowing Stone and Wayland Smith's "Cave," in the heart of "Tom Brown's" country and of Walter Scott's country too, we must go to these places without delay ; for who will have patience to examine even Uffington Church, with the care which it deserves abundantly, until he has seen these storied spots ? So, if you please, we will take the road marked as the Roman Way in the ordnance maps—and a very tiring road it is on a hot day—and we will refrain for the moment from turning aside to the right even for Childrey, or Sparsholt, or Uffington. At Kingston Lisle, the ancient seat of the de l'Isles, and of the Hydes, as we said at Denchworth, we cannot avoid noticing as we pass the trees of more than common grandeur, and that, really, is all that there is left to observe except the peculiarly pleasing formation of this northern slope of the Downs. Compared with the Hampshire Downs near Winchester they have, to my mind, a kindlier and less wind-swept look. Deep combes run up their sides, in them the grass is almost rich and luxuriant, and there is a good deal of wood—and altogether Nature smiles broadly, if indeed she be in the mood to smile at all.

But here we are at the Blowing Stone, found, it is said, somewhere on the Downs in days gone by, perhaps on White Horse Hill, perhaps at Wayland Smith's " Cave," but now converted to mere catchpenny uses. It stands, a Sarsen Stone—that is to say, a lump of hardened sandstone from the Bagshot Sands that once overlay the chalk—in a cottage garden by the wayside, with numerous holes in it, not unlike to those in a coarse sponge, but not nearly so numerous. The hole that matters, the one from which the skilful can extract a murmurous trumpet call, is covered with a padlocked lid, but any trifling sum will cause it to be opened. Into the hole, when the lid is removed, the wanderer may blow if he pleases ; he will most likely not produce any substantial volume of sound, and will probably bruise his nose into the bargain, if it be at all prominent. It is more satisfactory to fee the person who shows the stone—last time there was a maiden with a tip-tilted nose admirably suited for the task—and to do the blowing vicariously. But, frankly, the result is disappointing. The noise is of similar quality to that produced by blowing, in the proper way, through a conch with the pointed end filed off, a species of primitive "hooter" still used in Anglesey to summon the farm labourers to their meals. But a good conch-blower will beat a performer on the Blowing Stone hollow any day of the week. In fact the owners of the Blowing Stone have to thank Sir Walter Scott for having given to it a distinctly fictitious value. As for the theory that it was ever used to summon folks from a distance for any purpose, it does not appeal to my reason; but it is pleasant to think that cottagers gain an income, howsoever modest, in return for so poor a performance. To have written thus is by no means to have done the cottagers disservice; for—such is the perversity of human nature—the advice to leave the Blowing Stone on one side will doubtless inspire in others, as it did in me, an absolute determination to try it on the spot. So the sixpences will keep rolling in.

Now, with ardour cooled somewhat by an experience of the Blowing Stone, we will proceed along the same road, the Roman Way, as far as Compton Beauchamp, for so shall we climb up to the White Horse the more easily, and have time to glance at the interesting little church already mentioned, and the still more interesting Manor House. I know nothing quite like this house, the property of Lord Craven, but occupied for many years by the witty and wise Vice-Chancellor Bacon, and now the home of his son, his Honour Judge Francis Bacon. Certainly I know nothing more charming. Through an ancient gateway you enter an outer court; thence, crossing a moat—a real moat full of water and fish—you pass under an archway, probably eighteenth century, into a paved court-yard with a plashing fountain in its midst, surrounded on all sides by the walls of the house, walls of white chalk, mellowed by age. Then there is another archway in a straight line with the first and passing into part of the house, and beyond the house a narrow strip of velvet lawn; next the moat again, spanned by a wooden bridge. Beyond is a gentle slope, and above it a wide plateau of lawns, flanked on either side by immemorial brick walls of a tone of red to which no pen could do justice, whereon plums and peaches " drink the splendour of the sun." Past the lawn, and raised by a terraced stage above it, is an old-fashioned garden of yew hedges, rampant roses, and herbaceous plants without number. Up the middle runs a broad ribbon of path ending at a spacious gateway, having ancient gates of wrought iron, through which the rolling sea of the Downs may be seen for miles. Imagine first this ample expanse of softest green, with its margin of mellow brick walls, framed on either side with really fine trees, and you have the scene without life. Think of it, as it may be seen often, dotted with guests, some playing at croquet on the right, others at lawn-tennis or bowls on the left, and, costumes and some of the games apart, you have such a scene as might have been enacted in the days of Elizabeth. For all we know—perhaps it were as well not to know too much—the lawn may have witnessed such scenes in Elizabethan days, since, although the front of the house is of chalk, and of the eighteenth century, that side of it which faces the lawn, and is of brick, dates back to the sixteenth century. The whole has that indescribable fascination rightfully belonging to a house of individual beauty to which that tortured word "unique" is really applicable.

From Compton Beauchamp to the White Horse, to Uffington Castle, and to Wayland Smith's Cave, in the order named, is no difficult expedition, and one distinctly worthy to be taken. True it is that those plaguy folk, the antiquaries, have dissipated the specific halo of romance which hung round the White Horse, and have proved fairly conclusively that it was not set up by Alfred for a sign to the surrounding country of his victory over the heathen Danes at Ashdown ; but in dispersing one mist of halo they have but raised another, and one more dense and impenetrable. For example, some say that the horse is a rude presentment of the biga once figured on the stater of Philip of Macedon, which undoubtedly served as a model for the earliest British coins ; but the learned and voluminous writer on "Heraldry" in the *Encyclopædia Britannica*, not in one of the new volumes it is true, writes gaily and confidently of "the White Horse of Saxony, which still remains carved upon the chalk Downs of Western England." It is a little strained, perhaps, to include Berkshire in the West country, and it is true that there are other white horses of less account, but there can be very little doubt that the writer on "Heraldry" meant to refer to the White Horse of Berks, *par excellence* the "Eclipse" of the breed. Still less doubt is there that the White Horse was the Saxon emblem or totem : and we are left in this difficulty, that, if it be the Saxon emblem, it cannot be a British presentment of the "disjointed horse" of the early coinage ; and, if it be this latter, it cannot have been set up by Alfred as a sign of victory or by Saxons at all. So, to put the matter in a homely way, we do not know where we are. But it is always worth while to remember that while evidence showing that Alfred caused the outline of the horse to be dug would, if it existed, be proof corroborative of the theory that Ashdown was fought hard by, evidence to the contrary does not help us in the least to decide where the battle was fought. As for the artistic quality of the outline of the horse, without going to such lengths in admiration as the erudite Dr. Wise and his correspondents, one need not quite accept the view that it is "exceedingly rude." Reflect for a moment that it is 374 feet long, and visible, when "scoured," on a clear day for fifteen or twenty miles; and then think of the task of tracing the faintest approach to an equine figure on such a scale on a sloping hillside. The result of reflection is a decided tendency to take a lenient view of the artistic quality of the figure. And, if it be indeed so rude, what becomes of the argument based upon its resemblance to the disjointed horse on British coins ?

When I last saw the horse at close quarters he was sadly in need of that scouring rendered classic by "Tom Hughes," but perhaps most succinctly described by Lysons. It was said in his day that lands in the vicinity were held on the terms of cleaning it : "It is certain that the inhabitants have an ancient custom of assembling for this purpose, which they term scouring the horse. On these occasions they are entertained at the

R

cost of the Lord of the Manor, and keep a kind of rural festival
with various appropriate diversions. The last celebrity of this
kind took place in 1780." There has been at least one since—
it is cleverly worked into the tale by the late Judge Hughes
called "The Scouring of the White Horse," which all should
read—but the Lord of the Manor—that is to say, according to
the statute of 1777, of the manor of Uffington—might do a
great deal worse than organise the first scouring of the twentieth
century; for at present both horse and manger, a bank scarred
by little and straight ravines, are growing more difficult to distinguish every year.

At the very summit of White Horse Hill stands Uffington
Castle, all but 900 feet above the sea level and with as fine a
vallum, more than 200 yards in diameter, as man need desire
to see; but its history is lost in the ages and clouded by conjecture, and precisely the same observation applies to many
other ancient camps in the vicinity. That which will never be
lost is the memory of the splendour of the extensive view
over the smiling acres of the Vale to be obtained from
this lofty eminence. Here indeed the "Ayre is temperate,
sweet, and delightful, and prospect for pleasure inferior to
none."

If antiquaries have done lovers of romance some disservice
in relation to the White Horse, it is at least consoling to find
that the more one inquires into Wayland Smith and his "Cave,"
the stronger grows the fascination. In fact, to my mind,
Wayland Smith's "Cave" is the best dreaming spot in these
parts. Stand at the highest point of Uffington Castle and after
facing the view of the Vale for the last time be pleased to make
rather more than a half-turn to the left. There you shall
perceive, distant a mile and a half as the crow flies (and, saving
some ups and downs, you may walk as straight), a cluster of
trees, beeches of no great age, as they prove to be on approaching
nearer. Reaching them you find first a distinctly marked ditch
and mound of circular form, next a group of twenty or thirty

F L GRIGGS · 1906 ·

White Horse Hill.

WORKING MEN'S COLLEGE LIBRARY.

loose sarsen boulders, some of them of large size, and in the
middle the " cave," which is no cave at all in the ordinary sense
of the word, but a cromlech of familiar form, its central
chamber being, as it stands now, about three feet square.
And this is Wayland Smith's Cave, the centre of the local legend
of the mysterious smith who would shoe a horse left *in situ*
with sixpence and no more ; the peg, so to speak, on which Sir
Walter Scott hung one of his most stirring scenes. As for the
cromlech, it provokes as a rule the same observations by which
other cromlechs, if they had but ears, would be bored to stony
death. Somebody is sure to know enough to observe that it is
the central chamber of a barrow, which once contained the
body of somebody, a Briton for choice, and was covered with
earth. The presence of the stones is, in this case, sufficiently
explained by Lord Avebury. They are a group of lumps of
indurated sandstone, that part of the Bagshot Sands, formerly
covering this region, which has not been removed by wind and
water, to translate sub-aerial denudation into plain English.
Those of old time buried their chieftain here because the site
was commanding and the stones were placed conveniently.
How they piled the great slab on to the uprights is but the
question which presents itself at a hundred cromlechs more
remarkable than this, and the general tendency of the answers
to it, with their suggestion of inclined planes and the like, is to
indicate that " our rude ancestors " had really made a
considerable advance in the mechanical arts in a period which
used to be regarded as one of unmitigated barbarism.
Really, of course, the more we learn about the Druids the more
clear does it become that they had a civilisation of their
own, and a theology also, as described in *Mona Antiqua
Restaurata*, which were lost, as other civilisations have been,
and perhaps theologies also, elsewhere, in Africa and South
America for example. The movement of heavy stones is
not likely to have been an insoluble problem to the in-

ventors of scythed war-charriots, and, to be plain, we see
that it was not.

Wayland Smith is, on the face of things, a hero of Saxon
legend, of whom romancers have made grand use, domiciled
in the grave of a departed Briton.   But, when one comes to
look into the history of the legend, as I have been able to
look into it in a little book lent to me by his Honour Judge
Bacon, it is plain that Wayland Smith is quite an important
person in comparative mythology, or, to avoid scientific words,
the common traditions of many races.   The book (published
by Pickering in 1847) is entitled " Wayland Smith, a dissertation on a tradition of the Middle Ages, by G. B. Depping, and
Francisque Michel, with additions by S. W. Singer and
the amplified legend by Oehlenschlager."   In fact it is a
Northern saga which was "written up" in Danish by Adam
Oehlenschlager in 1800, and rewritten in German, and the
little volume has abundant notes.   You may trace Wayland
among many peoples.   He is the Voelund and Vaulundr of
Icelandic, the Wéland of Anglo-Saxon, the Weland and Velond
of Old English, the Galans and Galant of Old French.   The
Voelundarguida of the *Edda* has to do with a smith who made
magic swords and a flying machine.   In Beowulf's Anglo-
Saxon poem are the lines :

> " Send back to Higelac,
> If the war should take me,
> The best of warshrouds
> That guards my breast,
> The most excellent vesture,
> That is the legacy of Hræda,
> The work of Weland."

No common shoeing-smith is the true " Wayland " of romantic
legend, but an armourer of magic skill, and goldsmith also ;
for Boethius wrote of *Pocula quæ sculpsit Guielandus in urbe
Sigeni*.   In ancient French legend we read—that is to say,

Adam Oehlenschlager or his commentator did, and saved us the trouble—how Louis IV. girded Raoul (de Cambrai) with a magnificent sword forged in a dark cavern by Galans :

> " Li roi li caint l'epée fort et dure,
> D'or fu li pons et toute la hendure,
> Et fu forgie en une combe oscure,
> Galans la fist qui toute i mist sa cure."

Galans too is credited with having made, in addition to many other weapons, " Joyeuse," the sword, " cele tint Karle-maine longuement en certe," and our learned commentator notes that, like Hephæstus and Vulcan, he was lame, that, like them and every legendary smith, he worked underground, and that, like Dædalus, he invented a flying machine.

Many more legends there are of great exploits done with swords forged by this legendary tradesman—to use the word in its true sense—but enough has been written to show that in essentials he is the common property of many races. In fact, in Icelandic, Voelund simply means a " smith," so that Way-land Smith is equivalent to Smith-Smith, without the glory of a hyphen. But the direct source of the legend that haunts the vicinity of the White Horse is plain, for its story is that of Theodoric of Berne, of a smith who (for blaspheming on the death of his wife) was imprisoned in a cave and shod the horses of travellers in precisely the same fashion used by Wayland Smith of the pleasant county of Berks.

Was it, or was it not, in these parts, where Ashdown House (of which more later) stands on Ashdown, where a neigh-bouring camp is called " Alfred's Camp " to this day, that the battle of Æscesdune was fought ? Did the Danes occupy Uffington Castle ? Was it at Hardwell, the little camp close to Compton Beauchamp, that Ethelred lingered over his prayers, forgetting that God helps those who help themselves ? Are any of the stunted thorns that, as was observed previously, may be found on the Downs hereabouts and a little to the south, the descendants of the *unica spinosa arbor* round which

the battle-cries of Saxon and Dane rose fiercest in 871?
Without pretending to have read all that has been written
on this moot point, for much may have escaped my notice,
I am disposed to enlist myself under the banner of that
stout Berkshire man Judge Hughes, and to say that if the
battle was fought on the Berkshire Downs at all, as most likely
it was, Ashdown is the reasonable site to favour. We, who
would like to maintain this view, have two classes of opponents
to meet. There is the class of controversialists of the stamp of
Colonel Cooper King, who know the county so little that,
as has been shown, they apply to disprove local tradition
arguments which, if they have any force at all, tend to support
it. There is the class of opponents who say, " Quite unfounded
local tradition says that at the battle of Ashdown, Uffington
Castle was occupied by the Danes, Hardwell Castle by
Ethelred, and Alfred's Camp by Alfred." But that, with all
respect, is simply to beg the question. The onus of proof
lies upon those who set themselves up against local tradition,
for it, unless it be plainly absurd, or upset by good evidence,
is in itself the strongest of testimony. Our Berkshire folk
have many virtues, and some vices also, and whether the
power of imagination be virtue or vice it is not for me to say;
but it is quite safe to say that they do not possess it, although,
after the manner of all country folk, they can invent scandal
about their neighbours, especially if they be new-comers. If,
then, the Berkshire folk have no imagination to speak of,
whence came this tradition? The most likely answer appears
to me to be that it had its origin in truth, and that the
antiquarians and historians neglected to reflect, when they
discovered that Alfred could not have limned the White
Horse on the green hillside, that they had learned nothing
having the slightest bearing one way or the other on the
question where Alfred actually fought. That is the kind of
fallacy into which it is easy to fall. The fact is that the
kernel of a tradition may be true even though the shell be

false, and that, although Alfred probably did not make the Horse, the fact that the peasantry believed him to have made it is still evidence for the Ashdown site, rather than against it. What could be more natural than that they should think the visible Horse to be the witness to all time of the priceless victory, the tale of which had been handed down from father to son since time immemorial? As for the actual date of the battle, that, as those who have studied the country people in any part of England will be more than well aware, would become beautifully vague in a very short time. Both in Berkshire and in Hertfordshire it is no unusual thing to meet men, who must have passed through some kind of educational mill, who none the less will say, gravely and in good faith, that they remember hearing their fathers speak of this event or that, of at least two centuries' standing. The tendency in that direction must, one would think, have been far stronger in the days before the schoolmaster was abroad. A thousand years is to the peasant an expression as devoid of meaning, as difficult to realise definitely, as infinity is to us. But he does not invent legends, because he is not equal to the task. He brought Wayland Smith with him from his continental home; and if twenty families from the Vale were settled suddenly in the Argentine and survived, the chances are that their daughters would sing the old rhymes on the first of May, and their sons would introduce " King George " to the South American continent. But I feel very sure that they did not invent Alfred's Castle, or the theory that the Danes occupied Uffington Castle, and this conviction leads me to something approaching to a firm belief upon a point which has been treated with greater caution at an earlier point. In other words, I think that, while Æscesdun probably means the whole of the commanding range of the Berkshire Downs, Ashdown probably is that part of Æscesdun on which Alfred really began the great task of freeing his country. So I really feel at liberty to people these various ramparts with Danes and

Saxons as the case may be, to think of the fierce and irresistible onslaught of the Saxons as it swept up these steep slopes of grass, to believe that the country folk have some ground— other, of course, than scientific—for their belief that the flowerets of the Downs are brighter when they grow where brave men fighting fell :

> " I sometimes think that never blows so red
>   The rose, as where some buried Cæsar bled."

That, certainly, is the mood in which to approach Ashdown, and to tread lightly on the springing turf. Away with the dryasdusts who will balance to a nicety the claims of half a score of places, to decide in favour of none. It is not in such a temper that the mind of man is stirred by noble memories ; and, if he cannot be absolutely certain where he ought to cherish them, it is better that he should encourage them some- where, even in a doubtful place, than nowhere and therefore not at all.

It were a pity to descend at once from the Downs and Ashdown to the plain of the Vale, and to authentic history, however engrossing. So, if you please, we will make a little expedition such as you cannot, so far as I am aware, make anywhere else in England. A comfortable carriage and a sturdy pair of horses, which will be none the worse for being well covered with flesh, since there are hills to be overcome, has climbed the side of the Down, from Compton Beauchamp and is in waiting within a hundred yards or so of Wayland Smith's Cave. In it we will go, driving over a green track, so closely grown that it is not easy to follow, so elastic that the wheel- marks disappear as soon as the wheels have passed, in a direct line towards Lambourn ; it is some six miles of the most luxurious travelling, and the strangest, conceivable. One or two lonely homesteads of the Downs we shall pass, and no more. The rest is undulating space of green grass and herbage : and about half-way, amidst grass greener than the rest, will be seen solitary thickets of ancient thorn-trees and some of them standing singly, all stunted and storm-swept, which bring the *unica spinosa arbor brevis admodum* of Asser of Pembroke irresistibly to mind.

Then, in a moment, the scene is transformed. We turn suddenly from the green track, that has needed no care of man since the grass first grew on the chalk that had been under the sea, into a road that must needs be mended every year. We are in Upper Lambourn, and in the midst of civilisation. It is a trim and comfortable civilisation, for Lambourn, Upper and Lower, lives for racehorses now; and the racehorse may have a corrupting influence, but those who attend to him here seem to have more money than their neighbours of the purely agricultural districts. Nor, to all appearance, do they misuse their earnings. Children well grown and neatly dressed; gardens trimly kept and gay, with roses " that down the alleys shine afar " and " sweet-william with his homely cottage smell "; orchards in apple-pie order—a prolepsis this, but it flowed unasked from the pen—no lack of whitewash or of paint on the cottages;—all these symptoms of well-being disarm the moralist and dispose him not to pry too curiously into the sources of all this wealth. Is it really so very deadly a matter if some of it represents horses backed successfully by men in daily association with them, who are in a position to obtain information at the fountain-heads and even to guess shrewdly which fountains be pure and which foul? At the worst, if the sin of betting admit of degrees, this is its most venial form; and to know the lives of some other villages in the Royal County, where children are reared without milk, other than that of their ill-nourished mothers, because there is neither milk to be bought, nor money for the buying, is to be predisposed to raise the telescope to the blind eye when questions are raised as to the agency that has brought about this welcome touch of the magic wand of prosperity.

Lambourn may, perhaps, claim something of literary association ; it has certainly a venerable history. It has been suggested to me that Charles Kingsley may have had Lambourn and the Lambourn valley and river in his mind when he wrote the opening chapters of *Two Years Ago* ; and certainly little exercise of imagination, or allowance for novelist's licence, is required to read Lambourn into those chapters. True it is, no doubt, that, from the prosaic point of view, Newbury is in some material respects closer than Lambourn is to the " Whitbury " of Kingsley. For example, sixteen years before the date of Kingsley's tale, which was published in 1857, " Whitbury boasted of forty coaches per diem, instead of one railway." Kingsley, of course, died long before Lambourn had any kind of railway, and Newbury, situate on one of the ancient high-roads to the West of England that have played so important a part in history, doubtless boasted many coaches when Lambourn, in a byway, was lucky if it had more than one. But, after all, it is more than likely that Kingsley had both places in his mind and was guiltless of intention to limn one or the other of them with the particularity of a Memling portrait ; and such endowments of one place with the choicest qualities of two or more are not unusual in literature. Hence comes it, for example, that more than one of the little communities of England claims to have sat without knowing it for Mrs. Gaskell when she painted that inimitable portrait of a place and its people, *Cranford*, and that to the making of that strangely clever book of recent date, *The Nebuly Coat*, more than one old minster town has contributed.

So it is certainly no unwarrantable assumption to treat Lambourn as " Whitbury," especially seeing that Mark Armsworth, " banker, solicitor, land-agent, Justice of the Peace, guardian of the poor—in a word, Viceroy of Whitbury town," and gentle Edward Thurnall too, would far more conceivably have attained their commanding positions in the little society of Lambourn than among the larger population of Newbury.

The Guildhall, Newbury.

nursing old Dr. Thurnall, and awaiting the return of the wandering Tom, tamed by the world, fail to appeal more forcibly than the thought of Ealdswith? If it comes to that, who, without reading on a little, can say with certainty who Ealdswith was, or whether the name denotes man or woman?

Of a truth this Lambourn is a venerable place, a market town from time immemorial, according to Lysons, the right of fairs at which was granted to St. Paul's by Henry VI. It is one of the numerous places—Lyford is another of them, and so is Didcot—which have given rise to Berkshire surnames, and in Berkshire will be found many a William or a Robert Lambourn, or Lambourne, whose forefathers doubtless came from this happy valley. It is in connection with Ealdswith that we hear of Lambourn first, and Ealdswith, it may now be mentioned, was the widow whom King Alfred left behind him at the end of his priceless life. To her he granted a manor lying in the vicinity at any rate of the field of one of his first great victories against the heathen Danes, and this manor afterwards passed to the Fitzwarrens of Wantage fame, and eventually to the Cravens, of whom the time has not yet come to speak. But some of the other manors are really more interesting. That of Bockhampton was held in grand serjeanty by the De Bathes, the service assigned being the maintenance of a pack of hariers for the King's Hunt; hariers, be it noted, not foxhounds, for the fox was vermin in those days, and the hare was hunted for food, as well as for sport, the theory being that the flavour of a hunted hare was better than that of one killed in any other fashion. Did the De Bathes, of whom we hear first in connection with Strongbow's Irish campaign of the twelfth century, figure among the long series of benefactors to the noble church? That may not be averred with certainty; but there, on a brass, and above the arches in the church, or some of them, are to be seen the figures of hounds which pursue the same hares, year after year, and never decrease the intervals between themselves and their quarry; or it may be

since Lambourn was always celebrated for its coursing,
for stout hares and plenty of them, and for the illimitable
Downs on which to see the sport to advantage, that these
effigies represent the triumphs of some " Master McGrath " or
" Fullerton " of the Middle Ages. Another manor at Lambourn was held by the Blounts upon a tenure so shocking and
unusual that it will hardly serve even to follow good Gilbert
White's plan, when he had anything indelicate that needed to
be said, and to translate it into Greek. Suffice it to say that
it throws something like a searchlight on to the morality of our
early kings, and shows them as Solomons on a petty scale in
vice, if not in wisdom. The curious will find this tenure in
Lysons, who veils it in Latin. Girls, however, learn Latin in
these days. So in Lysons let the secret of the manor of
Lambourn lie hidden from those who do not wish to go out of
their way to disinter it.

" Pleasant old town, which slopes down the hillside to the
old church—just ' restored,' though, by Lords Minchampstead
and Vieuxbois, not without Mark Armsworth's help, to its
ancient beauty of gray flint and white clunch chequer-work,
and quaint wooden spire. Pleasant churchyard round it,
where the dead lie looking up to the bright southern sun,
among huge black yews, upon their knoll of white chalk above
the ancient stream." Let us hope that, in this particular
connection, Kingsley had not Lambourn Church in his mind,
although it is to be feared that he had. He wrote at a date
between two restorations, one in 1850, the second in 1861,
and, even from the most lenient and considerate point of view,
it is idle to argue that both these restorations were effected in good
taste. Surely it cannot have been necessary to substitute a
spiral iron stair for the ancient staircase leading to the parvise
above the south porch; and, if a curious and elevated piscina
on the side of the chancel arch could not be restored in something more worthy than plaster, it might have been omitted
altogether. But when all is said and done, and when indigna-

Lambourn Church.

F. L. GRIGGS - 1906

tion has been poured out in full measure over these individual outrages, the fact remains that the whole effect of the church, an exceptionally spacious building of the cruciform type, is dignified and imposing ; and inside are many interesting points, the quaintest of them, perhaps, being the medallion showing Charles I. being crowned by Religion and Justice, while two Puritans are seen fettered at his feet. Lambourn, indeed, hard by Newbury, and boasting that it was visited by Charles after his defeat by Manchester at Newbury in 1644, is just the place to preserve Stuart memories and relics of the Stuarts. The Estbury Almshouses, near the traditional site of one of Alfred's palaces, have been rebuilt to the comfort of their inmates, be it hoped, if not in a manner to please the eye. John Estbury's tomb, however, is still the meeting-place of the almsmen for prayer every day. In fact, take it for all in all, Lambourn is a place where the duly venerated past and the prosperous present meet in the most amiable and manifest fashion. The prosperity of the past was that appertaining to a trading town, and the chapmen's cross—the place was once called Chipping Lambourn—remains to this day ; nay, it has even a new top to it. The prosperity of the present is due to racehorses, and Lambourn may claim to be the chief of the training centres of the Berkshire Downs.

There is no reason in life against a night's sojourn in Lambourn, where there is an inn, and much reason for such a sojourn, since the Down scenery is at its best in the mornings and in the evenings. Be the decision on this point as it may, it will be well to execute the retreat from Lambourn in a northerly direction, with a slight tendency towards the setting sun, for thus the most western edge of this part of the county will be skimmed as far as Shrivenham. Metalled though the road be, it runs, for the most part, between such precipices of solitary downland as cannot be surpassed. No Northern or Western mountain pass is more lonely ; not in New Zealand itself is the name of the rabbits more absolutely

S

to be called legion. Before long upon the left appears a dark woodland, and soon the turf besides the road is sprinkled with "grey wethers," Sarsen stones in fact, of which the source has been explained already. The name fits the cluster well enough, and once they were many more in number, for the curious and commanding house known as Ashdown Park, now plainly in sight, was built out of them, and the grey wethers that survive are but the last relics of a mighty flock. The original gathering, by comparison with that which remains, must have been as a muster of 10,000 merino sheep, once witnessed by me on an Australian station, appeared by the side of memories of our more modest English flocks.

The house was built by Webb, and Webb was the favourite pupil of Inigo Jones, the inheritor of his designs; but it is so strange a house, consisting of two huge blocks of building with something approaching to a tower in the middle, as to lead to the conclusion that Webb did not have entirely his own way in the planning of it, and to give colour to the romantic, if mythical, story of the coming of the Cravens into Berkshire. Let me first endeavour to state the legendary story clearly. In the year 1665, the year in which the Duke of York introduced the naval tactics of fighting in line of battle with great success against the Dutch, London suffered from one of its very first visitations of the plague. Thereupon Sir William Craven, being Lord Mayor of London, took horse and rode away for his life in search of solitude and pure air. All the way to Reading he rode and thence, taking the southernmost of the two forks of the great high-road to the West, hied him on to Newbury. But Newbury was even then a prosperous community, and like enough there was plague there also, and so Sir William pressed on up the valley of the Lambourne, and through Lambourn town to the solitude of the Downs, and there he settled, at a spot whereof the loneliness is striking to this day; and there he built him a house with avenues leading north and south and east and west, and having rooms so planned that every one of them has windows on each side. The main objection to this story is that it is recent enough in point of date to be capable of absolute disproof; and it is vain to kick against the pricks of hard and sharp facts when they are almost modern. Still, the house and its position are alike strange, and, by virtue of their peculiarity, they leave a more clearly cut impression upon the memory than many other structures more historic and more taking to the imagination.

The road from Ashdown Park, or past it, to Ashbury, a village having more than one house worthy of passing and appreciative notice, runs at first through a deep ravine of the Downs, and then climbs to a height of nearly 700 feet as it crosses the Ridgeway at right angles. Having reached Ashbury, which probably owes its situation to the springs bursting out of the chalk at that point, as Childrey does also, most likely, and having observed, amongst other things, a moated house, turn to the right and follow the Roman Way, leaving Compton Beauchamp on the left, until the turning for Woolstone is reached. Here, in the summer of 1904, I saw not only the curious chalk-built church and leaden font spoken of in the guide-books, but also, in the course of a providentially vague attempt to find the field path to Compton Beauchamp, the most delightful of moated farmhouses, the moat still full of gleaming water, the space between it and the house a mass of gay flowers. What, it may be asked, is the explanation of such an abundance of moats in this corner of Berkshire? There is one at Ashbury, another at Compton Beauchamp (not marked in the 1-inch Ordnance map, though the others are, so there may be more), a third at Woolstone; and from Ashbury to Woolstone moat is exactly two miles as the crow might fly if he chose. The explanation is to be found, in part doubtless, in the springs, for they made moats easily available in these situations to those of old time. Perhaps the further explanation is that, without going into historical detail this time, it is pretty plain in a general way that this most tranquil and peaceful of districts in modern times, was doomed by its position to provide battle-fields for successive generations. Before made roads were it was near to the Ridgeway, then the natural highway between East and West. The Romans made their road straight through it. Saxon and Dane met in deadly combat, in the vicinity at any rate, time after time. King's men and Parliament's soldiers marched and countermarched across it a score of times. In fact the country must always have been full of the traditions of warfare, and it may well be that to these traditions we owe memorials of more stirring times, memorials all the more striking and alluring in that they now stand in absolute contrast to their placid environment. Prolong the little detour a mile or two, and you will find yourself at Uffington. It is the place above all others that English boys long to visit ; for it was at Uffington that " Squire Brown, J.P. for the County of Berks . . . dealt out justice and mercy in a rough kind of way, and begat sons and daughters, and hunted the fox, and grumbled at the badness of the roads and the times," as many a Berkshire squire does now. Here, too, Tom Brown heard, as one may hear still, " the legend of St. George and his fight," all " in true sing-song vernacular," fought the village boys, watched the barges on the old canal (that, alas ! is no longer possible), had his tussles with Charity Lamb, his rambles with old Benjy, his birds-nestings, his wrestlings with sturdy Job Rudkin and supple Harry Winburn. There still is the "old church . . . with its grey walls and lancet windows," happily unrestored, one of the most interesting in all the Vale. In a word, the wanderer can fill up every corner with personalities, as real as if they were flesh and blood, out of incomparably the best book about boyhood that ever was written by grown man. These words are written quite deliberately. There is no book in the world like *Tom Brown* ; and there will never be another like to it, until a man shall arise again amongst us who shall retain through life the irrepressible boyish spirits and the pure boy's heart that sustained Judge Hughes to the end of his long and often sorely-tried life.

Shall the wanderer lie to-night at Wantage or at Shrivenham ? He may make his own choice, provided he does not miss Shrivenham, rather a long way from Wantage, but more or less accessible by rail, or Sparsholt and Childrey, three and two miles from Wantage respectively and close together, before he leaves this part of the county. If there be a need to miss any of these let Shrivenham be omitted ; unless, indeed, there be private and special facilities for seeing Beckett House, itself modern, but possessed of Reynolds and Lawrence portraits. The church, however, is of real interest, both in itself and for the many monuments of the Barrington family, one of whom, an eighteenth-century Admiral, is honoured in an epitaph, too dull for quotation, from the pen of Hannah Moore.

For convenience' sake be it assumed that Sparsholt and Childrey are visited from Wantage ; and the prudent man will go to Sparsholt first, partly because it is the further away, but also because, once at Childrey, he will find it very difficult to leave it by daylight. Sparsholt Church has a shingle spire—I imagined it to be unique in the county, until I found one at Old Didcot—and statues of oak within, two ladies and a knight, to be matched, in point of material, only at Burghfield, a village half-way between Strathfield Mortimer and Reading. But Sparsholt is far better worthy of a visit than Burghfield, whither we do not go, for Burghfield Church is new, whereas Sparsholt is a good example of the Decorated style, not spoiled by restoration. That it has lost nothing cannot be said, for it once had a north transept, and that is gone. At least, however, nothing has been added to it ; and that, to put the matter in the Irish way, is really a great thing gained in these days.

From Sparsholt to Childrey there are two roads, but the better effect is produced on the mind by taking the upper route along the Roman Way, although it is something the

Sparsholt Church

WORKING MEN'S COLLEGE
LIBRARY.

longer of the two. Thus you shall approach most advantage-
ously one of the most typical of the villages wherein the Downs
and the Vale have each their share. On the right will be the
wide and rolling expanse of Childrey Field, part grass, part
plough-land, having many an abrupt depression and correspond-
ing hill, but a general level of some 500 feet above the sea.
Open freedom is the characteristic of the scenery. Turn down
to the left by the first road that opens itself, and, within half
a mile, you have descended a hundred feet into a village of
immemorial antiquity. When Childrey first came into existence
the most learned man may not tell with confidence; why
the houses grew in a cluster at this spot is obvious to the
meanest capacity. It was because the surrounding land is of
an extraordinary fertility—indeed the " blacklands " of Childrey
can hardly be matched in England—and because, where
Childrey now stands, the first settlers found the prime necessity
of human life, pure water, springing up in a perennial stream
at the meeting-place of the green sand and the chalk. There
are, of course, those who attribute all these villages to the
military needs of days gone by; but the water and the rich
soil are the more rational explanation of the sites chosen.

How much or how little shall be told of the history of this
venerable parish ? The practical answer to the question is not
a little perplexing to give. First and foremost, it was the
principal seat (deserted for Swinbrook later) of the Fettiplaces,
that great family whom the student of the antiquities of
Berkshire and of Oxfordshire meets at every turn. They have
been encountered already at Besselsleigh, but their property
was enormous and scattered far and wide. They did their
best to falsify old Fuller's saying that " the lands of Berkshire
are skittish and apt to cast their owners," for they endured in
the land from 1263 (no doubt they were there before) to 1805,
a long run for a single family. Theirs was not, it has been
hinted before, a very glorious story. The fifteenth-century
Sir Thomas probably married the illegitimate daughter of the

King of Portugal ; certainly she and Sir Thomas were buried in the church of East Shefford, and she quartered the arms of Portugal. But, on the whole, the Fettiplaces—there are a dozen ways of spelling the name—seem to have grown rich in comfortable obscurity. If they had not been obscure they would probably not have been so rich. There is no record that any one of them was beheaded during all the five centuries and more for which they held their estates ; and there are certainly few of 'the best families" of long standing of whom that could be written. Participation in the wars of the Rebellion they could not avoid, but it is not quite easy to understand the part that they took. Mr. Falkner tells us that Charles I. stayed at Childrey, as the guest of Sir Edmund Fettiplace's widow, on his way from Oxford to Banbury in April, 1644, and that Sir John Fettiplace paid a fine of £1,943 for delinquency during the Commonwealth, but was raised to the baronetcy by Charles II. On the other hand, Clarendon's account of the capture of Cirencester by Prince Rupert leaves a clear impression that a Fettyplace was taken among the Roundhead prisoners. Rupert, we are told, " enter'd their line with some loss of men, and many hurt, but with a far greater of the Enemy ; for there were not so few as two hundred killed upon the place, and above one thousand taken Prisoners, whereof *Warneford* and *Fettyplace* (two Gentlemen of good Quality and Fortune near that Town and very active in the Service), Mr. George, a Member of Parliament who served for that Burrough, and two or three *Scotish* officers of the Field, whereof Carr the Governour was one, were the chief." Possibly this " Gentleman of good Quality " may have elected there and then to throw in his lot with the King, thus becoming obnoxious to the Parliament ; but, on the whole, it is difficult to find a family of equal wealth and permanence in the land so little known to national as opposed to provincial history : and that, perhaps, accounts for the permanence of the Fettiplace family in the land. They eschewed fashion and avoided the block.

It is in its ecclesiastical history, enshrined in a noble church, exceptionally rich in details of interest, in monuments, and in brasses (the last some of the finest in England) that Childrey rivets the attention most closely. Here once were three manors; and of one of them, Maltravers, the house still remains. The mighty tithe-barn, still standing, bears silent testimony to the heavy tithes paid by these manors; and the church property was not confiscated at the Reformation, so the rectory was always one of importance. So heavy were the tithes, indeed, that time came when each of the manors gave up a portion of land to the benefice in lieu of tithe, with the result that the rector of Childrey from time to time is the largest landowner in the parish. He must have been hard pressed during the period of acute depression. Hence comes it that the rectors of Childrey have been men of importance, usually Senior Fellows of Corpus Christi College, Oxford, in the gift of which the living has been for centuries, and that the rectory is spacious and choiceworthy. One of these early rectors was Dr. Pocock, the first Laudian Professor of Arabic, and his memory is kept green by a noble cedar on the rectory lawn, raised by him out of a cone brought from the Lebanon. It is believed that the sapling was planted by Dr. Pocock in 1646. 1646! It is the kind of date that makes a modern reader shiver in surprise. It was the year when the despairing Charles left Oxford secretly to enter into treaty with the Scots, who made him a virtual prisoner, and finally, after their traditional custom, practically betrayed him for money, as David Hume, himself a Scotsman, must needs admit. The history of the preceding years, writ somewhat larger of necessity in another place, seems, when we read it, to have been a story of fighting and of nothing else, in which Berkshire had its full share. Adjacent Oxford had played, was indeed then playing, the part of capital for the King. Yet in the middle of it all the Professor of Arabic could go his ways in tranquillity, could procure, perhaps in person, from the

Lebanon a cone of one of the secular cedars ; could plant it so well and truly in the garden of his rectory and within fifteen or sixteen miles of Newbury itself that it flourishes to this day, having suffered nothing worse than the customary fate of cedars, that is to say, the occasional loss of limbs from the intolerable weight of snow upon the horizontal branches. This incident, and many others of a similar character, tend to excite a wonder whether England in the time of the Civil War was, as one might naturally imagine, harassed day and night, year in and year out, by the fear of violence and spoliation. Evidence is not wanting to show that the stolid Englishmen fought, because they had no choice in the matter, and fought well, since that is their nature, but that, so far as might be possible, they lived their ordinary lives also. Certainly there could be no more startling contrast than that between Charles, on his secret and ill-fated flight to Newark, and the Laudian Professor of Arabic sowing his cedar in the garden of Childrey rectory. The same rectory and its garden are the very soul of quietude, and a very ancient dovecot near " the old manor " breathes the essence of rest.

For many of the facts underlying the foregoing passages concerning Childrey a debt of gratitude is due to that sound naturalist and eloquent writer, the late Mr. Charles J. Cornish, whose father retired in 1904 from the rectory of Childrey. He added, kindly and characteristically, that the neighbourhood is a great haunt of carrion crows, of long-eared owls, and of hawks, and that the great plover breeds there. This leads me to say, since it may be said at this point as suitably as at any other, that so far as I have been able to judge, as a tolerably observant resident, with a bent for natural history of an unscientific type, there is nothing very remarkable about the ornithology of Northern Berkshire. It is not the kind of country wherein rare visitors would have a chance of surviving. There are no spacious and unconquerable marshes ; there are not many very extensive woods ; and on the Downs there is a great lack of

shelter. Kingfishers and the small birds of the waterside
are abundant along the Thames ; there was surely never such
a country for owls ; partridges, both English and French, thrive
amazingly ; but the only bird visitor that strikes a new-comer as
rare is the hoodie crow, who is usually seen in the vicinity of
the Downs, and sometimes in the Vale, in winter. A hoodie
crow was shot at Drayton a year or two ago. The fact is worthy
of mention because Mr. Seebohm writes, " Although it is a
permanent resident in Scotland, great numbers of the Scandi-
navian birds migrate to Holland, Belgium and Northern
France, and even to England, in the winter." Our only wild
beast of interest, so far as I know, is the fox ; and he receives a
full share of attention. The offer, too, is sought for now
and again in the Ock. Of botany I forbear to speak much,
for the best, or the worst, of reasons. Mr. Charles Druce has
enumerated "plants native to the county, 893 ; plants which
are denizens only, 45, and colonists, 56, making a grand total of
994 species." But Mr. Druce is a very learned man, who can
actually boast that a beautiful pondwed, bearing a hideous
name of its own, *Potamogeton Drucei*, takes its style and title
from him. He found it in the Loddon, and he has discovered
a good many other rarities of the kind that interest botanists.
Enough for us to specify some of the flowers that can be gathered
and enjoyed, and are not absolutely common everywhere,
or almost everywhere. First among them for beauty, not of
course for rarity, comes Solomon's seal, sometimes called Jacob's
ladder. Gentians are to be found on Down-land near Churn
certainly, and perhaps elsewhere. A peculiarly lovely forget-
me-not is to be seen near Hungerford, and orchids are abundant,
the fly orchis and the bee orchis being the most attractive. Bagley
Wood boasts the ivy-leaved campanula ; and the blue cranesbill
seems to me more frequent than in some counties. The chief
glory of our Northern Berkshire, however, is the snake's-head
or fritillary ; it grows freely in the Thames-side meadows, less
plentifully along the Kennet, and, besides being, as Mr. William

Robinson, the father of modern gardening in England, says, "an elegant native species . . . bearing a solitary drooping flower, beautifully tessellated with purple or purplish maroon on a pale ground," it takes kindly to the semi-domesticated grass of a lawn that is left a little long in spring for the sake of the bulbs mixed with the grass. Not so does the gentian, which I too have found, before the name of Mr. Druce as botanist was known to me, in the neighbourhood of Churn, and transferred, with a great sod of Down turf, to more confined quarters. The sod grew; the gentian it was that died; it was a warning, perhaps, against the wicked practice of spoiling the face of Nature. The name of the water-plants is legion, and some of them are rare, while others, without rarity, are graceful in the extreme. This is especially true of the reeds, flags, irides, docks, plantains, and bullrushes of the River Thames, but they are not peculiar to Berkshire, and if I, in my ignorance, were asked to name the chief floral glories of Berkshire, other than those to be found in many another county, the snowflake and the fritillary would be chosen for honour without hesitation. The former, as noted elsewhere, has its home near Shillingford, or rather, to follow Miss Austen, "one of its homes, for it has several." It will grow, men say, in a garden, but it is best in its true home by the waterside. So, in a minor degree, is the fritillary, but to transplant it is not so flagrant an outrage as the deportation of the snowflake, for the damp meadows are in large measure the work of man's hand, but the beds of flags wherein the snowflake rears its graceful head, like that of a giant snowdrop, are pieces of nature unspoiled. "To-morrow to fresh woods and pastures new"; but, before starting, hear the boast that nowhere in England shall you find such wealth of cowslips or of fragrant violets, white and purple, as in Northern Berks in the season of the year.

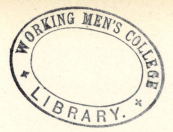
WORKING MEN'S COLLEGE LIBRARY.

CHAPTER X

BY THAMES' SIDE

ONE way of reaching Windsor from Northern Berkshire is by
river, and that route is described in this chapter from experience,
and for the sake of literary convenience. It has been pointed
out already that Berkshire's share in the glorious heritage of

the Thames is greater than that of any other county, and something of an effort has been made to indicate some of the natural beauties and equally attractive associations of those modest reaches above Oxford that are even now little known to the public. Still, there are left the noble and more familiar waters below; so let us take a voyage, not of discovery, but rather of renewal of pleasant memories, down the kindly stream of Father Thames, from Folly Bridge at Oxford to Windsor or thereabouts, keeping our mental eyes so far as may be possible upon the right or Berkshire bank, lest, by treating of places seen on the Oxfordshire side first and on the Bucks bank later, and of the thoughts stirred by them, the heinous offence of poaching on somebody else's manor should be committed. For such poaching there is no need; for the Berkshire bank abounds in scenes and places worthy of many more eloquent words than I can compass.

Travel by river is practically unavoidable, unless much that is interesting is to be omitted, for, except at rare intervals, as, for example, from Wallingford to Pangbourne, the roads do not follow the winding course of the river, and the tendency of them is to convey the wayfarer across from one county and its interior to the heart of the adjacent shire. Moreover, the river itself has a grand, a tranquil, and an ever-varying loveliness of its own, and this must on no account be missed. The only question is what method of travel to employ, and choice must depend partly on the time that is available. You may go by steamer, private or public; you may pass down stream easily in an ordinary pleasure boat, to be hired, by the way, at quite moderate rates at Oxford; or, if time be of no moment at all, and you can handle sails even in a moderately seaman-like manner, you may proceed at leisure in a roomy centreboard sailing-boat. *Experto credite*, all the methods are productive of no common measure of healthy delight; yet each has its individual drawbacks, and they have one disadvantage in common. In the public steamer your company, or some of it, chooses itself for you, and it cannot always be relied upon to be ideal.   Providence is not always to be trusted in matters of this kind ; and the public steamer goes too fast.   The private launch, even though you be the nominal master of its speed, does likewise ; it seems dull to travel at half-speed in a fast boat.   The row-boat, be it propelled by oars or sculls, costs some trouble and exertion, and, personally, I have always been of the opinion of the monk in *Hypatia*, who confided to Cyril (for whom he had been playing the part of a spy in the disguise of a galley-slave) that " of rowing, as of other carnal pleasures, cometh satiety at the last." Nay, more, in my judgment and experience, the interval between the first stage of eagerness to row and that of satiety of the thwart and the oar-handle is very brief in point of time.   To sailing the main objection is that, in spite of the gentle favour of the stream, it may consume an indefinitely long period of time, and that tiller and main-sheet, to say nothing of the jib-sheets, if you consent to the extra trouble that they involve for the sake of the aid a jib will give on occasion, call for some attention.   That, however, in time becomes instinctive or sub-conscious.   To resist the constant tendency of all good centre-boards to " gripe," that is to say, to point closer to the wind's eye than is necessary, to slacken sheet or haul it in as occasion requires, become almost reflex actions, and, while the breeze is gentle, one can go on handling the boat without conscious thought and, at the same time, drinking in the beauty of the scene, noticing the whitening of the willows and the shivering of the aspen—the Welsh call its foliage " leaves of girls' tongues "—the arrowy flight of the many-hued and frequent kingfishers, the graceful outline of an old-time bridge, or, in fact, any of the thousand and one beauties of life on our river.   All methods have this disadvantage in common ; they are so inter-esting and amusing in themselves that rarely indeed does the traveller by river halt to examine the things by the way that would certainly repay examination.   In the public steamer, of

rising in a glorious acclivity from its left bank. It is a noble spectacle, apart from the house, or houses, and it can be enjoyed best from the river, or from the Berkshire bank. Of the interesting story of Nuneham, of the removal of the original village from the spot where the mansion now stands, of its many successive churches, each uglier than the last, of the grand expanse of the park, of visits to the cottage by the waterside and the adjacent woodland during Commemoration week at Oxford, this is, more's the pity, not the time to treat. But a Berkshire man, even one of but short standing, with a grievance, is not to be muzzled, particularly when that grievance is public as well as personal. Let us suppose that, being located at Radley, a man desires to visit March Baldon, or Nuneham Courtenay, both of them distant a short mile across the river on the Oxfordshire side. Radley is over against the northern boundary of the park, and there are traces looking very like an old ferry there. Nor is it to be doubted that, when the village of Nuneham Courtenay stood on the slope by the river, and the mansion was not, a ferry existed, and the old path to it on the Oxfordshire side is obvious. You may cross the river, but that path must not be used, and it is the actual fact that, to reach March Baldon, you must needs go up river, by road or water, as far as Sandford, a mile or more, and then, crossing at the lock, make your way a full mile and a half southward along the London road. This if you be on foot, or riding a cycle ; the carriage must go round by Oxford or by Abingdon. Again, if you be at Abingdon, you must strike southward to Culham, and then upward, either through the park (an occasional privilege accorded but recently), or by way of Clifton Hampden, for an absolute right of way, before reaching March Baldon and Nuneham Courtenay. Both are interesting places that Berkshire folks would like to see, and their isolation, so far as Berkshire is concerned, is remarkable. I know nothing so complete of its kind in any reasonably populated part of England. Moreover, you shall note that at the end of the park over against Radley is one pier of an abortive bridge, and that on the Berks side is a raised causeway. This means that, before the succession of the late Sir William Harcourt's predecessor, a bridge was contemplated and begun. But Mr. Aubrey Harcourt would have none of it, and he left the pier standing as a reminder of his predecessor's intended bounty. Sir William Harcourt, it is said, would probably have continued the scheme, which would be of undoubted value, if he had lived, and both counties look hopefully to Mr. Lewis Harcourt in the matter. Since these words were written I have ascertained that both ferry and right of way undoubtedly existed.

The view down-stream in Nuneham Reach is sadly marred by the Great Western Railway Bridge. This monstrosity, like that at Appleford, less than two miles off by road, but nearly six by river, suggests that the projectors of the Great Western Railway made up their minds to punish the perversity of Abingdon (it will be remembered that Abingdon petitioned against the railway) in an exemplary fashion. Abingdon forced the company out of their planned route into two needless crossings over the Thames. The company revenged themselves by erecting two structures, marvels of ugliness even for railway bridges, to spoil the scenery as much as possible. Passing under the first of them—its piers are athwart the stream, and awkward, and the mast of a sailing-boat can be jammed under its girders, which is no fun at all—we are soon at the point where the Old River leaves the new, not but that the new river is much more than a thousand years old, to form the Andersey Island, that, as related in another connection, was so grievous a trouble to the Abbey of Abingdon. Here, near an ancient lock, its origin something of an enigma, is a backwater fringed with bulrushes, carpeted with water-lilies; and its grassy banks, within earshot of the tinkling murmur of water falling into the Old River (our old friend, *murmur desilientis aquæ*) are sheltered by splendid hawthorns and abundant willow-trees, the willows

T 2

WORKING MEN'S COLLEGE LIBRARY

pollarded, of course, but still effectual for shade.   There is no
better place on Thames' side for luncheon or tea, if they are to be
taken picnic fashion ; and no man says you nay.   Proceeding we
find the scenery of a normal riverside character.   Lush meadows
fringe the stream on either side ; the banks are low so that the
eye ranges far ; there is here and there a poplar-studded
island ; and so the river goes mecranking on, mecranking very
much indeed, towards Abingdon Lock.   Hence it is narrow as far
as the Abingdon Bridge, already introduced ; and the bridge
does not strike the eye of one travelling down-stream so grate-
fully as it does that of one voyaging against the current.   Also
its antique arches are parlous narrow and low ; so that a rowing-
boat must be steered delicately, and the mast of a centreboard
must clearly be lowered.

Soon the stream grows wide ; the Abbey and St. Helen's
Church are seen on the right, not seen for the first time, but
from a new point of view, and the river opens into the most
magnificent sailing reach on the Thames ; only, thanks again to
the early obstinacy of the burghers of Abingdon, it is not easily
accessible by rail.   There is no special beauty after this, save
of gleaming water, until we reach the beautiful stretch of river
leading to Sutton Courtney ; but that is part of another story,
so we leave it unexplored to-day, and pass by Culham Cut to
Culham Lock.   Below that is a pretty stone bridge, spanning
the straitened stream by a narrow arch, and after it the navigation route lies directly ahead.   But those who have leisure will
be well advised to turn to the right, to that part of Sutton
Courtney backwater inaccessible when we were at Sutton last
without making a breach through a disused paper-mill.   So
turning they will pass up a lovely piece of lively and natural
river, spanned by a really fine arch of old grey stone, past
meadows and willows on the one side, and a thicket of aspen
and poplar and sombre alder on the other, into the lagoon, so
to speak, of a magnificent lasher, a great sheet of water,
tranquil on the one side, churned into creaming foam by half-a-

dozen miniature Niagaras on the other, a haunt of fishers, of king-fishers and swallows too, and of bathers, altogether a most delicious and remote recess. Yet this rose has its thorn, for here the Berkshire man has another grievance. A moment ago mention was made of the grey stone bridge ; and it is obviously of respectable antiquity. It will hardly be credited, but it is the fact, that, while Abingdon Bridge has been free since it was built in 1416, this little bridge, called indifferently Sutton or Culham Bridge, is permitted to levy grievous tolls. It is, as a glance at any map will show, on the direct route between Sutton Courtney and Abingdon, and the alternative route, through Drayton, is not only more than twice as long, but also enters Abingdon at the end where there are no shops. It is certainly not too much to say that the tolls are an anachronism, or that they are a serious obstacle to commercial communications. Indeed, a Berkshire County Councillor, who resides at Sutton Courtney and catches a train at Abingdon or Culham on six mornings of the week, has recently entered the Council on what the Americans would call the free bridge ticket ; and small wonder either, when the local innkeeper can honestly say that the bridge costs him a £1 a week. Other bridges there are, all of them anachronisms in the way of levying tolls, at Clifton Hampden and elsewhere, but none of them is quite so oppressive in a small way as this, which cuts the people of a whole village off from their market town. All are doubtless doomed ; all are intolerable obstacles to free communication ; but the Berkshire mind moves slowly, and threatened bridges live far too long.

No sooner are we back in the main river than Appleford Bridge, twin brother (not sister surely, for nothing feminine could be so hideous) to Nuneham Bridge, heaves into sight, a black and uncompromising blot upon the peaceful scenery ; and behind it looms the swelling mass of Sinodun Hills, with their earthworks and their coronals of trees, dominating the view. They will go on dominating it for miles and miles, for they are high ; and the river winds in a gigantic horseshoe, north, and then west and south, before it meanders round their feet ; and they remain in sight for many a mile afterwards. So it is well to grow accustomed to them, and even to feel affection for them if possible, although that is sometimes difficult when they seem to mock your anxiety to make progress towards the end of a long day.

On this occasion we are absolutely resolved not to be in a hurry, and after Appleford Bridge is passed (by the way, it is neither easy nor worth while to land at Appleford) it is possible, if there be a disposition in that direction, to have some fine sport on a summer evening with the chavender or chub. In this broad and deep reach, under the shade of the pollard willows standing in orderly rows upon the right bank, casting their parti-coloured roots into the water like threads of coral or rare sea-weeds, and by the edges of the reed-beds that sway gently to the current, lie many mighty chub. Nor is it necessary, as our master Walton prescribes, to stalk them secretly from behind a tree in order to drop a grasshopper directly above their noses, for you may fish for them, ay, and catch them too, with a pale and mothlike fly of a summer's evening, casting from a gently gliding boat in such a fashion as to drop the fly just short of the edge of the bank. So, if your tackle be fine enough to make a fish that is not really much of a fighter seem an adversary worthy of your split cane or green-heart, you shall have good sport ; for your chub is " one of the leather-mouthed sort, of which a hook does scarce ever lose its hold." Having caught your " chavender or chub," you may, if you please, " hie you to a pavender, a pavender or pub," as the jingle goes. You may hie indeed very pleasantly to the " Plough " at Long Wittenham, by turning away to the right after passing through Clifton Cut and Lock, or to the " Barley Mow " at Clifton Hampden ; in both of which is fair entertainment for man, and doubtless for beast also. In any case the exquisite backwater of Long Wittenham should not be missed.

But as to your chub, you will be fortunate if, either at " Plough "
or " Barley Mow," the cook can be induced to dress him
as *Piscator* directed his more complaisant hostess of the
seventeenth century to prepare him for table. Here is the
direction, however. " First scale him and then wash him
clean, and then take out his guts ; and to that end make the
hole as little and near to his gills as you may conveniently ;
and especially make clean his throat from the grass and weeds
that are usually in it, for if that be not very clean it will make
him to taste very sour : having so done, put some sweet
herbs into his belly, and then tie him with two or three
splinters to a spit, and roast him, basted often with vinegar, or
rather verjuice and butter, with good store of salt mixed with it.
Being thus dressed, you will find him a much better dish of
meat than you, or most folk, even than anglers themselves,
do imagine." Perhaps you would ; but the trouble is that
none will be at the pains thus to dress a chub, and so all agree
with " the French, who esteem him so mean as to call him
Un Villain." In fact the best thing to be done with the chub,
after he is caught, is to give him away to a passing stranger,
who knows not how disappointing a handsome fish may be
when submitted to the supreme arbitrament of the dinner
table. No matter what the fate of the chub or his eater may
be, or whether he has been angled for or brought to creel at all,
the visits to the " Plough " and the " Barley Mow " should be
paid, for the former is not spoiled at all " for the accommodation
of summer visitors," and there is old-fashioned comfort there,
and the latter is not damaged much. Also the " Barley Mow "
has, as a rule, good roses and " fragrant stocks " and a lawn,
where tea, or anything else, may be consumed in mighty ease
and comfort, always barring the wasps, beneath the shade of an
ample apple-tree. It is on the Berkshire bank and accessible
from Oxfordshire only by another toll-bridge, an anachronism
economically, architecturally pretty, in red brick.

Passing onwards one sees Clifton Hampden Church and the

only piece of stone cliff on the river, a cliff that would certainly not attract attention if it were not aright in that respect; and so the boat glides, past meadows in Berkshire, and the pleasure grounds of private houses in Oxfordshire, to Day's Lock, with Sinodun towering rounded and insistent overhead. Incidentally it may be mentioned that on the Berkshire side is some very excellent partridge ground, and that, hard by Day's Lock, are the mysterious earthworks on the Oxfordshire side, supposed to have been an outpost of the fortifications of Sinodun. They are not lovely, in any sense of the word, but they are a gigantic relic of old time. From these, Lord Avebury the observant is able to form some idea of the level of the river-bed in a period almost, if not quite, prehistoric.

At Day's Lock, distinctly pretty, tea and the like may be obtained and the county of Berks has an amusing grievance. It appears that, not long since, the county authorities attempted to rate the lock-house on the ground that its keeper made profits from the sale of refreshments : and the Conservancy resisted the effort on the ground that their property was not liable to rates. What, then, would happen, say the county authorities, if the Conservators erected an hotel on their ground at the lock ? The answer seems to be pretty plain. The joint committee of Magistrates and County Council would refuse to license the hotel, which would have to be content with the exiguous profits that, in an unregenerate age, are earned by temperance establishments by the side of the thirst-provoking river. Besides, the area available is very narrow, and county councils are always capable of giving no end of trouble by judicious application of bye-laws. So the county grievance is mentioned *pour rire* only.

Day's Lock past we are at the very foot of Sinodun, and the hill with the great hundred-acre wood at its foot—we have visited it as sportsmen elsewhere—will keep off any southerly breeze. In a little while, on the left bank, enter Thame unobtrusively, and Isis and Thame become Thames—for the pedant. For a

time there is no feature of special interest, although there is a
perennial charm, about the meandering river; but in due
course Shillingford Bridge, a beautiful structure of white and
shining stone, is seen crossing above the river in a graceful
arch, having that well-known and ancient hostelry the "Swan"
standing at the Berkshire end, though Shillingford itself is in
Oxfordshire. It is a "Swan" sadly changed, from the selfish
point of view, since five and twenty years ago, when sundry
light-hearted undergraduates stayed there, at the end of a
glorious summer term, to read, and to fish, and bathe, and row,
and, last but by no means least, to gather not the lotus but
that gigantic water snowdrop, the snowflake, during the
intervals of sunny repose in a punt on the backwater. Or was
it during another visit, in spring, that the snowflakes were
culled? Then all was primitive, but comfortable. The worthy
Mr. Reynolds, true Boniface of the ancient type, spiced the
conversation with shrewd and pungent sayings, verging sometimes
on rudeness, causing all but the victim to laugh so heartily
that the victim himself was caught by the infection. Mine
host's multitudinous sons and a daughter attended to every
want, and the old-time avocations of the riverside, now
banished as unfashionable, were pursued without shame. For
example, the natural grass sloped down to the river-brink, where
a made lawn now lies; and on the bank was an ancient barn,
by the side of which the osier strippers, with their simple
apparatus, peeled the well-steeped and pliant wands grown and
cut in the osier-beds hard by. Now all is changed. The
"Swan" has an "annex," or it may be two, of flimsy make, by
comparison with the honest substance of the original hostelry.
The osiers are no more seen, and the basket-makers vow that there
are no such osiers to be obtained in these days. Houseboats
and steam launches may be seen moored to the bank; Japanese
parasols, fine ladies and finer clothes, give colour to the lawn
and to the river. Mr. Reynolds, father of many sons, sleeps
with his fathers, and his son, or one of his sons, reigns in his

Oxfordshire village, sadly ravaged by fires in the summer of 1905 and owned to a large extent by Christ Church, Oxford, another old inn, the "Beetle and Wedge," has gone the way of many like it, and the fashion of to-day, with real French cookery, has taken it captive. Herein, possibly, something is gained by way of compensation for the things that were; but that something is of surety not the twanging tinkle of the banjo, nor the pitiless patter of the latest and silliest music-hall song; and after all, in those old times, no man ever dreamed of staying the night at the "Beetle and Wedge," but all were contented to push on to Streatley after, it might be, a crust of bread and cheese and a draught of honest ale, or a dish of tea, according to the hour of the day and the disposition of the man who voyaged.

Streatley is still one of the most delightful places on Thames side, for it began to adapt itself to the imperious call for luxury made by the haunters of the river a good many years ago, so that it is accustomed to the business; and nothing could spoil the beauty of the white bridges, or of the network of foaming waters, crashing and roaring as it spreads itself out before the inn. Moreover, Streatley is not so painfully easy of access from London as are most of the places short of Reading; and Goring, across the river, absorbs a good many visitors. The village, too, which we have met before as the Berkshire starting-point of the Icknield or Ickleton Way, is not only beautifully situated beneath the shelter of the Downs, but also possessed still of quite a number of picturesque cottages. On the sheer slope of the hill are junipers, the only ones known to me in these parts, not but that there may not be more of them elsewhere and unknown; but they do not approach in point of size those on the Surrey Hills near the house and home that Miss Jekyll has rendered famous in literature. From Streatley downwards, except for an unlovely part near Reading, the river is, to use a feminine expression without shame, since it is precisely appropriate, sweetly pretty. We are now among

Place House, Streatley.

some of the reaches whereof the praises have been sung by writers without number. First comes Basildon, with its church hard by the river—the tower is of red brick—its great house rich in pictures, upon which it were wrong for him who has not seen them to dilate, and its memories of Jethro Tull, who is worthy of a pause. It would probably be quite safe to risk a modest wager that the name of the said Jethro is absolutely unknown to modern fame. The *Encyclopædia Britannica*, tripping airily from " Tulip " to " Tulle," affords no clue to the greatness of Tull except through the index. Nor, when one has read all that it prints concerning him under the title " Agriculture," does that severely practical work bring one face to face with the most attractive fact in the career of this for-gotten benefactor of our race. This is written in sober earnest. Tull was a really great man, as shall be shown shortly.

Jethro Tull, born at Basildon and buried there, may justly be described as the father of British agriculture, in the same way as, to use a modern parallel in the place of those that are too familiar, Gottfried Daimler was the undoubted parent of the petrol motor-car. " The first considerable improvement in the practice of that time was introduced by Jethro Tull, a gentle-man of Berkshire, who began to drill wheat and other crops about the year 1701, and whose *Horse-hoeing Husbandry*, published in 1731, exhibits the first decided step in advance upon the principles and practices of his predecessors." Later, after saying a good deal of " the extraordinary pains this ingenious person gave to his mode of culture," the writer of the article " Agriculture " tells us that Tull was vehemently opposed by his contemporaries, that " he occasionally showed an asperity in controversy which excites our regret," but that the soundness of his views and practice, in the matter of turnip-hoeing at any rate, only came to be acknowledged and generally adopted " some twenty-five years ago "—that is to say, about 1850. The grave work, excusably no doubt, since the article on " Agriculture " is nearly as long as this modest volume, omits all that human and, in its way, pathetic side of the story which aids the memory by quickening interest.

Jethro Tull was no ordinary gentleman farmer; rather was he among the first of highly cultivated men whose attention was turned by destiny, or providence if you will, to principles of agriculture. Born at Basildon in 1674, he went to Oxford, to St. John's College, to be precise, early, as was the fashion of his day; and, when the year 1699 found him twenty-five years of age, he had not only eaten his dinners at Gray's Inn, but also was a full-fledged stuff-gownsman. Nor need we doubt that he had mixed in the society of London during that stirring time of plots and counterplots, of innumerable foreign complications, and of brilliant wit also. In the early part of 1699 the world was open to him. He was newly married; he was called to the Bar; and (it is strange that this should be material) he was an accomplished musician who had mastered the mechanism of the organ. Suddenly, probably through the death of his father, Jethro Tull found himself transplanted to the paternal acres at Shalbourne in Berkshire, from the bustle of the town to the bucolic peace of that which is still one of the most slow-moving counties in England. Evidently the move was made unwillingly. "As to agriculture, it was not by choice, but by a sort of necessity, that I practised it"; but being transplanted, Tull was by no means content to vegetate. The intelligence that might have been expended on fines and recoveries, contingent remainders or pleas of the Crown, was applied to the land and its capabilities; and Tull's beloved organ suggested to him the idea of the mechanical drill. It may be that others had used drills of sorts before; but it is certain that Tull invented one of his own, less than two years after he began to deal with the rich land of Berks in the place of the dry dust of Gray's Inn; and the district of Berks that first knew the drill came in time to be called Prosperous Farm. There also he saw the advantage of frequent pulverisation of the soil, and, seeing it, acted upon what he saw. His mind, quickened by Oxford and London, was not content with the time-honoured customs of the country ; he was the last man in England to bury his talent in a napkin ; and, becoming a farmer perforce, he applied his intelligence to the mysterious problems of vegetable growth, its causes, and the most favourable conditions for its promotion. These problems had never obtained adequate attention before. It is easy to picture the scornful pity that the gentleman farmer from London excited amongst his contemporaries in an industry still, and in spite of many severe lessons, sadly slow to advance ; and it is the simplest thing in the world to sympathise with the "asperity in controversy" regretted by a cold-blooded nine-teenth-century annalist. In truth the crass stupidity of his neighbours must have been simply maddening to Jethro Tull, and he was more than human if he did not speak more harshly than he wrote. He was right in the main ; he was honestly convinced that he was right in all his views ; he was preaching to a deaf and stupid generation ; he could not console himself with the knowledge that his principles would be accepted when he had been lying in his grave at Basildon for more than a hundred years. By one man was he appre-ciated, perhaps by more ; but we know of one only during his lifetime. George Bellas, Rector of Basildon, added to the register of the innovator's death the words : "*Mem.* This Jethro Tull, Esq., was the author of a valuable book on agriculture, entitled *Horse Husbandry.*"

To the invention of the drill, like many an employer of labour before him, Jethro Tull of Prosperous Farm was driven by the discontent of the working classes. "Plough servants began to exalt their dominion above their masters, and a gentleman farmer could make little profit of arable land." So he resolved to plant the whole of his farm with sainfoin, and "contrived an engine to plant sainfoin more faithfully than hands could do it." This in 1701 ; in 1699 he was at Gray's Inn, remember, and in 1702 the labourers struck against his inovation and were dismissed *en masse*. It is the familiar story of many improvements in machinery. Workmen harass employers until employers are driven to thought ; employers find a machine that will dispense with workmen, or some of them ; workmen are left out of place, and, although increased production provides in the long run more employment for humanity at large, the offenders are more than likely not to secure any of it. The laws of economy do not concern themselves with the fates of individuals. They work on the grand scale. Similar was the origin of the planing machine, which arose out of a strike ; and of the apparatus known as " Billy Fairplay," invented by the late John Nixon, who, by the way, was the first man to realise fully the potentialities of the smokeless coal of South Wales. Mr. Nixon invented this apparatus for separating the large coal, for which miners are paid, from the small, then worthless, because on going up to his pit one day he found the " cropper " (the mere man whose business it was to guess the quantities of small and large coal) up to his waist in the canal, and the coal-hewers engaged in pelting him at their pleasure. In a word, discontent, with or without a strike, spurs invention ; the world gains ; the offenders suffer ; and, in a rude way, justice is done to all concerned.

Jethro Tull, a pathetic figure of bright intelligence, wasted, as it seemed, on a stupid generation, has beguiled us into something approaching to social philosophy ; from the peaceful churchyard of Basildon to the pit-mouth of Deep Duffryn. But the digression has been quite natural ; and it was made because the path seemed promising. More famous men than Tull, or the memories of such, we shall meet down stream, but surely none whose life's work has been more enduring for good.

Returning to the deserted Thames, we are at one of its very finest reaches ; for soon the woods on the Oxfordshire side— passing glorious were they in the autumn of 1904—rise sheer over the river to a height of 200 feet and more above its level, and every prospect pleases. Man, it must be confessed, is occasionally vile at the week-end. Try this reach in spring, summer, or autumn, when the sail scarce feels the faltering breeze up stream, and the bow creeps slowly round as any snail under the sway of the silent tiller, as the boat goes her dreamy way from bank to bank; or when a tearing wind from astern threatens to plunge the stem under water and the boat "gripes" for all she is worth, and the steersman has his hands full and muscles extended by straining sheet and tugging tiller—take it as you will, in fact, Pangbourne Reach is not to be surpassed in its kind. Here enters the River Pang, interesting, since it passes by Hampstead Norris, Yattendon, Bucklebury, and Bradfield (concerning all of which, but especially of Bradfield, there is gossip elsewhere); and here was a beautiful bridge; but it has gone the way of many another. Disembark at Pangbourne if you will, but it will be to find nothing remarkable, though the village is one of many trees, and the red brick of the church tower has a warm glow. Nor is Purley of striking interest, although it is worth while to remember that at Purley Hall, separated from the river by the railway and the high-road, lived, pending his trial, the much-maligned Warren Hastings, whom the fiery eloquence of Burke and the stately rhetoric of Macaulay covered with a cloak of disgrace that all the convincing but cold logic of Sir James FitzJames Stephen did not avail to remove. Such is the perversity of man. Many of us have read Sir James Stephen's *Nuncomar and Impey*, carrying away conviction, but we have read it once only. We return to Burke and Macaulay to be impressed anew, and in spite of ourselves, by the persuasive passion of the orator and the majestic indignation of the prejudiced historian.

Now we are drawing near to Reading. The hills have receded on the left bank; the monotonous embankment of the Great Western Railway, a piece of artificial Berkshire, hides the natural Berkshire from all eyes. Tilehurst (it is true that it is not worth a visit) is almost as far distant as Reading; but Tilehurst station, with extensive platforms and the other appanage of a

U

WORKING MEN'S COLLEGE LIBRARY.

railway station, is perched close to the river. Why does it exist at all? Did the railway company at any time venture to cherish the hope that upon some future day the vicinity of Tilehurst station might blossom forth as a "riverside resort"? If so, the gloomy rampart of their own embankment should have warned them of certain failure. Or is it possible that the importance of the station is not entirely disconnected with the presence of an unassuming bungalow across the stream, where

The Old "Angel" Inn, Theale, near Reading.

the late general manager of the railway, one of the most genial of men, was wont to make occasional holiday? To these questions there can be no answer; but it is certain that this is a dull piece of river, and that the Thames has but little charm until Caversham Bridge has been reached and passed. Neither, just now, will we halt to look at Caversham, unlovely suburb of Reading, nor to linger in Reading itself.

For Reading, rich in memories and in history, is poor in relics and in beauty. Most of it looks as bare and newly baked as one of the biscuits of Reading fame, and the one tolerable thing seen as you pass in the train is found in the flashing bands and beds of colour from Messrs. Sutton's nursery grounds. Nothing, or next to nothing, is gained by entering the town ; for reading may be accomplished elsewhere and there is little to see. The castle is completely vanished ; of the Benedictine abbey, once third of the English abbeys, only pitiable traces remain, and the same sorry fragments represent the palace that Henry VIII. made out of the abbey buildings. Some of the churches possess features of interest in detail. But on the whole the town that was taken by the Danes in 871, burned by them in 1006 ; the town where Parliaments were often held and kings and queens were frequently entertained ; the town, above all, which was of such tremendous importance during the Civil War—is as plain and prosperous a conglomeration of dull houses, and one seeming to breathe the air of history as little, as any that is to be found in England. Its importance during the Civil War, when the soil and roads of Berkshire played a principal part, is sufficiently emphasised elsewhere. So let us away down-stream to-day, leaving the ugliness and the prosperity of modern Reading behind us with such speed as may be vouchsafed by breeze, or oars, or throbbing engine.

A few miles from Caversham Bridge—through them the river runs between low banks—bring us to Sonning, formerly Sunning, where the Bishops of Salisbury once held the manor. Leland speaks of "a fair old house of stone at Sonninge by the Thamise ripe, longing to the bishop of Saresbyri, and thereby a fair park" ; and before that Sonning was the residence, in Saxon times, of the Bishops of the combined diocese of Berks and Wilts ; but of the palace, their "fair old house," not one stone remains upon another. Sonning none the less, with its fine trees, its really picturesque old houses, its mellow red brick, its steep acclivities and declivities on the Berkshire bank, is fair still, what though the palace be gone, and the church

E L GRIGGS · 1906

Sonning.

WORKING MEN'S COLLEGE
LIBRARY.

—doubtless it served for cathedral once—has been modernised
not a little, and within the venerable walls of the vanished
deanery's garden a structure of modern date has arisen. This
brings us to a point of some interest. Sonning has suffered,
from the artistic point of view, a little from the inroads of
fashion, of sorts, but its remoteness from a railway station—it
is about four miles from Reading and a little less from Twyford
—has saved it in some measure, and this new house, in the
old deanery garden that has been mentioned, is one example
among several of the fact that Sonning has been fortunate
in the architects who have invaded it. This particular house
was designed by one of the well-known architects of our day
who has a real reverence for antiquity and a genuine appreciation
of its spirit ; by one who errs, if he errs at all, in the direction
of excess of veneration for the antique. Again, the "French
Horn," on the Oxfordshire bank, and the "White Hart," on
"Thamise ripe" on the Berkshire side, are new hotels on the
sites of ancient and well-known inns. With the "French
Horn" we have no legitimate concern, but the most perverse
lover of antiquity, and there are such, would hardly venture to
say that the remodelled "White Hart" is not a very appropriate and unobtrusive structure, or is in any way unsuitable to
its surroundings. It was the work of Mr. Campbell Jones ;
the house in the deanery garden was shaped in the mind of
Mr. E. Lutyens and built to his designs.

The river ramifies not a little immediately above Sonning,
and all of its many channels are very beautiful. From them
rises the necessity for many bridges, rather than one long
bridge, and those on the Berkshire side, built of ancient brick-
work and of good design, are likely to remain a joy for ever, or,
at any rate, for many years to come. That on the Oxfordshire
side is quite new, and by no means restful to the eye. It was
in 1902, if memory serves accurately, that the joint county
authorities of Berks and Oxon were apprised by their surveyor
that a new bridge was required. I inspected the old bridge at

the time, since there was loud outcry from the friends of the river, and came to the curious conclusion that, so far, both the surveyor and the friends of the river were in the right. The surveyor had reason when he said that the existing bridge was inadequate to the traffic of the district, since traction engines and the like, which after all are entitled to exist, could not cross it with safety. Moreover, he was not wrong in asserting that,

Sonning Lock.

supported as it was upon an inordinate number of piles, many of them rotten, the old bridge must needs catch the weeds as they floated down-stream, and so interfere with the management of the flood-water, the curse of the Thames valley. Since, however, public sympathy does not exactly flow out to traction engines, the æsthetic objection to the removal of the old bridge might have prevailed, through the channels of public opinion, if that old bridge had really been a thing of beauty.

In truth, and apart from the piles, to which irregularity of angle and the marks of decay may have added some kind of charm, the bridge as a whole was not attractive. Its superstructure was just a roadway, with iron balustrades, of tubular railings about an inch and a half in diameter, jointed in the same fashion as gas-pipes, having plain iron supports at intervals of six feet or so, and painted white. The controversy was keenly waged, but nobody went out of his way to mention this fact. It would not have suited the argument of those who were for retaining the old bridge at any price ; and the surveyor, probably, did not care to advance it. Still, there it was, and it cannot have failed to rob the opposition of some of the weight belonging to sincere conviction. Nobody could possibly have fallen into architectural love with the old bridge at first sight. Still, the æsthethic opponents of its removal were wise in their generation none the less. The old bridge was inoffensive, or, at worst, the frequenters of the river had grown accustomed to it ; and that makes more difference in men's judgment of scenic effects than most folk realise. They had a lively apprehension that, if the county authorities had their way, a worse thing might befall them ; and that apprehension has turned out to be only too well-founded. The new bridge is a " lattice girder " bridge. That is enough ; no more need be said about it. Something, however, must be said upon the systematic and progressive destruction of picturesque Thames bridges, rightly or wrongly alleged to be past their work, and of the substitution for them of monstrously ugly structures. To love of beauty it is, presumably, hopeless to appeal. The blessed institution of local government makes it a moral certainty that county councillors, with a few exceptions, will not be men to whom that kind of appeal has any sort of meaning. Let us try to take them in a tender place, to appeal to their pockets. Do they reflect that the ancient and comely bridges across the Thames are, so to speak, county assets ? Do they realise that to erect ugly bridges instead of those inoffensive ones that might be

built, at a little more cost perhaps, to carry the traffic of the day,
is to turn the faces of visitors to other parts? Do they remember that the advent of these visitors tends to the prosperity of
the riparian population, and to the raising of ratable values?
If not, let the county councils of Berks, Oxon, and Bucks look
to their rate-books for fifty years past; they will very soon
realise the additional value, combined with increased liability

Sonning Bridge.

for rates, which the silent stream of the Thames has given to
scores, nay, hundreds, of riverside hostelries. Fifty, even
thirty years ago, humble inns stood where large hotels stand
now, and, although there be many to regret the change, it
certainly is not to the commercial interest of the counties to
stand in its way, or to drive visitors away from the river.

From Sonning to Wargrave the Thames follows a sinuous
course in a nor'-nor'-easterly direction, the ground being low
on the Berkshire side and the country solitary. Note the

"brimming Loddon" as it enters, a short half-mile above Wargrave. Elsewhere we follow it from its entry into Berkshire through the park of Strathfield Saye and join Miss Mitford in joy over its tranquil passage through her country. North of Miss Mitford-land it has passed Twyford, of no interest except as the junction for Henley, and Ruscombe, where William Penn died. But there is nothing remarkable about the country it flows through, and there is no use in going to Ruscombe to see the house in which Penn died, for it is standing there no longer.

At Wargrave by all means disembark, for it is a lovely village, and the "George and Dragon" offers not only good entertainment for the lower part of the inner man, but also refreshment for that part of man which is higher, in every sense of the word. Those great artists, Mr. George Leslie, R.A., and Mr. Broughton, R.A., to the former of whom lovers of the river owe an incalculable debt of gratitude for his readiness to come forward at all times as the champion of the Thames never did a kinder act than when they collaborated to paint a sign for this house of call. It hangs within the house and a copy is suspended outside; but no man who eats or drinks "for the good of the house," and sees the original picture, is likely to regret either act. St. George himself, by the way, is represented on one side of the sign tossing off a tankard of ale. It is the fashion to speak scornfully of the church, because it has been restored, but the ivy-covered tower of brick has considerable fascination. In fact Wargrave is a delightful little place, and near it we find three place-names not without their special interest in connection with a question raised in another part of this volume. They are Bear Place, Bear Park, and Bear Hill; and elsewhere we have Bear Wood, Mr Walter's seat near Wokingham. All three, it will be noted, are within the limits of the ancient forest, having the Loddon for its eastern boundary in mediæval times, although at an earlier date it stretched up the valley of the Kennet. In dealing with Bear Wood, and for reason duly given, it is suggested that it may mean no more than it appears to mean, that is to say, that Bearroc Wood, which, like the old forest, would include all these places, was the wood of bears. But the good Lysons, writing at the beginning of the last century, says that these places near Wargrave were reputed to be named after the A'Bears, a family who were still in the land in his day. Does this militate against the theory outlined above, and explained with more elaboration in connection with Bear Wood? Surely not; for, although many places in Berks are named after former lords of the manor, Sutton Courtney for example, it is still the most usual thing in the world for families to use for surname the name of the place from which their forbears came, in Berkshire and in other counties. To take the first examples that come to mind, the honest man who attends to the needs of my cabbages is named William Lambourne, and an old Mutiny veteran who occasionally uses a spade in my service is named Didcot. The A'Bears are just as likely to have taken their name from Bearroc, or Bear, Wood, as Bear Wood, Park, Place, and Hill are to have taken their names from the A'Bears. Apart from that, it is quite possible that bear-baiting may have been practised at the Park, the Hill, or the Place. The last-named, it may be added, is singularly beautiful, and the river, flowing beneath its hanging woods, is at its very best, for the woods are raised on a mighty cliff which gives a suggestion of that element of towering grandeur which we sometimes miss in Thames-side scenery.

Proceeding northward, up the map and down the stream, the passage of Marsh Lock is made. The wooded hills on the Berkshire bank recede; a couple of eyots in mid stream are passed, and Henley Bridge, model of what a Thames bridge should be, faces us a quarter of a mile off. Henley itself is in Oxfordshire, so it is outside our purview, but the bridge joins it to Berks; the river, presumably, is "land covered by water," and Berkshire land at that on the right side, up to its *medium filum.* The "Red Lion" may be in Oxfordshire; its classic meadow and the towing path are in Berks, and the Royal County is thus entitled to claim its full share in Henley Regatta. The question is, what shall be said of Henley and Henley Regatta? And, since volumes might be written concerning it, the simplest plan is to take a sentence from a practical authority, comment upon it a little, assume the existence of a good deal of general knowledge of Henley Regatta, and throw in one or two individual views.

The worthy Mr. Taunt, of Oxford, writes thus: "Henley Amateur Regatta is the largest and most important of the English Regattas : it is visited by the *élite* of the aquatic world, and during its continuance the town is the centre of a very fashionable gathering." Mr. Taunt is enthusiastic, elegant in phraseology, almost one might write *recherché*, but not quite accurate. On the one hand, he overstates the greatness of Henley Regatta, for it is but the largest of English freshwater regattas, and Cowes has at least equal importance ; on the other hand, he understates the case, for Henley is really the most celebrated, in the classic sense of "crowded" no less than that of "famous," of the freshwater regattas that the whole world can show. There are those, indeed, who fear that its celebrity, and the apparently irresistible attractions that it holds out to oarsmen from overseas, may ruin it as a pleasant gathering. That is a large question, into which it is not fitting to enter here. Suffice it to say, that although English oarsmen and athletes generally prefer not to take their sport quite so seriously as some others, and in spite of some unpleasant disputes concerning the precise definition of an amateur, English oarsmanship still has things quite sufficiently its own way at Henley. Relentless truth, however, compels a gentle protest against Mr. Taunt's "very fashionable gathering," unless indeed the word "very" be (impossible suggestion!) "wrote sarcastic"; for of course Henley cannot be compared in this respect with Cowes among regattas, or with Goodwood among race-meetings. In suggesting this, no disparagement of Henley is intended. It is altogether desirable that the pleasures of Henley should be shared by all sorts and conditions of men and women. They cannot be excluded from ground subject to public rights ; they come in great numbers ; and they enjoy themselves to the full. In fact, racing apart, Henley Regatta is emphatically the resort of the middle classes and the multitude ; and, since the middle classes, or some of them, have plenty of money, and of gay house-boats, fine clothes, and at least as much taste and culture as the highest classes, and all classes are bent on enjoyment, the result is a moving picture of exceptional brightness and gaiety, with an accompaniment of cheerful noise that is distinctly exhilarating. All of this is entirely as it should be , but to say that Henley Regatta is " very fashionable " is a double injustice, for it gives a false impression, and it might easily lead those who know "very fashionable " society, but do not know Henley, to avoid the Regatta, lest it should be found prim and dull. In fact it is neither the one nor the other, but in its kind perfectly enjoyable. No foreigner should miss it ; no English man or woman knows English life who has not been to Henley during the Regatta ; and, even if custom withers somewhat the enjoyment of those who, merely as spectators of the scene, know Henley well, it is always a gathering to be anticipated with pleasure, to be looked back upon with pleasure also.

To those who are intelligently interested in oarsmanship Henley Regatta appeals with irresistible force. The course, as now arranged, is perfect as it is possible for an up-stream course to be ; it stirs up memories of great achievements and glorious struggles in the past ; and the meeting is only equalled, not surpassed, by the University Boat Race in the number of opportunities that it presents for the foregathering of veterans of the thwart and the oar, and for the fighting of friendly battles o'er again. There is no place that can touch Henley for possibilities of observing the best rowing that the

world can show, exhibited not by two crews only, as it is from
Putney to Mortlake every year (not that even Oxford and
Cambridge crews are always quite beyond criticism), but by
many crews from many sources.   The pick of the Universities
are there, contending for their colleges, rather than for Alma
Mater ; the London and Thames-side clubs generally, recruited
largely from the Universities ; eights from Eton and Radley
always, sometimes from other schools ; crews from the
provinces and from Ireland, Colonial crews, American boats,
Continental eights and scullers.   Nowhere can you see, on the
same day, so many styles of rowing ; nowhere can you meet so
many men entitled, and sometimes more than willing, to speak
with authority on the whole art, science, and practice of
rowing in fresh water.

Yet Henley Regatta is not of great antiquity.   The first
race over the Henley course, or rather over more than the
Henley course, of which the record survives, was rowed
between Hambledon Lock and Henley Bridge in 1829, and it
was also the first University Boat Race.   Let the brief account
of it be quoted in the words of Mr. Edward Dampier Brick-
wood, who, as oarsmen and as critic of oarsmanship, held in
his time the highest possible position.   He died at the close
of 1905 while these pages were awaiting correction, and his
death left the aquatic world much poorer.

"Considerable correspondence passed before it was agreed that the
course should be from a point above Hambledon Lock to Henley Bridge,
a distance of 2¼ miles against stream, and that the race should be rowed on
the 10th of June, in the evening.   The Cambridge crew, whose colour was
pink, won the toss for position, and took the Berkshire side.   Before
reaching Remenham the Cambridge coxswain fetched out into the stream
as if he desired to pass on the Bucks side of the island, while the Oxford
crew had made up their minds to pass on the inner or Berkshire side of it,
and as the competing boats were not clear of one another at the corner
below the eyot, a collision occurred.   The eights were ordered to row
again, and Oxford won by five or six lengths, though details of the race are
not extant.   The coxswains were both amateurs, and members of their respec-
tive Universities, and Bishop Selwyn rowed No. 7 in the Cambridge crew."

This first University Boat Race is interesting in itself; for 2¼ miles up stream, rowed at high pressure, once and a half on the same evening, to say nothing of paddling twice to the starting-point, in primitive eight-oars with keels, without outriggers, and on fixed seats, must have made it a struggle fully as trying as any of those that have followed it. It was not, however, until 1839 that the first Henley Regatta was held, the Grand Challenge Cup for eight oars having been founded by public subscription. In early years the Universities, or rather the colleges and esoteric clubs of the Universities, were the principal competitors. Thus in 1839 First Trinity, in the "Black Prince," beat the Oxford Etonian Club in the final heat for the Grand Challenge; but other events were soon added; crews from elsewhere began to enter, and Henley grew from strength to strength, and, though Oxford and Cambridge colleges always kept up their interest in it, time was when the London clubs quite held their own. The present course is but a mile and a quarter in length, a trifle when compared by admeasurement to the 2¼ miles, rowed over once and a half, of the first University Boat Race, but perhaps it is every whit as exhausting to men who lay themselves out to row for all they are worth. Apart from Regatta time Henley Reach is a quiet and restful part of the Thames, and Remenham is a quiet riverside village with a fascinating background of tree-clad hills.

Shortly below Temple Island, the starting-point for the races, the river turns sharply, almost at right angles, to the East, before reaching Hambledon Lock, and below Hambledon Lock there is quite a miniature Archipelago of islands. Boating is pleasant, the river is good, but there is nothing calling for special observation on the Berkshire side until Hurley is reached. This Hurley, with its remains of the Benedictine Monastery, including a very fine barn and dovecot, its timber houses, and the legends of Lady Place, is a village of extraordinary fascination. It has its place in history. Here the sister of Edward the Confessor was buried, here Sir Richard Lovelace is said to have built Lady Place out of "money gotten with Francis Drake." So Lysons, and thus the more sonorous Macaulay, in relation to Richard Lord Lovelace of 1688.

"This mansion, built by his ancestors out of the spoils of Spanish galleons from the Indies, rose on the ruins of a house of our Lady in this beautiful valley, through which the Thames, not yet defiled by the precincts of a great capital, rolls under woods of beech, and round the gentle hills of Berks. Beneath the stately saloon, adorned by Italian pencils, was a sub-terranean vault, in which the bones of ancient monks had sometimes been found. In this dark chamber some zealous and daring opponents of the Government held many midnight conferences during that anxious time when England was impatiently expecting the Protestant wind."

Lady Place is gone ; but, as has been stated, some of the buildings of the Benedictines remain, and the grand barn in particular serves to remind us of the priceless services rendered by the Benedictines of Hurley and elsewhere to British agriculture. Berkshire seems to have been particularly fortunate in attracting their attention, and, with the Benedictines, Jethro Tull of Basildon, the late Prince Consort at Windsor, and the late Lord Wantage at Lockinge, she may claim to have been the home of some of the most valuable leaders of the agricultural movement, ancient and modern. Others there have been some, like Sir John Throckmorton of Buckland, who are known to me by name (Sir John, by the way, was the Squire who sat down to dinner at the Pelican in Speenhamland in a coat which had been wool on the skins of two sheep 13 hours and 20 minutes before). Doubtless there are many others, living and dead, but unknown to me, who have done yeomen's service to the agricultural community in Berkshire. Still, it would be hard to match, and impossible to surpass, the Benedictines and those who are named with them above.

Immediately below Hurley Lock, where again are many islands, comes a broad stretch of water in relation to which a true account of personal misfortune may amuse some and be of service to others who choose to go idly down stream in a sailing craft. It was in 1882, and in the second week in June, that I sailed with a friend down the narrow stream from Hurley Lock, before a summer gale so violent that the jib alone served to take us tearing through the ruffled water. The broad and straight reach after the confined stream looked glorious and half a mile

F.L. GRIGGS - 1906

Dovecote, Hurley.

was accomplished at a great pace. Then came unforeseen catastrophe. Who would have dreamed, without looking at the chart—*alias* Taunt's map of the river—of finding another lock within six furlongs of the last. Certainly neither of the occupants of the sailing craft looked for the indications of the lock so early, and the river stretched broad and tempting ahead ; so on we sped, careless of mankind, our bows hissing through the water, until, to our horror, we found ourselves in a *cul de sac* under the very windows of Temple House, then, and until this

WORKING MEN'S COLLEGE LIBRARY

very year of writing, the Berkshire home of that really great sportsman the late General Owen Williams. Sailing men will know that trespass was inevitable. It is childishly simple to let a boat run under a jib only before a strong gale and with the stream ; but, before we could beat up stream to the turning for the lock it was necessary to close-reef and hoist the mainsail, and before that could be done the good ship had to be moored to the bank, else should we have drifted into Temple Mills. The storm-driven but cheerful mariners were not interfered with in any way, but it was a long time before they weathered the point for the lock, and there was then too much of occupation for desultory talk. Afterwards, I remember, there was mention of General Owen Williams, who had been a hero of my boyhood in Wales, by reason of an exploit not recorded in any of the " obituary notices " after his death in 1904. He had made a modest wager with the King, then Prince of Wales, that he would kill a hundred couple of snipe in a single day to his own gun on the Anglesey marshes that he owned, and he had won it ; and the feat had been equally creditable to the sportsman who performed it and to the very sporting island where it was possible. Whether the famous yachtsman, the owner of the *Enchantress*, whose pluck Mr. Montague Guest tells us, " was almost a proverb with his friends," would have welcomed two young mariners, who had overshot their mark in a cockleshell, cannot be said with certainty. Trespass, even involuntary, is not always well received on the banks of the Thames ; and no wonder. But the bold sailor, who answered his apprehensive skipper with the words " No, we will not shorten sail, we will let her feel the full fury of the gale," and brought the *Enchantress* safe into port after sustaining damage to the extent of 500 pounds, would most likely have shown sympathy if he had seen us. We had, however, no wish for sympathy ; no wish at all, except to escape as soon as might be. So Temple House is associated in my mind with the memory of a great sportsman and with that of an exciting little episode.

In treating of Bisham, the next point of interest on the Berkshire bank, and, in its way, one of the most attractive places in England, both by virtue of its present appearance and of its memories, candour and inclination alike compel an acknowledgment of the help given by Mr. Falkner in Murray's *Berkshire*. Sometimes, in the byways, he stumbles, but it is the stumble of a spirited horse, jogging along an uninteresting road. Where, as at Bisham, he has history, ecclesiastical and personal, and really good architecture to attract his attention, he is to be relied upon to tell the whole story, omitting no point of legitimate interest, and to tell it passing well. In such a case it is mere waste of time to refer to the authorities, as was speedily discovered by me in attempting that long process, and so, after that labour in vain, nothing remains save to condense the story and to tell it in new language, not a whit better than that of Mr. Falkner; perhaps, indeed, far worse than that of one who is historian and novelist, as well as a writer of exceptionally interesting guide-books.

Bisham, then, once styled Bustleham, still stands, in part at any rate, a mile or so from Cookham by road, and about twice as far by river. Behind it the Quarry Woods, rising to a great height, and, running far down stream, make a magnificent background. On the level space below them and by the water's edge the Knights Templars raised a preceptory in the troublous days of Stephen. There the Knights Templars abode until the foreign orders were suppressed during the reign of the unhappy Edward of Carnarvon; but, very shortly after his murder in 1327, in 1333 to be precise, an Augustine Priory was settled at Bisham by William de Montacute, Earl of Salisbury. (Mr. Falkner says 1338, but this is probably a misprint, for 1333, when written, may look very like 1338, but MCCCXXXIII, as the date appears in the *Denchworth Annals*, could not be mistaken for MCCCXXXVIII, and, as has been seen in another chapter of this volume, accident and a piece of Vandalism revealed in the remote church of Denchworth, in the Vale of

White Horse, the original brass commemorating the foundation of this priory.) For 200 years and more the Augustine Priory lasted, and it was the chief of five monasteries. In 1536 it was surrendered—reluctantly, no doubt—to Henry VIII., but in the following year it was refounded as a Benedictine Mitred Abbey. That lasted but two years, and the abbey passed into lay hands in a curious and interesting way. The story takes us back to Henry VIII. in his most characteristic mood. We see the robust king, not long after the death of Jane Seymour, whom he really held in affection, thinking of yet another wife.

Bisham Abbey.

We think of him gazing eagerly at Hans Holbein's all too flattering picture of Anne of Cleves ; we sympathise with the disappointment of the ardent monarch when, having ridden to Rochester to meet the original of Holbein's portrait, he found the living woman plain, awkward, and a monoglot Dutchwoman. How he married her ; how he divorced her on flimsy pretexts and settled £3,000 a year on her, all the histories tell. Not everybody, however, is aware that the house of the Benedictines at Bisham was settled on her, perhaps then, probably later ; for Henry died before the privy seal was affixed to the grant, and the matter seems to have been forgotten in the time of

Edward VI. ; but Mary confirmed the grant, and Anne, with the leave of Mary, exchanged Bisham for Sir Philip Hoby's house in Kent. Sir Philip Hoby, as the last English papal legate at Rome (his brother Sir Thomas was English ambassador in France), was doubtless *persona grata* to Mary. It was the widow of Sir Thomas who in after years brought her husband's body, and that of her brother-in-law, to be buried among the illustrious dead at Bisham, and this Lady Hoby, daughter of Sir Anthony Cooke, had for sisters Lady Bacon and Lady Cecil, the guardians of that Princess Elizabeth who was to be the greatest of English queens before Victoria ; and hence it came that Elizabeth, half-prisoner and half-guest, passed three years of her life, happily as she herself said, in this lovely place. Sundry alterations in the abbey date back to the time of her stay, but the hall is doubtless fourteenth century and so is the barn.

That is a little piece of history, and the names of "the illustrious dead" interred in the church suggest much more. First comes the founder of the Augustine Priory, who described himself as "Sire William de Mountagu." With him sleep his son William, Earl of Salisbury, a hero of Poictiers, and John, the son of William, betrayed by the Duke of Rutland, and beheaded for treason in the second year of King Henry IV., and Thomas, the son of John, who died before Orleans in 1428. Here too lay the bodies of Richard Neville, also Earl of Salisbury, beheaded in 1460 ; of Richard Neville the king-maker, of his brother John who fell at Barnet in 1471, and of that luckless Edward Plantagenet, Earl of Warwick, Richard Neville's grandson, who was beheaded in 1499. Almost, in an age when anything unprecedented is glorified as a "record," is one inclined to say grimly that Bisham holds the record among small places, both for the number of its illustrious dead and for the percentage of them who died by violence, either on the field of battle or under the headsman's axe. In a more serious mood, when one thinks of the dangers which beset the nobility of old times at home as well as abroad, and in peace no less than in war, the wonder is not that so many of the old families have vanished, but that any of them have survived.

Bisham abbey has its ghost story, of course, and it is one of rather a more perplexing character than is usual. It is said that the ghost of Lady Hoby, the widow of Sir Thomas, and afterwards the wife of Lord John Russell—of the sixteenth century, not the nineteenth—appears in a certain bedroom with face and hands of an inky black, but dressed in white. Tradition has it that the ghost is compelled to wander thus because the woman in her days on earth beat her child William Hoby to death by reason of his inveterate habit of blotting his copy-books. Mr. Falkner adds, " It is certainly curious that about 1840, in altering the window shutters, a quantity of children's copy-books of the time of Elizabeth were discovered, packed into the rubble between the joists of the floor, and that one of these was a copy-book, which answered exactly to the story, as if the child could not write a single line without a blot." He adds that in the dining-room is "a picture of Lady Hoby, with a very white face and hands, dressed in the coif, weeds and wimple then allowed to a knight's widow." Mr. Falkner does not say that he believes the ghost story ; but to the matter-of-fact man who does not place a particle of reliance on any ghost story that ever was told, or, like Topsy, grew, there is a good deal of interest in some of them. The ghost does not walk, of course. There is no sort of use in arguing with those who believe that it may, unless by urging that it really would be very silly and unfair of Providence, merely because Lady Hoby was a cruel and, possibly, murderous mother, to punish her by sending her ghost to frighten innocent servant-maids when she has been dead nearly 300 years. It might be a very painful exercise to Lady Hoby, in her present indefinite state, or again it might not ; but it would assuredly be cruelly unjust to the maids ; and, the story being well known, nobody need doubt that plenty of fanciful persons are convinced that they have seen the ghost. There is nothing wonderful, either, in the prevailing notion that the blackness and the whiteness of the portrait are exactly reversed in the ghost. That is the kind of detail that might easily grow up round the portrait and the story of the copy-books. "But," the believer in ghosts may urge, "surely this strange discovery of the copy-books supports the legend." He (or she) might even add :

> " There are more things in heaven and earth, Horatio,
> Than are dreamed of in our philosophy."

But one who cannot endure it that ghosts should be treated as a serious possibility, because when they are so treated foolish persons are badly frightened, and because, as a child reared in a remote environment, he long went in terror of ghosts, may be permitted to point out coldly that the whole account, minus the ghost, may be perfectly true and consistent. More than one recent trial in the criminal courts of our country makes it all too plain that, even in this enlightened age, it is not impossible, not even very unusual, for highly born and well-educated women to show a perfect savagery of cruelty in the treatment of their offspring ; and the days in which Lady Hoby lived, including at least the last fifty years of the sixteenth century and the first nine of the seventeenth, were not mild. It is quite possible that the boy William perpetrated the identical blots that appear in this pathetic little copy-book, that his mother flogged him brutally, that he died, and that the neighbours laid his death at his mother's door. If so there is quite enough, without any ghost, to account for the ghost legend. No theory in life, even in these days, is so enduring as oral tradition in country districts. From father and mother to son and daughter the evil deeds of the cruel Lady Hoby would be handed down in the natural course of things. There is nothing more strange in the permanence of this legend than in a score of other instances of tradition that may be found in the country. If the jingle verses concerning Saint George, of which mention is made elsewhere, have been handed down orally for generations in Berkshire, as they have ; if every street-child in London or the provinces knows the immemorial, mysterious, and immutable laws of "hopscotch," how much more would a horrified village in a remote part of rural England hand down to posterity the memory of Lady Hoby's barbarous deed ? That a ghost story should grow up round the legend, a false story round a true legend, is simply and perfectly natural.

These mysteries of female cruelty seem to be a kind of passionate madness beyond the understanding of man ; but it certainly gives the visitor something approaching to a shock to enter the church by the riverside, there to find that Lady Hoby mentioned her offspring, perhaps William, perhaps another, in the epitaph that she placed on the ornate tomb of alabaster raised by her to honour the memory of Sir Philip and of her dead husband Sir Thomas, of whom it is written :

> " In his floure in Paris town he died,
> Leaving with child behind his woeful wief,
> In foreign land opprest with heapes of grief.
> The corps with honour brought she to this place,
> Performing here all due unto the dead.
> That doon, this noble tombe she caused to make."

Here again are other tombs, one of a Margaret Hoby who was certainly not the wicked Lady Hoby of the legend, for she was "never mother" ; some of no interest, and "a small sculptured monument to two children whose mother, a very old legend says, was Queen Elizabeth !" Truly, between those who vow that our Virgin Queen was never maid at all, but man, and those who deny that she remained a virgin, Elizabeth's fair fame has been most unkindly treated ; but at least her admirers may console themselves with the certainty that she could not have been both a man in disguise and a mother.

For its memories, then, Bisham is an interesting and an eerie place. Yet in the present state—the abbey is inhabited, and the surrounding parts open to the public—things seen from without, the barn, the parsonage, the church, with a window of enamelled glass, besides its curious monuments, are amongst the objects that none who aspire to know England, be they British born or no, should be contented to live without seeing. The whole, certainly, is best approached by the river, but if road be preferred, a drive of a mile and a half from Cookham station will serve the whole purpose.

Our craft, whatsoever it may be, has now travelled fifty-four miles from Folly Bridge at Oxford in rather more than as many pages of closely written manuscript, and there are nearly seventy miles in all to accomplish before reaching Windsor. Those remaining may be passed over in a brief space, not because some of the scenery to be enjoyed is not of the sweetest and best known on the banks of the Thames, but because, for a while, most of the interesting places are on the Bucks side, and it were an idle exercise to go on rhapsodising for ever on those fascinations of hanging woods and gleaming water which are the making of the river. At Cookham we will pause, to look at the curious church of mixed flints and brickwork, and to note, in addition to some brasses of no striking interest, the medallion commemorating the late Fred. Walker, A.R.A., friend and associate of Sir John Millais, engraver, too, for Thackeray, Walker who in the thirty-five years that were allotted to him on earth painted so many pictures of startling and sterling merit that his early death was a bitter disappointment to the world of art. He was born in Marylebone in 1840, and, after working as a wood-engraver, and in black and white for sundry magazines, he became an Associate of the Society of Painters in water colours in 1864. A year before that he had secured admission to the Royal Academy for the first time as an oil painter, and in 1871 he was elected an Associate of the Royal Academy. Dearly as he was beloved by his friends, who were many, for by all accounts he was the most lovable and the brightest of men, the gods loved him all too well, and he died young in 1875. How far he would have gone if he had lived it is idle to speculate.

He went far enough to occupy a very high, and in some respects unique, position in the English school. He was at once a real lover of nature, a master of harmonious colouring, and a correct draughtsman, who revelled in landscape ; and it may well be that the Berkshire which he came to know so intimately supplied him with more than one of his unnamed rural subjects. Let us lay our willing tribute to his memory.

As we proceed down stream from Cookham all the glory of Cliveden Woods is spread out for our enjoyment, but Cliveden is on the wrong side of the river for us, and so is Taplow. The Berks side is interesting only for the view of Bucks that can be obtained from it and from the river, and it is distinctly not worth while to leave the water and to walk a short mile in order to see Maidenhead. With the Berkshire bank at any rate lying very low, 77 feet above sea-level at Maidenhead, whereas Cliveden rises to 256 and the Quarry Woods that we passed some time ago to 351, we are badly off here for striking scenery ; and, as it happens, there is no store hereabouts of legends or architectural attractions. So we may hasten without regret. Still, in the few miles of our voyage that remain is a place irresistibly suggestive of a really old song. It is the village of Bray, famous for the song about the Vicar of Bray, whom the good Fuller shows to have been an historical personage. He was Simon Aleyn, who clung to his benefice under Henry VIII., Edward VI., Mary, and Elizabeth, making all the necessary professions of faith with alacrity as occasion required. So the song that celebrates his practical and pliant conscience is really old ; but, since few songs of ancient or modern date are so familiar as it is, probably by reason of its rollicking tune and chorus, it would be bold as well as superfluous to quote it. Apart from this, it is well to land at Bray for a visit to the Jesus Hospital, founded by William Goddard, of the Fishmongers' Company, in 1627, and built in a quadrangle of red brick, which clipped yews and gay flowers combine to render a scene of calm and sequestered beauty. This quietude is, in very truth, apt to be refreshing after the lower reaches of the river in summer, for we are now at that part of the Thames easily accessible by train, which is prone to be crowded to inconvenience by all manner of craft, frequently steered and propelled without regard either for prudence or manners; and here, especially on Saturdays and Sundays, the din of cheerful gaiety is too often excessive. There are two views of Boulter's Lock, " where as many as 1,000 boats have been dealt with in a day "; and one of them is that to have seen it once on such a day is enough for a lifetime. In truth, it is well for quiet folk so to time a journey down stream as to traverse this part of the river in mid-week.

Another place suggests a well-known melody. Half a mile below Bray Lock comes Monkey Island, called after the monkeys that Clermont painted in a pavilion for the Duke of Marlborough, and, exactly sixty-six miles from Folly Bridge, was (alas, that it is necessary to write in the past tense!) Surley Hall. Half a mile lower comes Boveney Lock. Each and all of these places bring to Etonian memories the glorious recollections of boyhood's days, the procession of boats, the suppers, the loud-throated shouting of the " Eton Boating Song," on the Fourth of June in these later days, but formerly on Election Saturday also. (Parenthetically it may be added that in 1869 or 1870, having been a candidate for election, I saw the riot, a glorious thing from a boyish point of view, which caused Election Saturday to go the way of Montem and of other fine old institutions.) In 1904, for the the first time, apart from years when public or domestic calamity had put a stop to festivity, the row up stream to Boveney was perforce abandoned. For form's sake the boats rowed up stream for a mile or so, that they might be seen of spectators on the Brocas, but then they sped down again and supper was provided in the Home Park. A few days later the King, with the Queen and the Prince and Princess of Wales, watched the same boats in procession from a pavilion by the waterside, and then,

themselves carried in the ancient state barge propelled by
Royal watermen in scarlet, proceeded down stream ; and again
the crews were entertained at supper in the Park.   It was as
pretty a sight as the heart of man might desire, and again,
indeed on both occasions, the " Eton Boating Song " was roared
amain.   Who has failed to notice, at balls and places where they
dance, that when this tune is played in waltz time, human voices
are frequently heard above the instruments ?

So, having reached Windsor insensibly, let us leave the river
before quite reaching the point at Old Windsor where it deserts
the county that it has bounded, save for here and there a
wandering island of Oxfordshire, for more than a hundred miles.
This is not to say, of course, that there is not good boating for
a few miles more with Berkshire, in the form of Windsor Park,
on the right bank, but there is nothing on the bank or in mid-
stream to be mentioned particularly, except Old Windsor, and
Runnymede, and Magna Charta Island, the last half a mile
below the boundary of Berks ; and, as is explained in another
place, there is little or nothing but their memories to recommend
any of these.   We have seen our last of the river.

CHAPTER XI

WINDSOR AND ITS CASTLE

Madame Waddington—Windsor Castle and Moscow—A contrast—
English and American views of antiquity—Windsor's "prospects
unconfined"—Early History—The Conqueror—Queen Adelais and
the Harcourts—Magna Charta—Henry III.'s work—Recent Excavations—Edward III. and William of Wykeham—Wykeham as architect
—Eton College, indirectly Wykehamist—Wykehamists at Windsor—
Building work of Edward III.—Impressed workmen—Plague—Con-
flicting authorities—Windsor, fortress, home, and prison—Illustrious
prisoners—David of Scotland to John of France—James I. of Scotland
—The " King's Quhair "—The " garden fayre "—Growth of Windsor
Castle—First view—Windsor Town Hall—Windsor's citizens—From
the White Hart balcony—A royal wedding, and a personal adventure
—A rash sentence—King Henry VIII.'s gate—A contrast—St. George's
Chapel—Its abundant light—Its memories—Burial of Charles I.—
Funeral of Queen Victoria—An impression of it—A Garter ceremonial—
Foundation of Order of the Garter—Origin of motto—Conflicting
theories—Dr. Brewer to the rescue—St. George's Chapel and royal
funerals—Royal marriages—Points in St. George's Chapel—Despoiled
by Puritans—Clarendon's account of funeral of Charles I.—Clarendon
prejudiced?—A recent visit—The Chapter Library and the *Merry
Wives*—Curfew Tower—Chambers under St. George's Chapel—
Horseshoe Cloisters—Gilbert Scott—Winchester Tower—*hoc fecit
Wykeham*—Round Tower—Tradition of King Arthur—Well in Round
Tower—Prince Rupert as man of science—The North Terrace—The
lists below—The Great Quadrangle—View down Long Walk—The
" Copper Horse "—Treacherous Elms—The private apartments—State
apartments described—Rubens in England, and as diplomatist—Many
portraits—Quintin Matsys, painter not iron-worker—Vandyck room—

"THE old grey fortress and its towers and crenellated walls, the home of
the sovereign who lives there with little pomp and few guards—guarded
by her people in the same castle and the same surroundings as when she
began her long reign, a mere girl. When one thinks of all the changes she
has seen in other countries—kingdoms and dynasties disappearing—one
can realise what a long wise rule hers has been. It is such a contrast to
my last Royal Audience at Moscow, which now seems a confused memory
of Court officials, uniforms, gold-laced coats, jewelled canes (I can see one
of the chamberlains who had an enormous sapphire at the end of his staff),
princes, peasants, Cossacks, costumes of every description, Court carriages,
Russian carriages, the famous *attelage* of three horses, every language under
the sun, and all jostling and crowding each other in the courts of the
Kremlin—with its wonderful churches and domes of every possible colour
from pink to green—only soldiers, soldiers everywhere, and the people
kept at a distance—very unlike what I have just seen here."

Thus, in those full, frank, and artless, and therefore infinitely
charming, *Letters of a Diplomat's Wife*, published in 1903,
Madame Waddington summed up her first impressions of life
as a guest at Windsor Castle. The letter was written in
December of 1883, and the contrast between the majestic
simplicity and confidence of life at Windsor and the splendid
anxiety of that of the Russian Court impressed her the more
deeply in that she saw the two Courts in rapid succession.
Earlier in the same year she had been a witness of the world-
renowned magnificence of the festivities and ceremonials
connected with the coronation of the Emperor Alexander III.
at Moscow. How infinitely more striking has been the
contrast of late.

An Englishman is inclined to say that the human spirit of
Windsor inspires these simple words more completely than it
has inspired those of many a more sonorous writer; but that the

WORKING MEN'S COLLEGE LIBRARY

architectural spirit of Windsor is entirely absent from them.
To the daughter of the President of Columbia College, New
York, and the granddaughter of the second Minister sent to
England by the United States after the adoption of their
Constitution, it was the venerable age of "the old grey
fortress" that appealed. To us, accustomed to ancient edifices
wearing the obvious signs of their antiquity upon them,
Windsor Castle hardly appeals on that ground at all, because it
appears to be, and it is, kept in such excellent repair; and it is
one of the standing puzzles of history that the story of
Windsor Castle should be so short as it is; for its situation
is the most admirable and commanding to be found in
Southern England. It is not described amiss in a forgotten
poem quoted by Lysons :

> " Hail, Windsor, crowned with lofty towers,
> Where Nature wantons at her will,
> Decks every vale with fruit and flowers,
> With waving trees adorns each hill.
> Like Mars with Venus in his arms,
> Like his thy strength, like hers thy charms.
>
> " When o'er thy plains I stretch mine eyes,
> Pleased with thy prospects unconfined,
> A thousand scenes before me rise,
> A thousand beauties charm my mind :
> Though different each, yet each agrees,
> Not this or that but all things please."

So some unknown versifier wrote, and so the forgotten Mr.
Lowe sang "to the flute in unison"; and if the verse-maker
was not a poet of the first water, he had at least an eye to see
the principal and abiding charm of the site of Windsor Castle.
It is to be found in the "prospects unconfined," in the
unrivalled view of the rich champaign of the valley of the
Thames from that isolated chalk knoll now veritably crowned
by Windsor Castle. Those of old times, very sensibly no
doubt from their point of view, concerned themselves mainly

over considerations of convenience when there was a question
of building a great house. The Saxon Kings built their
palace at Old Windsor, possibly by reason of its propinquity to
the river, or possibly because it was, as some have it, on the
Roman road to Silchester. Brickwork shows that the
Romans also had a settlement at Old Windsor. The Windsor
of to-day did not possess so much as a name—it was included
in the manor of Clewer, said by some to be called after the
"men of the cliff" of Windsor. The summit of the knoll,
the point at which the Round Tower now stands, had
commended itself to the Saxon Kings as a suitable site for a
fortress, and Harold had held $4\frac{1}{2}$ hides of land there, "et
castellum de Windesores est in dimidio hida." Of the
surrounding forest much must have been included in the
Confessor's grant to St. Peter's, Westminster, of "Windsor and
Staines and all that thereto belongs." To the Conqueror,
warrior and sportsman as he was, both site and forest appealed
very strongly, and, the site being already his by right of conquest,
he agreed to give Wokendune and Feringes in exchange for
them. These were fat manors of Essex, and the "venerable
abbot" was no doubt glad to make the exchange.

At any rate the Conqueror obtained the forest and the sheer
knoll that looked then, as it looks now, down upon the valley
of the Thames and commands it for many miles; and on the
eminence he built him a fortress, for which he had need; and
he dotted the forest with hunting lodges for the convenience
of the sport that, after warfare and after warfare only, was the
consuming passion of his life. Kings and Emperors have
taken their pastime in Windsor Forest from that day until this,
but there has been no mightier hunter among them than the
Conqueror, of whom the Saxon chronicler wrote that "he
loved the tall game as if he had been their father," and there
is nothing in the character of that strong and ruthless King
that brings him so near to the affections of modern Englishmen
as does his love of sport.

Such was the beginning of the real Windsor, called New Windsor for many a year, the Windsor that Shakespeare knew, that Falstaff revelled in, the Windsor now famous all the world over. It soon became a favourite residence of the Conqueror's successors, but, for our purposes, only two events with which the Castle was connected, before the reign of Edward of Windsor, the third Edward, need be named. The first is, so to speak, of local interest to Berkshire and the adjoining county of Oxford. At Windsor Henry I. married Adeliza or Adelais of Louvain, who interests us not so much because she was niece of Pope Calixtus, not, as Hume has it, because she was "a young princess of an amiable person," not because the Archbishop of Canterbury all but struck the King for allowing the Bishop of Salisbury to crown her, as by reason of a gift of lands made by her, either before or when, a childless woman, she left this world. For Queen Adelais gave lands near Bablockhithe at Stanton to Millicent de Camville; and those lands passed to her daughter Isabel, and with her, on her marriage, to Richard de Harcourt. So Stanton, if Stanton it was, became Stanton Harcourt, and it remains the property of that historic family, now most worthily represented by one beloved alike of friend and opponent—he has no foes—in the political world of Great Britain. So I wrote in the middle of 1904, but early in October the words were falsified. On the day following that on which these later words are written, within five miles of the spot at which they are being penned, Sir William Harcourt was laid to sleep with his fathers. May he rest in peace, and of his son and successor let it be said, " *Uno avulso non deficit alter, Aureus.*" One other event of Windsor's early days no Englishman may omit to mention. It was from Windsor that the meanest King who ever ruled England slunk to a camp on the Bucks bank of the Thames, near Runnymede, before signing Magna Charta, still a name to conjure with, still the foundation of our liberties.

Palace and Castle grew gradually in early days, their nucleus and centre being the stockaded mound, relic of the Saxon fortress, still the basis of the Round Tower. To this mound the Conqueror added a stone-built rampart and on it Henry III. built the first Round Tower. Henry, indeed, was a builder on the grand scale, but little of his work now remains. His great hall, kitchen, and chapel have perished long since to make room for St. George's Chapel. His chapel, dedicated to the Confessor, was rebuilt as to its upper part by Henry VII.

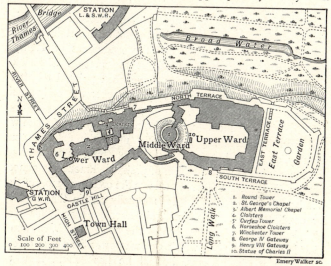

1. Round Tower
2. St. George's Chapel
3. Albert Memorial Chapel
4. Cloisters
5. Curfew Tower
6. Horseshoe Cloisters
7. Winchester Tower
8. George IV Gateway
9. Henry VIII Gateway
10. Statue of Charles II

Emery Walker sc.

and has now become the Albert Memorial Chapel; and of the works that were done in his day the only intact pieces surviving are one of the many minor towers with which he surrounded the Castle as with a garland, and the south wall of the Dean's Cloisters, where man may still see the head of the mural portrait of Henry painted by William the monk, of Westminster. Most of Henry's creations have perished, and the Windsor Castle that we know now is, in the main, attributable to Edward of Windsor and to William of Wyke-

Y

ham. Here let us pause for a moment. Since the above words were written, it has been my privilege to examine much of the vicinity of St. George's Chapel, and to see something of the excavations that have been and are being made in order to discover traces of Henry III.'s work. The effect of these excavations and of laborious examinations of the "Close Rolls" has been to show that much of the generally accepted story of the building of Windsor Castle is incorrect on a large scale ; the result of the discoveries and the studies will, in due course, be a monumental and authoritative work, in which the history of every fragment will be traced with certainty. But until that work is published and the exact lines of Henry's great hall, running to the north of the present Chapel of St. George, and of his cameræ, have been pointed out, it is mere waste of time to linger very long over the early architectural history of Windsor.

Even with the mention of Edward III. and Wykeham we find ourselves treading reluctantly upon the field of controversy, and it is but fair to state that this commentator on controversy is the willing victim of prejudice amounting almost to piety. It is certain that Edward was the creator of most of the Windsor Castle of to-day. It is equally certain that he had for coadjutor no less an historical personage than William of Wykeham. But what exactly was the position of Wykeham ? That is a question upon which one who owes his whole career —nothing much, perhaps, but all he has behind him—to Wykeham's magnificent bounty cannot be an absolutely impartial judge. So, as to many of the words which follow, words showing a willing acceptance of the time-honoured view that William of Wykeham was, in truth and in fact, architect of Windsor Castle, of Winchester College, and of New College, Oxford, it is necessary to avoid misunderstanding. I am perfectly well aware that Mr. Arthur Leach, sometime Fellow of All Souls', and second to none in authority upon the antiquities of education, maintains the contrary view in his

Windsor from the Meadows.

WORKING MEN'S COLLEGE LIBRARY.

History of Winchester College. He holds that Wykeham, as *supervisor*, or " maystre of the works " (in the case of Winchester his own works), was merely business manager, and that the true architect of Winchester was William Winford, the *cementarius*, or " mason." He would doubtless write in like terms of Wykeham's position at Windsor. But in relation to the whole of this matter his tone is less positive than is customary in him. Moreover, he admits with all candour that in Horman's *Vulgaria* (1519), a work of which some learned men may have heard the title before, " master of the works " is translated *architectus*. So, on the whole, there is less reason here than antiquaries are in the habit of producing for the destruction of a cherished idea. Usually they are dull, but detestably convincing. In this case the conviction is not absolute. We need not assume that the relations of architect and builder were so completely defined in the fourteenth century as they are now, but surely it is not necessary to assume either that *cementarius* connoted many more qualities than " mason," or that " master of the works," translated indifferently as *supervisor* or *architectus*, was not the title of the man inspired by the mind that devised and designed the whole of the glorious structure.

Edward III., then, had for coadjutor in his great work at Windsor Castle that fourteenth-century architect-bishop who is still held in grateful and reverent memory by every man educated at the College *Beatæ Virginis Mariæ Winton prope Winton*, better known in these days as Winchester College, or at the " New College," that has been one of the glories of Oxford for more than 500 years. The consequences of the lives of men of Wykeham's type are incalculable, and one of the most remote and indirect of them is the writing of this book by him who writes it ; a matter which is mentioned mainly by way of excuse for a tone savouring of panegyric, and, some will add, of perversity, concerning the principal architect of Windsor Castle and of "the mother of schools." Another indirect consequence of William of Wykeham's fruitful life, and a far more important, is to be seen in architectural embodiment with the naked eye from Windsor Castle every day; and its influence is to be traced in every corner of the English-speaking world. It is nothing less than Eton College. The spires and "antique towers,"

> " That crown the watery glade,
>   Where grateful science still adores,
>   Her Henry's holy shade,"

were, it is true, erected by the sixth Henry, whose benefaction is thus celebrated by Gray in a poem that is in itself a miniature handbook of familiar quotations. But it is not so generally known as, in the opinion of a Wykehamist, it ought to be, that Henry was prompted to his great foundation by Wykehamist advisers, that Eton's buildings are in large measure a replica of Winchester, and that the Etonian system was at the outset simply that of Winchester translated. A Wykehamist of the twentieth century, visiting Eton for the first time, is disposed to describe School Yard as an inferior Chamber-Court. How much greater, then, must the disposition to do likewise have been among those scholars of Winchester who, when Eton College was opened, were transported, with a master in charge, from the banks of the Itchen to those of the Thames, to be the first Etonians and to guide their schoolfellows in the true way?

Modern fashion to the contrary notwithstanding, I venture to attribute to Providence, not to blind chance, the fact that, in 1347, Edyngdon, Bishop of Winchester, brought William of Wykeham, then but twenty-three years old, to the notice of his great master, Edward III. Educated at the old Priory School at Winchester, at the cost of a patron, the yeoman's son William had entered the service of the bishop, and had clearly shown no little tact in business affairs and taste in architecture. So, in architecture, had the King, who was engaged on the Round Tower at Windsor Castle, and, when he appointed Wykeham

his chaplain, although the bishop of the future was not yet
ordained deacon, it was doubtless with a view to making use of
him as an architect as well as a man of business. Ten years
almost passed, years during which the King, one of the most
sagacious as well as one of the strongest of our long line of
sovereigns, had every opportunity of realising the fine quality
of the instrument that lay to his hand : and, perhaps, recognition of the genius of the young man may have helped the King
to perceive that in him he had found the one man capable of
creating a worthy habitation for the Kings of England. There
is nothing in this inconsistent with the pretty theory that
Edward's honoured prisoner, the French King, prompted him
to architectural ambitions. Be that as it may, in 1356 Wykeham, who had already held a number of appointments involving
duties similar to those of a modern land agent, was appointed,
according to Lysons, a clerk of the works at Windsor, at the
rate of one shilling *per diem*, save during absence from home,
when he was entitled to receive two shillings. In 1359 he was
made keeper of the manors of Old and of New Windsor. In
1359 also began his principal work at Windsor, the building of
the Great Quadrangle, which was ten years in the building.
More than 500 years later, in the summer of 1897, I happened
to be present when the Winchester College " eleven," being at
Eton to play the annual cricket match, were invited to the
Great Quadrangle in the evening as the guests of Queen
Victoria, and sang their school song, " Dulce Domum," of great
antiquity and of pathetic if mythical origin. I think they sang
it, and certainly an equerry in waiting must have had some
reason for being kind enough to tell me about a tenth of what
I already knew of " Domum." But it would have added an
immense amount of real interest to be reminded, as the
cricketers very likely required to be reminded, that the noble
proportions of that Quadrangle were due to William of
Wykeham himself.

It was an arduous business of building   That elementary

work *The Student's Hume* (useful for reference because, unlike many more profound works, it condescends to hard facts) says : " The magnificent Castle of Windsor was built by Edward III., and his method of conducting the work may serve as a specimen of the condition of the people in that age. Instead of engaging workmen by contracts and wages, he assessed every county in England to send him a certain number of masons, tilers, and carpenters, as if he had been engaging an army." Hume's complete history makes substantially the same statement. These are dry bones indeed, but with the help of Lysons, they can be made to live and to tell more of the whole truth better than they can be said to tell as they stand. They omit, for example, the commanding figure of Wykehem as clerk of the works. That, perhaps, is *omissio* rather than *suppressio veri*, and a small matter beside the doubtless unintentional *suggestio falsi*. The impression left by the sentence, with the emphasis laid on what Carlyle used to call the "great condition-of-England question," is that the Great Quadrangle of Windsor Castle was raised in blood and tears, as we suppose that the Pyramids were, by the labour of men who were practically slaves. In justice to the memory of Edward III. be it remembered that if the men were impressed, as the first batch of 360 were, and if some of them were committed to Newgate for absconding, it was "at King's wages." When they had been impressed the tall fabric was not erected without difficulty. In 1361 came the second of the three visitations of the plague in Edward's reign, and "many workmen were carried away." One may realise what this meant among workmen not, in all probability, too well housed, by remembering that in 1352 twothirds of the University population of Oxford perished, a colossal bill of mortality. One of its effects was that much of the country went untilled ; and another was the necessity of issuing new writs for the supply of workmen, to the sheriffs of Yorkshire, Shropshire, and Devon, who were each compelled to find sixty masons and diggers of stone. Glaziers were not

called for until 1363, and the work was not completed until
1369. But it included most of the best parts of Windsor
Castle, that is to say, the Great Quadrangle, the " Palace," the
Round Tower, St. George's Hall, St. George's Chapel (not of
course the existing chapel), the lodgings on the east and south
sides of the Upper Ward, the Canon's houses, the circumference
of the outer walls with towers and gates. Such is the account
given by Lysons, and as a rough summary, apart from the
inclusion of St. George's Chapel and of the Canon's houses, it
will serve indifferent well in the present very incomplete state
of knowledge on the subject. It leaves, at any rate, one abiding impression, that Edward III. was the greatest of the
builders of Windsor Castle ; and that is unquestionably correct.
The rest we shall learn when the great work already mentioned
sees the light of day.

For my own satisfaction, I have employed in my notes
" the deadly method of the parallel columns " to a number of
the authorities who discourse on the dates of various parts of
the Windsor Castle of to-day ; but the discrepancies, numerous
as they are, do not matter, and the method is as deadly in its
dulness as it is destructive of error. Moreover, it results in
confusion rather than in clarification of ideas, and it does not
help one at all towards an intelligent understanding of
Windsor. That comes far more readily from reflection upon
the part which Windsor has played in history than from
laborious investigation into antiquarian works and architectural
discussions. Windsor, then, has been, since the time of
Henry II. at any rate, not only a fortress and a castle, but
also the principal home and State residence—the two things
are by no means synonymous—of our sovereigns and their
suites. It has also served as a State prison. Hither David
of Scotland was brought after Neville's Cross by Edward III.,
to be ransomed in due course for 100,000 marks. Here John
of France was kept by the same Edward, who at times treated
his royal prisoner with great consideration. There is even a

suggestion that Edward's great scheme of enlargement was inspired by the observations of one or other of these distinguished if unwilling guests, and that their ransoms went a long way towards paying the cost. The first part of the theory may stand, but the second cannot; for the ransom of David was small, although it was paid in 1357; and that of the French King was handsome, being equivalent to a million and a half of our money, but it was never received. In fact King John of France returned to England because he could not fulfil the terms of his agreement with Edward—for he was an honourable man—and he died in the Savoy in 1363. To Windsor Castle James I. of Scotland was brought by Henry V. from the Tower; here he courted Jane Beaufort, whom he married in 1424, and here he wrote *The King's Quair*, or *Quhair* (meaning "book" in either case), concerning his love for Jane Beaufort. The manuscript is at the Bodleian, and may be described as mildly and tediously Chaucerian. (The "garden fayre" whereof he wrote used, in Victorian days, to be "carpet-bedded" with the semblance of the insignia of the Garter. Now, at the instigation of Queen Alexandra, it is a paradise of tender-hued tea and rambling roses.) Besides this, accommodation had always to be found for a guard of soldiers at Windsor, and, since the foundation of the Order of the Garter and the subsequent erection of St. George's Chapel, it has been the centre of the ceremonies of the principal order of knighthood in Great Britain, and the abiding place of a considerable ecclesiastical community. Like many a great country house, but upon a far grander scale, it has grown with its needs; and different parts of the area enclosed within the walls have been used for many purposes in successive periods. Thus the present palace on the summit of the eminence was built, partly at any rate, by reason of the need for accommodation for ecclesiastics and officers in the Lower Ward, a need which grew pressing after the foundation of the Order of the Garter; and the growth of Windsor has been, in some measure, commensurate with the increase in the importance of our Kings and of their country and ours.

The most simple, perhaps the only practical way, of examining Windsor Castle, is to take it piece by piece, as you see it. And first, travelling to Windsor by the Great Western Railway, it is seen as a majestic whole some time before the line sweeps round Eton to reach the station. It matters but little what be the point of view, so long as it is far enough off to escape the distressing but inevitable appearance of newness that is Windsor Castle's chief, if not its only, drawback. Bathed in summer sunlight, with the red roofs of Windsor glowing below, and with the green foliage of many trees clustered beneath the terrace; or against a background of grey cloud, when the Royal Standard on the Round Tower, of small size by reason of a storm, streams straight before the gale; or, perhaps most of all, when towers and battlements are wreathed in snow; Windsor Castle is always perfect in its kind. The very best of all views is from the river-bank at Clewer. There is little, if anything, in the Royal Borough to detain the visitor, except the Town Hall, quite a characteristic, but altered, structure by Sir Christopher Wren, adorned by statues of "glorious Anna" and Prince George of Denmark. For the story that Wren inserted additional pillars to satisfy the timorous burgesses, but, to show his contempt for their fears, did not permit the pillars to reach that which they were supposed to support, the gaps between the pillars and the floor above still vouch. Near the Town Hall are some nice old houses (to look at, not to inhabit), and a few in Peascod Street. Not a vestige remains of the inns that Falstaff and, as we need not doubt, the creator of Falstaff, knew full well. There is indeed a " Star and Garter," but it is in Peascod Street, and the probabilities are that Shakespeare's house of call stood where the " White Hart," familiar to all Etonians, stands to-day. But the " White Hart " is, from an æsthetic point of view, sadly modern, having been completely rebuilt at some time, probably

Windsor, Church Street.

quite recent, within the last twenty years. It is a hotel, however, at which man may stay in reasonable comfort, though there are London hotels where more comfort can be secured for less money. They have not, however, as the " White Hart " has, a full view of the Castle Hill, so that, when the King and Queen are at Windsor, or when any great ceremonial is to the fore, Royalties and distinguished visitors may be seen at any odd moment. In truth, to sit on a balcony of the " White Hart " on such occasions, in delicious scorn of the crowd jostling on the pavement beneath, is to enjoy the sensations of one in the Royal Box at the theatre, as compared with that of men who have had to wait at the pit door. It is true there may be no play, and that in any case it is impossible to tell in advance when the curtain will rise or what scene will be enacted; but experience shows that some interesting episode nearly always comes, and the uncertainty as to the *dramatis personæ* adds to the pleasure of seeing that of anticipation.

A Quarter of a century ago it was my fortune to stay at the "White Hart," then an old fashioned inn, but still not Falstaff's haunt, several times as a solitary traveller; and, in the smoking-room, not in the body of the house, was held a nightly parliament, quite informal, of the civic worthies of Windsor. It left the impression that the social tone of Windsor men pure and simple, of the natives as distinguished from local residents, attracted entirely, and for the most part temporarily, by the presence of the Court, was, if possible, more narrow, and certainly more pompous, than that of their equals in station in the average provincial town. These not very considerable tradesmen, perhaps they were warrant-holders, seemed to set themselves up as superior to others of their class, and one of them, who was a hatter, was also a knight. Now a barber may be a "tonsorial artist," a butcher a "purveyor of meat," a grocer an "Italian warehouseman"; but a hatter is always a hatter, and a hatter who was also a knight seemed an incongruity. At any rate, rightly or wrongly, the nightly parliament left the impression described, and the opportunities of studying this stratum of society in Windsor further, numerous as they have been, were deliberately neglected.

The sights on which I have looked from the window of the "White Hart" would fill a book, writ out large. Among the persons—one ought perhaps to write personages—seen from that balcony have been many Kings and Queens, and an Emperor and Empress, to say nothing of minor potentates, statesmen, and diplomatists. Among the scenes witnessed from it have been some of the brightest and some of the most solemn and affecting in the history of the Royal Family of England. When the brighter occasions are to the fore it is certainly not too much to say that an occupant of that pleasant balcony can hardly look up and down the street, or up the Castle Hill, without seeing somebody who is illustrious.

Once, however, that favourite balcony went near to playing me a mischievous trick, to be forgiven because an episode that opened awkwardly closed in merry laughter and the cheerful clatter of tea-cups. Some fifteen years ago, on a sweltering day in summer, I walked down to my room at the "White Hart" to describe, in the capacity of "special correspondent," a state wedding witnessed in St. George's Chapel. Time crept on, sheets were filled with writing, the heat grew intense, and, one by one, superfluous garments were cast aside. A pleasant commotion became audible from the street without; cheers signified that the bride and bridegroom were driving to the railway station to begin their honeymoon. Noting the hour I wrote on. Suddenly there was a rustle of drapery at the open window, and I looked up to see ladies' faces withdrawn rapidly at the sight of an unexpected man in habiliments that, amply sufficient as they would have been in a boat or on the cricket field (not to say ludicrously excessive on the running path), were exiguous in a sitting-room. Followed a parley, wherein the voices of the parties, actually separated by a foot or so of wall more substantial than that through which

Pyramus and Thisbe whispered, travelled through the open window; and after that a man clothed and in his right mind, a very fortunate man he counted himself, had the honour of entertaining at tea sundry ladies, of whom one had actually been a Royal bridesmaid. Hence came, as Mr. Pepys might have said, mighty entertainment in the first place, and, in a great newspaper of the next day, such minute accuracy in matters of millinery, and such apt use of terms in description. as could not have been attained save for this happy accident. For—this is quite by the way, but not an uninteresting little secret out of the prison-house of journalism—to describe dresses in cultivated terms is passing difficult. A man cannot do it, because he knows too little ; a dressmaker cannot do it, because she knows too much about technicalities of dress ; a " lady journalist " often fails because she knows too little of English ; and the true opportunity comes only when chance throws together the man who has to write and the lady who has worn the dress to be described. Is this a digression ? Of course it is. So are half the best things in *Tristram Shandy ;* .and Laurence Sterne, dead as he is this many a year, shall have no monopoly in one of the most attractive and seductive of literary artifices.

One might linger on this balcony, in the spirit as in the flesh, long and with enjoyment, were it not for the imperious necessity of attacking the Castle itself in detail. Concerning this matter that most learned antiquarian and my honoured friend, John Meade Falkner, has written many wise and thoughtful sentences, and one—in a guide book it is true—that is astonishing : " Three hours are hardly enough to see the Castle, the State Apartments, the Albert Memorial, and the North Terrace." This has been equalled once, in a somewhat diversified experience, by the conductor, so to speak, of a party of pilgrims from the United States, who had " done " Stratford-on-Avon, as the saying goes, in a morning. For that they might be pardoned, since nothing that man can effect to make

Shakespeare's town intolerable to the tranquil traveller has been omitted. But when the conductor of this "handful of American citizens travelling simply for recreation," and taking it laboriously and for instruction consumed in a highly condensed form, proceeded to add that there was nothing in Oxford to keep them for more than "half a day," my heart sank : Mr. Falkner cannot have meant to be taken literally ; for he would be the first to agree that it is impossible to visit Windsor Castle too often, or to spend too much time in St. George's Chapel, in the Cloisters, or on the Terrace, and that each fresh visit leaves one the richer by some new point of interest unobserved before and the more conscious that there is still much more to see and to learn. Indeed, the careful and affectionate tone of Mr. Falkner's treatment of Windsor Castle is proof positive of many days and weeks spent in loving study of his subject. The guide-book he wrote bears the honoured and familiar name of Murray, and it is by my side as I write, and in my pocket whenever I go to Windsor Castle, because Mr. Falkner is no ordinary and commonplace writer of guide-books. He is, in his tastes and training, a scholar, a man of letters, an antiquary, and a profound student of architecture. He writes, as the linnet sings, because he must, and because he finds, in the production of novels of no mean merit and of learned histories, much-needed relaxation from the labours incident to high place in an industrial enterprise of world-wide fame and of striking prosperity and volume.

So, starting up the Castle Hill, we turn " stunt to the left," as they say in the West Country, through King Henry VIII.'s Gateway, so called in spite of the fact that it marked the entrance to the Lower Ward long years before the many-wived King saw the light, and the south side of St. George's Chapel faces us in all its glorious and airy majesty. This have I done a hundred times, perhaps more often, but never without a first feeling that there is something of incongruity about the things seen and heard in these most dignified surroundings. Through the

Windsor, Henry VIII.'s Gateway.

imposing entrance, past the sentry, always a Guardsman and therefore the most majestic of foot-soldiers, into the cloistered peace of the Lower Ward, the stranger walks with the glamour of the place on him. A thousand memories crowd into his mind. Suddenly there is a clatter of hoofs and a tradesman's cart, butcher's, fishmonger's, or dairy-man's, dashes in, seeming to be no part of the picture: and next comes the quick thought that this sense of incongruity is really a wrong sense, that these necessary vehicles of everyday life are properly significant in their little way. They serve to emphasise at once the variety and the numbers of the normal population of Windsor Castle. It is in very truth this very fact that makes Windsor Castle the most remarkable of royal residences. Apart from the Court, here are the Dean's household, those of the canons and the minor canons, of the lay clerks and of the military knights.

The sense of incongruity may be felt, rightly or wrongly, justly or unjustly, upon entering the Lower Ward. It is lost entirely as one passes by the south door into St. George's Chapel. Here three thoughts force themselves into the mind in quick succession. The first is that St. George's Chapel is the absolutely right thing in the absolutely right place; the next that it is, if the sun be shining at all, flooded with pervading light as few structures, if any, of an ecclesiastical character, are in this or in any other country; and the third is that there is an infinite amount of detail, here a monument, there a chapel, here beautiful carved work, there iron-work of extraordinary merit and intricacy, calling for much time to be spent with equal profit and pleasure. There shall be no essay written now on St. George's Chapel, its history, and its beauties, general and particular, partly because such essays have been written often before, written well, and written ill, but even more because it is one of the very few amongst our sacred edifices where those who guide the footsteps of the visitor are, if they find him or her to be cultivated and sympathetic, themselves patient, suggestive, informing, and unobtrusive. Its harmonious char-

South Transept of St. George's Chapel, Windsor.

acter and suitability to its position and surroundings are so obvious that they need no emphasis. It is a perfect example of Perpendicular architecture, spacious enough to be worthy of the Kings and the illustrious Order for whom it serves as a place of worship and of ceremonial, yet not so large as to remind one of a stately cathedral. Its delightful abundance of light, due partly to the airy character of the buttresses, and partly to the scanty supply of stained glass in the windows, suggests the thought that elsewhere the "dim, religious light" may be in the nature of an error; and then comes the reflection that few indeed of our sacred edifices can boast interiors able to bear so well as St. George's the searching light of day. As for the details, they must be seen to be enjoyed and understood to the full, and studied as well as seen. To catalogue them, giving inscriptions and dimensions, would be tedious alike to writer and to reader. A sufficiency of them, perhaps, will come into the picture, so to speak, if I attempt to reproduce one or two of the impressions that St. George's Chapel has made upon me on majestic and memorable occasions; and to do this with any measure of success will be to pass on to others an idea of this beautiful and holy place far more complete than could be produced by transcribing and elaborating notes made diligently on the spot or collected as the result of studying many authorities. The notes exist, of course, but they are no more than the dry bones.

Many great scenes, majestic, affecting, have been enacted within the four walls of St. George's Chapel, and it would be an endless task to enumerate them. The most pathetic of them, perhaps, was the silent burial of the body of Charles I., in February of 1648. But for grandeur and pathos combined surely the scene of the 2nd of February, 1901, can never have been surpassed, perhaps never equalled, since St. George's Chapel was built; and this sentence is equally applicable whether it be applied to the chapel in its present form and position, or to the earlier work, on a slightly different site, of Henry III. or of Edward III. A spectacle that can never be erased from memory was the final scene in the funeral of Victoria the Good. It was an occasion unutterably affecting, a solemn ceremony of unspeakable majesty and meaning, and its stately course comes to mind irresistibly whenever I revisit St. George's in the spirit or in the body. Did I write "irresistibly"? Who that was present would desire to thrust back a reminiscence so infinitely sad and yet of such incalculable value? Let me go back a little, only a few days. During the week preceding that gloomy Saturday I had been one of the few who moved, sad, silent, all but stupefied by the silent evidence of the kingdom's loss, through the room at Osborne where the body of the Queen lay,.watched by Grenadiers bending over their reversed rifles, and draped in the folds of the proud flag that she had loved full well. I had looked while it was borne down the hill from Osborne and laid on the deck of the *Alberta*. I had seen the *Alberta* steam slowly towards the East between the lines of Great Britain's colossal ships of war ; had listened to the thunder of mourning guns, each sounding like the beating of a nation's broken heart. Very early on the next morning, that dull and grey and cold morning of the 2nd of February, I walked through the beautiful Horseshoe Cloisters, past the west door, and to an appointed place in the organ loft. The nave, with a carpet of soft green over a broad path running from west door to choir screen, with tiers of purple seats on either side, had not its normal aspect. The choir, empty as yet, was as usual. Away on the north side, above the altar, was the oriel balcony of the Queen's "closet," never to be occupied by Queen Victoria again. There, close to it, visible to the eye of knowledge rather than actually, was the screen for the tomb of Edward IV., the masterpiece in wrought iron of Quintin Matsys, or, if not, of a worker no less cunning of hand. (So, at least, I thought then. Now I know that if any Matsys made the screen it was Josse, not Quintin, that it was used for a gateway first, and that it very likely may not be wrought iron at all, but cast.) The sombre fifteenth-century oak of the carven stalls was in shadow, although here and there a light flashed from the enamelled brass of this or that Knight of the Garter in days gone by; and the banners, helmets, and swords of the existing members of the highest of our Orders of knighthood made a brave show of colour above. In the holy of holies of the Order the body of its Sovereign Lady was about to be buried with every circumstance of solemnity. Even before the funeral service began in the chapel, in fact before the Queen's body had left London, the close connection between St. George's Chapel and the Order of the Garter began to take personal shape and colour, and figures recalling bygone years in the history of Windsor Castle apart from the Order of the Garter were seen to be assembling. The Bishops of Winchester and Oxford and the Dean of Windsor appeared, not in their accustomed vestments as ecclesiastical persons, but in the gorgeous and old-world robes belonging to their positions as Prelate, Chancellor, and Registrar of the Garter. The Yeomen of the Guard, in their scarlet and with their halberds, carried back memory to the days immediately after Bosworth Field, to which they trace their history. Of the old world spoke the uniforms of the King's Bodyguard of the Honourable Corps of the Gentlemen at Arms, and of the Military Knights of Windsor; and one remembered that these last were the direct successors of the "alms knights," or "poor knights," for whom Edward III. made first provision, for whom Queen Mary built houses and Elizabeth gave lands. It seemed as though the centuries were assembling to pay the last honour to Victoria's memory, since for the nineteenth century too there were many and illustrious witnesses. It is no figure of speech to say that these thoughts came to the mind unasked. There were hours to wait and they really came.

Followed something in the nature of a shock. The Arch- bishops, the ecclesiastical officials of the Garter, the clergy, and the choir had gone to the closed west door. It opened to disclose, at first, greyness and bare ground. Then suddenly the void was filled, not by artillery horses, as men had expected, but by straining sailors, and a thrill ran through the waiting assembly, ignorant of the misadventure, a happy one it seems now, that had brought about the change of plans. Up the nave, very slowly, came the coffin, the insignia of the Sovereign and of the Most Noble Order of the Garter, and behind them the King and the German Emperor, both of them the very embodiment of grave sorrow and of earnest dignity. The broad passage up the nave, that had been empty, was now a mass of colour and of glittering uniforms, testifying not only to the honour in which Queen Victoria was held, but also to the greatness of the Order whose head had passed away. What more needs to be written? The music throbbed and wailed; the beautiful service was said and sung; and the last words that rung in all ears were those which proclaimed King Edward to be "*now*, by the grace of God of the United Kingdom of Great Britain and Ireland King, Defender of the Faith, Emperor of India, *and Soverign of the Most Noble Order of the Garter. God save the King.*" In those italicised words is embodied the essential and singular significance of St. George's Chapel at Windsor. It is the very heart of a glorious Order of knighthood, the first in the civilised world in point of honour and antiquity, whose head and corner-stone is the sovereign for the time being.

Historians and heraldic experts have disputed not a little as to the date of the foundation of the Order and concerning its origin. Dr. Stubbs, for example, wrote that "Edward III. celebrating his great feast on the institution of the Order of the Garter in the midst of the Black Death" was but acting in the spirit of complete lack of sympathy between classes that was characteristic of his age. But the Black Death was no respecter of persons, and the opinions of the learned vary concerning the precise date of the foundation of the Order. The Black Death ravaged the country in 1348-9. Froissart, delightful, contemporary, but not always accurate, says the Order was founded in 1344; Mr. Longman is in favour of 1347; Ashmole and Dr. Stubbs support April and St. George's Day of 1349; and the Wardrobe Accounts are not conclusively in support of any of the theories. So there is not enough evidence on which to convict the founder of the Order of an act of "heartlessness," even if it were justifiable, after an endeavour to assume a fourteenth-century point of view, to say that it would have been heartless to found a great Order with every circumstance of joyous festival at a time of national calamity. Indeed, the one thing that remains certain is that Hallam was right in saying the Order was founded when England "was the sun, as it were, of that system which embraced the valour and nobility of the Christian world . . . when chivalry was in its zenith, and in all the virtues which adorned the knightly character none were so conspicuous as Edward III. and the Black Prince."

As for the origin, not so much of the Order, as of its insignia, riband, and motto, it is in much doubt. True it is that Ashmole speaks of "the vulgar and more general story" concerning the accidental dropping of the garter of a Countess of Salisbury—nobody knows which of two ladies who bore that name—with some contempt. Still he does not repudiate it absolutely, and it must be remembered that the age was robust and not unduly refined, and that the words "*Honi soit qui mal y pense*" fit in more neatly to some such incident than to any more solemn theory. On the other hand, the Black Book of the Order, compiled at least 150 years later by some person or persons unknown from materials no longer accessible, but at a date much nearer to the initiation of the Order than that of any commentator of weight, gives a more dignified theory. It is that when Edward founded the Order he had in view the fact, if fact it was, that Richard I., when he was fighting in Cyprus at the end of the twelfth century, selected some of his knights to wear a special garter round their knees, the intent of such garter being to impress their duty of gallantry upon them. That, however, sounds a little fanciful, and it does not harmonise in any striking measure with the motto. Still, this was the view advanced in 1527, when Francis I. was invested as a Knight of the Garter. At that precise time, however, Henry VIII. had every reason for desiring to make himself pleasant to the King of France, and it is quite within the bounds of possibility that the theory may have been invented to foster the *entente cordiale*. Certainly the view ultimately adopted by Ashmole would not have tended to conciliate the French King. It is that "King Edward, having given forth his own garter as a signal for a battle which sped fortunately," the said battle being that of Crecy, "took occasion to institute this Order, and gave the garter eminence among the ensigns of it, whence that select Order whom he incorporated into a fraternity are frequently styled *Equites aureæ periscelidis*, and vulgarly 'Knights of the Garter.'" The upshot of the whole matter is that the circumstances are so remote, not merely in point of time, but in their whole character, from the ideas of the present day, that imagination is baffled not a little in the endeavour to weigh the probabilities. Even in an age of message by token a garter, one would think, could hardly have been an appropriate vehicle of information and command. Yet a theory attaching some importance to a King's garter was undoubtedly considered probable enough to be offered to a King of France in the sixteenth century, either in good faith, or to soothe his sensibilities. Again, if the theory of a King's garter, whether the King were Richard I. or Edward III., be reckoned the most tenable, what becomes of the meaning of "*Honi soit qui mal y pense*"? Can it be that it has been erroneously construed for more than 500 years? What impropriety, or shame, is connected with the garter of a man, King or commoner?

Left unsatisfied by the learned upon this perfectly trivial but quite amusive question ("amusive" is Wordsworth's word and

Gilbert White uses it far more effectively than "amusing"),
I had recourse to that little treasury of quaint information, the
Dictionary of Phrase and Fable, whereof the 100th thousand
appeared in 1895, when its author, Dr. Brewer, was in the
eighty-sixth year of his age. It is a volume that often proves
useful, in spite of frequent inaccuracies and of neglect to state
authorities, when those of higher reputation are found wanting.
In this case it is any rate suggestive. Dr. Brewer tells us that
"wearing the garters of a pretty maiden either on the hat
or knee was a common custom of our forefathers. Brides
usually wore on their legs a host of gay ribbons, to be distributed after the marriage ceremony among the bridegroom's
friends, and the piper at the wedding dance never failed to tie
a piece of the bride's garter round his pipe. If there is any
truth in the legend given above" (that of Joan, Countess
of Salisbury, and her garter) "the impression produced on the
guests would be wholly different to what such an accident
would produce in our days." In passing this last sentence
will not bear examination, for the essence of the Countess
of Salisbury legend is that the garter was displayed by accident,
and that of the bride tradition that the garters were intended
for distribution. But there may be a great deal of substance in
the next suggestion. "Perhaps the 'Order of the Garter,
after all, may be about tantamount to 'The Order of the
Ladies' Champions.'" That, if Dr. Brewer is right about the
"common custom of our ancestors"—would that he had told
us how he knew it—would fit in well with the spirit of the age,
with the theory of Sir Harris Nicholas that the Order first
originated in connection with a tournament, and with the fact,
established by the Wardrobe Account, that garments similar to
the Garter vestments were issued for the Christmas games at
Guildford in 1347, and for sundry tournaments. Nor would the
motto be then ill fitting. It would say roughly, "The gage
which we wear may be unusual; none but a foul mind will
construe it amiss."

No apology need be offered for this gentle effort to add a little stone to the cairn of literature concerning the date of the foundation of the Garter, and the occasion of founding it ; since we are at St. George's Chapel, and it is as the chapel of that genuinely noble Order that St. George's Chapel chiefly strikes the imagination. A Valhalla it is not, in the national sense. To be that is the privilege of St. Paul's and of West-minster Abbey. But it is the primary burying-place of royal personages, of Edward IV., Henry VI., Henry VIII., Charles I., a host of Hanoverian kings, princes, and princesses, the Duchess of Kent, the Prince Consort, the Duke of Clarence and Avondale, the Duchess of Teck, and last, but not least by a long way, of Queen Victoria. The word " primary " has been used, for lack of a better one, to indicate the comforting fact that, while in modern times the burial service has been said and sung over the bodies of royal personages in St. George's Chapel, they have not been permitted to remain there. Even the Royal Tomb House has not been employed for its appointed purpose since 1878. Its place has been taken by Frogmore ; and the chapel which Henry VII. once intended for that purpose, where Wolsey began his own monument (part of it used for Lord Nelson's tomb in St. Paul's), where Verrio lavished his art on the ceiling, and under which are buried George III. and all his family, has become the Albert Memorial Chapel, the work of the late Sir Gilbert Scott ; a gorgeous affair of mosaics, inlaid marbles, marble pictures, lapis lazuli, alabaster and porphyry and malachite ; but, apart from the actual memorials of the Prince Consort, and the Dukes of Albany and Clarence, not in the least pleasing to a not too punctilious sense of art.

However, the essential thing is that the dust to which all men and women, kings or peasants, must come at last, is far away from a structure that, besides being exceptionally bright and airy, for a place of worship, is also a favourite scene for illus-trious marriages. Of these the most interesting was that of

March, 1863, when the Prince of Wales, now King Edward
VII., led the "sea-king's daughter from over the sea," who
is now Queen Alexandra, to the altar. Here, too, have been
celebrated several other royal marriages, notably that of
the Duke and Duchess of Connaught; but others, of at least
equal importance, have taken place elsewhere, in Buckingham
Palace and St. James's Palace for example, with a considerable
loss of effect, if that matters. For prettiness, surely a desirable
attribute of a joyous wedding, a marriage in one of the private
chapels is not to be compared with one at St. George's, and by
all contemporary accounts that of our King and Queen was an
occasion of unexampled splendour and solemnity.

If St. George's Chapel is impressive principally by reason of
its proportions, its light, its associations with Royalty and the
Garter, and its fitness for those associations, it is also
remarkable for containing points of beauty and interest
greater, perhaps, in number, in proportion to its size,
than any other sacred edifice can show. If the west window,
where ancient and modern stained glass are used together
without success, will not bear close examination, the stained
windows of the choir show portraits of sovereigns, beginning
with Edward III. and ending with William IV. and his
Queen Adelaide; and other portraits, of Edward III.,
Edward V., and Henry VII. may be seen in the Aldworth
Chapel, besides windows representing the Coronation of
William III. and Queen Anne giving her bounty. Again, the
tracery on the roof of the nave, with a touch of colour added
by the arms of Knights of the Garter, is very fine. Of
monuments, too, there is great store, the most noticeable for
interest being Boehm's figures of the late Duke of Kent, of
Leopold I., King of the Belgians, the "Uncle Leopold,"
who is referred to constantly in the published correspondence
and memoirs of the Royal Family in early Victorian days,
and of the Prince Imperial. Whether this last is more or less
pathetic in the death that it recalls than that to Princess

Inscriptions and those Land-Marks pulled down by which all Men knew every particular place in that Church, and such a dismal mutation over the whole, that they knew not where they were : nor was there one old Officer that had belonged to it, or knew where our Princes had used to be interred. But there was a Fellow of the Town who undertook to tell them the place, where, he said, ' There was a vault, in which King Harry the Eighth and Queen Jane Seymour were interred.' As near that place as could conveniently be, they caused the Grave to be made. There the King's body was laid without any words, or other Ceremonies than the tears and sighs of the few beholders." (Another account tells us that the Bishop's lips were seen to move.) " Upon the coffin was a plate of silver fixt, with these words only, ' King Charles, 1648.' When the Coffin was put in, the black Velvet Pall that had covered it was thrown over it, and then the Earth thrown in ; which the Governour stayed to see perfectly done, and then took the keys of the Church."

Of a truth, and in spite of a certain superfluity of personal pronouns, this is a noble and affecting passage of English prose ; although it is always necessary to remember that Clarendon was violently prejudiced in his views. But the words are quoted mainly to show how wonderful it is that the chapel, after suffering " so dismal a mutation " in those days as to puzzle those who knew it well, after losing much of its beauty of detail in the days of the Reformation too, should be now, as it has been for many years, a veritable treasure-house of memorials of the past, as well as, perhaps, the most perfect example of Perpendicular architecture to be found in England. It is but fair to add that some of those best qualified to know describe Clarendon's passage as mere invention, point out, with some truth, that the Commonwealth soldiers at least left a great deal behind, and assert that Charles II.'s only reason for failing to find his father's body was that he desired for his private purposes the money granted for a tomb.

Yet once more, since the last preceding words were written, have I visited St. George's Chapel under accomplished guidance, to find all sorts of new points of interest ; for example, the lovely ironwork of all the locks ; the ingenious peep-hole permitting those who desired ingress

to the Royal Closet to be scanned without their knowledge from the stairway; the ancient lean-to wherein the
acolytes kindled their incense and the new stone in the pillar
they had chopped away with their carelessly swung censers—
this last is close to the Hastings Chantry. On the same day,
but away from the chapel, were visited the chapter library, rich
in black-letters, including a Caxton, and famous as the place
wherein the *Merry Wives* was first played by lay clerks and
choir boys, in the presence of Elizabeth, who was doubtless the
more delighted in that the Pages and the Fords and the rest of
them bore names that, as the ancient leases show, were real
Windsor names. In the Curfew Tower, too, I saw the cannon
trained by Cromwell on the bridge to Eton, the clock, with
works that have lasted since Stuart times at any rate, and the
dungeons, and, lantern-bearing, penetrated by the passage leading to the sally-port and under the cabstand in the public road
outside the Castle. Noteworthy in this tower is the colossal
timber-work within, standing independently of the walls, so
that the ringing of the bells might not affect the masonry.
Again, under the building of St. George's, we inspected the
chambers allotted to two of the chantry priests, with the little
recesses for books at the head of the bed-place, and their fine
fireplaces. One of them is now used as the home of the
machinery for blowing the organ, the other as a toolhouse, and
it was amusing to note that the massive oaken door had been
adorned, on the inside, with innumerable midget photographs
from packets of cheap cigarettes! Irreverence for antiquity
could surely go no lower.

Windsor Castle is all impressive, much of it very beautiful,
all instinct with story, and the difficulty besetting the writer is
not so much what to say about it as where to begin and where
to end, since it would be easy to go on writing for ever. The
safest plan, therefore, will be simply to go on. We entered
St. George's Chapel by the south door, but the most noble
entrance, reserved for State occasions, joyful and solemn, is by

the western door, and in any case the visitor must needs go
thus far, even if he may not pass through, unless he is to miss
one of the most picturesque corners of Windsor Castle, the
Horseshoe Cloisters. These have an air of immemorial,
exquisite, and well-preserved antiquity. In fact they are not
older than the flight of broad steps, quite modern, by which
the west door is reached. It is almost hard to believe that
they were not built in their present form in the glorious days
of Elizabeth or of her father Henry, but that to Sir Gilbert
Scott belongs the credit of having reared in the place of an
insignificant and unlovely range of buildings an edifice easily
to be mistaken for a piece of genuine Tudor work. Somewhere
one would like to see an inscription, " *Hoc fecit Gilbertus Scott*,"
after the model of " *Hoc fecit Wykeham* " on the Winchester
Tower, and for good reason. There may be doubts, to be
spurned as destructive of pious illusions, whether Wykeham
was really an architect : there is no question whatever that
Scott achieved this particular work, and there is still less that
he perpetrated many other works by no means so well calculated to enhance his reputation in after ages. Hard by are the
Canon's Houses, nestling round a cloister of immemorial oak,
interesting and secluded, to be reached also by the vigorous
after ascending the Hundred Steps from Thames Street. This
ascent is worth making even for the middle-aged. It offers to
them many physical inducements to turn round and regard the
surrounding country ; and the view, as soon as it becomes
possible to look down on the red tiles of Windsor, on the
winding river, on Eton in its girdle of trees, and on the champaign beyond and on all sides, is of unexampled fascination of
the tranquil kind. Here, too, are the early sixteenth-century
Deanery, the exquisite Dean's Cloisters built in the time of
Edward II., and the Winchester Tower with its inscription, " *Hoc
fecit Wykeham*." All the world of course knows the story to
the effect that the King saw the inscription and was jealous, and
that the ready scholar turned the tables on his patron and

Edward III., then, with Wykeham to advise him, raised the Round Tower on top of the mound fortified since the days of the Heptarchy, and he raised it to be the meeting-place of that glorious Order of knighthood of his foundation. If old Froissart may be believed, the site of the Round Tower was chosen for other reasons in addition to its commanding eminence; for it was on this very spot, according to the legend quoted by Froissart, that King Arthur used to sit surrounded by

> " The goodliest fellowship of famous knights
> Whereof this world holds record."

It is a fascinating suggestion. There may have never been a Table Round; Arthur, Launcelot, Galahad, and the rest of the glorious company, may never have lived and fought; that true and untrue woman Guinever and the hapless Elaine may be alike fables and myths of ancient time; but since their story is infinitely human, and since it has been celebrated in matchless verse, to say nothing of Malory's direct and vivid prose, we are entitled, if we please, to believe with Gibbon rather than to be sceptical with Milton. Such, at any rate, was the sober and considered opinion of Sir Edward Strachey, who performed a real service to the public by introducing the original edition by Caxton, revised for modern use, of Sir Thomas Malory's *Morte Darthur* to the public through the house of Macmillan more than a generation ago. In any case it may be taken for certain that Froissart found the legend, and did not invent it; for the " little secretary " and indefatigable gossip was much in England, in the confidence of the Court, and particularly in that of Queen Philippa; and, if he had not critical judgment, he was an ardent and painstaking chronicler. At least it may be taken as proved that the tower that was to be the first house of the Sovereign of the Most Noble Order of the Garter and of the Knights thereof was reared on the site assigned by tradition to Arthur and the Knights of the Table

Round : and that is fascinating. There could have been no more appropriate hearth upon which to light anew the sacred fire of British chivalry.

Was it Edward or another who, mindful that the Palace of Windsor might be called upon to serve as fortress and to withstand a siege, caused a deep well to be dug under the Round Tower and down to the level of the bed of the Thames? No man knows. In truth, the very existence of the well had been forgotten until it was discovered afresh, in quite modern times, when Sir John Cowell was Master of the Household; and it was natural that its existence should have passed out of memory, for centuries have passed away since the very idea of a siege of Windsor Castle has been conceivable. Its most potent charm, indeed, is that, fortress-like as it is architecturally, it is in its essence the undisturbed and inviolable home of our sovereigns and of the ecclesiastical and knightly communities of which the sovereign from time to time is the living centre. The Round Tower has its memories, none the less, although they are not memories of storm and stress. It has housed many illustrious prisoners, besides those named already. Henry IV. kept here, in honourable custody, the child of seven years old, Edward Mortimer, Earl of March, the rightful heir to the throne. The same King held the lad James I. of Scotland captive in the Round Tower, making some amends by providing his prisoner with an excellent education. A willing resident was Prince Rupert after the Restoration, and, if the effeminacy of the pictures and tapestries in his bedchamber horrified Evelyn, in their contrast to the martial furniture of "the huge, steep stairs," it is at least worth remembering that the wayward genius had useful occupations in the Round Tower. Engraving, chemistry, the perfecting of gunpowder, had engaged Rupert's attention in Paris during the years of his exile, and, when he came back to prosperity, he used the Round Tower as laboratory and workshop. An inanimate, but by no means voiceless, object there is also in the Round Tower ; nothing less than the great bell, weighing nearly a ton, brought from Sebastopol to England after the Crimea. The prospect from the top of the tower is magnificent in the extreme, being more extensive than that from the steps or any of the terraces, for the point is higher and the eye can rove in every direction ; and when distinguished visitors are at Windsor it is practically a rule of the household that a Lord in Waiting should attend them up the 150 steps of " the huge, steep stairs " leading to this matchless coign of vantage.

Passing away from the Round Tower, and dealing first with the things visible elsewhere than under a roof, let us make in the spirit the tour of the terraces, of which the northern, looking down on Eton and the Thames, beloved of Elizabeth, Charles I., Charles II., and of homely George III., who did not hesitate to walk there with his family among the crowd, is perhaps the most choiceworthy. From it fall the steep slopes, well planted with trees, and beneath them is a riverside plain made by nature to be the scene of human pastime, and converted by English kings of old days to the uses of the tournament. Perhaps the most memorable occasion when it was employed for this purpose was the splendid tournament instituted, not long before Crecy by Edward III. Fain would one attempt to reproduce the scene, in spite of surroundings, many of them, the South Western Railway station for example, distressingly modern. If the truth may be told, the more one knows of mediæval tournaments, the more difficult it becomes to think of them as gallant spectacles. The ladies and the lists, the gorgeous pavilions and the heralds in their tabards, one can imagine to have made a brave show. That is really all ; there can have been very little dash or life about the fighting. The horses were heavy—the shire horse is supposed to be their lineal descendant. The few tilting helmets that remain, unsightly steel boxes commanding absurd prices, show that it was quite impossible for the knight wearing one to see what he was doing. The spears—there were some in the temporary ante-room to Westminster Abbey at the Coronation, and they adorn many a hall—were of cumbrous weight. The armour was so ponderous that an unhorsed knight must needs be put in the saddle by others, and, last absurdity of all, the chargers were led at one time by the squires of the knights. That quenches the ardour of the imagination. Glorious accounts of old time notwithstanding, it is abundantly clear, even from Malory, that a tournament must always have been rather a ridiculous business. This sounds well : " Then Sir Lavaine met with Sir Palamides and either met other so hard and so fiercely that both their horses fell to the earth." The next words destroy the glamour. "Then they were horsed again"—and so it must have been with all tournaments.

Towering above the North Terrace are the State Apartments ; and, round the corner, above the East Terrace, the Private Apartments look over a flower-garden and into the face of the rising sun. State Apartments, Private Apartments, and the Visitors' Apartments on the south side, where there is an entrance by George IV.'s Gateway, form, with the Round Tower at the western extremity, what is sometimes called the Great Quadrangle of the Upper Ward, but it is really, and by reason of the abundant space at the western end, rather a spacious rectangular trilateral of gravel ; its one note-worthy feature is an equestrian statue of Charles II., and here the pedestal, carved with fruits and fishes by Grinling Gibbons, is far more worthy of admiration than the statue. Sooth to say, the tawny gravel and the trim grey walls present a somewhat dull and monotonous appearance, except when the band of this or that regiment of the Foot Guards is playing in the morning, and looking bright as it plays ; and the trilateral must have presented a far more noble spectacle before " the magnificent dragon-fountain of Queen Mary " was destroyed. Owing to the height of the surrounding buildings, too, and the perverse arrangement of Nature causing the sun to appear to rise in the

Windsor, Market Street.

east and to seem to travel by the south to the west, the interior of the trilateral is apt to be chilly and sunless, particularly in winter. It is, however, an open question whether to prefer the ample prospect of country that may be enjoyed from the Private Apartments or the view down the Long Walk from George IV.'s Gateway. The former, of course, is unconfined, but it is not for everybody. From the gateway the eye passes first along a gentle and artificial slope, the foot of which appears to be occupied, as of traditional right, by the Eton boys on State occasions ; and then the view is strictly bounded on either side by a magnificent double avenue of fine elms, bordering a perfectly straight road for some three miles, and ending in a colossal equestrian statue of George III., known to the scoffer as "The Copper Horse." The elms, it must be confessed with sorrow, are not what they were, here or elsewhere. It is indeed a thousand pities that the forest tree which, with the possible exception of the beech, undoubtedly makes the most imposing avenues, while they last, the tree endowed by Tennyson for ever with the epithet immemorial, should really be short-lived, and remarkably dangerous into the bargain. For it is to be noted that the elm not only succumbs readily to storms, but also has an inveterate habit of dropping huge branches without warning in still weather. Apart from its majestic height, its spreading branches, and its graceful form, there would be no tree more unsuitable for planting by the side of ground habitually frequented by man. Yet it excels so much in the respects named, and it grows so readily where the beech will not thrive at all, that it is *par excellence* the tree chosen for the adornment of such places ; witness Windsor Park, the adjacent Playing Fields at Eton, and, if an example on the borders of Berkshire may be given, the familar Broad Walk in the meadow of Christ Church, Oxford. In all these, interspersed among secular trunks that have stood for centuries, will be found numerous young trees of varying ages, testifying to the one serious drawback to planting an avenue of elms.

These elms have taken us away from the interiors of the great ranges of buildings forming three sides of the Upper Ward. That, perhaps, is not entirely to be regretted by either reader or writer. In regard to the private apartments the reader is not likely to desire description based on other descriptions, which, in their turn, do not for the most part appear to have been written at first hand. Let it be enough for one who has never entered the private apartments, and is not in the least likely to be invited so to do, to state, on the authority of others, that access to the various rooms is by a corridor, over 500 feet in length, having on its walls paintings illustrating the principal State events of Queen Victoria's reign—more attractive, it may be conjectured, from the historical point of view than from the artistic—that there are some interesting Tudor portraits, and one of Luther, in the passage between this corridor and St. George's Hall; that " the Great Drawing Room is noticeable for its magnificent furniture of red silk ; the White Drawing Room and the Green Drawing Room for their decorations in these colours ; the Dining Room for its rich mirrors and gilded Gothic tracery." Most of these startling facts might have been discovered by the simple process of natural inference, and there is the less excuse for any attempt here to describe things unseen in that King Edward and his Consort are reported to have made a great many alterations inside Windsor Castle no less than outside.

The State Apartments and the Royal Library are another matter. These it has been my privilege to see, and the difficulty which presents itself is to be summed up in the phrase " embarrassment of riches." An art critic might say with justice that in these grand rooms and their staircase there was ample material wherewith to fill a volume ; and he might add with equal justice that, if so much space were denied to him, he would really choose to say nothing at all. Let a plain man endeavour to hit something approximate to the golden mean. Having chosen a time when the Court is absent from Windsor, having studied the special regulations touching the dates for inspecting the State Apartments, and having obtained the necessary ticket in the Lord Chamberlain's office in the Lower Ward, the visitor will begin his tour of inspection at the Grand Staircase. Here he, or she, will be impressed first, as he would be in a less degree at Sandringham, by the magnificence of the collection of mediæval armour ; and at sight of the wondrous shield ascribed to Benvenuto Cellini he will be disposed to say that, if that most adventurous and versatile artist did not execute this marvellous work, another must have rivalled him in skill of hand and design. Up to a point the history of the shield seems to be fairly well established. The view that Francis I. gave it to Henry VIII. on the occasion of the Field of the Cloth of Gold is not generally disputed. On the other hand, the workmanship is doubted ; but on that point it is well to remember that Francis and Benvenuto Cellini were closely associated. So to the State Ante-room, where the Verrio ceiling is not worth the stiff neck its study involves, but the carvings, by Grinling Gibbons, are superb ; the pictures, by Zuccarelli and Domeni-chino, fail of their effect for want of well-directed light. It is a curious little fact, by the way, that of this Verrio whose "sprawling saints" Pope and Walpole treated with satire, many books of reference, even the multifarious and excellent Pierre Larousse, and the monumental *Encyclopædia Britannica*, make no mention whatsoever.

It is in the next room, known indifferently as the King's Drawing Room or the Rubens Room, that the real joy of the picture-lover begins. Here are a round dozen of paintings, many of them in the best manner of the great Fleming, and, if every touch was not in all cases laid on by his brush, the other hand that is to be traced in "St. Martin and the Beggar," and perhaps in the whole of the group of Sir Balthazar Gerbier's family, is almost equally worthy, for it is that of Sir Anthony Vandyck. It is not for me to discourse on the genius of Peter

Paul Rubens : so far as the artistic feast goes it is enough to
say that the pictures are there, visible without charge or
difficulty at the appointed times, and that among them are the
painter's portraits of himself, and of his first wife, Elizabeth
Brandt, and his celebrated picture " Winter." Still, apart from
their undoubted excellence as works of art, the pictures serve
to bring up a whole train of memories eminently characteristic
of the early seventeenth century. Let the meaning be illustrated. The portrait of Rubens was once the property of
Charles I. ; the picture " Summer " belonged to Villiers, Duke
of Buckingham ; there is an equestrian portrait of Philip IV. of
Spain ; and there is the Sir Balthazar Gerbier group already
mentioned. The five combine to carry one back to those early
days in the seventeenth century when James I. ruled in
England, when the beauty of Henrietta Maria took captive the
heart of Charles, Prince of Wales, when Buckingham abetted
Charles in a flying visit to Paris and in playing fast and loose
with the Infanta of Spain. Rubens was intimate with Charles
as Prince of Wales and as King, and with Buckingham. He
painted a portrait of the former that would be worth a mint of
money if it could be found now ; he was present at his marriage
with Henrietta Maria at Notre Dame in 1625, and all but lost
his life there and then through the collapse of a scaffold. When
difficulties arose later between Spain and England, difficulties
arising equally out of *spretæ injuria formæ* and political complications, Rubens and Gerbier, Flemings and artists both,
were chosen as unofficial negotiators, Rubens for Spain and
Gerbier for England. They met in Holland. Mr. Dudley
Carleton writes to Lord Conway in 1627 : " Rubens is come
hither to Holland, where he now is, and Gerbier in his company, walking from town to town upon their pretence of
pictures." This mission produced, as its best and most lasting
fruit, a sojourn of nine months by Rubens in the Spanish
Court, where he attracted the King not less as artist than as
diplomatist. In diplomacy, indeed, he was more than

commonly successful, for on coming to England in 1629 he was welcomed by Charles and knighted by him, and received the honorary degree of Master of Arts from the University of Cambridge. Did the Cambridge Chancellor of 1629 use towards Rubens terms equally happy to the "*splendidè audax*" with which, in 1904, Lord Goschen admitted Mr. Sargent to his honorary degree at Oxford? The King's Closet, with its landscapes by Van de Welde and by Teniers, and its characteristic Venetian scenes by Canaletto, will detain the visitor for some time, but it need not delay us here. In the Queen's Closet are two Claudes, two Poussins, sundry portraits by Hanneman, a Lely (Elizabeth Hamilton, Duchesse de Gramont), and Holbein's portraits of Henry VII. and Edward VI. These last, with other pictures at Windsor, numerous drawings, and above all that of Sir Thomas More's head, serve to remind us of the generosity of the reception met by Holbein in England when he came over first, on the introduction of Erasmus to Sir Thomas More, and next, at a time when More's patronage would have been of less than no value if he had been living to extend it.

In the Picture Gallery is that famous picture "The Misers," whereby Quintin Matsys is stated to have won his wife. The worst of this romantic legend, as of a good many others, is that it is most likely quite untrue. The story is that Quintin Matsys or Massys, being a smith, learned painting and achieved this picture in order to prove himself worthy to become the son-in-law of an artist in painting. But the truth, which may have bearing also on the origin of the vision in iron in the chancel of St. George's Chapel, is probably that Quintin's brother Josse was the smith, and that Quintin was never anything more than a painter. Nor, for his time (he lived from 1466 to 1530), was he of the highest order of merit. "The strength of the picture lies essentially in the effort at character in the painter's conception of the subject." That is Kugler's view. Another, not entirely mine, is that his efforts to display concentrated character degenerated into something approaching caricature, redeemed by glowing colour. But there are other and nobler pictures. Here are a very excellent and well-known Holbein, Thomas Howard, and other portraits by the same master, a Correggio, a Rembrandt, two Claudes, an Andrea del Sarto, a Canaletto, to name a few, and, best of all, Titian's portrait of himself and a friend.

To an Englishman, the Vandyck Room, boasting more than a score of pictures, portraits all, from the hand of Sir Anthony Vandyck, appeals with exceptional force. Among them is the master's portrait of himself, and it hangs among those of the Stuarts whom he limned with such surpassing skill that other contemporary portraits of them have passed out of mind. He painted them very often too. Here we have Charles I. on horseback, the well-known group of his children, his head, painted separately that Bernini might make a bust for Whitehall from it, Prince Charles (Charles II.), in armour (at the age of nine years!), a complete Stuart "family group," as the photographers would say, four versions of Henrietta Maria, and other famous portraits besides, to say nothing of Vandycks elsewhere, in St. George's Hall. They vary a little in quality of course, but, take him for all in all, Vandyck was perhaps the greatest and the most valuable to posterity of the painters to whom England, and England's Kings, extended willing and eager hospitality. Of him it may be said, as was written by Opie of Titian, in words well worthy to be quoted for their own beauty, "that he combined resemblance with dignity, costume with taste, and art with simplicity." England may congratulate herself that, if she could not produce a Vandyck, she could recognise him. She gave him honour, a rich reward in money, rapidly gained and swiftly expended, a noble wife, and a worthy resting-place for his ashes. He was Sir Anthony within three months of his first landing on our shores; he married Lady Mary Ruthven; he was buried in 1641 at old St. Paul's; and King Charles himself composed his epitaph. Need the twentieth century regret that the master of portraiture was extravagant and fond of pleasure, possessed in fact of the artistic temperament, so that he painted few pictures in England besides portraits, and more of them perhaps than he was able to finish as he alone could finish them? Surely this was all for the best; for every portrait that Vandyck painted, in whole or part, no matter how hurriedly, is an historical document, and not one of them could be spared. He, above all others, has handed down to posterity the presentments of many of the most interesting personages during a critical period of English history; and he has touched them all with a nobility and a refinement above price. The Stuarts, as we know their faces, are the Stuarts as they presented themselves to Vandyck; and it may well be that, for that reason, they seem to us somewhat more attractive than they were in life. If that be so there is an illustration of historical justice working by devious ways, for the most prominent of the Stuarts atoned for his errors so painfully, in his later years, and by his death, that we would fain think of him as possessed of a more noble presence than, perhaps, exact truth would warrant. In one point certainly the portraits make for an appreciation of history. Those of the unhappy Charles help one to understand why his followers were devoted not merely to a cause and to a principle, but also to a man; those of Henrietta Maria, combined with Howell's description of the Infanta, drive me to a view of the failure of the Spanish marriage more human and more probable than that usually adopted by historians.

The keynote of the whole business may be found in the portraits, and in the descriptions by Howell (quoted in the *Life and Letters of Mr. Endymion Porter*, by Dorothea Townshend : Fisher Unwin, 1897) of Henrietta Maria and of the Infanta. Henrietta Maria, when she reaches England in March, 1625, is thus painted in words : " A most noble, new Queen of England, who, in true beauty, is beyond the long-wooed Infanta, for she is of a fading flaxen hair, big-lipped, and somewhat heavy-eyed, but this daughter of France is of a more lovely and lasting complexion of a dark brown. She hath eyes that sparkle like stars, and as for her physiognomy she may be said to be a marvel of perfection." Let me endeavour to state the facts of the whole story, as they are likely to impress everybody who is a man, as Charles was, and not always able to say of himself, as David Hume did, " I was a man of mild dispositions . . . and of great moderation in all my passions." The facts, apart from the glosses of historians, seem to indicate that, although political considerations and schemings may have had much influence on others than the principal parties, it was love, after all, that made the world go round. The best of the historians, perhaps, is Endymion Porter, who did not mean to be an historian at all, who tells us only what he thought it worth while to tell his wife, and less of the visit to Paris in 1623 than we should like to know. The disadvantage of him is that he was too much surrounded by the trees to be able to see the wood as a whole. Clarendon, dramatic and prejudiced, was notoriously wanting in deep insight into human character. David Hume was essentially phlegmatic, incapable of sympathy in such a case.

At this point it is desirable to say that the ensuing recitation of facts must be understood to be made with a full knowledge, so far as such knowledge is attainable by fairly diligent study, of the then state of international politics, and that an account of this is omitted simply because it would be inappropriate to the character of this volume. The human side of the business, however, is of no less importance ; and other, not to say infinitely more eminent, writers have done ample justice to the political side. Early in 1623, then, Buckingham suggested to Charles that they should journey informally to Spain so that Charles might woo and win the bride whom, on terms, others deemed it might be advantageous for him to marry. Charles, barely twenty-three years of age, was nothing loth, not because he cared or had enjoyed the opportunity of caring for the Infanta personally ; but because the project had been before him for some time, and the delays had been sufficient to stimulate his obstinacy into desire. About the political aspect of the projected visit he probably cared very little, although in laying the matter before his father he was shrewd enough, probably at Buckingham's instigation, to use the political considerations for all they were worth. The King consented at the time. Of his subsequent repentance of his consent, of the stormy scenes which followed, and of the final renewal of the consent, Clarendon gives a vivid account ; but of the events immediately following he omits the most material part :

"The manner, circumstances and conclusion of that voyage, with the extraordinary accidents that happened in it, will no doubt be at large remembered by whosoever shall have the, courage to write the transactions of that time with that integrity he ought to do : in which it will manifestly appear how much of the prophet was in the wisdom of the King ; and that that designed marriage, which had been so many years in treaty, even from the death of Prince Harry, and so near concluded, was solely broken by that journey."

So it was, but for a cause not so much as mentioned by Clarendon. The Prince and Buckingham left England as John and Tom Smith, servants to Sir Francis Cottington (who was bitterly opposed to the whole journey), and were joined at Dover by Endymion Porter. They went to Madrid by way of Paris, and one day and night in Paris changed the course of history. "I give God thanks," writes Endymion Porter to his wife on the 22nd of February, 1623, "we are all arrived safely at Paris, where it hath pleased his Highness and my lord to stay this day to see the town." From Porter's letters we betake ourselves to Hume, who writes : "The Prince and Buckingham . . . passed disguised and undiscovered through France ; and they even ventured into a Court-ball at Paris, where Charles saw the Princess Henrietta, whom he afterwards espoused, and who was at that time in the bloom of youth and beauty." There is no doubt, really, that their thin disguise was penetrated, and was meant to be penetrated, that "John Smith " was recognised as a royal incognito, that they were hospitably received at the French Court ; or, to my mind, that Charles lost his heart on the spot. Henrietta's fair face worked the old miracle that women's faces have accomplished from time to time since men were men, and will continue to accomplish while the world endures.

Is there anything in the sequel running counter to this view ? Charles and Buckingham went on to Madrid with their companions. They were received with the utmost warmth by King, Court, and populace ; and, at first, only the poor Infanta, her fears worked upon by her confessor, was opposed to the idea of the match. Certainly it cannot have been encouraging to a girl to be adjured thus : " What a comfortable bedfellow you will have ; he who lies by your side, and will be the father of your children, is certain to go to hell." Royally entertained, but seeing nothing of the Infanta except in public, Charles was again the victim of the desire fostered in an obstinate man by denial. He forgot the charms of Henrietta in his eagerness to break down the barrier of formality erected by the timid and unwilling Infanta around herself. So, early one morning, he went with Endymion to waylay the Princess in the Royal Garden, whither she was in the habit of going "to gather May dew with her ladies." But she shrieked when he jumped down from the wall ; "so the door was opened and he came out under that wall over which he had got in." Let us put the politics aside for a moment, not ignoring their existence, but not forgetting either that princes are human, and let us endeavour to read this riddle either as men with the warm blood of manhood coursing in their veins, or with a vivid memory of the days of early prime. Charles had seen Henrietta Maria, in the pride of her youth and beauty, once and once only. He can hardly have failed to be attracted by her. He had journeyed on to Spain to woo the Princess whom he had been taught that he ought to marry for reasons of State. He had probably reconciled himself to the necessity, sometimes falling to the lot of princes of the blood, of marrying without love. (Let it by no means be supposed, however, that a princely marriage, dictated by reasons of State, may not also be a marriage of affection.) He found the Infanta determined to deny herself to him in every possible way; he became, naturally, the more eager to win her. At last he forced himself into her presence; and she fled, shrieking, timorous, unlovely most likely, in her morning attire. His imaginary passion was naturally quenched at once. All this was perfectly human and manlike; and so was the momentary forgetfulness of the beautiful French Princess, if forgetfulness there was. Probably Charles had made up his mind that Henrietta Maria represented unattainable felicity, and that he might as well make the best of things; but the coy stupidity of the Infanta threw him back on Henrietta.

So it may well be that " Buckingham, sensible how odious he had become to all Spaniards "—he had, indeed, done his utmost to offend them—" resolved to employ all his credit in order to prevent the marriage," as the worthy Hume has it. It may be also that his domineering character had obtained " a total ascendency over the modest and gentle temper of Charles." But there is no wisdom or knowledge of masculine nature in this : " By what arguments he could engage the Prince of Wales to offer such an insult to the Spanish nation, from whom he had met with such generous treatment, by what colours he could disguise the ingratitude and imprudence of such a measure ; these are totally unknown to us." The main argument is presented in imperishable terms and many times over by Vandyck in the portraits of Henrietta at Windsor and elsewhere ; and the " fading flaxen hair," thick lips, and heavy eyes of the spiritless Infanta gave it irresistible force. Historians of Hume's phlegmatic temperament forget that princes, hedged in by restrictions as they are, remain human beings notwithstanding.

The task of persuading Charles to continue his suit formally, but to relinquish all idea of actually marrying a plain woman, can have presented no difficulties to Buckingham ; and on this occasion he can have felt no need to be domineering.

Noting the fine Gobelins Tapestry and the portraits, especially that of Mary Queen of Scots, in the Audience Chamber, and the Gobelins Tapestry in the Presence Chamber (the continuation of the story of Esther and Mordecai from the room first mentioned), we find in the Guard Room, among much armour and many arms, a case containing three swords, full of pathetic interest from their juxtaposition. There is the sword of Charles I., and, close to it, is the weapon John Hampden drew against the King who esteemed him so highly that the King was willing, if there had been any hope, to send his own surgeon to tend him after he was wounded at Chalgrove Field. With them is the sword of Marlborough, a greater soldier than either, but not of stainless honour. Here, too, are the busts of Marlborough and of Wellington, the banners by the annual presentation of which their descendants hold their lands. These, and more portraits and busts, are the objects that stir the mind, and the counterfeit presentment of Dymoke, the King's Champion, in the original Elizabethan armour, gives an appropriate finish to the whole.

Most attractive of all the rooms, with its coats of arms and banners of Knights of the Garter, its splendid series of royal portraits, its magnificent trophies of armour, and the miniature armour, in blue and gold, worn by Prince Harry, eldest son of James I., and by his ill-fated brother Charles, is St. George's Hall. One memory of it lingers with me. It is one of a scene rarely witnessed, save as a whole, even by the guests of Royalty, and it was in detail no less than as a whole that it impressed the imagination. Candidly there is hesitation whether to say it was nothing more, or nothing less, than the table set for a State banquet with all the gold plate that Windsor Castle can boast ranged upon and around it. Was it vulgar and small-minded to be impressed? Possibly it was; but, passing that on one side, it was a most imposing spectacle, and that, doubtless, was the effect it was intended to exercise upon the minds of the German Emperor and other notables who were to be the honoured guests of the evening. Let those who think it may have been a sight to be forgotten and passed over, pause until they know the facts. Along the centre of the long table ran a broad river of mirrors, doubling the effect, and the plate ranged upon and alongside of them was worth at least two millions of our money. The amount was stupendous, when you come to think of it, and perhaps it is not too much to say that it is not for those who have not looked at such wealth of cunningly wrought gold all at once to know how it would have impressed their minds. Such a sight can be seen only at Windsor: for those who have not seen it to scorn one who was impressed by it, almost to stupefaction, is much the same thing as for a man who has not been under fire to avow that he would not feel afraid if he were. As a fact all men are, at first, and nearly all confess it, but they conceal their feelings at the time; and that is courage. In the case of this gleaming glory of gold there is no adequate reason for concealment. Why on earth should there be any shame in saying that our sovereigns' possessions in this kind of treasure are simply stupendous? Should we not rather feel honest pride that, on a suitable occasion, they can make so brave a show of "pieces," many of them, especially those of Indian work, taking us back to some of the most glorious and terrible days in the making and the keeping of the Empire. In fact St. George's Hall is a most noble banqueting hall, worthy alike of those who entertain in it and of those who are honoured as guests. Sometimes, too, it serves for supper room after a theatrical performance. On such occasions the Waterloo Chamber, with its glorious gallery of portraits by Lawrence, serves for theatre. Possibly, however, if the opinions of our leading actors and actresses were asked, they would say that, while Windsor is the more accessible place at which to give a command performance, to say nothing of the fact that there are hotels at hand, Sandringham, when it has been reached, is preferable by virtue of its facilities for the actual representation of a piece.

And now this peregrination of apartments, byways not always open to the wanderer, is almost over. The grand Reception Room is in Louis Quinze style, with fine tapestry ; over the ante-room and the vestibule it is not necessary to delay save to mention that in the latter is the celebrated foot-stool of " the tyrant Tippoo " of the old camp-song, a massive tiger's head in pure gold with fangs of crystal. But there must be a word of the Throne Room. Here it is, in an apartment hung with Garter Blue and adorned with the insignia of the Order, that the silver-gilt throne of the ancient kings of Kandy is kept. It carries us back to a time of stress and storm ; for, in the present prosperity and peace of Ceylon under British rule, we are apt to forget that, so lately as 1803, the British garrison of Kandy was massacred after capitulation, and that only three months before the Battle of Waterloo was our authority over the island finally recognised. A modern Kandian chief, by the way, and an ancient Kandian king doubtless, would require an unusually ample throne; it is the immemorial custom of Kandy that in proportion to the honourable position of a chief is the number of yards of costly material wound about his waist, so that he appears at a Durbar—he did before the Prince of Wales in 1901, for example—with his diameter at the waist increased by a full foot or more. Here, too, are likenesses of Queen Victoria and the Prince Consort by Winterhalter, portraits of the first and second Georges by Kneller, an excellent George IV. by Lawrence, and Sir Martin Shee's presentment of William IV. In these days, once more, the Throne Room is mainly used for investitures, which,

WORKING MEN'S COLLEGE LIBRARY

judging by one once seen in St. Patrick's Hall in Dublin
(when the Prince of Wales, then Duke of York, was invested
as a Knight of St. Patrick), must be vastly fine. In Queen
Victoria's later days the full ceremony of investiture was rarely
accomplished, for two good reasons. As Sovereign of the
Order of the Garter she invested with her own hand two of the
most unhappy knights ever admitted into the most noble Order,
Louis Philippe and Napoleon III. ; and both these unfortunate
sovereigns were regarded by the Royal Family with warm
personal attachment. Then the Prince Consort was also, and
as of course, a Knight of the Garter. So it is easy to understand why Queen Victoria felt a natural repugnance to
ceremonies irresistibly associated in her mind with painful
memories.

Of one more room at Windsor Castle I would like to write,
but may not, for want of knowledge at first hand. It is the
private library with its matchless collection of drawings by the
old masters, especially Leonardo da Vinci, Michael Angelo,
Raphael, and Holbein, including the beautiful drawing, often
reproduced, of Sir Thomas More's head. Here, too, are the
English historical prints, in the collection and arrangement
of which the Prince Consort and Queen Victoria worked
together. But, when there has been so much to deal with in the
open air and at first hand, there is no justification for remaining
within the Castle walls in order to discourse at second hand.
So let us leave it, with three general impressions. The first,
that the Castle is of no common majesty and worthy of its
occupants ; the next, that it is a casket containing jewels of
art and treasure worthy of the building that enshrines and
of the sovereigns who own them ; and the third, homely.
Windsor Castle covers a vast area of ground ; it contains an
immense number of rooms ; but, when the King is at home,
there is no space to spare in it. It is indeed almost amusing
to one not connected with the Court, if he or she should
happen to call on an acquaintance in the royal household,

when the Court is at Windsor, to note how narrow is the accommodation provided for them, and how peers and peeresses, honoured by official positions in the household, have, so to speak, to work for their living. There could be no greater mistake than to imagine that the office of a Lord or Lady in Waiting is a sinecure.

CHAPTER XII

IN THE FOREST COUNTRY

Boundaries of the Forest Country—Famous parts—Miss Mitford—Charles
Kingsley—Settlements in the Forest—its space—A recipe for rest—
Windsor for centre—The Great Park—In the footsteps of Falstaff—
" From Frogmore, over the stile "—Herne's Oak "—Who was Herne
the hunter?—An Elizabethan poacher—Elizabeth as huntress—A
legend of Lancelot—Malory quoted—True description of Great Park
to-day—Old Windsor and the Confessor—Cock and bull miracles—
Runnymede and Magna Charta Island—By coach to Virginia Water—
An amateur coachman *in statu pupillari*—A sarcastic lesson—Virginia
Water, artificial—Paul Sandby, an artist—William, Duke of Cumber-
land—A good word for " the martial boy "—Ascot and its glories—
Easthampstead once a Royal residence—Richard II.—Wellington
College—No romantic history—Qualities of Wellingtonians—Royal
Military College—Roman Road, Silchester to London—Wokingham
—Binfield " Rape of the Lock "—" Here Pope sang "—Beeches as
name preservers—Œnone and Paris—Francis Cherry's stratagem—
Bear Wood—Seat of the Walter family—Determination of the Walters
—A premature death—Bear Wood, why so called?—Included in
Bearroc Wood—Why not called after bears?—Bears not extinct in
tenth century—Persistence of country traditions—Rustic inability to
compute time—Arborfield Cross—Miss Mitford's country—Described
in her words—" The old house at Aberleigh "—A beautiful quotation—
fate of the last Standen—Miss Mitford's view maintained—" Molly
Mog " discredited—Murray dozes a little—The Roman road to
Silchester again—Silchester outside purview—Remains at Reading—
a short expedition—Hampstead Norris, picturesque, but poor—
Yattendon, tidy, pretty, and prosperous—The late Mr. Waterhouse,
R.A.—Canon Beeching—Mr. Robert Bridges—A holiday party—
Bradfield College—Mr. A. F. Leach, and his history of it—An

IF, taking a map of Berkshire, a line be drawn due north and south through Sunningdale, it will bisect Virginia Water and it will form the eastern boundary of so much of the " Forest District " as lies within our subject ; and the River Loddon, entering the county from Hampshire, near Strathfield Saye, and discharging itself into the Thames a short mile above Wargrave, may be taken for a western limit ; while the Blackwater may serve for the southern line, as the Thames does for the northern. Within this very irregular polyhedron, apart from the well-known spots, dealt with elsewhere, on the right bank of the Thames, are comprised a number of places that must needs be visited. They are, to name the chief amongst them, Windsor Castle, already disposed of, Windsor Great Park, including Frogmore and Virginia Water, Old Windsor, Ascot, Sandhurst, Wellington College, Wokingham, and the little corner about Arborfield and Swallowfield rightly described as Miss Mitford's country. Yet it is also Charles Kingsley's country, for, although Eversley has the bad taste to be beyond the county boundary, in much of Kingsley's prose is to be traced the spirit of the Berkshire Forest, and he has many a tale to tell of the ways of the Berkshire broomsquires.

Of these places the interest is in the main human, and none the worse or the less attractive for that ; but the country also has a character of its own, a character gradually vanishing as London spreads out its tentacles, but still wonderful when we remember how very near London is. Hardly anywhere in Southern England, except where this forest-land stretches beyond Berkshire, shall you find such vast expanses of barren and sandy heath, such ragged growth of firs and bracken and gorse, so much wild nature or so many solitudes. They are being invaded fast in these days. Trim villas and rows of houses rise as if by magic among the firs ; at least three railway companies contend for the privilege, and the profit, of carrying bread-winners up to London every morning and back into the pure air when the day's work is done. Unaccustomed hands take to digging and planting; amateur gardeners struggle amain to make good the deficiencies of the soil, and wonder more and more every year at the amount of "nourishment" that it will absorb. The forest, in fact, is disappearing gradually, but the process is very slow; for Nature is intractable and the earth is not responsive, and there will be plenty of forest open for matchless rambles and rides for many a long year to come. At any rate it would be churlish to complain, for it is too obvious to need argument that this exodus from the cities, this migration of children to districts simply overflowing with health, this bringing of a part of the rising generation face to face with Nature, is all for good. Amongst other things it must serve to check, in part at least, that physical degeneration of our people of which we hear on all sides. There is exaggeration in the cry doubtless; but there is some substance in it also, and one of the cures for it is to be found in the settlement of such regions as the forest offers.

At present there is abundance of free and open space, enough to get lost in sometimes, and it may be enjoyed in all sorts of ways, none of them very definite. You may ride on horse, or on cycle, as far as you will; you may walk almost where you like with none to say you nay; and you may lie, in the sun or under the shade of a fir-tree, gazing at the sky, listening to the hum of insects or to the murmur of the scarcely perceptible breeze among the vocal needles of the pines and firs. You may picnic, with others or alone; you may read; you may do nothing at all; and that sometimes is the best of all. Once, in idle curiosity, a wise and very hard-worked man was asked how he meant to employ his holiday at a place that sounded distinctly dead-alive. "What shall I do, you ask? Why, I shall lie on my back in the sun and do nothing. I shall not even think more than I can help." This pleasure, and easy-going rambles to see nothing in particular, save the stretching undulations of the moorland and the rosy flush of the stems of Scotch firs in the sun, is easily accessible in the country where we now are. For a centre Windsor may be recommended, although Reading is far more suitable and convenient from what may be called a Bradshaw point of view. But Reading, rich as it is in railways and in history, is a distressingly unlovely and bustling place, whereas at Windsor there is always the Castle to look at, and it never palls ; and besides that there is always the park, with its green turf and graceful deer, and stately, if not immemorial, elms.

To that Great Park we shall betake ourselves shortly, after only one more preliminary remark concerning the invasion of the forest country by man. This, as we have often been told, is a crowded land ; one in which it is hard to find places for the due exercise of soldiers, or for the education of youth amidst free and open surroundings. So it was but natural that as soon as railways offered the necessary facilities for locomotion, the forest should be used in part for these purposes. Hence come the Royal Military College at Sandhurst, and, beyond the border, that large military community of Aldershot ; so that in the extreme south-eastern corner of the county you will meet more soldiers in a day's walk than in any other district north of the Thames. Hence also comes Wellington College, not to be matched for the beauty of the situation in which its boys are reared, for the freshness of the air that they breathe, and for the freedom of the ground over which they may roam at will, so far as the law of England is concerned.

Windsor, then, is our centre, and first let us wander in the Home Park, using none other than Shakespeare for guide. Rooms in the Garter Inn, at Ford's house, or Page's, or that of Dr. Caius, we cannot see ; but, following the present road to the park, we can hardly fail to move in the footsteps of Mistresses Page and Ford as they started with Dr. Caius along "a street leading to the park," to quote the stage direction,

Surely it was but little beyond the top of Peascod Street that
Mistress Page told the doctor her daughter was "in green";
and it may have been in the shadow of those ancient houses
past the Town Hall that the two merry wives chuckled over the
coming mockery of Falstaff and fury of Page. Once in the
park we are not far certainly from that "field near Frogmore,"
where Sir Hugh Evans was "so full of chollors and of trempling
of mind" that he betook himself to singing of "shallow rivers,"
"melodious birds,", "peds of roses," and "fragrant posies,"
mingled with "a great dispositions to cry." Where an iron
gate is we can see, in imagination, and with Slender, "my
master, Master Shallow, and another gentleman" come "from
Frogmore, over the stile, this way," and can laugh with a will
over "good Sir Hugh's" trembling bluster. Of a truth these
memories are more willingly conjured up now that we are in
the light of day and among the trees and grass than those
more solemn memories that Frogmore must needs recall. Those
other memories are by no means ignored. Rather are they
taken as understood and passed on one side because, in walking
through St. George's Chapel and the adjacent structures, we had
enough of tombs. For the moment let us rejoice in sun, the
grass, the trees, and the air, giving the go-by to melancholy.

Can we localise "Herne's Oak"? The tree, certainly, is
gone, though there was a remnant of an oak among the elms,
known as such, and duly protected; a mere sapling in point of
age reigns in its stead. Any gnarled oak, so it be within an
easy walk of Windsor, for Falstaff was, by his own confession,
"in the waist two yards about," will serve; and there are
plenty of such to be peopled round and about with the
lightsome scene that ends the *Merry Wives*. Who, after all,
was Herne? It does not much matter, perhaps, save for the
fact that all mysteries are provoking. So it may be as well to
state that, after more than one learned work had been con-
sulted in vain, recourse was taken to Mr. Falkner, who says:
"According to tradition Herne was a woodman, who had in

some way incurred the displeasure of Queen Elizabeth and hung himself on a tree that she would have to pass." Now Herne, as Page reminded Falstaff when he was pulling off his buck's head, was "Herne the hunter." His offence against Elizabeth was doubtless that of making too free with the Queen's deer : for Queen Elizabeth was a huntress, ardent as a more legendary lady to be mentioned ere long.

The Long Walk passes from the Castle along the eastern edge of the Home Park, and then to Snow Hill and the very heart of the magnificent Great Park of 1,800 acres, stretching southward to Sunningdale, across Virginia Water and into Surrey, and at the south-west almost to Ascot, the most thickly wooded parts being on the west, near Cranbourne Tower, and on the south-east, near Virginia Water. It is, to put it in a phrase, an altogether noble domain, possessing trees that are hard to match ; and within its limits are contained Frogmore House, frequently occupied by the Prince and Princess of Wales ; Cumberland Lodge, long associated with the names of Prince and Princess Christian of Schleswig-Holstein ; Lower Lodge, said to have been built by Nell Gwynn ; and the Royal Farms, including the Flemish Farm ; for the King, like his father before him, is an enthusiastic and a judicious breeder of cattle, and Queen Victoria kept up all the agricultural enterprises started by the Prince Consort. With its broad stretches of green grass and its abundant trees, Windsor Park is a most choiceworthy place in which to ride or to walk ; but sooth to say it is singularly wanting in legends. After that of Herne the hunter, which is not full enough to be engrossing, perhaps the most interesting legend of Windsor Forest is one told by Sir Thomas Malory concerning an incident, though Lord Tennyson omitted to translate it into noble verse, in the life of Sir Launcelot du Lake. All the world knows the piteous story of Elaine le Blanc, the Lily Maid of Astolat who died for love of Launcelot. No man can forget how Guinever said, to quote Malory, not Tennyson : "Ye might have showed her some bounty and gentleness, that might have preserved her life " ; for Tennyson wrote the memorable lines :

> " Ye might, at least, have done her so much grace,
> Fair Lord, as would have help'd her from her death."

Everybody is familiar with Guinever's apology, as Tennyson phrased it, so let us quote Malory again. " The Queen sent for Sir Launcelot and prayed him of mercy for why she had been wroth with him causeless." At this point Tennyson relinquishes the episode, to proceed to others of undying grace, and, since Malory's version is less familiar than it deserves to be, not all men know of the sequel. Shortly, it was that a great tournament was arranged for Candlemas to celebrate the admission of Sir Lavaine, Elaine's brother, to the Round Table ; that Guinever charged Launcelot to wear her sleeve of gold, so that his kinsmen might know him in the fray ; and that Sir Launcelot, as we should say, went into training with Sir Lavaine, retiring " unto the good hermit that dwelled in the forest of Windsor, his name was Sir Brastias, and there he thought to repose him, and to take all rest that he might, because he would be fresh at that day of justs."

" So Sir Launcelot and Sir Lavaine departed, that no creature wist where he was become, but the noble men of his blood. And when he was come to the hermitage wit ye well he had good cheer. And so daily Sir Launcelot would go to a well fast by the hermitage, and there he would lie down, and see the well spring and bubble, and sometime he slept there. So at that time there was a lady dwelled in that forest, and she was a great huntress, and daily she used to hunt, and always she bare her bow with her ; and no men went never with her, but always women, and they were shooters, and could well kill a deer both at the stalk and at the trest ; and they daily bare bows and arrows, horns and wood-knives, and many good dogs they had, for the string and for a bait. So it happened that this lady, the huntress, had baited her dogs for the bow of a barren hind, and so this barren hind took her flight over heaths and woods, and ever this lady and part of her gentlewomen coasted the hind, and checked it by the noise of the hounds, to have met with the hind at some water. And so it happed the hind came to the well whereas Sir Launcelot was sleeping and slumbering. And so when the hind came to the well for heat she went to soil, and there she lay a great while ; and the dogs came fast after, and umbecast about, for she had lost the very perfect track of the hind. Right so, there came that lady the huntress, that knew by the dog she had that the hind was at soil in that well. And there she came stiffly, and found the hind, and she put a broad arrow in her bow, and shot at the hind, and overshot the hind, and so, by misfortune, the arrow smote Sir Launcelot .in the thick of the thigh, over the barbs. When Sir Launcelot felt himself so hurt, he hurled up woodly, and saw the lady that had smitten him. And when he saw that she was a woman, he said thus, ' Lady, or damsel, what that thou be, in an evil time bare ye a bow, the devil made you a shooter.' "

The exquisitely quaint passage goes on to show how the lady apologised briefly and departed, how Sir Launcelot " as well he might, pulled out the arrow, and the head above still in his thigh ; and so he went weakly to the hermitage, evermore bleeding as he went." We hear, too, of the wrath of Sir Lavaine and the hermit ; of their efforts to heal the unhappily located wound, " for it was in such place that he might not sit in no saddle " ; of Launcelot's resolve to be in the field " whatsoever fall of it " ; and, as of course, of Launcelot's mighty deeds in the tournament ; but that is another story, and the delightful features of the passage for our present purpose are the chaste huntress, the curious words of venerie (all clear except " trest," which, to be frank, is a puzzle), the vision of the knight seeking vigour from repose, a valuable suggestion this, to our athletes of to-day, and that of the hind taking her flight over heaths and woods, many of them surviving to this day. They are all perfect in their kind. Most perfect of all is the unconscious picture of the loneliness of Windsor Forest conveyed and the thought that, of the Windsor Forest remaining to us, much is as wild and solitary as it was in Malory's days, and as he supposed it to have been in the days of Arthur. The Great Park has, however, shrunk not a little in the course of ages, for Lysons says that by Norden's survey it was 3,650 acres, rather more than twice its present area.

In any map marking woodlands and parks green it is easy to

realise first the vast size of Windsor Great Park even now, and
then to notice, in the north-east corner, an uncoloured patch.
That is Old Windsor, now of no sort of interest, save for the
tradition that Edward the Confessor had a palace there, the very
site of which is forgotten, and because hard by, down river, are
Runnymede and Magna Charta Island. The Confessor is said to
have worked sundry miracles there, but one really cannot write
down in cold blood in these days so much as the stories of
miracles wrought by men of flesh and blood similar to our own.
We know that the Confessor " touched for the evil " ; to believe
that he touched efficaciously is impossible. One cannot even
contemplate the idea seriously. On the other hand, since Earl
Godwin undoubtedly died suddenly at the King's table, it is
more than likely that he did so at Old Windsor ; but the
crumb of bread story will not go down any more easily than
the crumb itself went in the myth. As for Runnymede and
Magna Charta Island, all the powers of memory and imagination are needed to make them interesting, to the eye at any
rate, in these days. They are easily found ; but to one who has
reached them down-stream, they seem sadly tame after Hurley,
Bisham, and Cliveden, and that is why, in the chapter dealing
with the river below Oxford, an end was made near Windsor.

A most pleasant way of travelling to Virginia Water is to
take a coach from London, which involves a drive through
some charming country having but one fault, to wit, that it is not
a part of the Royal County of Berks. There is, or there used
to be, a possible drawback. Coach and teams were of the
best ; the guard was past-master in the art of extracting
exhilarating melody from a yard of veritable silver, not of tin,
a trophy of his prowess in preceding years. But the worthy
proprietor of the coach had a habit of taking pupils, to whom
he imparted the science of driving a coach and four, and my
own experience of being driven by such a pupil was almost
disconcerting at the time, although it is very funny to look
back upon now. Off we started nobly from Northumberland

Avenue ; but in Piccadilly our troubles began, or rather the troubles of the amateur driver and his four-in-hand whip became manifest. It was clear that the near leader was shirking his work, that he needed a reminder from the lash. But to hit the near leader was beyond our Jehu's powers, although his lash blundered upon most of the other horses and some of the passengers. Hence came it that when we reached comparative quiet beyond Knightsbridge a truly horrible affront was offered to the coachman ; for the proprietor, who sat close to him (in case of emergency and to give instruction), said loudly to the guard, " Get down and give that near 'orse one "; down the guard slipped, and, keeping pace with the moving coach and team by hanging on to the traces as he ran alongside, brought " that near 'orse " to a sense of duty by the aid of a knotted cane. At Richmond there was a brief halt, and it occurred to me to ask the amateur whether it were not a nervous business to drive a coach through the complicated traffic of Piccadilly. The answer was, " Not a bit of it ; I don't feel the least nervous "; and the retort was irresistible, " Perhaps you do not ; but what about your passengers ? "

For this and for other reasons, the chief of them being the sylvan beauty of Windsor Great Park, it is just as well to approach Virginia Water from the north. The journey is more than worth making. True it is that the water and its surroundings are all artificial. Nature did not cause the wood-girt water to meander as it does. History has nothing to say to those ruins. The whole is simply a magnificent piece of landscape garden-ing, as landscape gardening goes ; it is now attaining quite respectable antiquity, and many of our Kings, to say nothing of William, Duke of Cumberland, have been much attached to it. The truth of the matter is that Paul Sandby, the creator of the whole design, was not merely a gardener and favourite of the Duke of Cumberland, but a water-colour artist of no mean repute and power, and a foundation member of the Royal Academy, whose views in "aqua tinta" still command high prices. So the general plan of Virginia Water is distinctly good. Amongst its curious structures it has an interesting relic. In the belvedere is mounted a battery of artillery, and it is the very same battery that was used by William, Duke of Cumberland, against Charles Edward at Culloden. William IV. caused a model frigate, now vanished, to be made and floated on the waters. In days when Queen Alexandra, as Princess of Wales, used to skate, Virginia Water was a favourite resort for her ; and in these days, when shooting is to the fore at Windsor, it is a frequent venue for luncheon.

Let us have a kindly memory of this last-named Duke of Cumberland, the "martial boy," the victor at Dettingen and Culloden, who outlived his popularity, who even got a worse name than he deserved, and as we proceed to Royal Ascot let us remember that he earned the gratitude of generations to come as the founder of Ascot Races, and as keen a sportsman as ever lived in England. What is more, he bred, at Ilsley, as noted elsewhere, Eclipse, the most famous of all English-bred horses. The Duke, it is true, never saw the triumphs of the renowned chestnut with a white blaze down his face and those black spots on the rump traceable in nearly all his produce ; for Eclipse was born on the 1st of April, 1764, and the Duke died in the following October. Hardly less eager was Henry, Duke of Cumberland, whom we find among the subscribers to the Gold Cup in 1771. It would be wrong to describe the greatness of Ascot as a meeting, and it is unnecessary its follow its growth from strength to strength under steady royal patronage. Suffice, to say, without fear of contradiction, that in Ascot Berkshire boasts a racecourse of world-wide celebrity and quite *sui generis*. Ascot is not so popular as Epsom, not quite so aristocratic as Goodwood ; its course is one on which the "going" frequently leaves much to be desired. Still, it is emphatically a great meeting, fitly described as the State event in the annual history of the sport of kings. Need it be added that, with the exception of Goodwood, Ascot is, from a scenic point of view, far and away the most choice-worthy of English racecourses? It is just the wildness of the country and the sterility of the hungry soil, the main causes of Ascot scenic beauty, that make it difficult to keep the Ascot course in proper order. It is not an ideal place for a racecourse as such; on the other hand, it is an ideal place for men and women to reach from London in order to see horses run and to meet one another. Finally, it is within easy access of Windsor Castle. So the advantages more than counter-balance the drawbacks, and Ascot will surely live so long as horses are matched against one another for speed.

From Ascot you may go through the pine-country to Brack-nell, a quiet village in the heart of it, and turn by the left to Easthampstead, of almost forgotten fame. Few there are now who remember, with Lysons, that there was a royal residence at Easthampstead whence the hapless Richard II. was wont to start a-hunting in days before treachery and rebellion drove him from the throne—there is much forest left hereabouts still—or that James I. resided at Easthampstead in 1622-3; for James, too, was a mighty, or at any rate an ardent, hunter. In these days the two things to do at Easthampstead are to enjoy the fresh air, and to forgive the modernity of the church for the sake of the beautiful Burne-Jones windows it contains.

Hence we pass, still in the pine-country, undulating and at its best, by way of Cæsar's Camp (just like a hundred places of the same name) to Wellington College. Here you will find none of the architectural charm marking Eton or Winchester; indeed, the buildings may almost be called unattractive. You will find something nearly as good, a school for English boys in a situation that, if it had but a river, would be absolutely ideal; you will find manly lads, many of them, as befits the eponymous hero of the school, intended for a military career, growing up with as much of wholesome *esprit de corps* as may be discovered at the oldest and greatest schools. If there is no long delay here over Wellington College, as there is elsewhere over Radley and over Bradfield, that is in no sense to the disparagement of Wellington. It is, from one point of view, in the happy position of having no history. It was not founded by an eccentric enthusiast and it has never trembled on the verge of bankruptcy. Its foundation was business-like; it has been remarkably well managed; and it has flourished accordingly under Dr. Benson, who became an archbishop, under Dr. Wickham, who went away to a deanery, and under Dr. Pollock, who still reigns. There, amid the rhododendrons, and the Wellingtonias and the pines, are reared generations of boys before all of whom is set the grand example of the great duke. All of us have met them in the wider world, and have observed how conspicuous most of them are for manliness, straightforwardness, and absence of affectation. Surely this is due, in part at any rate, to the fact that the King's Gold Medal is given each year to the boy who, in the opinion of the master, has most nearly approached to the character of the great duke. At any rate it is a very happy idea that this standard should be officially recognised, by the master and the sovereign, as the one to be aimed at beyond all others.

Two miles away, or a little more, in the same kind of country, although preserving less of its original character, is that Royal Military College, whither many of the pupils of Wellington migrate. We are here on the confines of the settlements arisen since the establishment of Aldershot. They have their uses, but they are very far from being lovely. It is, however, worth while to go from Sandhurst to Finchamp-stead, on the borders of the county and almost on the bank of Blackwater, for the sake of crossing the Finchampstead ridges. The church too, standing clear of the village to the north-west, and on a hill 100 feet higher above the sea than the road leading through the village, is distinctly attractive. In all the adequate maps will be seen, a mile or so north of

Finchampstead, lines of uncompromising straightness indicating a Roman road. This is the old Roman road from Silchester, only partially within our purview, to London. From Silchester it starts as if it had been drawn with a ruler; then it becomes more difficult to follow, but north of Finchampstead, through the woodland known as California

Lucas's Almshouses, Wokingham.

(one knows not why) and along the " nine-mile ride," it goes absolutely straight to King's Beeches and Sunningdale. Of this last place, since it has come in accidentally, it may be said that it is a typical and well-to-do settlement in the pine-country ; and that is enough.

These recently-named places might just as well be visited from Wokingham, which is picturesque and old-fashioned—

witness the Hospital of Henry Lucas—as from Windsor. Hence you may go to see Binfield, keeping Pope in mind the while, remembering that he wrote here, amongst other things, " The Rape of the Lock " and, more appropriately, the Pastorals. Here it was, too, that Lord Lytton carved on a beech-tree (now perished) the words " here Pope sang." Does everybody remember how the fashion of inscribing in beech-bark, names of lovers for the most part, was set ? In me the very mention of it stirred a memory fully six and thirty years old ; but candour compels the confession that reference only enables the quotation to be given. The deserted Œnone is repre-sented as writing to the faithless Paris.

> " Incisæ servant a te mea nomina fagi
> Et legor Œnone falce notata tuâ."

> " Deep-carved by thee the beech-bark holds my name,
> Thine was the blade that graved Œnone's fame."

It is but a rough verse ; but a faithful version. Alas ! Pope's beech is vanished from Binfield as completely as Œnone's from Mount Ida. Pope spent most of his boyhood at Binfield, whither his father, a City merchant, retired not long after the birth of the sickly son who was to make so distinct and individual a figure in literature. Warfield, two or three miles to the east, is worth a visit for its church ; but Winkfield, a little further to the east, and White Waltham and Waltham St. Lawrence, some four miles to the north of Binfield, are hardly worth the detour. Shottesbrooke must on no account be missed for its noble church, a happy hunting ground of archi-tectural enthusiasts, with many curious brasses, and for the legends attached to its great house. Here, as we learn from the *Memoirs of the Pious Robert Nelson*, Francis Cherry, whom Queen Anne described later as " one of the honestest gentlemen in her dominions," kept open house, to the extent of seventy beds, for his non-juring friends ; amongst them the pious Robert, practically forgotten, Bishop Ken, and others. Mr. Cherry, by the way, was also the brilliant horseman (admired and emulated by King William as such) who tried to tempt the Dutch King, then following him close in the hunting field, to his death, by jumping his horse into a deep part of the Thames. An unthinking mole succeeded where the plotting Cherry failed ; for Dutch William came by his death from a fall over that which Herefordshire folk call an "oonty tump."

About two and a half miles north of Wokingham is Hurst, with nice old almshouses, a fine old inn, and a magnificent yew. A little to the west of Wokingham lies Bear Wood, the house standing on an eminence, and house and estate a monument of the position won by the Walter family as faithful servants of the public and honourable conductors of a great newspaper. The house was the work of the third John Walter, and about the building of it a characteristic anecdote is told. There was a strike of bricklayers. " Mr. Walter "—the quotation is from *The Times* of November 5th, 1894—" was not a man to be beaten by labour troubles. He at once mounted the scaffolding and began to lay the bricks with his own hands. 'You see I can get on without you,' he said, turning to the men on strike, who were watching him ; ' it will take a little longer, perhaps, but I shall get it done in the end.' The men returned to their work forthwith, and there were no more strikes at Bear Wood." Here was a trait of the father repeated in the son, for it is recorded of John Walter the second that, when the London compositors attempted to dictate terms to him, he worked for thirty-six hours at case and at press with a few apprentices, and brought *The Times* out as usual. Surely, then, the Walter family is one of which Berkshire may be justly proud. The house contains some notable treasures of art, and hard by is a large piece of artificial water, where, as an epitaph in the church records, he who should have been John Walter the fourth, of Printing House Square and Bear Wood, " died rescuing his brother and cousin from the frozen lake at Bear Wood, Christmas Eve, 1870."

WORKING MEN'S COLLEGE LIBRARY

Why is Bear Wood so called? That is just one of those
little questions arising by the way that are apt to suggest interesting thoughts. Here, in the heart of Berkshire we have Bear
Wood and, near Wargrave, Bear Place, Bear Park, and so forth.
The Saxon chroniclers called the county " Bearrucsire "; Asser
says that Berkshire or, as an equal number of old-time writers
had it, Barkshire, took its name from " the wood of Berroc, where
the box-tree grows abundantly." Green, in his *History of
the English People* (vol. i., p, 33, Macmillan), publishes a map,
entitled " Britain and the English Conquest," showing a vast
" Bearroc Wood," having an area of some 500 square miles,
and certainly including Bear Wood. Finally, we know that the
Romans were in the habit of importing bears for their games
from Britain, and that bears were certainly not extinct in
Britain in the tenth century. So, while Bear Place may
possibly have been one of the sites of a pit for baiting bears,
there seems to be no sufficient reason why the title of Bear
Wood, beyond question of great antiquity, should not be due to
a tradition, founded on fact, that this once pathless wood was
haunted by bears. It may be that here we have lighted on the
explanation of the origin of the name of the county also. There
is really nothing against the theory, except the fact that nobody
seems to have thought of it before, unless the etymologists have
something to say on the subject. For them, frankly, I have an
ever-present distrust. They never weary of reminding the
inquirer of the obvious fact that the men and women of old
time cared not a straw how they spelled even their own names.
Yet, in the same breath, or in the same dip of the pen in the
ink, they will pronounce in favour of a derivation based entirely
on spelling. So let them be passed on one side, and that all
the more readily since we know not what they might say. Let
us reflect that the tenth or eleventh century are but as yesterday
when it comes to a question of the origin of place-names; and,
thus reflecting, let us ask what could be more likely than that
Berkshire, with its huge tract of forest, was in very truth one of

the last haunts of the savage bear in Southern England, and that Bear Wood was called after its own bears. Sometimes, too, one comes across traces of forgotten fauna in the sayings of the people of the country, which the learned call folk-lore, and in the games of country children, which never change. For example, at Sutton Courtney not long since, as noted in the opening chapter, was encountered a rhyme entering into a childish game which mentioned the wolf. Elsewhere, but near enough to Berkshire for the purposes of this argument, I had occasion once to tell a countryman that I was going to Wales, and it is a serious fact that the ingenuous rustic replied, " Ah ! Wales : that's where the bears are." The fact of the matter is that the traditions of these peasant folk are handed down from father to son, from generation to generation, that time is as nothing to them. My friend of the bear quotation, a typical son of the Hertfordshire soil, is convinced that his grandfather remembered the time when the sea came up to Hertford. Our Berkshire peasants speak of the wars, always meaning the civil wars, as if they had been waged a century back at most. Their minds will not take in the idea of the lapse of centuries, and it would not surprise me in the least to meet a native of the Bear Wood district who should say " Ah" (they always open with a long-drawn " Ah "), " my faather used to tell oi as 'is faather minded the days when bears used to be just about plenty in Bear Wood." So, in an inarticulate fashion, he might embody a tradition containing a kernel of historical truth.

From Wokingham a good road, with no serious variations of level, runs to Arborfield Cross, leaving Bear Wood on the right hand. At Arborfield it "trifurcates," to coin a word, going north-west by west to Shinfield, south-west to Swallowfield, and southward to the Blackwater and Eversley. Here the lover of good literature about rural scenes and rural folks is on holy ground ; for this is the country of Mary Russell Mitford, and the country, too, to which Mrs. Thackeray Ritchie, in the

Arborfield

edition of *Our Village*, published in 1902 (Macmillan), has even given something of added fame. Pope wrote a poem, too, on the Loddon, entitled " Lodona," but he who opined that "the proper study of mankind is man" was not instinct with the spirit of wild nature. The great mass of trees at Bear Wood, or of Bear Wood, is not long passed before Arborfield is reached, and there stands a modern Arborfield Hall, in place of "the old house at Aberleigh." When we have gone so far as Swallowfield we are in the quiet village rendered famous for ever by virtue of Miss Mitford's pure and graceful prose, the retreat where the Duke of Wellington, Mr. Ruskin, Charles Kingsley, and James Payn used to visit her, the starting-point of her delightful drives, one of them to see the Queen and Prince Albert returning from their visit to the Duke of Wellington in 1844 ; for Strathfield Saye is but a mile or two from Swallowfield across the Hampshire border. It is in the village churchyard that Mary Russell Mitford (blessed be her gentle memory !) lies buried.

" The old house at Aberleigh " is no more, but the way to it is, as in the middle of the last century, "pleasant in every sense, winding through narrow lanes, under high elms, and between hedges garlanded with woodbine and rose-trees, whilst the air is scented with the delicious fragrance of blossomed beans." If " Emily " were in our company, we, too, might cry out in innocent ecstasy, " This is the Loddon, Emily. Is it not a beautiful river ? rising level with its banks, so clear and smooth and peaceful, giving back the verdant landscape and the clear blue sky, and bearing on its pellucid stream the snowy water-lily, the purest of flowers, like the lady in ' Comus.' That queenly flower becomes the water, and so do the stately swans who are sailing so majestically down the stream, like those who—

> " ' On St. Mary's lake
> Float double, swan and shadow.' "

In the absence of " Mary " it is submitted with confidence that

Miss Mitford has drunk in, and pours out again, the essential character of the beauty of this tranquil and sequestered country, and that it is impossible to describe it more aptly than in her words. Let us take one passage as typical, making the choice with difficulty owing to embarrassment of riches.

"Over every part of the picture, trees so profusely scattered, that it appears like a woodland scene, with glades and villages intermixed. The trees are of all kinds and of all hues, chiefly the finely-shaped elm, of so bright and deep a green, the tips of whose high outer branches drop down with such a crisp and garland-like richness, and the oak, whose stately form is just now so splendidly adorned by the sunny colouring of the young leaves. Turning again up the hill, we find ourselves on that peculiar charm of English scenery, a green common, divided by the road ; the right side fringed by hedgerows and trees, with cottages and farmhouses irregularly placed, and terminated by a double avenue of noble oaks ; the left, prettier still, dappled by bright pools of water, and islands of cottages and cottage-gardens, and sinking gradually down to cornfields and meadows, and an old farmhouse, with pointed roofs and clustered chimneys, looking out from its blooming orchard, and backed by woody hills. The common is itself the prettiest part of the prospect ; half-covered with low furze, whose golden blossoms reflect so intensely the last beams of the setting sun, and alive with cows and sheep, and two sets of cricketers ; one of young men, surrounded by spectators, some standing, some sitting, some stretched on the grass, all taking a delighted interest in the game ; the other a merry group of little boys, at a humble distance, for whom even cricket is scarcely lively enough, shouting, leaping, and enjoying themselves to their hearts' content."

The passage is matchless, perfect, true in every detail and infinitely human. Indeed, there is but one thing to be regretted in connection with "this shady yet sunny Berkshire" and *Our Village*. It is that at no time did Miss Mitford have occasion to describe the full glory of golden colour in the trees during so gorgeous an autumn as that of 1904. Something of the kind she essayed, it is true, in the concluding picture entitled "The Fall of the Leaf," but in this the colouring is but pale and weak in comparison with that which surrounds me as I write. For now—it is in the last week of

October—there have been many still and sunny days, and an equal number of windless nights with just a suspicion of frost in the air, and the consequence is that the colouring is deeper, richer, and shown upon more countless leaves of elm and poplar, than in any previous year within the memory of man. So, at least, it seems, while we are face to face with so much beauty; and it is very certain that, if Miss Mitford had looked upon a scene equally remarkable, she would have painted an imperishable picture in words warm, glowing, and accurate.

Yes, "the old house at Aberleigh" has perished; but there need be no apology for quoting Miss Mitford's description of it, not merely for the sake of stirring vain regrets concerning architectural beauty lost, but because it needs something of elucidation. Its references, indeed, may not have been too clear even in her day. Here are Miss Mitford's words:—

"And crossing the stile we were immediately in what had been a drive round a spacious park, and still retained something of the character, though the park itself had long been broken into arable fields—and in full view of the Great House, a beautiful structure of James the First's time, whose glassless windows and dilapidated doors form a melancholy contrast with the strength and entireness of the rich and massive front. The story of that ruin—for such it is—is always to me singularly affecting. It is that of the decay of an ancient and distinguished family, gradually reduced from the highest wealth and station to actual poverty. The house and park, and a small estate around it, were entailed on a distant cousin and could not be alienated; and the late owner, the last of his name and lineage, after long struggling with debt and difficulty, farming his own lands, and clinging to his magnificent home with a love of place almost as tenacious as that of the younger Foscari, was at last forced to abandon it, retired to a paltry lodging in a paltry town, and died there about twenty years ago, broken-hearted. His successor, bound by no ties of association to the spot, and rightly judging the residence to be much too large for the diminished estate, immediately sold the superb fixtures, and would have entirely taken down the house, if, on making the attempt, the masonry had not been found so solid that the materials were not worth the labour. A great part, however, of one side is laid open, and the splendid chambers, with their carving and gilding, are exposed to the wind and rain—sad memorials of past grandeur! The grounds have been left in a merciful neglect; the park, indeed, is broken up, the lawn is mown twice a year like a common hay-field, the grotto mouldering into ruin, and the fish ponds choked with rushes and aquatic plants ; but the shrubs and flowering trees are undestroyed, and have grown into a magnificence of size and wildness of beauty, such as we may imagine them to attain in their native forests. Nothing can exceed their luxuriance, especially in the spring, when the lilac, the laburnum, and double-cherry put forth their gorgeous blossoms. There is a sweet sadness in the sight of such floweriness amidst such desolation ; it seems the triumph of nature over the destructive power of man."

Miss Mitford goes on to tell Emily, and us, that the "soft and soothing melancholy" of the place reminds her of the novels of Charlotte Smith, which almost inclines one to visit the British Museum or the Bodleian and to recall Charlotte Smith from oblivion. But it is more practical to follow Miss Mitford's reference to local history, since Charlotte Smith's charms as a writer were probably due to Miss Mitford's appreciative imagination. That possibly played upon local history also, but on the whole we think not. *"Our Village"* began to appear in the *Ladies' Magazine* in 1824, and other authorities have it that Edward Standen, the last of his lineage who owned Arborfield Old Manor House, died at least 90, and not 20 years before Miss Mitford wrote ; died too, not in a paltry house and in a paltry town, but in the old house at Arborfield. The balance of probability is in favour of Miss Mitford's version : indeed doubly in favour of it. First it fits in with things as she found them in 1824, whereas it was not likely that the house would have been left desolate for 90 years and more. Next the other version, in order that it might be connected with the story of "Molly Mog," the inn-keeper's daughter of Wokingham, required to be dated back to the days of Gay, Pope, Swift, and Arbuthnot. The story is that the last of the Standens was hopelessly enamoured of Sally Mog, one of the daughters of the Rose Inn at Wokingham, and that the literary verses wits beguiled a wet afternoon by drinking and by writing in turn about the despairing lover and his lass : finally the wits seem to have mixed up the two maidens and to have sung of "Sweet

Molly Mog " when they meant Sally all the time.   In any case as there is no doubt when Swift, Gay, Pope, and Arbuthnot lived and died, the " Molly Mog " story will not fit in with Miss Mitford's date, and her story may be accepted by preference. Of course it does not matter at all really to the progress of the world whether there is any truth in either story, and there is no doubt as to the existence of the song ; but Miss Mitford's version is the more dignified and, in an age which regards drunkenness as disgusting rather than amusing, it is the more acceptable of the two.

So let us take leave of Miss Mitford's country, part of which, including Shinfield, with its warm-toned church tower of brick-work 300 years old, or thereabouts, and Three Mile Cross, where Miss Mitford's home was until she went to Swallowfield, is outside the boundary of the " brimming Loddon " that was set before us at the outset of the chapter.   No better advice can be given than to take Miss Mitford for guide, for the pure spirit of the country is in her ; nay, even is it so strong in her, and so infectious, that the wanderer imbued with Miss Mitford's mood hardly feels that change in the surroundings which impressed itself on Mrs. Thackeray Ritchie's mind. But, then, Mrs. Thackeray Ritchie drove from Reading, and that is the wrong way to approach Arborfield and Swallowfield if the object be to reach the appropriate frame of mind. Again, *aliquando dormitat Homerus* ; in this country the infallible Murray is not entirely to be relied upon.   He may possibly be right in telling us that Three Mile Cross is " Our Village," although the better opinion points to Swallowfield where Miss Mitford lived and wrote in her later years, and was buried ; but he is certainly wrong in writing, the reference being to Shinfield (with those abbreviations and italics dear to his soul), " 1 m. E., on the Basingstoke road, is *Three Mile Cross*" for East is East and West is West, and Three Mile Cross and its inn lie due West of Shinfield.   Let it be added that, to a writer conscious of infinite fallibility, it is a genuine consolation to discover a good thumping error of this kind in a volume usually infallible and precise.

Going due South from the inn at Swallowfield for a little more than a mile the wanderer will reach simultaneously the ancient Roman road to Silchester and London, and the border of the county of Berks. Time was when, with a superb disregard for the fate imprecated on him who removes his neighbour's landmark, there was an intention of writing at some length of Silchester, and of the interesting results of excavations there stored in the Reading Museum. That was before the wealth of memories and associations possessed by my legitimate territory was realised thoroughly. Now that it is realised there is almost comfort in the thought that Calleva Atrebatum is a good mile inside the Hampshire boundary, and that hardly enough of its outskirts to justify more than passing allusion are to be found in Berkshire. None the less, the models to scale of unique Roman houses and the actual relics contained in the Reading Museum are things to be regarded with attention. Otherwise there is nothing much to detain the visitor to this part of the country, apart from places mentioned in another connection, principally that of the Civil War, and from its general beauty, except the queer church of Sulhampstead Bannister.

Geographically the brief remainder of the chapter is hardly to be justified; but we must go to Hampstead Norris, Yattendon, Stanford Dingley, and Bradfield, whereof the last but one has an ancient church of St. Denis, wooden-towered, and standing in a grove of Spanish chestnuts. My own first pilgrimage through it, from the direction of Didcot as it happened, was made by train and bicycle, influenced partly by the direction of the wind—it was blowing briskly from the West—and governed finally by a determination to see Bradfield College, since here was yet another public school of Berkshire, having a short but very exciting history. The choice therefore lay between taking train to Pangbourne, and riding against a head wind to Bradfield, or travelling to Hampstead Norris by train, and having a stern wind for a longer but by no means alarming distance. No cyclist will be surprised that the wind settled the question of choice of routes. The ride was delightful, and the impression left by the first part of it was not entirely scenic; rather was it of the contrast between the appearance of a village apparently untouched by the magic wand of prosperity, and that of one that had been more fortunate. Hampstead Norris was and is picturesque, but, in the spring of the year, it seemed also somewhat squalid and unkempt. Yattendon told another and a very much more pleasing story. It has antiquity enough to satisfy the most fastidious in the shape of its fifteenth century church; it has also modern prosperity and comfort, engineered, so to speak, by men of literary and artistic taste, inspired by just regard for antiquity. The late Mr. Waterhouse, R.A., was then the dominant landowner; Canon Beeching had been, until recently, the incumbent; among the names of Parish Councillors was to be seen that of Mr. Robert Bridges, the poet. The whole village was not, in the contemptuous sense of the word, "model," but comfortable, prosperous, and tidy. The inn afforded good refreshment, of a plain kind, set out decently and in order. The roses on the cottages were carefully tended and trained. Hammered copper work of excellent design showed that, with guidance, the English country folk are quite capable of being warrantable craftsmen. The whole, perhaps, had something of an artificial origin. Natural taste may not have dictated the planting and tending of the roses and general appearance of trim neatness, so much as a feeling that these things pleased the fancy of the leading persons of the community. In any event the effect was exceptionally pleasing to one who knew how much of grinding poverty is to be found in the smiling hamlets of Berkshire.

Our route led us to Burnt Hill, where a merry party of excursionists, probably biscuit "hands" from Reading, were making the most of a breezy Bank Holiday, and then through a gloriously wooded country, with the fragrance of bracken in the air, and with no hedges to speak of, until we were on the brow of the valley of the Pang, with Bradfield College, our goal, facing us. There, before returning to the railway at Pangbourne, some hours were spent with equal pleasure and profit, with all the more of both, no doubt, in that the "History of Bradfield College" by Mr. Arthur F. Leach (Henry Frowde, 1900) had been assimilated beforehand. It had been read not merely because Mr. Leach is an authority of the highest order, a friend and connection of my own, and before this little book had been conceived, simply because, as our public schools are among the most distinct and characteristic of English institutions, so the history of their development is, to one of the opinion just expressed, an absorbing story to read. Of its separate chapters that relating to Bradfield College is one of the most exciting. Stevens of Bradfield, like Sewell of Radley, never counted cost beforehand in relation to his own enterprises, although, as a Poor Law Commissioner, he showed no mean aptitude in managing the affairs of others. He was impelled, as Mr. Leach puts it, "by his own momentum"; he would comfort an assistant master, whose salary had not been paid, by recommending him to repeat the Nicene Creed (parts of the Athanasian would have suited the tutor's mood better); before he died his manor and lands had been sold, his Rectory had been sequestrated. Yet when Mozley wrote, in 1882, "Bradfield College survives, but has ruined its founder," and finally "Bradfield College has now that touch of tragic interest which in one way or another is ever to be found in the noblest of human enterprises," he was not only writing hysterically, since there are plenty of human enterprises, noble and educational, free from all touch of tragic interest, but also saying that which was to be proved unhistorical with quite remarkable rapidity. The school was opened, with one boy, in February 1850; it passed through a long period of stress and storm; the man who was to save it, and to convert it into a thoroughly solvent and valuable public school, appeared in the person of Mr., now Dr. Gray, in 1880, an ardent Wykehamist and scholar of Queen's College, Oxford, who had enjoyed some experience as a school-master at Westminster, besides a little that did not count at Louth, in Lincolnshire. Dr. Gray worked the miracle; and the result is entirely satisfactory. At Bradfield one sees boys admirably housed, a school perfectly equipped, possessed of good tone, *esprit de corps*, traditions. What struck me most, on the occasion of my visit, was the excellent physique of the boys and their appearance of robust health. Beyond that it was interesting to see how the school had grown out of and round the red-brick and flint Manor House, now occupied by the headmaster, who is also warden, to note the handsome gateway, the modern, but pleasing, buildings, an ancient wall of red brick, having at one end the hexagonal chamber called Tom o' Bedlam's Hole, probably of fourteenth century work. Very much more attractive, however, is the exact reproduction of a Greek theatre in a chalk pit adjoining the college, with a Greek Temple for stage-building or scene. In it have been produced a long succession of Greek plays, causing the fame of Bradfield to go out to all the world. The excellent idea was conceived by Dr. Gray himself; his boys helped him in the preliminary work of hewing out the tiers of seats; he himself took the part of Coryphæus in the original production of the Antigone; and since advertisement of a really good thing is not merely harmless but positively good, it will not be offensive to say that the Greek theatre at Bradfield ranks equal to "Tom Brown's Schooldays" as one of the two most effective advertisements ever exhibited, without meaning to advertise at all, for public schools.

D D

CHAPTER XIII

BERKSHIRE AND THE CIVIL WAR

Berkshire's importance in the Civil War—A question of roads—Importance of defence of Basing, Donnington, Wallingford, and Faringdon—Abingdon a grievous loss to the King—Siege of Reading—Ill-treatment of Colonel Fielding—Essex loses an opportunity—Charles, commanding Berks roads, compels detour by Essex—Hungerford—A glance at early history—First battle of Newbury—Rupert's impetuosity—Essex carries his plan through—Falkland's death and character—Sir John Boyes at Donnington—The fruitless siege—Manchester, Essex, Cromwell—Second battle of Newbury—Royalist ignorance of Parliamentary army's movements—Compare Boer War, and forgive—Northampton's departure, an error—Shaw House and its defences—The Royalist positions—Relics of Charles—he fights hand to hand—Scene little changed—King's retreat to Oxford—Essex hampers Cromwell's pursuit—Charles returns to Hungerford—Seventeenth century military pocket maps and guides—Buried in the Bodleian—Colonel Gage, the De Wet of the Civil War—His personality—Experience in Flanders—the Governor of Oxford—An importunate Marchioness—Charles leaves authority with Gage, and places Lords of Council above the Governor—Jealousy of the Governor—Gage to relieve Basing—His force—night march to Wallingford—His plans—A messenger to Winchester City—Another to Lord Winchester in Basing House—English temper makes disguise in vain—Skirmish at Aldermaston—A weary night march—A disappointment—Relief of Basing House—A clever escape—Gage compared to De Wet, French, Morgan, and Stuart—The loss of Abingdon—The Ill Humour and Negligence of Wilmot—Effects of Parliamentary occupation of Abingdon—After all it hastened the inevitable end—*Finis*.

IT is fairly safe to say, in an anticipatory sentence, that almost every place of interest in Berkshire not already named, as well as many that have been mentioned, must needs come forward in this chapter, for Berkshire had a great share in the Civil War and, as there has been occasion to point out, the country-side still preserves an inarticulate memory of the time, the winter of 1644 was its worst period, when "hardly a sheep, hen, hog, oats, hay, wheat, or any other thing for man (or beast) to feed on" could be found in that sorely overrun county. Let there be no alarm, however. It is no part of the present purpose to tell the whole of the story of Berkshire's share in the Civil War, partly because that story is involved inextricably in that of the whole war, but even more because, apart from pitched battles, nothing is more remarkable than the absence of connected purpose in individual operations in Berks and elsewhere during the Civil War, on both sides, during the intervals between battles. Still Berkshire was the scene of many battles, some of them more important in their results than the general run of historians are disposed to allow, of gallant exploits, and of brave defences still living fresh and green in historical memory ; so that in this chapter topographical and antiquarian gossip may well be relegated to a secondary place.

Why was the county fated to be the field of so many fights? The answer is to be found in any seventeenth-century map showing those main roads of England which, when the ill-fated Charles raised his standard at Nottingham in August, 1642, were practically the only means of communication. On them it will be seen that three principal roads, and three only, led from London to the west of England, and commanded much of the avenue to the north-west. The most southern of them ran through Basing to Salisbury, and thence to Exeter. The central road, on reaching Reading, bifurcated, following one route north-west by west to Wallingford and Faringdon, thence leading to Cirencester, where it forked again for Gloucester and Hereford to the north-west, and to Bristol. The route of the southern fork was by Newbury and

Chippenham, and so to Bath and to Exeter. The northern-most road ran straight to Oxford, forking there for Rugby and Leicester, on the one hand, and Edgehill and Worcester on the other. There was also direct communication between Walling-ford and Oxford. If one bears these roads in mind, re-membering at the same time that Oxford was virtually the Royalist capital during the whole course of the war, and that there was a constant tendency for the Parliament to become stronger and stronger in the country to the south and west of these roads—we may leave the north untouched—much of the story of the Civil War assumes not exactly a new, but a very clear aspect. One sees at once how vital to Charles, how exasperating to his opponents, were the heroic defence of Basing, the ceaseless energy of Blagge at Wallingford, the unflinching gallantry of sturdy Sir John Boys at Donnington Castle, and the prolonged resistance of Faringdon. They commanded the roads, kept the Parliamentary forces of the west and south from easy access to those of the north and east, provided Charles with a country more or less his own, within the limits of his nominal kingdom, and once at least, before the first battle of Newbury, allowed him to execute a masterly movement on interior lines. In like manner one perceives how grievous a thorn in the flesh must have been the Parliamentary occupation of Abingdon to Charles—it was most stupidly lost by Wilmot, as is recorded later—and how serious a blow to him was the capture of Reading by Essex in April of 1643. The capture of Windsor, grave perhaps as a matter of prestige, was strategically unimportant.

Let us begin with Reading. Late in 1642 Reading fell into the hands of Charles, in the course of the King's famous march from Banbury to Brentford, where, finding himself too weak to face the train bands of the City under Essex, he thought well to retire, again *via* Reading to Oxford. Looking back now it seems that Martin, the Parliamentary Governor, had every excuse for thinking that all was going well for the

King and that discretion was the better part of valour.
Certainly he made no resistance, but fled in advance with his
garrison. Charles, who was no mean general, although he
more than once showed himself a mean man, by no means
ignored the importance of Reading, where 3,000 foot and 300
horse were quartered under Sir Arthur Aston throughout the
winter; but the fortifications were "very mean to endure a
formed siege," and there were not forty barrels of powder.

The Kennet and Avon at Westfields, Newbury.

The former weakness might have been remedied; the latter
was incurable, unless indeed Charles had established a powder
manufactory of his own. As Clarendon puts it, "the King
had no port to Friend, by which he could bring up Ammunition to *Oxford*," and all the powder he possessed during the
early part of the campaign was "the remainder (after
Edgehill) of the 400 Barrils brought by the ship call'd the
Providence, before the setting up of the standard." In fact
the plan of the Royalist Council of War had been to draw off
the garrison of Reading to the King's headquarters at Oxford,

and it was only the promptitude of Essex, in marching on Reading as soon as the days of truce for the abortive negotiations for peace were ended, that rendered a siege necessary. Nevertheless a fairly stout resistance was made against a strong force. The siege began on the 15th of April. On the 22nd Major Vavasour attempted to take the city by assault, and perhaps it was on that day that Sir Arthur Aston was stunned by a " Brick-tyle " dislodged by a cannon-ball, so that the command devolved on Colonel Fielding. Charles, too, made an effort to relieve the town, and was driven back with heavy loss, but not before General Wilmot had succeeded in furnishing the beleaguered garrison with some powder and reinforcements. It was not until the 27th that the garrison surrendered on the terms that they should march out with flying colours, have a free passage to Oxford, and fifty carriages for baggage, sick and wounded. Clarendon says that, in fact, they were plundered and disarmed by the mob as they left the town, and gives this as an excuse for " barbarous injustice of the same kind " committed by the King's troops, as well as those of the Parliament, during the remainder of the Wars. Accusations of this kind are, however, familiar in time of war, and Clarendon is not the witness from whom one would accept them uncorroborated. Both sides seem to have been satisfied with the result for the time. The Parliament had gained Reading, a point of vast importance, cheaply ; Charles, who was sadly in need of men, received valuable reinforcements. Even Clarendon, however, is compelled to admit that Charles treated Colonel Fielding ill afterwards, allowing him to be tried by a Court of Inquiry, and depriving him of his command, although " I do believe him to have been free from any base compliance with the enemy, or any cowardly declension of what was reasonable to be attempted. So fatal are all misfortunes, and so difficult a thing it is to play an aftergame of reputation, in that nice and jealous pro- fession." There are those who will think these words might have been written with equal justice in the twentieth century. The real, but not the logical or the confessed reason for the undeserved disgrace of Colonel Fielding, may well have been that, while the Earl of Newcastle (whom the recent reprint of his devoted wife's book has taught us to know better than before) was doing well for his King in the North, the Midlands were in a bad way; and, in the South and West, Portsmouth, Chichester, Winchester, Hereford, and Tewkesbury, to say nothing of many other places, were in the hands of the enemy. So weak did the King deem his position to be, short of ammunition as he was, that, to quote Clarendon on a point wherein he is certainly credible, "If the Earl of *Essex* had, at that time, but made any show of moving with his whole Body that way, I do verily persuade my self, *Oxford* it self, and all the other Garrisons of those parts had been quitted to them."

Essex made no movement, but that immobility of his was not conspicuous early enough to save Colonel Fielding. Essex, says Clarendon, failed to move because it was too early in the year for campaigning, so that his troops had suffered from exposure to frost and rain during the siege, and were stricken with disease. Well, it was April and the siege had lasted less than a fortnight. Were our fore-runners of the seventeenth century much less robust than ourselves? Was Essex even less wanting in dash and vigour than his reputation shows him? Or, as is more likely, had the besiegers also suffered heavy loss in Vavasour's assault, and in repelling the relief force at Caversham. No man can tell with certainty; all we know is that Essex did not move, and that his men were raw and untrained.

It was not long, however, before events outside Berkshire brought Essex back into the county he had left. Charles had set about the siege of Gloucester, after a series of victories by Rupert in Somersetshire; and the Parliament had all but lost the West, where it had been strong. Essex, after marching his army through the Cotswolds (the houses as well as the hills of which probably looked the same as they do now), had

alarmed Charles sufficiently to make him raise the siege ; but
Essex himself, being without artillery, deemed it wise to make
his best speed for London.   Here it was that the command of
the Berkshire roads possessed by Charles gave him a great
advantage.   Passing through Evesham, North Leach, Faringdon, and Wantage, he left Essex no alternative save to come *via*
Cirencester and Swindon, and when Essex reached Hungerford
on the 19th of September, Charles was already in the neighbourhood of Newbury.

Hungerford was already a considerable place, celebrated then
as now for its great trout, and named after the Hungerfords, the
original holders of the Manor, one of whom, Sir Thomas, was
the first Speaker of the House of Commons ; its inhabitants
owned " the riall fishing from Eldren Stub to Irish Still," by
grant from John of Gaunt, and possessed the horn given by
John of Gaunt as an emblem of their tenure.   Possibly it may
have witnessed, Streatfield thinks it did witness, a battle royal
between Saxon and Dane in 871.   Certainly there was something appropriate in 1643 about the fact that the birthplace of
the first Speaker of the House of Commons was destined to be
uncomfortably near the fringe of a battle between the Commons
and King, more decisive than some historians are ready to
recognise, appealing more perhaps to our emotions than is due
by reason of the prominence of some of the brave men who fell.
Before that battle began, Essex had to march through Kintbury,
noteworthy only apart from our present topic as being the
nearest railway station to the highest point in the county,
Inkpen Beacon, and Enborne, remarkable mainly for a "custom"
hard to match for ribald obscenity even in mediæval times.

The two armies met and the battle began to rage, the
" precipitate courage of some young officers " having hurried
the King into action.   But I am not going into the details of
the fight from a military point of view because, not being
interested in that aspect of the affair personally, and being
reasonably sure that, from the details of a battle fought under

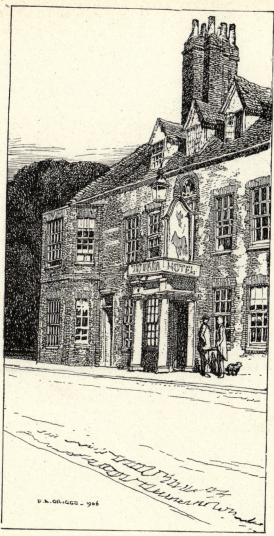

The Bear at Hungerford.

seventeenth century conditions near Newbury, few lessons useful for modern conditions could be learned while some fossilised
ideas might be confirmed, I should, in such a case, probably fail
to write in interesting fashion. It is grand, however, to read, how
the London Train'd-bands and Auxiliary Regiments "stood as
a Bulwark and a Rampire to defend the rest"; and it is worth
while to note that, while some more modern historians affect to
regard the battle as having been indecisive, Clarendon was
under no such misapprehension. Essex meant to make good
his march to London; Charles did all that he could to check
him. Essex succeeded partly by good generalship partly
through the impetuosity of some of his opponents, and
although harassed a little by Rupert at Aldermaston, Padworth,
and Bucklebury, he won through, leaving, it is true, Reading to
be reoccupied for the King, but well deserving the thanks of
the London people for an action "perform'd by him with
incomparable conduct and courage . . . it may well be
reckoned among the most soldierly actions of this unhappy
war."

The "Bill," as soldiers have it, was heavy, and, even while
perceiving the wrongheadedness of Clarendon's description of
it, it is difficult not to share his feelings :

"On which side soever the Marks and Publick Ensigns of Victory appeared most conspicuous, certain it is, that according to the unequal fate
which attended all the skirmishes with such an adversary, the loss on the
King's side was in weight much more considerable and penetrating ; for
whilst some obscure, unheard of Colonel or officer was missing on the
enemy's side, and some Citizen's Wife bewailed the loss of her Husband,
there were on the other above twenty officers of the Field, and Persons of
Honour, and publick Name, slain upon the place, and more of the same
Quality hurt."

Nothing, in reality, could be more cruelly wrong; but if most
modern readers would examine their hearts and confess the
truth, it would be found that they shared some of Clarendon's
feeling. The Earl of Sunderland, "a Lord of great fortune

and tender years," may not touch them more than the vision of the Citizen's mourning widow, all the more affecting now because she is thrown off in a sneering phrase.   Even the fact that Sunderland's death left the poet Waller's "Saccharissa" a widow may not rouse their deepest sympathies.   The Earl of Carnarvon's fate may leave them unmoved.   But the fall of Falkland, "the virtuous and the just," whose monument stands at Newbury, having been erected in 1878, still compels the sorrow of every feeling man and woman.   Clarendon devotes to his memory sundry pages of genuine grandeur and eloquence. His praises have been sung in verse and celebrated in pure and noble prose.   His fame is world-wide and everlasting.   It will be enough to say here that no man ever began life under happier auspices, with instincts more refined, with keener intelligence or with more just taste ; that no man ever deserved happiness more completely ; and that no man of his age saw with more unerring an eye the certain coming of the Civil War, did his duty according to his conscience in a grave crisis more consistently, or felt the sorrows of his country more deeply than Falkland.   They produced in the once happy and eager mind an abiding and depressing melancholy.   The only consolations we have for the early death of one from whom much good fruit might have been justly hoped are, that it was an escape from grief almost intolerable and that he fully expected to meet on Newbury Field that day the fate he was too good a Christian and too loyal a gentleman to invoke with his own hand. That were, indeed, sufficient consolation but for the fact that Falkland did not live to see how, in the fulness of time, England settled down into a life of orderly progress and of that "Peace" for which he yearned day and night.   In truth he must have lived far beyond the allotted span of man before he could have been quite assured on this point that, for him, was incomparably above all others.   Whether he knows now, is one of those ever-present questions that successive generations have asked earnestly, appealingly, and always in vain.

May one word be added in justification of those men of to-day who, in the never-dying argument on the rights and wrongs of the Great Rebellion, feel that while the Parliament could hardly have acted otherwise in the main, and that Charles was wrong in most of his acts and utterly mean in many of them, they would still have taken up arms for him if the unhappy choice had been placed before them? In truth they stand in need of no apology. To have followed Falkland's model would have been to act in unquestionable obedience to true principle, and those of the contrary inclination are equally entitled to quote Hampden as an imperishable example. There are crises in the lives of men and of nations when there can be no true guide but conscience, and conscience may inspire two men, equally pure in principle, to conduct diametrically opposite. The lives and the deaths of Falkland and of Hampden are proofs that the controversy is undying, and that good men will always be found to take both sides of it. To have written this is by no means to have expressed so much as a shade of sympathy or of anything less than contempt for the foolish frippery of modern Jacobitism. That is puerile pantomime, tasteless trifling with a memory which, for those who really cherish it, has no little measure of sacred quality. If Falkland could revisit this earth to-day, King Edward would have no more loyal or able subject, and the League of the White Rose, or whatsoever it be called, would be regarded by him with superb scorn.

A year and a little more, of misery and fighting elsewhere, and not without little skirmishes in Berkshire, passed before Newbury was destined again to witness a pitched battle between Cavalier and Roundhead. It came about in this wise. In October the King was at Andover—Waller's force having declined battle—and, finding his army in the best of spirits, determined to relieve the sieges of Donnington Castle, Banbury, and Basing before retiring to Oxford for the winter. At Donnington the stalwart John Boys—he had not been knighted yet—had rendered an excellent account of his charge, " making merry of the high and threatening language " of his besieger Colonel Horton, although the latter had been reinforced and had beaten down three towers and a part of the wall. To Colonel Horton then came the Earl of Manchester, and the two generals would fain have attempted to take the castle by storm ; but their troops had no stomach for the enterprise, and a sally of his garrison was not only successful but also proof positive of their unbroken spirit. Still the besiegers went on pounding at the walls, expending " above one thousand great shot" in nineteen days, and did not retire (Clarendon omits to tell us whither) until they heard of the approach of the King's army. As a matter of fact they went no further than Swallowfield, where Manchester made his headquarters. So Miss Mitford's country had its share of excursions and alarms. There Essex came, with a considerable force, although he was himself sick ; and Cromwell also, who appears in our story for the first time. These facts are known to us now ; the probability is that they were hidden from Charles and his advisers, and that their first intimation of the recovered courage and the increased strength of their adversaries came when the combined Parliamentary forces appeared at Thatcham, less than three miles away, on the eve of the second battle of Newbury.

Charles and his generals were in a fool's paradise—a state of things for which we can hardly blame them much when we remember that the same kind of mistake has been committed over and over again quite recently by commanders possessing field-telegraphs, balloons, and all manner of apparatus for obtaining intelligence as to the movements of the enemy. Quite ignorant that a force far superior to his own was being marshalled within a day's march or so of Newbury, the King stayed at Newbury, converted plain John Boys into Sir John (an honour richly deserved), and detached forces under the Earl of Northampton to relieve sorely-pressed Banbury. The task was accomplished, but more might have

F. L. GRIGGS ~ 1906

Shaw House, Newbury.

WORKING MEN'S COLLEGE
LIBRARY.

been gained by maintaining the strength of the King's force, soon to be subjected to a crucial ordeal. At the same time the dashing Colonel Gage, as recorded more fully shortly, rode to the relief of Basing. Gage was at Oxford; but Northampton was detached—a grave error, if the enemy's position was known; a fatal misfortune in any event.

Were the movements of the enemy known? Clarendon writes as if their appearance at Thatcham had been a complete surprise. The earthworks at Shaw House, their traces still not the least interesting feature in the environment of one of the most noteworthy houses in the kingdom, may seem to tell another tale, for Shaw House was the strengthening buttress of the right of the King's position on the north of the Lambourne River, just before its junction with the Kennet. *Non sequitur*, however, that the earthworks were thrown up then, for Shaw and Donnington were, and are, adjacent, and Donnington had long been blockaded and often hotly besieged. Possibly, then, Charles, taken by surprise, had works already to his hand at Shaw House, as he had at Donnington, to which additional defences of earth and turf had been given immediately upon the raising of the siege. At any rate the King's position, you may see it plainly now, was that his left rested on Speen Hill, on that very tableland where the Romans once had a settlement, hastily entrenched; that the village of Shaw, with every convenient house loopholed and fortified, was occupied to protect the ford across the Lambourne; that Donnington and its works strengthened the centre and Shaw House the right. It was a fine position; its details are set forth because they are still plainly to be seen, and the wanderer may conjure up the whole picture, if he pleases, without difficulty. In Shaw House he may notice many relics of the war and of Charles. In the drawing-room, close by the identical hole made by a bullet in the wainscot, he may picture the King himself in converse with Mr. Dolman, descendant of the wealthy clothier who built the noble house. They may go in the

spirit, as Charles II. went in the flesh with Mr. Dolman in
1663, through the garden where Dolman and Charles are said

The Bath Road at Speen.

to have fought the enemy hand to hand. He may fancy Sir
Bernard Astley in Shaw Village, Sir Thomas Hooper and

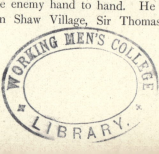

WORKING MEN'S COLLEGE LIBRARY.

Sir John Brown on the ground between it and the house, Sir
John Boys still in command of his inviolate if battered castle,
St. Leger at Speen Hill, Prince Maurice and his foot at Speen
Village, Newbury occupied by soldiery.

Changes there have been, of course, in the aspect of town,
villages, and country : but there is surely hardly any other
battle ground in England, of those in which the positions of
buildings and fences were important, that may reasonably be
imagined to have been modified less than that of Newbury in
shape and appearance since the day that made it greatest
in history. Then, as now, Newbury was a flourishing market
town, had been such, indeed, for many centuries. It is no
longer the seat of a prosperous woollen industry, but the Cloth
Hall stood, in sound repair, where it now stands decayed. So
did the noble church of St. Nicholas. The wooded hills, the
fat cornlands, the water-meadows, almost everything that is at
Newbury to-day, except the railway, the new houses, and the
Town Hall, were there, in the same positions, "on *Sunday*
morning the seven-and-twentieth of October," when the great
fight began. It is possible, book in hand, to follow every
detail of the fight. Having accomplished this task with one
book, Clarendon if "you'm a mind to," as a Berkshire man
would say, you can do it over again, quite differently, and in
more than one new fashion, with other books. Is this any
grievous misfortune ? Surely all that is of moment at this date
is that in the end the King, not realising how near he had been
to escaping defeat, elected to retire to Oxford by way of
Wallingford, choosing that route, no doubt, because the far
more direct way was now barred by Abingdon, in the hands of
the Parliament ; and that Manchester lost a great opportunity.
Of course he ought to have harried the King during his retreat.
Cromwell pressed that course upon him again and again ; but
he consented too late, and, having consented, repented him of
his compliance. Hence came it that Cromwell, Waller, and
Heselrige, with their horse, effected nothing, got no further

E E

than Blewbury, Hagbourne, Chilton, and Harwell, all villages familiar to readers of these pages, bivouacked there, and were then ignominiously recalled. By the way, there is a Chipping Cross broken at East Hagbourne. Did Waller cast it down, crying " Nehushtan " ?

The King's artillery and baggage, or much of it, remained at Donnington in the custody of Sir John Boys, who again repulsed an assault ; and so nerveless was Manchester that the King was able to return to the district, relieve Donnington and provision it, draw off his arms and ammunition, march to Lambourn, and thence to Marlborough. In a little while he was back again at Hungerford, to find the enemy departed for Basing, and in November, " a season of the year fit for all the troops to be in their winter quarters," he had returned by way of Faringdon to Oxford.

These are minor movements, alluded to mainly by way of suggesting the sufferings of Berkshire during the Civil War generally, and especially at this period. The naturally tranquil county was, it is plain, in a constant state of unrest, and the sight of the troops of both sides hurrying over it, leaving empty barns and henroosts behind them, must have been painfully familiar. So much was this incessant wandering regarded as a matter of course that I hear mention, not in any written book, of county maps, including one for Berkshire, prepared on the instructions of the King's Council at Oxford, of a kind calculated to make our military advisers of to-day think. They showed the roads and every village in the county described, and gave an estimate of the number of men that might be billeted in each. They were seen a score of years ago in the Bodleian Library, but, in the absence of any title to facilitate reference in the catalogue, repeated personal research, aided by the willing help of assistants in that sadly undermanned institution, has failed to discover them anew. Apart from this, the mere fact that Charles, upon reaching Hungerford, having being permitted to recover his strength after the second battle of

Newbury, found the enemy gone to Basing, is another and a sufficient justification for having followed these movements in a cursory fashion, because it brings us to a desired point.

Berkshire cannot claim the honour of having Basing within its borders ; it can claim to have rendered possible that gallant ride to the relief of Basing justifying the description of Colonel Gage as the De Wet of the Civil War, in point of mobility, if not of character, wherein the seventeenth-century colonel had the advantage over the Boer general. For dash, cleverness, and aptitude of resource there is nothing in the history of warfare to beat Gage's ride to and from Basing—a ride rendered feasible only by the hold the King's forces had over Northern Berkshire, Abingdon excepted ; a ride, further, wherein many miles of Berkshire country were traversed. The whole story of the manner of its happening is keenly interesting, and it reveals so much, with humour too, of the way in which matters were managed, and mismanaged, at the headquarters in Oxford, that it is worth telling.

When Charles started for the West, a little time before the second battle of Newbury, he left Oxford in very sorry condition. Provisions were scanty, fortifications poor ; there was a superfluity of peers, " with very many ladies who, when not pleased themselves, kept others from being so." Constant watchfulness was needed, for Major-General Brown, " a citizen of London and a stout man," was but six miles off at Abingdon, and " he infested *Oxford* very much." Amongst the unemployed officers were Colonel Gage and his comrade Colonel Webb who, like himself, had served in the English regiment in Flanders. Of Gage more shall be written in a short time. To complete the rough sketch of the Oxford society of the moment two more figures are needed : the first, that of the Governor, Sir Arthur Aston ; the next, that of the Marchioness of Winchester, sister, be it observed, of the same Earl of Essex who was fighting for the Parliament. Her business in Oxford was to press, with that delicate and effectual importunity wherein great ladies excel no less than small, for measures to be taken towards the relief of her husband, who had now held Basing House against a strong Parliamentary force for more than three months. As for the Governor, if Clarendon had been an English schoolboy he would have described him succinctly as "a beast." Being a master of gentle sarcasm—witness the remark concerning the ladies, recently quoted—and of stately periphrasis, he tells us, in a good many sentences, that Charles had made a great mistake in appointing Aston to be governor, and that Charles had become conscious of his error when it was too late to amend it. Aston "had the fortune to be very much esteemed where he was not known ; and very much disliked where he was." Before leaving for the West, Charles had particularly assigned to Colonel Gage the care of one of the quarters of the city, and he had made the Lords of his Council, by an extraordinary Commission, superior to Aston in authority.

An unpleasant man, as it would seem, at best, Aston · was left in the worst of moods, prepared to quarrel with anybody, and eager to thwart any plan suggested by Gage, for whom he had the instinctive dislike of a churl towards one of more noble character. Gage was certainly a fine fellow, not merely, or, for that matter, at all, for one of the reasons assigned by that pompous and delightful snob, Clarendon, that his grandfather had been a Knight of the Garter, but in many other ways. He was "of a large and very graceful person"— a good many of Matthew Arnold's barbarians are so much, and no more. Gage was a great deal more : an accomplished scholar, a wonderful linguist; a soldier of experience : and Aston's jealous hatred of him was inflamed the more by the fact that the Council, who had been placed in authority above Aston, frequently availed themselves of the valuable advice of the veteran soldier Gage.

In these circumstances came an earnest appeal from Lord Winchester—who, by the way, was a Roman Catholic—that "his person, and a place from which the rebels received so much prejudice," might be saved from delivery into their hands." The appeal was backed by the earnest solicitations of the Marchioness, and eagerly supported by the Roman Catholics. Well knowing that only pressure of necessity had prevented Charles from taking this matter in hand before pro-

Gateway at Hampstead Marshall.

ceeding to the West, sensible of the importance of Basing, influenced perhaps by the attractions of the Marchioness, no less than by her rank and position (in Clarendon's view the only thing about her worth mentioning), the Council, " both upon publick and private motives," were well disposed towards the idea. Aston would have none of the enterprise, on the ground that it was too difficult, and calculated to weaken the garrison unduly; and the first conferences were a failure.

Followed an interval, a more despairing appeal from Lord Winchester, " new instances from his lady " ; and we may be very sure that, during that interval, Lady Winchester used, and used legitimately, every feminine artifice to cause the adventurous Gage to be even more than naturally inclined towards a hazardous expedition. A novelist might do worse than weave a veil of romance around the great lady on the one hand, pleading for her husband's safety, and the polished soldier, " of a large and very graceful person," lending a willing ear to pleadings he had every disposition to favour, and at the same time feeling warm pleasure no less than true sympathy. Be that as it may have been, the upshot was exactly what Gage and Lady Winchester desired, and, in spite of Sir Arthur Aston, Gage was entrusted with the enterprise.

Sir Arthur Aston so far succeeded in carrying his way that the normal garrison was not weakened for the expedition except by the departure of Gage and his old comrade in Flanders, Colonel Webb. Four hundred men came in with Colonel Hawkins from Greenland House, where surrender had been compulsory ; and besides these Gage had only irregular horse, noblemen's servants mounted upon their own cattle, and volunteers, the whole mounted force amounting to " two hundred and fifty very good horse." They had need to be ; and they proved themselves such. With these, early on Monday night, Gage started for Wallingford—again the importance of Governor Blagge's tenure of that stronghold is manifest—and in the morning horse and foot halted for rest and refreshment in a wood near Wallingford. It was a piece of good marching, and it had been accomplished without arousing the unwelcome attention of the sleepy guards at Abingdon. During the rest Gage sent on an express to Winchester—a long way in any case, but we are not told the route—asking Sir William Ogle to send a hundred horse and three hundred foot from his garrison to fall on the besiegers of Basing in the rear, at a given hour, when Gage himself intended to be attacking them in front. At the same time he despatched a secret messenger—that he should penetrate the besiegers' lines is taken as a matter of course—to desire the

Gateway at Hampstead Marshall.

Marquis to make simultaneous sallies. He laid, in short, the most elaborate plans, and then rested his troops, since he must needs wait to give the express time to reach Ogle at Winchester.

At this point occurs what the old commentators would have called *hiatus valdè deflendus*. Clarendon continues, "After some hours of refreshment in the morning, and sending this express to Winchester, the troops marched through by-lanes to Aldermaston, a village out of any great road, where they intended to take more rest that night." But which way did they go? Aldermaston exists still, a secluded haunt, out of any great road, famous for its osier-beds and the magnificent park attached to Aldermaston Court, surrounded by wooded hills, not far from Silchester, and some eight miles to the east of Newbury. The easiest, and probably the safest, route would have been to keep on the Berkshire side of the river, pass through Cholsey and Moulsford, cross the Downs by way of Compton Parva, and then, proceeding by Hampstead Norris, Yattendon, Frilsham, Bucklebury, and Woolhampton, to cross the Kennet where the road from Aldermaston to Reading crosses it now. It was sixteen or seventeen miles as the crow flies, anyhow a splendid piece of marching that it would be sheer pleasure to trace in detail, over good walking country, for the Downs are grand going ; so is all the Bucklebury district—and the character of the ground has not changed in either.

At quiet Aldermaston came the first *contretemps*, serious enough to deprive the troops of their sorely needed rest. Gage, reckoning to deceive the enemy, had provided his men with orange-tawny scarves and ribbons ; but he had reckoned without the fighting instinct of Englishmen. No sooner had his advance party entered Aldermaston than they discovered there a party of Parliamentary horse. Their masquerade was immediately thrown to the winds ; and they had killed some of the Parliament's troopers, captured some more, and put others to flight, and to apprise the Roundheads of their coming, before it occurred to them to remember their disguise. Gage was angry, perhaps ; certainly he changed his plan of operations with prompt decision. The enemy would know of his raid by now; he must needs push on; and so, after marching well during the day, on top of a long night march, his weary troops were set marching again.

They started at eleven *post meridiem*; they were within a mile of Basing between four and five in the following Wednesday morning. Which route they took in the darkness is not stated, but the account of their manner of marching is vivid, almost pathetic. "They continued all that night: the horsemen often alighting, that the foot might ride, and others taking many of them behind them; however, they could not but be extremely weary and surbated." To the tired men came a new disappointment at Basing—to their leader, at any rate; to them, most likely, nothing was told. An officer from Winchester brought the unwelcome news that Ogle, by reason of intervening forces of the enemy, could not attempt to create a diversion by taking the enemy in rear. Disappointed, by no means daunted, ready for any emergency, Gage prepared his men to deliver an assault on the enemy in one body. Away went the tawny scarves and ribbons; white armlets, as prearranged with Lord Winchester, were substituted for them, lest the sortie party should mistake the relief expedition for besiegers in a *mêlée* where all would be Englishmen; and finally, addressing stirring words to his men, squadron by squadron, "which no man could more pertinently deliver, or with a better grace," he instructed them to use the time-honoured English battle-cry of "St. George." Gage was one of those rare commanders who, combining scrupulous forethought upon detail with the capacity to devise the boldest plans, command success as nearly as may be in a fallible world.

How complete was the success, how Basing House was provisioned afresh and furnished with twelve barrels of powder and twelve hundredweight of match, all probably that Oxford would afford, how it stood until Cromwell took it, much later, putting "most of the garrison to the sword," this is not the place to tell; but Gage's return to Oxford, almost as

F. L. GRIGGS - 1906

Newbury Bridge.

WORKING MEN'S COLLEGE LIBRARY.

masterly a movement as his outward expedition, is very much within our scope. It threatened to be no child's play. The besiegers under Norton had plucked up their courage and "appeared within sight of the house more numerous and gay than before." Gage's spies let him know that, if Brown, the stout citizen, had allowed himself to be passed in his sleep during the Monday night, he was awake now. He had occupied Aldermaston in the interval. "Two other villages upon the river Kennet"—Woolhampton and Thatcham, most likely—had been filled with Parliamentary troops from Reading and from Newbury. Things looked black for Gage, but he was more than equal to the emergency. Knowing well that the news would be sent to the enemy, he warned sundry villages, none of which he had the remotest intention of visiting, that they must provide stated supplies of corn for Basing House by noon of the next day, or he would come with 1,000 horse to burn their villages. This was on Thursday night; but, instead of appearing to terrorise the villagers, before noon of the next day, having marched all night, he had come back again into Berkshire, forded the Kennet at some point unknown, where the enemy had destroyed the bridge, ventured within a mile of Reading, where he crossed the Thames. Before night he was safe again at Wallingford, the priceless Wallingford, and could rest his men in security before returning at his leisure to Oxford, the hero of an exploit worthy to be remembered for ever in the annals of forced marches by horse and foot. "It was confessed, by enemies as well as friends, that it was as soldierly an exploit as had been performed in the war on either side." It was, in truth, an achievement worthy to rank with the greatest of De Wet, of Sir John French, or with Morgan's famous raids during that other Civil War where men of the Anglo-Saxon race met one another in deadly combat, where brother fought brother, and father and son were more than once found on opposite sides. Seriously, it is more than doubtful whether Morgan's Kentucky raid in 1862, though he travelled 300 miles in eight days, or Stuart's raid of the same year in Pennsylvania, were greater performances than that of Gage ; for they were not hampered by foot, as he was ; nor had their worn-out troopers to dismount in order that infantry, more tired than themselves, might clamber on to their hard-pressed horses. Of a truth, the army learned something more than the habit of swearing in Flanders at that age.

Gage's expedition was, as has been noted, before the second battle of Newbury, and the second battle of Newbury was the last important action of the war fought on Berkshire soil. The stubborn defences made by Donnington, Wallingford, and Farringdon, and their value, have been noticed, not duly, perhaps, but partially, in this chapter and elsewhere. They were as safe rocks round and past which the tide of the yearly campaigns ebbed and flowed. The capture of Reading, and the unmerited disgrace of Colonel Fielding, have been chronicled. One grievous loss to the King only has been postponed lest it should break a feeble thread of narrative. It was that of Abingdon, which, at one time, had ever so many mayors in a single year by reason of the ascendency of this or that party. Time after time have we seen how unmitigated a nuisance to the King's party was the presence of Major-General Brown at Abingdon. It compelled Charles, for example, to retire from Newbury to Oxford by the round-about way of Wallingford ; it involved Gage in a prolonged detour when he was going to the relief of Basing, since but for the fear of General Brown he might have saved many miles by marching direct to Ilsley from Abingdon, and so on to Aldermaston and Basing. It commanded one of the few bridges across the Thames, and Brown, as we have seen, was enabled by its possession to "infest Oxford very much." Its importance was obvious, almost paramount ; and it was recognised. Abingdon was in the King's hands, for the most part at any rate, until May, 1644 ; it had been the headquarters of his horse ; it had been honoured with a royal visit in April. In May it was finally lost, mainly through "the ill-Humour and Negligence of Wilmot." Charles had left Wilmot at Abingdon, with all the foot, instructing him to quit the town, if need be, supposing Essex to advance from the undefended west, but even in that case to make a fight of it first unless Essex were in greatly superior force, when he might retire with the whole army on Oxford. If Essex advanced from the east, giving Wilmot the advantage of the river, to say nothing of weak works of defence, Wilmot was to fight seriously. Essex, with a powerful army it is true, but from the east, advanced in a leisurely fashion. The news of his advance was enough for the pusillanimous Wilmot. He turned tail with his army, leaving the horse to cover his retreat, without attempting to strike a blow; so expeditious was his flight that his army was within sight of Oxford before a special messenger from Charles arrived to countermand the fatal movement. It was too late. Charles, apparently, was at Oxford, and Wilmot had sent Sir Charles Blount, the Scout Master General, to tell him of his faint-hearted purpose. Oxford was, and is, but six miles off by way of Bagley Wood, a mile more by way of Radley—the Radley Road may not have been made then—and a little further by the London Road behind Nuneham to Oxford. Wilmot would have run the risk of meeting Essex by going that way. In any case the distance was trifling, and it is impossible to avoid the thought that something more despicable than ill-humour, and more contemptible than negligence, hindered Wilmot from staying to hear his royal master's wishes.

Of course the King desired that Wilmot should fight. Charles proved, not perhaps in Berkshire, but in other counties, that he had an eye for country from the military point of view; and a child in strategy could not have ignored the vital importance of Abingdon. Now there was no help for it. The wrong man had been trusted; the false move had been made; it was past remedy. "Abingdon was in this manner, and to the King's infinite trouble, quitted." How dire that trouble was we have

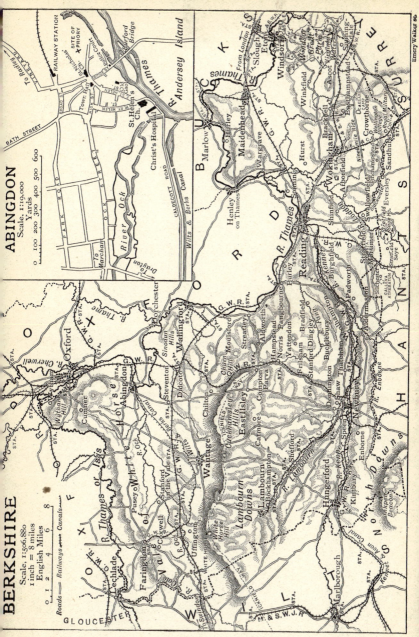

ABINGDON

Scale, 1:19,000

Yards
0 100 200 300 400 500 600

BERKSHIRE

Scale, 1:506,880
1 inch = 8 miles
English Miles
0 2 4 6 8

Roads ═══ Railways ──── Canals ┅┅┅┅

Emery Walker sc.

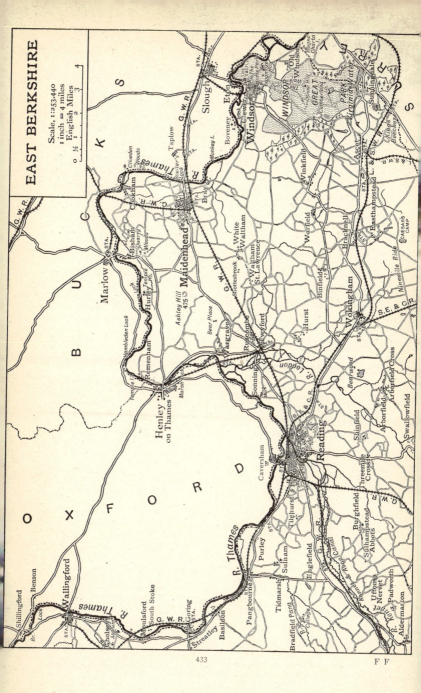

EAST BERKSHIRE

Scale, 1:253,440
1 inch = 4 miles
English Miles

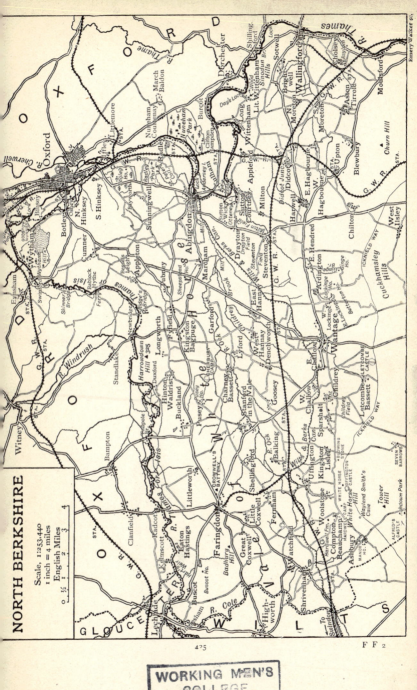

NORTH BERKSHIRE

Scale, 1:253,440
1 inch = 4 miles
English Miles

0 ½ 1 2 3 4

WORKING MEN'S
COLLEGE
LIBRARY.

INDEX

WORKING MEN'S
COLLEGE
LIBRARY.

Highways Berkshire.

G G

INDEX

THE END

PRINTED IN GREAT BRITAIN BY R CLAY AND SONS, LTD.,
BRUNSWICK STREET, STAMFORD STREET, S.E. 1, AND BUNGAY, SUFFOLK.

THE
HIGHWAYS & BYWAYS SERIES.

Extra crown 8vo, gilt tops, **6s.** net each.

London. By Mrs. E. T. Cook. With Illustrations by Hugh Thomson and Frederick L. Griggs.

GRAPHIC.—"Mrs. Cook is an admirable guide; she knows her London in and out; she is equally at home in writing of Mayfair and of City courts, and she has a wealth of knowledge relating to literary and historical associations. This, taken together with the fact that she is a writer who could not be dull if she tried, makes her book very delightful reading."

Middlesex. By Walter Jerrold. With Illustrations by Hugh Thomson.

EVENING STANDARD.—"Every Londoner who wishes to multiply fourfold the interest of his roamings and excursions should beg, borrow, or buy it without a day's delay."

DAILY TELEGRAPH.—"A model of its class, for it is difficult to see how descriptive work of the kind could be performed with a more sympathetic and humane touch."

Hertfordshire. By Herbert W. Tompkins, F.R.Hist.S. With Illustrations by Frederick L. Griggs.

WESTMINSTER GAZETTE.—"A very charming book. . . . Will delight equally the artistic and the poetic, the historical and the antiquarian, the picturesque and the sentimental kinds of tourist."

ST. JAMES'S GAZETTE.—"Cram full of interest and entertainment. The county is singularly rich in material for gossip and comment, and Mr. Tompkins has made a very charming book from it. Nothing more can well remain to be said, yet all that is said in these pages is to the point."

Buckinghamshire. By Clement Shorter. With Illustrations by Frederick L. Griggs.

WORLD.—"A thoroughly delightful little volume. Mr. Frederick L. Griggs contributes a copious series of delicately graceful illustrations."

OBSERVER.—"A very full, pleasant, and informing book. . . . Mr. Griggs again gives us of his best."

Surrey. By Eric Parker. With Illustrations by Hugh Thomson.

DAILY TELEGRAPH.—"Author and artist have combined to give us one of the very best books on the most variedly beautiful of the home counties."

SPECTATOR.—"A very charming book, both to dip into and to read . . . Every page is sown with something rare and curious."

Kent. By WALTER JERROLD. With Illustrations by HUGH THOMSON.

PALL MALL GAZETTE.—"A book over which it is a pleasure to pore, and which every man of Kent or Kentish man, or 'foreigner,' should promptly steal, purchase, or borrow. . . . The illustrations alone are worth twice the money charged for the book."

Sussex. By E. V. LUCAS. With Illustrations by FREDERICK L. GRIGGS.

WESTMINSTER GAZETTE.—"A delightful addition to an excellent series. . . . Mr. Lucas's knowledge of Sussex is shown in so many fields, with so abundant and yet so natural a flow, that one is kept entertained and charmed through every passage of his devious progress. . . . The drawings with which Mr. Frederick Griggs illustrates this charming book are equal in distinction to any work this admirable artist has given us."

Berkshire. By JAMES EDMUND VINCENT. With Illustrations by FREDERICK L. GRIGGS.

DAILY CHRONICLE.—"We consider this book one of the best in an admirable series, and one which should appeal to all who love this kind of literature."

Oxford and the Cotswolds. By H. A. EVANS. With Illustrations by FREDERICK L. GRIGGS.

DAILY TELEGRAPH.—"The author is everywhere entertaining and fresh, never allowing his own interest to flag, and thereby retaining the close attention of the reader."

Shakespeare's Country. By The Ven. W. H. HUTTON. With Illustrations by EDMUND H. NEW.

PALL MALL GAZETTE.—"Mr. Edmund H. New has made a fine book a thing of beauty and a joy for ever by a series of lovely drawings."

Hampshire. By D. H. MOUTRAY READ. With Illustrations by ARTHUR B. CONNOR.

STANDARD.—"In our judgment, as excellent and as lively a book as has yet appeared in the Highways and Byways Series."

Dorset. By Sir FREDERICK TREVES. With Illustrations by JOSEPH PENNELL.

STANDARD.—"A breezy, delightful book, full of sidelights on men and manners, and quick in the interpretation of all the half-inarticulate lore of the countryside."

Wiltshire. By EDWARD HUTTON. With Illustrations by NELLY ERICHSEN.

Somerset. By EDWARD HUTTON. With Illustrations by NELLY ERICHSEN.

DAILY TELEGRAPH.—"A book which will set the heart of every West-country-man beating with enthusiasm, and with pride for the goodly heritage into which he has been born as a son of Somerset."

Devon and Cornwall. By ARTHUR H. NORWAY With Illustrations by JOSEPH PENNELL and HUGH THOMSON.

DAILY CHRONICLE.—"So delightful that we would gladly fill columns with extracts were space as elastic as imagination. . . . The text is excellent ; the illustrations of it are even better."

South Wales. By A. G. BRADLEY. With Illustrations by FREDERICK L. GRIGGS.

SPECTATOR.—"Mr. Bradley has certainly exalted the writing of a combined archæological and descriptive guide-book into a species of literary art. The result is fascinating."

North Wales. By A. G. BRADLEY. With Illustrations by HUGH THOMSON and JOSEPH PENNELL.

PALL MALL GAZETTE.—"To read this fine book makes us eager to visit every hill and every valley that Mr. Bradley describes with such tantalising enthusiasm. It is a work of inspiration, vivid, sparkling, and eloquent—a deep well of pleasure to every lover of Wales."

Cambridge and Ely. By Rev. EDWARD CONYBEARE. With Illustrations by FREDERICK L. GRIGGS.

Also an *Edition de Luxe.* Limited to 250 copies. Royal 8vo, 21s. net.

ATHENÆUM.—"A volume which, light and easily read as it is, deserves to rank with the best literature about the county."

GUARDIAN.—"Artist and writer have combined to give us a book of singular charm."

East Anglia. By WILLIAM A. DUTT. With Illustrations by JOSEPH PENNELL.

WORLD.—"Of all the fascinating volumes in the 'Highways and By-ways' series, none is more pleasant to read. . . . Mr. Dutt, himself an East Anglian, writes most sympathetically and in picturesque style of the district."

WORKING MEN'S COLLEGE LIBRARY.

Lincolnshire. By W. F. Rawnsley. With Illustrations by Frederick L. Griggs.

PALL MALL GAZETTE.—"A splendid record of a storied shire."

Nottinghamshire. By J. B. Firth. With Illustrations by Frederick L. Griggs.

Northamptonshire and Rutland. By Herbert A. Evans. With Illustrations by Frederick L. Griggs.

Derbyshire. By J. B. Firth. With Illustrations by Nelly Erichsen.

Yorkshire. By Arthur H. Norway. With Illustrations by Joseph Pennell and Hugh Thomson.

PALL MALL GAZETTE.—"The wonderful story of Yorkshire's past provides Mr. Norway with a wealth of interesting material, which he has used judiciously and well; each grey ruin of castle and abbey he has re-erected and re-peopled in the most delightful way. A better guide and story-teller it would be hard to find."

Lake District. By A. G. Bradley. With Illustrations by Joseph Pennell.

ST. JAMES'S GAZETTE.—"A notable edition — an engaging volume, packed with the best of all possible guidance for tourists. For the most part the artist's work is as exquisite as anything of the kind he has done."

The Border. By Andrew Lang and John Lang. With Illustrations by Hugh Thomson.

STANDARD.—"The reader on his travels, real or imaginary, could not have pleasanter or more profitable companionship. There are charming sketches by Mr. Hugh Thomson to illustrate the letterpress."

Galloway and Carrick. By the Rev. C. H. Dick. With Illustrations by Hugh Thomson.

Donegal and Antrim. By Stephen Gwynn. With Illustrations by Hugh Thomson.

DAILY TELEGRAPH.—"A perfect book of its kind, on which author, artist, and publisher have lavished of their best."

Normandy. By Percy Dearmer, M.A. With Illustrations by Joseph Pennell.

MACMILLAN AND CO., Ltd., LONDON.

C 5.3.6.19.